290/400

Anarchy in the Year Zero

The Sex Pistols, The Clash and the Class of '76

Clinton Heylin

route™

First published by Route in 2016
PO Box 167, Pontefract, WF8 4WW
info@route-online.com
www.route-online.com

ISBN : 978-1901927-66-5

FIRST EDITION

Photograph section:
All photographs by Peter Lloyd, taken at the following gigs:
P1 – Northallerton 19th May, 1976.
P2,3 – Penthouse, Scarborough 20th May, 1976.
P4-9 – Screen On The Green, London 29th August, 1976.
P10,11 – Fforde Grene, Leeds September 12th, 1976.
P12 – Coatham Bowl, Redcar November 11th, 1976.
P13-16 – Leeds Polytechnic, December 6th, 1976.

Cover concept by Clinton Heylin
Cover Layout:
GOLDEN

Typeset in Bembo by Route

Printed and bound by CPI Group (UK) Ltd, Croydon, CR0 4YY

This book is dedicated to the Free Trade Hall,
home of many a revolutionary rave.

This is the story of the birth of Punk, with a capital P, in the only country where it was a mainstream movement: the UK; told entirely by eye-witnesses (myself included) whose words, then and now, have been held up to the light of history's hindsight.

This is also the story of the rebirth of Rock, by a bunch of bands who set out to deconstruct and destroy the form, on the island that largely invented it and reinvented it at least twice in the fifteen years before Punk.

And it is the story of the ex-Catholic, semi-Irish, snot-nosed, working-class Cockney oik who dealt the final, fatal blow to England's dreams of empire when he became a Rotten revolutionary.

But most of all it is the story of a handful of British youths who were inspired to raise their voice in song, and allow it to echo around the world.

It is a story that, till now, has only been told piecemeal: of one band blazing a trail gig by gig, convert by convert, to the pre-set agenda – not always adhered to – of a fetish shop owner until, within a single year, the whole island rocked to the sound of ANARCHEEE.

How did this happen…

and why does it still matter?

Read on.

INTRO: THE BIG BANG THEORY OF PUNK

This is the period cited by people such as Adam Ant, Morrissey and Billy Idol as [among] their greatest influences – The Pistols in '76.

– *Glen Matlock,* I Was A Teenage Sex Pistol

The Pistols' ultimate mark wasn't left by recording. We were a *threat.*

– *John Lydon,* No Irish, No Blacks, No Dogs

The universe began with a bang. A big bang. The effects of which are still being felt, and disputed. Punk's version of the big bang was not quite so instantaneous – it took a year of laying depth charges underground before it burst upon the world in a single cussing media blitz – but when all around was a great big void, it brought heat and light; and its aftershocks still resonate today wherever Rock has an identity beyond what simply sells.

Without the Sex Pistols, it probably all falls apart as Prog and Metal conspire to take rock & roll all the way down to the pit. Beyond the spiky quartet lies something else, raw and vital. Everything Rock does that actually matters in the next quarter-century will spring forth from their bondage-trousered loins.

And what is truly remarkable is that they never needed to make a record or a national TV appearance to have such a profound effect. In fact, by the time the dust settled on their incendiary fourteen-month career, the *original* Pistols had released just one single ('Anarchy In The UK') which EMI deleted just as soon as it began entering the charts.

All it took was a single two-minute live interview on local London teatime TV to sound the bugle call on Rock's last apocalypse; and it was fanx ta-ra to ELP, Yes and all their ilk. Year Zero.

If 'modern music begins with the Velvets' (as dead rock scribe Lester Bangs once posited), it required the Sex Pistols to add social autonomy (aka anarchy) to the equation and take it out of the art colleges and the Lower East Side, where it had languished, largely unloved, since the New York Dolls vacated the frame. And they did it in a blink of pop culture's myopic eye, in the face of apathy and antipathy in almost equal measures – using ideas mapped out by ex-Dolls manager Malcolm McLaren, articulated by a manic frontman and aligned to a decidedly retro, Britpop sensibility.

They did it while most everyone else was sleeping and only the chosen few were looking for a lapsed-Catholic Antichrist. And when I say a chosen few, I mean just that. Across a matter of months the pre-EMI Pistols played seven-dozen gigs at the midpoint of the seventies to audiences so small no one can agree where and when they played, or who was there.

We're talking about less than a hundred true converts *in total* – an elite by self-selection. There was something in this band's unique DNA which spread the punk virus selectively and seditiously.

Beforehand, the only people who seemed to believe this was destined to happen worked at a fetish clothes store at the World's End (i.e. arse-end) of Chelsea's King's Road. Afterwards, there was an unseemly scramble from the same neck of the woods for most of the credit, forcing chroniclers to come down on the side of either McLaren or Rotten.

Wherever the balance of credit (and blame) truly lies, one undeniable fact underlines all this anti-social, anti-apathy activity: the Sex Pistols were always knowing carriers of the punk plague.

Anyone who thinks that they *accidentally* inspired a generation of bands to shatter the template of modern pop and rebuild it in their own iconoclastic image simply ain't been to no school of Rock. The very first interview the band gave, in early April 1976, just five months after their infamous St Martin's debut, contains a complete manifesto:

Johnny Rotten: I hate shit. I hate hippies and what they stand for. I hate long hair. I hate pub bands. I want to change it so there are rock bands like us … I want people … to see us and start something.

No one had made such a self-conscious demand for a cultural movement this side of André Breton; certainly not in popular music, where the aim was to please, please, please. Rotten was making his outlandish demand when the Pistols had mustered exactly two live reviews in the music press. One of these, by *Melody Maker*'s Allan Jones, famously concluded, 'They do for music what World War II did for peace.'

And yet the most famous convert to the Pistols' cause – Clash frontman Joe Strummer – saw the light the same night Mr Jones heard the sound of war. On that very Nashville night, the future components of The Damned came to see what all the fuss was about; as did the core figures in the original Clash. Even Buzzcocks sent their future manager, Richard Boon, as an emissary. Such were the signals the Sex Pistols sent at a frequency few could find.

It worked. From gig one – which itself challenged a future Adam Ant to question all he had previously held dear – to the Anarchy tour itself, attended by most of the elements that would make up bands as radical and forward-thinking as Gang of Four, The Pop Group and Joy Division, they sailed this sea of possibilities with a motley crew of converts.

The seeds of sedition, which before Year Zero was done would sprout a dozen vital bands playing follow the leader, were mainly sown in those first six months. This bumper crop of 'bands like us' also ensured the ongoing pre-eminence of English Rock. Of course, with such a disparate set of agendas even this tight-knit cabal of confidants soon fractured, the rock archaeologists giving each chip off the ol' block its own name: New Wave, Neu Musick, Afterpunk, Post-punk, Oi, Two-Tone, Hardcore, Thrash, Thrash-metal, Grunge. But the roots of them all – if one dug deep enough – could be traced to one band's clear vision of the way forward, and usually a single show from Year Zero.

Because, as Pistols drummer Paul Cook later opined, 'The strange thing was that people latched on to us straight away.' These people turned out to be just like them – angry with the status quo, frustrated by a broken society and betrayed by the music that had once been their solitary solace. Outsiders. Such was certainly the recalled response of one attendee at the Pistols' legendary first Manchester show:

Ian Moss: I thought, 'Wow, they're my age, they look great, [and] they're untamed … These people are me, I'm not alone. [All] these years I felt a misfit. [But] these are exactly the same as me.'

Something about those early Pistols shows transmitted a form of teen-angst that defied all conventional means of communication. Even that June '76 Manchester gig, the most famous of them, yet attended by just seventy hardy northerners, proved influential enough to inspire a book, two films and at least four seminal punk and post-punk bands. Considered by many informed souls to be the most significant show in rock's tangled history, it convinced untutored musicians to walk the walk:

Una Baines: It was a shift in consciousness – something that had to happen, almost like people were linked up on a psychic level.

Ian Moss: From that first gig I knew it was about more than [the] music: this is empowering – nothing else has made me feel like this. I knew this was challenging, a new way of going about things.

If Manchester's musical misfits – Buzzcocks excepted – took their time turning into bands, it wasn't for want of trying, but for want of tuning. When future members of The Fall, Joy Division and The Smiths were poleaxed by the two Lesser Free Trade Hall performances, on June 4th and July 20th, there was barely a musician among them. But they still took to their calling like men – and woman – possessed.

As Ian Curtis's widow, Deborah, put it in her evocative memoir, *Touching the Distance*, 'After the [second] performance [at the Lesser

Free Trade Hall] everyone seemed to move quickly towards the door. It seemed as if we had all been issued with instructions.'[1]

So much we know. Where not the detail, the general outline. Yet, even as the historical ground has hardened the worm has started to turn. Forty years on – and a full quarter century since Jon Savage's *England's Dreaming* provided that first authoritative historical reference point – we are in danger of forgetting just how unique this mo(ve)ment was; and how much momentum the Pistols achieved by sheer force of will and singular vision between November 6th, 1975 and November 26th, 1976.

★ ★ ★

Although the young Savage did an admirable job contextualizing the rise and fall of the Sex Pistols twenty-five years ago, he could only scrape away at this hard rock with the tools he had to hand. Some of the heavy excavating equipment has only become available in the last fifteen years.

In that time, the number of eye-witnesses who have opened up to punk chroniclers has more than doubled, while important recordings have emerged (notably complete sets of the Pistols, Clash *and* Buzzcocks at The Screen On The Green in August and Manchester on the December Anarchy tour); reports have been collected and collated from hard-to-find fanzines and local papers; and, partly thanks to the internet, the voices of many who did not change the world but did see the chimes of anarchy flashing have added a much-needed static charge to any ongoing debate about the Pistols' importance.

At the same time, the punk memoir – good, bad and indifferent – has become a mini-industry in itself. Fortunately, not all of these subjective self-chroniclers have sought to dilute the scale of the Pistols' impact. Recent memoirs by Viv Albertine of The Slits, Billy Idol of Generation X, Berlin of the Bromley Contingent, Richard Dudanski of The 101'ers (and PiL), scribes Nick Kent and Paul Morley, Buzzcock Steve Diggle and Pistols soundman Dave

[1] The Pistols even reinforced their message to all Mancunian mavericks (and gave Curtis his entrée to Joy Division) with two further forays to the Electric Circus on the Anarchy tour.

Goodman (published posthumously, edited by Phil Strongman), have all helped redress deficiencies in detail.

Ironically, the two least edifying recent 'punk' memoirs have been those attributed to Vivienne Westwood and John Lydon, each of whom was caught in the eye of the Year Zero storm. Both volumes were ghosted by a.n. other, as if the act of setting down one's memories in one's own words was beyond the two former iconoclasts. Neither, it seems, had learnt a great deal from their experiences or remembered any credible detail which turned history on its head. Each garnered more headlines than their worthier rivals collectively, though in each case next to nothing was revealed.

Nor does it seem this pair are alone among the recent spate of punk memoirs – at times more torrent than spate – when it comes to failing to set the record straight, or straighter, for those who want it so. In fact, some have taken us in the opposite direction, into reactionary revisionism.

And the most unexpected arch-revisionists are the very figures who helped to save punk from itself in the dark days of post-punk but would now like to lead it down the garden path. As the two Manchester LFTH gigs have slowly but surely become the defining gigs of the era, due in no small part to David Nolan's *I Swear I Was There* (2001) documentary/book and, I must suppose, *24-Hour Party People,* four of those changed from the creatures they once were have started denying they heard the sound of Rock shattering.[2]

For Mark E. Smith of The Fall, who has made a career out of contrariness (to the point of having two mutually contradictory 'as told to' autobiographies to his name), 'It was crap … and anyone who says differently is lying … We came away certain that we could do a lot better than that.' But no matter how much he thinks he speaks collectively for the fallen – adopting that royal 'we' on behalf of Tony Friel, Martin Bramah and Una Baines – neither Baines nor Bramah, both of whom I have interviewed, concur with his assessment or affirm his memory.

At least that other cantankerous contemporary, Mr Morrissey, realized he had less wriggle room for such a post-revisionist about-

[2] These fabled shows are assigned less than three pages in Savage's chunky 600-page tome.

face. After all, he had been inspired by the June 4th gig to write not one, but two letters to the music papers, both of them published. His solution when writing a best-selling 2013 memoir was to essentially ignore the first two Pistols gigs – to deny their impact by omission, rather than revision.

From Peter Hook and Bernard Sumner – the two surviving members of Joy Division/New Order who were there at the dawn of it all – one might have expected more. Yet each has displayed a commensurate desire to shatter the 'myth' of that first Manchester gig:

Peter Hook: Fucking hell, what a racket. I mean, they were just dreadful; well, the sound was dreadful ... It was almost as though the Pistols' sound guy had deliberately made them sound awful ... because it was all feeding back, fuzzed-up, just a complete din. A wall of noise. I didn't recognize a tune, not a note, and considering they were playing so many cover versions ... I surely would have recognized something had it not sounded so shit. [2012]

To write these words thirty-five years after the concert in question first circulated seems wantonly contrary on Hook's part. Self-evidently, the sixty-minute tape of the show – bootlegged on both vinyl and CD – is an accurate audio document of a surprisingly well-mixed gig by a remarkably fine rock band. As for not recognizing a single tune: are you seriously telling me, Hooky, that 'Substitute' passed you by?

(If others hadn't confirmed Hook's presence, one might almost believe that for all his swearing, he wasn't there – as Simply Red's Mick Hucknall certainly was not. Hucknall got to hear about this band and movement from fellow Frantic Elevator, Neil Moss.)

Bernard Sumner's account, published in 2014, showed an even more tenuous grasp of the Mancunian milieu he (and I) inhabited. For him, 'Punk was an interesting, exciting new movement of which a few people in Manchester were aware ... [who] attended that concert as a result. I'd seen the Buzzcocks before I saw the Sex Pistols ... and they were also an influence on us.'

In June 1976 there was exactly one *English* punk band; and in order to see Buzzcocks 'before I saw the Sex Pistols', he would have needed to invest in a Tardis. Steve Diggle met Pete Shelley and Howard Devoto for the first time at the June Pistols gig, as Sumner('s copy-editor) should have known.

Contemporary accounts, whatever their other failings, do not carry the same historical baggage.[3] Whereas David Nolan's oral history, no matter how well-intentioned, does. As does John Robb's, and Stephen Colegrave's. All three commendable works, published in a five-year period at the start of the noughties, connected some necessary dots Savage could not. However, readers of all of them could still come away thinking the two Manchester shows were acts of *happenstance*.

In reality, Morrissey, Hook, Sumner and Smith were caught up by a phenomenon which claimed outsiders like them at every turn. What happened in Manchester on June 4th and July 20th, also transpired – in almost identical ways – at gigs in St Albans and Weybridge in November, 1975; at the Chelsea School of Art and Ravensbourne in December 1975; at the Marquee and Andrew Logan's loft in February 1976; at the Nashville in March and April; at the 100 Club every other Tuesday from May through August; at Northallerton in May; at Hastings and the London Lyceum in July; at Birmingham and The Screen On The Green in August, and Newport in September. 'Tis the punk version of the domino effect, hinted at in all that has come before, but here <u>Writ Large</u>.

* * *

Forty years after the fact, this necessary revision has only been possible with a little help from both familiar and unfamiliar musical converts, among whose recollections I have selectively sprinkled the thoughts of photographers and writers, as well as the fashion-

[3] The other subtle enemy of historical truth is the kind of pseudo-academic who posts and re-posts versions of an article riddled with factual errors about the two Lesser Free Trade Hall gigs and then gives it the hubristic title, 'Print The Truth, Not The Legend'. The article in question singularly fails to acknowledge the historical primacy of photos of both shows, 8mm silent film of the second show, the atmospheric audience tape of the first show, and the contemporary published accounts by *Penetration*'s Paul Welsh, *Out There*'s Paul Morley, inveterate letter-writer Steve Morrissey and *Sounds*' very own Jonh Ingham; as well as being hopelessly confused about who attended which show/s.

conscious friends and enemies that McLaren made, cultivated and alienated in the fourteen months him and 'his' band were cultural magnets; before the big bang blew up in all their faces.

Naturally, questions remain – not just the how and why, but the who and when. As the inspirees are dying off – Steve Strange being the latest – it's now or never for a book like this which attempts to reconstruct the narrative of 'Punk '76' – the real Year Zero – authoritatively, if not dispassionately; to connect the dots not only literally (providing, for the first time, an accurate chronology), but laterally – by showing how many of the characters that circle the band spin off into new vistas of music, fashion and pop culture.

For, lest we forget, Pistol proselytizers were to become almost a roll call of music-makers who matter in the decade ahead, starting with the three bands who embraced the message with such immediacy that they were all up and running by July 1976: Buzzcocks, The Damned and The Clash. If Buzzcocks came closest to emulating the Pistols' real directive, The Damned were responsible for punk's vinyl debut, while the influence of The Clash – for good *and* bad – would most endure.

But there were other, more radical voices from the outset. Subway Sect would become the grey men that punk forgot – though not before they issued two of its greatest 45s, 'Nobody's Scared' and 'Ambition' – while Siouxsie & The Banshees would go on to fame and fortune. Both bands would be inspired by the same night of Marquee mayhem, pursue the same initial anti-rock agenda and debut the same night at the 100 Club Punk Festival. But it would be the Banshees who would find their sound as punk mutated into post-punk, leading Rock away from the centre ground while still making the Top Ten.

Also up and running by the end of 1976, after experiencing the Pistols in all their shape-shifting glory, were the likes of The Jam, The Adverts, Generation X, Wire, Penetration and X-Ray Spex, all names to conjure with. Yet most of the bands founded and forged by Pistols apostles only finally took their place on stage in 1977.

But what names: The Slits, Joy Division (né Warsaw), The Fall, Alternative TV, The Pop Group, Gang of Four, Dead Or Alive (né

Nightmares On Wax), The Nipple Erectors, The Prefects, even the Tom Robinson Band, were among those sprouting up from that initial harvest.

All these seeds were as straws in the wind the year the Pistols blasted on through. Thankfully, most of those I name and shame remain grateful they were in the right place at such a righteous time. Some even have almost perfect recall of the first time they ever saw the Face of punk or heard its primal howl.

As punk panned out, there were more than enough wannabes with the whiff of Pistols in their nostrils massing on the borders of propriety and deference, prepared to pogo to the sound of cultures clashing. Every man, woman or child who ever caught a Pistols show soon seemed to be wielding a guitar, bass or mike stand in a highly threatening manner. And as of January 1st, 1977, they began to break on through.

The initial elite faced a stark choice. They could be leaders of men (and/or women) or be trampled underfoot. Among the former was one guy calling himself Adam Ant who had finally decided to front a band of Ants. And underneath the undertaker make-up and bondage clothes, he bore an uncanny resemblance to the bassist from Bazooka Joe, a pub-based rockabilly outfit who back in November 1975 had had to fend off a support act which was going around calling itself *Sex Pistols* – a quartet of musical misfits the like of which the rock world had not seen. One thing was apparent to 'Adam', even on first listen: these guys meant it, maaaan…

– Clinton Heylin, April 2015

IGNITION

1. BELOW THE RADAR, BENEATH SOME ROCK

[November 6th, 1975 – February 14th, 1976]

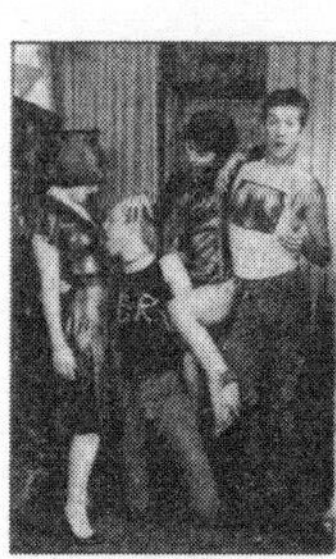

The people behind "Sex" hard at work in their Chelsea HQ. Must have sex on the behind.

How did Sex begin?

Vivian Westwood and her boyfriend Malcolm McLaren started Sex as a Rock n' Roll shop four years ago. "We were interested in the Teddy Boys", Vivian explains, "so we moved into the back of this shop on King's Road with a collection of 1950s records and about 40 pairs of Lurex (cloth interwoven with gold threads) trousers. We became popular with the Teds right away.

"The 1950s appealed to Malcolm and I because that was the first time the kids really had a culture of their own in which they established their own cults. Before we started the shop, I was a schoolteacher, and Malcolm was a student. He didn't like me very much then, but we've both changed a great deal and he likes me a lot now."

Vivian and Malcolm don't sell Rock n' Roll records any more. But they still sell 50s clothing, some of it altered for sexual purposes. The wall of Sex now displays an amazing variety of "hip" sex gear including rubber and leather fetish clothing; high heeled boots, rubber panties, leather bras, leather wrist and ankle restraints ("Bound to please"), rubber mini-skirts (for £12), T-shirts with a page from a porno novel written across the front (for £4), a genuine "dirty old man" raincoat (£25), and six different styles of rubber masks and hoods (£20-£50).

"I want to make rubber and leather sex stuff easily accessible to those people who feel strongly about it," says Vivian Westwood. "I usually wear a T-shirt around the shop that reads: 'Be reasonable, demand the impossible', and people are always coming up to me and asking: 'Excuse me, but what's the impossible?' They think it must be the ultimate kink, and they're missing out on something. They want to find out what it is so they can be part of the inner circle.

"To some people the ultimate is certainly wearing tight fitting black rubber gear (red is the second most popular colour). Most of our rubber masks fit entirely over the head and cause restricted breathing, which of course is part of the turn-on. A few of them lead to almost total occlusion of air, allowing only the thinest thread of breath.

1

Can rock & roll [really] still speak with this kind of power and glory?

– Jon Landau,* The Real Paper, *May 1974, quoted in November 1975 CBS ads for Bruce Springsteen's London concerts.

Although the [Sex] Pistols have an admirable physical energy … it will take a far better band than them to create a raw music for their generation.

– Phil McNeill,* NME, *July 3rd, 1976 reviewing a June 1976 show at the 100 Club

It is the midpoint of the seventies, the day after Guy Fawkes Night, and twelve days before the latest 'future of rock'n'roll', Bruce Springsteen, lands in London to confirm the hype (or not) that his brand of retro-rock is proof positive that the decade is still idling its way out of the sixties.

A surreal sight greets passers-by at the Centre Point end of Charing Cross Road, cutting a swathe through London's West End: half a dozen of the weirdest looking individuals this side of a Fellini movie are pushing amps and drums, carrying guitars and mike stands across from Denmark Street, once London's answer to Tin Pan Alley and the home of Regent Sounds Studio. A place where The Beatles, the Stones and Van Morrison's Them once recorded important chunks of the sixties soundtrack, it has since fallen on hard times.[4]

Next door to the former studio there now stands a Greek bookshop, Zeno, and it is from the courtyard behind Zeno's that the sextet emerge, four of whom seem young enough and spotty enough to be

[4] Among the tracks recorded at Regent were numerous early Stones demos, Them's 'Story of Them' and 'Friday's Child' and The Beatles' 'Fixing A Hole'.

a boy band. They just don't look like any boy band from this austere time and place.

The weediest of the quartet, the one doing the least heavy lifting, is wearing an ill-fitting kiddies' jumper, ripped at the seams and held together with safety pins – Oxfam chic when it wasn't chic, just scruffy. The look is as anti-glam as it gets, at a time when T. Rex, Sweet, Gary Glitter and Slade have only just started surrendering their grip on the upper echelons of the singles chart.

His real name is John Lydon. Of fiercely Irish Catholic stock, he lives a stone's throw from where his beloved Arsenal FC play. But he is now calling himself Johnny Rotten, a self-conscious retort to his religious upbringing – much as Richard Meyers, New York's original punk, reinvented himself as Richard Hell when forming Television in 1974.

By now Rotten knows Mr Hell was the preferred choice of his band's manager, self-styled fashion guru Malcolm McLaren, who had travelled to New York the previous spring, anxious to hear his ideas for a new punk rock. (Thankfully, Hell attached little credence to McLaren's account of the band awaiting him in Blighty.)

It is McLaren who has cast himself as a leather-clad Pied Piper this damp autumn day, leading the troupe across the busy thoroughfare, through the entrance of St Martin's College of Art and down to the spit'n'sawdust bar. In this arty setting he intends to unveil his latest Situationist statement.

Or so he would later come to believe. As he told the *NME* in 1980, after losing all legal rights to 'his' band, 'With the Sex Pistols I was always behind the curtain.' (More Wizard of Oz than Pied Piper, then.) But as we shall discover, here was someone with a particular penchant for rewriting history with added smoke'n'mirrors. It is time to tell the true story; one which casts neither McLaren nor Rotten as the Sultan of Punk, but rather its joint viziers.

* * *

In truth, McLaren only entered the punk parable in chapter three. For all of 1974 and the first half of 1975, McLaren had taken little or no interest in the trio who rehearsed down the road in Hammersmith: bassist Glen Matlock, guitar/vocalist Steve Jones and drummer Paul

Cook, or their erstwhile friend, Wally Nightingale, who professed to play guitar but more importantly held the keys to a rehearsal room at Riverside Studios.

As long as they called themselves Swankers and continued to humour Wally, McLaren considered their extra-curricular activities entirely their affair; even though his clothes shop continued to employ Matlock on Saturdays to keep an eye on the notoriously light-fingered Jones.

Through the early seventies the shop was called Let It Rock; and with a name like that and a King's Road address, it naturally attracted every pop star – from Mick Jagger to Bryan Ferry – who still had money to burn after a trip to Granny Takes A Trip. Though friendly with the latter, McLaren refrained from telling the foppish frontman what he thought of Roxy's recent records when he came to Let It Rock after banking his latest royalty cheque.

But the music he selected for the shop jukebox said it all; songs like 'Have You Seen Your Mother, Baby (Standing In The Shadow)', the last Rolling Stone A-side McLaren really rated. Ex-shopworker Glen Matlock points out its appeal, 'Everything's in the red, and [when] it was on this big old jukebox … [it sounds like] there's one riff, and everybody in the whole band … plays everything together always, all the time. It's just like this incessant row … a glorious racket.'

The most modern 45 on there was the Flamin' Groovies' 'Shake Some Action', a 1972 track belatedly released on a 1975 Skydog E.P. by Malcolm's Algerian friend, Marc Zermati. Otherwise, it was filled with the likes of 'Psychotic Reaction' (Count Five), 'Through My Eyes' (The Creation), 'Have Love Will Travel' (The Sonics) and 'I Put A Spell On You' (Screamin' Jay Hawkins).

But if the jukebox said let it rock, as of the winter of '75 the shop sign no longer did. Matlock et al were now Sex shopworkers. The shop had received a radical refit along with its dramatic name change. Its new clientele no longer came for the brothel creepers that had been Let It Rock's best-seller, but for something creepy to wear to the nearest Madame – preferably made out of rubber or leather.

McLaren's business partner and live-in girlfriend, Vivienne Westwood – who performed roadie duty that November day – had finally found her transgressive niche. Westwood may even have been responding to a change she had noted in her partner's whole outlook. Fashion alone was not enough for either of them. They were looking to strike at the very heart of pop culture, to stir things up.

The 29-year-old McLaren – an ex-student of Croydon Art School who had tried (and failed) to organize a student occupation at the height of the Paris '68 riots – had recently fallen for camp-rockers the New York Dolls, after seeing them trash the Paris Hippodrome in autumn 1973. In the winter of 1975, he flew to New York to work with them further, only to find a band riddled with dissension and addled by drugs. So much for shaping the Dolls into a band transgressive enough to shake society's foundations.

If McLaren was convinced that Rock had forsaken its revolutionary edge – as it assuredly had – his great white hope for the future of rock & roll had proven to be three junkies and a cabaret singer. Fortunately, his decision to let Westwood steer the shop through its sea change to Sex proved a blessing in disguise. She was a businesswoman and he was a dreamer. What bound them together was a resolute belief in creating ferment.

He returned to London a wiser, if no less idealistic, iconoclast, and almost immediately took charge of another set of rock hopefuls, leaving Westwood to steer Sex through any choppy waters. His decision to become involved with the local likely lads – Matlock, Jones and Cook – was a direct result of that chastening experience managing Manhattan's most infamous set of musical misfits as they went through their death pangs. His vision had also been sharpened by nights spent downtown at New York's sleaziest rock & roll club watching Television trash the rock aesthetic.

The demise of the Dolls, which McLaren proved powerless to prevent, convinced him he needed the rock equivalent of a tabula rasa onto which he could imprint his master plan. The Swankers, who needed him as much as he needed them, would be the band to wipe the slate clean. He articulated his scheme to a number of confidants, including (ex-)rock photographer Ray Stevenson, 'I'm going to change the face of the music scene! All the music at the moment is by and for thirty-year-old hippies. Boring.'

In fact McLaren bounced his ideas off any number of sounding boards with connections to the rock industry. Stevenson wasn't even the only rock photographer to whom he spouted ideas of revolution. Also on the receiving end was Joe Stevens, an established *NME* photographer then living with Kate Simon, a young *Sounds* photographer and a feisty member of an all-American coven comprising her, Chrissie Hynde, Judy Nylon and Patti Palladin. Whenever Joe seemed inclined to hear his friend spout forth, Simon would flee round the corner to see her friend, *Melody Maker* journalist Caroline Coon:[5]

Kate Simon: Joe was always hanging out with Malcolm, he was always coming round to our house, which was a drag, because he was really boring – I couldn't follow him. I just glazed when he opened his mouth … He wasn't talking about punk, he was talking about boring political stuff.

The 'boring political stuff' was actually the 'politics of sexual anarchy' which McLaren outlined to three separate interviewers who came to his door in the first few months of the Sex Pistols' existence. To David May in December 1975, he was particularly direct: 'If people were upfront about their sexual responses, the whole politics of this country would change … I'm saying that if everyone did wear [fetish] clothes, then this particular island and all the violence that has been pushed down, would actually *explode*.'

He also confided to May that he was 'primarily concerned with … young people, eighteen, nineteen years of age, who need to find expression in what they are doing'. The Pistols – now up and running – went unmentioned in the piece, but that says more about May's angle than McLaren's. He *was* invited to attend the Sex Pistols' very next gig but declined.

Although the thoughts of manager Malcolm at this juncture remained confined to the adult-only pages of *Forum* and *Gallery*

[5] Nick Kent's then-girlfriend, Chrissie Hynde, who was also writing the odd piece for the *NME*, did not share her friend Simon's distaste for McLaren's worldview. In fact, she later told Chris Salewicz about an occasion in 1975 when she 'was sitting in this cafe in Soho with Malcolm, who was fresh from managing the New York Dolls, and we were talking about how to form the ideal rock band. "What we need," said Malcolm, "is someone who's young, intelligent, looks great and is totally dedicated to rock'n'roll."' When both came up with the same individual, her beau, they wondered aloud, what if?

International – the latter devoting a five-page spread to Sex called 'Sado Sex for the Seventies', in which the shop's striking assistant, Jordan, posed in its designs – his focus was turning slowly to the music papers. This was a natural progression given that the people to whom he vented his ideas were mainly obsessed with rock music. In April 1976, he was quoted in a brief article in *Street-Life*, a short-lived fortnightly rival to the music weeklies, saying, 'Kids have a hankering to be part of a movement … that's hard and tough … like the clothes we're selling.'

If Kate Simon, a self-confessed prude from Poughkeepsie, couldn't see the connection between the shop and the band, she was better off at Coon's. However, once there, Simon had to listen to Coon complaining about how reactionary and unexciting Rock had become; unaware that the seeds of revolution were being sown by the motormouth she had left revving up the rhetoric in her Chelsea apartment.

When it wasn't Stevens who was on the receiving end of McLaren's Situationist spiel, it was other *NME* employees like star-reporter, Nick Kent. In his 2010 memoir, Kent recalls how the pair 'spent most of our times together [that year] verbally plotting out the revolution we both recognised that rock music needed to undergo in order to be truly relevant again'.

The circle in which Malcolm and Vivienne moved tended to place Rock at its core. Even the husband of the husband-and-wife team who arranged to have her relatives sow and stitch the racy designs Westwood was churning out, revealed himself to be a secret singer.

Future Only One Peter Perrett never heard Malcolm 'mention that he was getting a band together at all until he came to Kidbrooke in May 1975 and I played him some of my music. I'd just done a demo with Squeeze.'[6] Only then did the haberdasher reveal his scheme for putting together a band who were 'like the Bay City Rollers, but bad boys'. Perrett interpreted this to mean 'linking it with fashion'. That meant stripping the Swankers of any desire to be the next (Small) Faces, making them instead a refraction of the Sex jukebox draped in the Sex shop's more provocative attire.

[6] The Perrett-fronted Squeeze also played three shows at the Marquee in the summer of 1975; while Glenn Tilbrook was for a short time part of the nascent Only Ones.

Perrett didn't treat his friend's ideas seriously, mainly because 'he gave the impression it was all haphazard, and he [was always] do[ing] things on the spur of the moment', but openly admits, 'in retrospect, maybe he was a lot cleverer than everyone thought.'

For whatever reason, probably because McLaren realized this self-assured singer would be almost impossible to manipulate, Perrett was never courted as a potential Pistol. But he was duly introduced to 'the boys' at their new rehearsal studio in Denmark Street: 'They had a little Dansette and they put "Roadrunner" on. That was all that was played for an hour – that was all part of [Malcolm's] indoctrination – what he wanted their approach to music to be.'

The track in question was the one solid outcome from a brief flirtation with a second guitarist. McLaren had somehow convinced Kent to temporarily front the Pistols, which largely involved the critic sitting 'around with Matlock and Steve Jones for hours and hours and hours playing The Modern Lovers' "Roadrunner" – John Cale had given me a tape – and The Stooges. Endlessly.'

But Kent already had a career in rock, thankyouverymuch, as the pre-eminent scribe at that weekly gospel of youth, *NME*. And it was one which brought all the sex and drugs he desired, without all the travails membership of an actual rock & roll band brought. And, as he says, his status as 'a kinda celebrity writer' already 'cast a long shadow, whether I wanted it to or not', which meant, 'the whole focus would have been on me if the group had started out with me in it.'

At least he might help them pick a suitable moniker, one that suggested bad boys on the loose. Marc Zermati, who aside from running London's Bizarre Records had already set up the Skydog label in Paris, recalls the day the band was christened. Matlock, Jones and Cook hadn't even been invited:

Marc Zermati: I had a meeting with Nick, me, Malcolm [and] Jamie Reid at my flat to decide what the name of the band was. There were two names: the Young Bloods and the Sex Pistols. The next day we learnt that Nick Kent was out. It was a bit like that with Malcolm.

McLaren's next thought was to bring Richard Hell over from New York, much as Chas Chandler had brought the equally unknown Jimi

Hendrix to Rock Central in autumn 1966. But, as Matlock ruefully notes, that idea 'was doomed to failure because we … couldn't go over there, and he couldn't come over here'. Well, not without McLaren dipping his hand into his rarely visited pockets, and Hell was not exactly keen to leave behind his rent-controlled Lower East Side apartment, at least not on the word of someone as notoriously flighty as McLaren.

The search for a singer continued into the summer of '75. In fact, as bassist Glen Matlock later recalled, they had gotten so desperate by then that 'if someone had short hair, we would stop them in the street and ask them if they fancied themselves as a singer'. Imagine everyone's surprise when London's answer to Richard Hell walked through the doors of Sex uninvited, with his friends John Grey and John Beverly (aka Sid Vicious):

Glen Matlock: When John came in the shop he looked exactly like Richard Hell. He had the torn t-shirt, the sticky-up hair and all that lark, [but] it was a total coincidence … It was kind of weird. Instead of having Richard Hell over from America we had Johnny Rotten from Finsbury Park.

Anyone looking to garner a sense of McLaren's priorities at this stage should perhaps consider the subtext to Johnny Rotten's audition at Sex: stood in front of the AMI jukebox singing along to Alice Cooper's 'Eighteen', which rather suggests he wanted to see how Rotten *looked* as a singer, and was not so concerned about how he sounded.

In fact, Rotten had already told the assembly it would sound awful. That one-woman sandwich board for Sex, Jordan, vividly remembers Rotten 'standing by the jukebox … and being asked to do something – and him saying he could only play a violin, out of tune'. Which is pretty much how he expected his vocals to sound. As he admitted the following year, when the import of that moment was still sinking in, 'I was frightened of going near the microphone … I had no ambition towards it at all. I just knew I was sick of a lot of things and [had] no way of expressing it.'

He was also afraid that the 'other' musicians in the band would baulk at his ineptitude, and subject him to a level of ridicule even his withering sarcasm could not withstand. Imagine his delight when, at their first rehearsal as a four piece, in late August, he discovered they were as much novices as he was: 'They were trying to do early rock & roll, but it weren't right. The notes were wrong, but the patterns were right!'

This is how Lydon describes that first rehearsal now. But back in 1975, he no more knew a wrong chord than a lost chord. England's premier rock critic had no such concerns. Two months earlier, hearing the pre-Rotten Pistols rehearse, Nick Kent ventured the opinion that he 'hadn't heard straight rock'n'roll sound this spry and impactful since The Stooges were still firing on all cylinders back in 1972'. Whatever Rotten's real first impressions were, the former Swankers were no slouches when it came to playing with themselves.

Perhaps Rotten had spent so much time listening to Can, Captain Beefheart and Van Der Graaf Generator that he had forgotten what 'early rock'n'roll' sounded like. In fact, as late as 1978 he was still insisting, 'It should've been called … Rubbish Rock when we started. I just loved the cluttering of it all. Complete breakdown of music.'

The others, though, were determined to get steadily better. Matlock, for one, felt a whole lot better after a conversation with Rotten's oldest friend, John Grey, who told him, 'If John had the band sounding the way he wanted, it would have been unlistenable. Great lyrics but no one would have wanted to listen to it, because it would have been such a horrible row.' A 'complete breakdown of music', by any other name.

At this stage Rotten wasn't looking to destroy the passer-by, he was looking to destroy rock. Not because he had no appreciation of the form, but because he felt let down by those acts who had once been groundbreaking, but were now just money-making. And in this, at least, he found common ground with Westwood.

Indeed, it was the Sex proprietor who was first to fire a shot across the bows of one particularly self-satisfied seventies rock icon. And no one seems to know why. Two weeks before the Pistols made their frontal assault on London clubland, Vivienne joined Nick Kent at the front of Wembley Empire Pool to see the return of Roxy Music. But she hadn't tagged along to 'do the Strand'. She had gone there to tell Ferry what she thought of him, and specifically what he had become. She made such a nuisance of herself that two of Sex's better customers, who had also gone there that night because there was not a lot else happening, vividly remember the commotion Vivienne caused.

The young Marco Pirroni, already an accomplished guitarist and a regular at Sex, knew 'Viv' well, but had only recently discovered she 'had' a band. He had been 'walking down Denmark Street looking at guitars and I suddenly saw Vivienne wearing Malcolm's black leather coat carrying a coffee cup. "What are you doing here?" "Oh, we're rehearsing with the band." "What band?" That was the first I ever heard of the Pistols.' And now, here she was 'getting up and pointing at Bryan Ferry and shouting, "You're disgusting, you're disgusting."'

Simon Barker, a music fan who had travelled all the way from Bromley to Wembley to shout Viva, knew about Sex but had no idea who Westwood was. He simply remembers, 'When Bryan Ferry came on, wearing army clothes or something, suddenly this woman with white hair and tight trousers and big shouldered jacket, jumped up and started shouting obscenities at him. Nick Kent was with her, and she was going crazy. They had all this security … trying to throw her out, but she was in the middle of the row. She looked so brilliant, but I couldn't understand what she was shouting, or why she was doing it.'

Judy Nylon, Eno's then-girlfriend and one of Hynde's quartet of brash American girls, was also there with Westwood at Wembley. In fact, they nearly came to blows over the incident, but Westwood would not back down. She wanted to see just how far one could push the audience/artist envelope before blood was spilled. Already she was a willing, even zealous, advocate of the Situationist schtick her partner would spout when his enthusiasms got the better of him. Rotten could learn a lot from the two owners of Sex. But only if he was prepared to open his eyes.

* * *

Whatever Rotten's concerns about the original trio's musical chops, McLaren knew that his presence gave renewed purpose to his own great plan. Starting the third week of September 1975, he agreed to rent the band a rehearsal room and studio flat behind Zeno's bookshop, having answered an ad in *Melody Maker* which began, 'Tin Pan Alley. Must be useful for some musicians, agents or such…' His hero, fifties impresario Larry Parnes, would have been proud of him.

(Later on, McLaren would begin to parrot Lydon, asserting that 'the music wasn't [ever] important. It was just a declaration of intent and an attitude.' But such post-Pistols statements are belied by his every action in the year the Pistols mattered.)

Having spent months looking for grade-A Attitude, McLaren had stumbled on someone it spumed from like some great geyser. Once Rotten found a 'way of expressing it', bile gushed forth in all the lyrics he wrote in the months before the band found a public platform for this loaded Pistol. The songs had titles like 'Submission', 'I'm A Lazy Sod' and 'We're Pretty Vacant', to which Matlock, Cook and Jones set their own Small Faces-but-for-the-seventies sensibility. McLaren couldn't wait to tell one former incumbent:

Nick Kent: The first time Lydon's presence was made known to me was when McLaren and I were walking down Denmark Street, and he turned to me and said, 'We've found a singer. He's the best thing in the group. He looks like a spastic, and he's just written this song, "You're only twenty-nine/ You got a lot to learn."' ['Seventeen']

As for Rotten, he couldn't wait to unveil his own version of punk rock on a London that still hadn't quite recovered from the Blitz. Years of being ignored, put down and put upon had produced a genuinely angry young man who, like an automaton of hate, one only needed to wind up (and stand back) to see folk scatter. Unless one felt just like him. And Rotten now had a remit, planted there by the equally iconoclastic McLaren:

Johnny Rotten: We didn't stay in a rehearsal studio until we were so perfect we were boring. The whole idea was to get out and have some fun … and we hoped that some people would see us and go away and form their own bands. We wanted to make a new scene. [1977]

The 'we' in question was not the royal 'we'. Rather, it represented the philosophical union of manager and man-at-the-mike which would last until the darling buds of May, that is, the first flickers of infamy. For now both were equally anxious to smelt the Sex Pistols in the furnace of public opinion and see if it still stood up. But neither of them had a clue as to how one actually secured gigs. McLaren's last resort was literally called The Last Resort, a late-night restaurant/club on the Fulham Road, which agreed to allow them to play, then at the last minute changed its mind.

When this potential avenue fell through, the Pistol with the greatest pop sensibility, Glen Matlock, took matters into his own hands. He convinced the social secretary at the art college he was ostensibly attending – thus receiving an annual government hand-out without having to 'sign on the social' – to let them play. St Martin's College of Art had several things going for it. It was not only slap-dab in the heart of the city, it was across the road from their new rehearsal room. Most importantly, it was *not* a pub.

All it took was Matlock's request. There were many tin-pot colleges in the South East that needed bands willing – for 'beer money' at best – to provide support for an evening's entertainment in front of apathetic students pissing away their grant at the subsidised bar of a weekend. When there were no Christians available, even a band calling itself the Sex Pistols would do. The bassist promptly decided to visit other art colleges in the environs to see if it was just as easy to get gigs elsewhere:

Glen Matlock: Just before that [St Martin's] gig, I went over to Central School of Art in Holborn and swung us another gig there … 'I'm in a band and we're looking for a gig.' 'What's the name of the group?' asked [social secretary] Al [McDowell]. 'The Sex Pistols.' [His friend] Sebastian [Conran]'s eyes lit right up … 'With a name like the Sex Pistols, we must have you.' So I invited them to the gig at St Martin's.

This meant at least two people would be there to see the Sex Pistols – as opposed to the headliner, Bazooka Joe. However, if Matlock was relying on the band's manager to fill out the sparse throng from his address book of contacts, he was to be disappointed. McLaren wasn't yet sure they were ready. The extent to which he drummed up interest was mentioning it to the fashion-conscious boy and girl who ran Sex, Gene Krell and Jordan, and its accountant, Andy Czezowski, a colourful character but hardly a music buff.[7]

On the night, though, McLaren was a most willing rabble-rouser. Bazooka Joe's bassist well remembers at the soundcheck, 'Malcolm standing at the front, orchestrating them, telling them where to stand.' When they did start playing, at ear-splitting volume, Krell, who was standing alongside his boss, remembers, 'Malcolm looking perplexed and then curious. I think he could see what a lot of the clued-up amongst us could see – this raw talent.'

If so, he had a musical antenna like few others. The drummer pounding away at the back of the stage is not so convinced it was 'raw talent' McLaren heard, and not the sound of a penny dropping: 'I don't know what he thought about the music … but he did know we were able to shock, … and I think he [then] made a decision to get more involved.'

At the time, McLaren was as likely as the band to draw others' attention. St Martin's attendee Paul Madden, for one, noticed some 'weird bloke … wearing peg-leg trousers … [who] kept running back and forth', and formed the view, 'He was trying to start trouble.'

He need not have bothered. When it came to looking for trouble, the mere presence of the Pistols would more than suffice. And St Martin's was the living proof. As Madden told punk chronicler John Robb, 'They had an attitude that was basically, "Fuck off, we're the Sex Pistols." … They had a confidence in what they were doing.' Even from the makeshift stage the band could see that they had set something in motion as yet unnameable – but explosive:

Steve Jones: We'd start[ed] playing live shows before we could play, really. I mean, we could make noise and some sort of construction of the songs and stuff; but it was madness, it was total madness.

[7] That first show still left enough of a mark for Czezowski for him to recall, 'They upset everyone … it was racket upon racket'. (Both Caroline Coon and Roger Armstrong claim they attended the St Martin's gig in a recent article in *Mojo* [Feb. 2016]; but their memories are playing tricks.)

John Lydon: The college audience had never seen anything like it. They couldn't connect with where we were coming from, because our stance was so anti-pop, so anti-everything that had gone on before.

Paul Cook: We went on and it was really loud. It was *deafening*. And we were going really mad, 'cause this was our first gig and we was all really nervous. And suddenly you had this great big hand pop out, and someone pulled the plug out. [1977]

That someone, possibly chewing gum, was in the employ of Bazooka Joe, whose drummer John 'Eddie' Edwards had stuck around long enough to see Rotten 'get up and sing in his torn woolly, [before] everyone said, "Oh, they're not much good, are they?" and went and sat in the bar ... [We just thought] they were a bit untogether and a bit messy.'

Bazooka didn't stay in the bar for long. By this time the Mandrax Jones had popped shortly before hitting the stage was beginning to kick in and, as the boy looked at Johnny, he began to think, 'This is fucking fantastic ... I've made it. We're actually playing in a band.' (By his own admission, he '*was* fucked up'.) Jones started to get a bit carried away, turning his amp up full and aiming swipes at the PA the headliners had never been entirely happy sharing, sending a Bazooka Joe roadie scuttling across the road to the pub where the band had settled:

Robin Chapekar: We were sat in the pub and one of our roadies came running in, shouting, 'You'd better get back! They're trashing the gear and everyone is leaving in droves.' We shot back. They were making a massive noise ... They were kicking the amps, the drummer was trashing the drums. We went over and said, 'Enough is enough!' Danny took the mike off John and I took the amp off Steve and pulled the plug on him ... They were too loud and the space wasn't big enough.

Not every member of Bazooka Joe shared the general distaste. In this particular boot camp, bassist Stuart Goddard comprised a minority of one, 'The rest of my band hated them … They thought they couldn't play … I thought they were very tight.' But even he had to admit, 'They *were* abusing the instruments.' The abuse didn't stop there. When the plug got pulled, there was either 'a brawl' (Chapekar), 'a bit of a fracas' (Matlock), or 'a huge scrap' (sayeth Lydon).

Predictably, the cause was Rotten who, according to Goddard, 'slagged off Bazooka Joe … [so] our guitarist Danny Kleinman leapt from the front row and pinned John against the back wall.' So much for inter-band camaraderie. For Goddard, it would prove a turning point, 'I came out of that gig thinking, I'm tired of Bazooka Joe, I'm tired of Teddy boys.' (It would still take several top-up doses of the Pistols in performance for Adam Ant to emerge from Goddard's febrile imagination.)

Matlock convinced himself the evening's events had put the kibosh on the following night's Central School of Art gig. To his mind, the whole performance had come across as 'something of a racket. Plus, Bazooka Joe kept on pulling the plugs on us, trying to get us off the stage … [But Al McDowell] kept roaring with laughter all the way through the set – well, what we managed to do of it. I really thought we'd blown it … In fact, he really liked us.'

The following night they succeeded in getting the whole way through their eleven-song set. Indeed, Matlock would subsequently insist the Central was 'one of the best gigs we [ever] did'. And the reaction was largely positive, aided as it was by a few familiar faces. As Steve Jones observes, 'They pulled the plug on us [at St Martin's], but the next gig, all the [same] crowd was there again.'

McLaren immediately realized art colleges were the best way to acquire valuable stage-time and hone the Pistols' performance-art, while distancing the band from the current pub-rock revival which, to McLaren's mind, was giving 'rock revivals' a bad name.

After the Central School of Art, he set about phoning round all the art colleges and technical colleges he could find. As one social secretary he phoned that month recalls, McLaren claimed to have got his number from *Time Out* (not true) and proceeded to explain 'that he used to manage the New York Dolls, and he had a new band he was looking for gigs for. He said they'd only done one gig so far.

[I told him I] wasn't planning on a support band and there wouldn't be much money, maybe some beer. Malcolm said fine.'

But such a pragmatic approach was never going to suit any burgeoning McLaren myth. By the following April he had constructed a better-sounding account of the birth of a revolution. When Jonh Ingham wrote the first profile of the Pistols in *Sounds*, he was informed, 'The Pistols found their first public by gatecrashing gigs, pulling up and posing as the support band.' The willing Ingham printed the legend as is, but a legend is all it ever was.[8]

In reality, art colleges were the 'safe' option for a band with this much capacity to shock. The kind of direct, physical confrontation some pub bands faced weekly was rare within the hallowed halls of further education. It was also among arty teenagers, or so McLaren reasoned, that they would most likely find kindred spirits. In fact, what took everyone in the band by surprise was the sheer level of apathy and conservatism which greeted them whenever they assailed collegiate cloisters:

John Lydon: After [St Martin's], for the next few months, we'd play every college and university we could, in and around London. I [discovered] that the student body was not the volatile hotbed of rebellion we were led to believe. They were a very conservative bunch ... [but] we loved the college gigs because there was always free sandwiches, and union prices on the beer. [2014]

Despite such innate conservatism, there were those at these early art college gigs who recognized revolutionary performance art when they saw it, responding directly to the humour that was an essential component of these early, anarchic performances. The Pistols' next notable convert was actually doing a foundation course at the Hertfordshire College of Art and Design in St Albans when – the weekend after the Central School of Art – the Pistols drove out to darkest Herts to play their third 'beer money' gig:

[8] By July 1977, McLaren was telling *Melody Maker*, 'What we used to do was turn up at the college, never tell them, said we had a gig and blagged my way through to the social sec saying that we're [the] support group.'

Shanne Hasler: A band just turned up and played ... We thought they were a piss-take of a 60s group ... They were terrible. Very slow, very amateurish ... But really posey as well ... The first time [I saw them] I thought they were so bad [yet] something came through as really good ... They had the same hairstyle as I had. I was going through this thing, chopping my hair off and dying it ... That was how I got talking to them. John Lydon came up to me 'cause he couldn't believe I dressed like that. He asked if I'd ever been to a shop called Sex ... He said there was a girl there called Jordan, who dressed like me.

Hasler would soon become punk's first cheerleader, convincing her college to book the Pistols twice more that winter before converting her on-off boyfriend Shane MacGowan, and generally championing the band at a time when most feedback was negative, sometimes physically so.

(Her reward for these good deeds was Rotten writing the scathing 'Satellite Kid', in which he described 'her', somewhat unkindly, as 'a big fat pink baked-bean'. Evidently, Rotten read a whole lot more into their 'relationship' than Hasler ever did and then, as was his wont when rejection even breathed its name, lashed out in song.)

For now, though, it was simply a case of spreading the word in some very unpromising places. An All Night Ball at Queen Elizabeth College in South Kensington – where they once again 'played for expenses' – almost resulted in a review, but part-time *NME* writer Kate Phillips arrived too late to catch their set. She did, however, give the band a plug at McLaren's prompting: 'They're managed by Malcolm, who runs "Sex" in the King's Road, and they're going to be the Next Big Thing. Or maybe the Next Big Thing After That.' Right, first time.

Never one to overlook an opportunity to expand his personal network of contacts, McLaren assured Phillips and her then-boyfriend, fellow *NME* scribe Tony Tyler, he would let them know when the Pistols were next playing. But McLaren wouldn't make that call until the following February, perhaps because he knew they weren't quite *ready*.

Though they were actually playing the following night, McLaren didn't think *NME*'s own were likely to trek all the way out to the National College of Food Technology in Weybridge to see a support act, even 'the Next Big Thing'. This was suburban Surrey, hardly the most promising breeding ground for musical ferment. All of which was seemingly confirmed the minute Rotten hit the stage with his opening verbal volley, 'Hello, you student piss-pots,' which promptly got 'all the students' backs up' – though it brought a broad grin from Pete Hawkins, the social secretary who had booked them in the first place.

The frontman of a 'tartan-dressed teenybop band' called Jimmy & The Ferrets, hailing from nearby Hersham, had apparently turned up unnoticed and unknown, and came away convinced teenybop was dead and rabble-rousing might be the future. Still not sure he was reading the tea leaves of pop culture right, Jimmy Pursey eventually informed his fellow Ferrets they were now a garage band from Hersham, truncating it to Sham 69.

Somewhat more attuned to the Pistols' wavelength were a handful of students from the food college itself, equally inspired by what they saw though not because *they* wanted to ride the right bandwagon to glory. At the head of this college cabal was Simon Wright, a musical novice who nonetheless felt enough of a surge of energy coming from the stage to carry it into his designated role as leader of the first band to take Rotten's raw wail to its logical conclusion: the spectacularly unsuccessful, long forgotten Trash:

Simon Wright: They were fairly extraordinarily dressed. I remember Vivienne being there, and Jordan. They'd bought an entourage with them. They started off with probably two hundred people in the hall, but by the end there was about six. But the six that were left thought it was the best thing they'd ever seen … We were huge fans of The Who and the Stones, but you didn't really have the chance to see them anymore … I remember them playing very well. I don't go for all this shit about [how] they couldn't play. They started in time and they stopped in time, and they didn't waffle on. So as far as I was concerned they were good … When I saw them at Weybridge, it was the shock of the new. I didn't know what to expect from a band called the Sex Pistols … One of the six who lasted out the gig at Weybridge was Jane Wimble; another legacy of the Weybridge gig is we formed our own band. Jane and I were the vocalists … We were called Trash, after the New York Dolls track. 'Cause we thought, 'Bloody hell, if they can do that, we can do that.' If you grew up through Prog, it was all complicated stuff. No one would see ELP and think, 'I could do that.' The [Trash] guitarist was there, I was there, Jane was there and our [eventual] manager was there. We [all] got the bug.

Trash were starting from scratch, so not surprisingly it would be the following October before they were ready to strike up the band. In the interim, Jane and Simon renewed that initial hit whenever they knew the Pistols were coming to London town. As for Jane's own memories of the Weybridge gig, they now largely focus on the extraordinary people the band had brought with them:

Jane Wimble: Vivienne Westwood was quite a stand-out character [with her] leather jacket on and her spiky peroxide hair. Her and Malcolm [were] in the hall, and there was only them, pretty much, dancing to them. Everybody else, except for Simon and a couple of others, was watching from a distance because they were really loud. They cleared the room.

She was not alone in gawping. At this juncture, the band's fetishistic retinue drew almost as much comment as the onstage t-shirt salesmen. The visuals were proving just as arresting as the aggressive punk rock the Pistols played, and a lot easier to assimilate.

Meanwhile, the Weybridge social secretary ventured backstage to pay the band their fifteen-quid fee and to tell them how much he personally enjoyed it, only to find McLaren laying into Steve Jones verbally for 'playing too many Johnny Thunders licks'. Such criticisms notwithstanding, the manager sensed they were building enough of a head of steam for Rock to finally blow a gasket. Just as he intended.

★ ★ ★

To further that goal, a mere month after St. Martin's and a week after Weybridge, McLaren arranged for the Sex Pistols to play their most notable gig to date: the Chelsea School of Art. Its proximity to Sex, its prestigious past, and the promise of a famous Rock photographer in situ, all convinced McLaren that now was the time to spread the word further:

Peter Perrett: There were probably a handful of people like me and Zena who had been invited by Malcolm, 'cause he used to send out written invitations to the gigs. They were quite neatly done – he tried to do them [like] an invitation that made you curious. It wasn't just scribbled out, and [he] tried to make it look like an interesting thing to go to.

Bernie Rhodes, a business associate of McLaren's without obvious means of support, was also informed about the Chelsea gig. He took it upon himself to inform a loose conglomerate of young musicians he had taken under his wing about the Pistols, hoping to offer them a glimpse of their own possible future. He already had ambitions to ride McLaren's tailgate to boy-band glory, lacking only the faintest idea as to what it took.

Rhodes' inchoate amalgam of so-called musicians went by the 'provocative' name London SS, but line-up changes were almost as common as rehearsals, and they were going nowhere fast. At least he was right about one thing: they needed to know where the bar was.

In fact, the primary recollection of the Chelsea gig by London SS bass player Tony James is that 'it was all quite chaotic, [but] they had a frontman. And we still hadn't found a frontman.' And they never would. James's best friend, London SS guitarist Mick Jones, was so worried they might be beaten to the punch he refused to attend. But his girlfriend Viv Albertine trundled along, and what she saw that night permanently rocked her world:

Viv Albertine: I hadn't been to a rock concert for a year … I'd look through the papers and there was nothing I wanted to see … And I couldn't understand why. Then, when I saw the Pistols, I knew … It was a matter of attitude – and fuck everything else. I can't remember the [actual] music … It was just something I understood, and that was it. [1976]

Albertine may not have been able to put down in words what she felt at the time, but in her evocative 2014 memoir she referenced having 'seen bands [with] this anarchic quality before: the Pink Fairies, The Pretty Things, the Edgar Broughton Band.' The difference this time was that 'there's no fake American twang ... All the things I'm so embarrassed about, John's made into virtues ... He's brave. A revolutionary. He's sending a very powerful message, the most powerful message anyone can ever transmit. Be yourself.'

Although converting other seasoned gig-goers might take more than 'a matter of attitude', McLaren had decided it was time he invited Roger Armstrong, who had recently set up Chiswick Records with Ted Carroll, to a Pistols gig. Armstrong, another music-man friend of McLaren's, had already told him he couldn't have singer Mike Spencer from The Count Bishops – because the Bishops were *his*. Yet relations remained cordial and all it took was a phonecall.[9]

Even at this early stage, he was interested in Armstrong's reaction, believing it would be a likely litmus test for other music contacts whose opinion he respected. His response was fairly typical – one quarter bemusement to three-quarters amusement:

Roger Armstrong: They were a total mess, but it was fun; Johnny just slagged the audience off, basically, and the audience slagged him off and threw things at him, and that encouraged him. But it wasn't as if they were playing to people who would throw bottles and glasses at the slightest encouragement.

Jordan also enjoyed the experience, knowing she wouldn't have to put up with the sort of unwanted attention her fetish wet-dream look tended to draw in any West End pub; and after the gig she could still make the last train back to the south coast. She was anxious to see how the band had come on in the few weeks since last she'd caught them. The answer was: a lot. Eighteen months later, she described

[9] Mike Spencer, who independently attended the Chelsea School of Art show, only later found out McLaren was interested in him as a potential Pistols frontman.

this very gig as the moment she 'really got the feeling that the Pistols were bound to make it – because there were people going crazy and dancing. I really defy anyone in those days to go to a Pistols concert and not be excited by what was going on … There was definite static energy.'

That 'static energy' transferred equally well to the Perretts, who were as amused as Armstrong and as enthused as Albertine (and Jordan) by the way the band set about challenging the whole post-Pepper edifice that had made 'learning to play' a prerequisite of getting up on stage. Having only just decided to form another band himself, to replace the inglorious England's Glory, Perrett took a great deal of heart from the night's experience:

Peter Perrett: Most of the audience were [standing there] with open mouths, thinking, 'How have they got the nerve to stand up there?' I thought it was highly amusing, very funny. The majority of the audience hated them, but in a benign way. They weren't throwing bottles or anything. I was laughing because I thought it was the most entertaining thing I'd been to [in ages]. I went to see the Sex Pistols because Malcolm was so insistent. But I actually enjoyed it. Because it was different – it was definitely different. Later [on], I can remember [Johnny] abusing the audience, but I don't think he had the confidence to abuse them at that time … The main thing that came across was that they had the nerve to do it, which I found inspiring. It must have been *very* inspirational for any young kid learning to play guitar that they didn't have to wait till they mastered the guitar. And it was valid, because it definitely got a reaction, even if it was an open-mouthed reaction.

If Perrett was still undecided whether to tie himself to the Squeeze mast or find a more rocky alternative, the Pistols helped tip the balance. Nine months later, The Only Ones would start preparing to run along parallel lines to punk.

For the Pistols, the Chelsea gig was enough of a homecoming for Rotten to wear Sex's hot-off-the-press Cambridge Rapist t-shirt and for Jones to wear the equally notorious Two Cowboys t-shirt as ex-Bowie and Syd Barrett photographer Mick Rock snapped the first professional shots of the band live and the latest line in Sex shock tactic t-shirts.[10]

McLaren only had one problem – he was fast running out of inner-city art colleges to play, having yet to find an alternative that would catapult his band of 'bad boys' into instant notoriety. Their next gig, four days later, was at the Ravensbourne College of Design & Communication in Chislehurst, Kent; where McLaren again dutifully escorted the band in to the premises. When journalist David May, who had just interviewed him for *Gallery International*, failed to take up his invite, he harboured little hope that anyone there would 'find expression in what they are doing'. But he was wrong:

Simon Barker: It was Saturday night in Bromley and [as per usual] there was nothing to do. There was a band called [Fogg] on, we were just going for something to do, not to see them. It was 50p to get in. I got there, and I saw Malcolm. I'd seen him in the shop and I knew he'd managed the New York Dolls. We were big New York Dolls fans. I thought, 'Wow, what's he doing here?' Then the Sex Pistols came on, and I just thought they were really brilliant. I was the only person clapping ... All the students there were just going mad, shouting and crap... You could tell what they were trying to do, that sleazy rock'n'roll ... It had some style to it, even though it was so badly played ... Steve and [Sue] came afterwards, and I told them about it.

So, contrary to legend, this was not the fabled Ravensbourne gig witnessed by Steve Bailey and Sue Ballion (aka Steve Severin and Siouxsie Sioux), co-founders of the Bromley Contingent's most enduring musical refraction, Siouxsie & The Banshees. Rather, as Severin informed me in 2006, 'We arrived a bit late. I went to the bar, and Simon went into the hall and saw the last song that the Pistols played. [He] just said, "I've seen the English Stooges."'

The pair would have to wait for an opportunity to replay Barker's epiphany. And wait. And wait. Because, for reasons that are still

[10] The Two Cowboys t-shirt famously depicted two butch cowboys naked from the waist down greeting each other, with their penises almost touching.

unclear – but were probably the result of McLaren being distracted by other business matters (one of them a still-unresolved obscenity charge relating to that Two Cowboys t-shirt) – over the next two months the Sex Pistols disappeared below the most sophisticated gig-goers' radar. Just two confirmed gigs separate their December 10th, 1975 gig at a London City Polytechnic hall of residence – the day after Ravensbourne – from their seditious assault on Soho's Marquee Club, the second week in February.

But gig they did, even if no one can quite remember where. According to latterday Lydon, there were shows at the West Ham social bar, where he 'won them over with love and charm', and a Hounslow Teddy boy convention, just the kind of audience McLaren would have wanted to expose them to. Paul Cook also remembers a show in East London somewhere, 'around Christmas. By then John handled himself so well onstage. He had everyone in stitches.'

Perhaps those revellers included a certain Bill Dyke, from Lewisham, who wrote a letter to *Melody Maker* in October 1976 informing its readers, 'The only time I have ever come across these punker-wallahs live was at a gig ... at my old college. Within two minutes I and half the audience were rolling about laughing. The other half had fled for the bar.' Evidently, an early gig.

Dyke's old college might have been North East London Polytechnic where, according to Jonh Ingham, 'they succeeded in emptying the room' that winter.[11] This could also have been the first time that the Pistols supported Ian Dury's band, the Kilburns (shorthand for Kilburn & The High Roads), North East London Poly being a favourite haunt of theirs.

Dury biographer Will Birch, for one, is sure 'the Sex Pistols supported the Kilburns at North East London Poly ... Malcolm knew Ian from two years before, in the King's Road ... and Malcolm [was there, holding] Ian up to Lydon: "See how good he is – see how he draws the audience in – he stands behind the mike – one hand on the mike – hangs on it Gene Vincent-style."'

If McLaren was this intent on inculcating stage-craft in his own

[11] Ingham makes this observation in his original April 1976 article on the band, so he must have heard about this otherwise-undocumented gig at the time.

Artful Dodger, then the gig in question must have been early on, before egos got the better of them both. These shows, lost in the mists of myth, were witnessed by few folk and fewer still came to see the Sex Pistols. But Viv's Sex workers remained loyal to the cause, even when things got hairy. The girls, in particular, were increasingly amazed at how the once-diffident Rotten lost his chronic shyness whenever he hit a stage, ruling each potential mob with an iron stand and a lashing tongue:

Tracie O'Keefe: In those days John used to swear a lot at the audience. The equipment used to pack up and stools used to break, and stuff like that, and so he used to stand there and swear at the hall and throw beer at people and tell them they were stupid.

Jordan: There were times when it didn't work. A lot of it involved the audience, John couldn't work with an audience that wasn't feeding something back to him … There had to be some sort of buzz going on with the audience for it to work.

If the girls and boys from Sex were for now the Pistols' only regular fans, it wasn't for want of trying on Steve Bailey and Sue Ballion's part. They continually phoned up the shop. But, as Barker recalls, 'They'd cancel all the time. You could phone up on the day, and people would say yeah, they're gonna play tonight.'

The suburbanite lovers didn't catch up with the band until the first week of February, when the Pistols returned to Ravensbourne. This time Steve and Sue were down the front (though Barker, mysteriously, was not). The dolled-up Siouxsie even ran into an old school friend, Pete Long, and they exchanged 'embarrassed greetings across the hippie/punk divide', or so writer Nigel Williamson recalled twenty-six years later, putting pen to paper to offer his own impressions of that wintry evening:

> A cold and cheerless Saturday night … [Shall we] spend the rest of Saturday evening getting pointlessly drunk in Henekey's Wine Bar in Bromley High Street, or go the short distance to Ravensbourne College of Art to see an unknown band called the Sex Pistols? We

> opt for the latter ... Within minutes we wish we'd stayed in the pub, for there is more future in getting mindlessly obliterated on Newcastle Brown than in listening to this racket. The Sex Pistols can barely play their instruments. Each tuneless thrash that passes for a song sounds the same as the one before. And while the spotty, under-nourished frontman knows how to sneer, he certainly doesn't know how to sing.

Siouxsie's equally vague memory of that gig, which she mistakenly thinks 'might have been Beckenham', was of 'just a few students wandering about ... Everybody kept their distance ... [The Pistols] just played their music. Rotten didn't ... really glare at anyone the way he did later. Glen was the loudest ... He used to do backing vocals and ... he'd do them in tune!' Who did he think he was? Ronnie Lane?

The Bromley pair were hooked. Severin remembers, 'We met them in the bar afterwards. We [already] knew Malcolm and Vivienne a little bit from going up to the shop, and Glen said, "We're playing the Marquee next week. Why don't you come along?"' It was the sort of invitation they'd been waiting for ever since that evening, two months earlier, when their friend Simon told them he had just 'seen the English Stooges'.

★ ★ ★

Little did Steve and Siouxsie know they were being invited to the Pistols' calculated entry into the annals of London clublore, a head-on confrontation with the very embodiment of English pub rock, Eddie & The Hot Rods. The conflagration that night appears to have been part of McLaren's plan all along – even as he impatiently awaited the band developing enough chops to scythe down Southend's favourite musical misfits.

It had required two months off the radar, reliant solely on the drip-drip effect of word of mouth, before he felt they were ready, switching his strategy from art college gigs to a full frontal assault on the citadel of West End rock clubs. Time, he felt, was not on his side.

But by Thursday, February 12th, McLaren had all his ducks in a row. The band had by now dropped 'Through My Eyes' (a Sex jukebox favourite) from the set, concentrating on the five originals and six covers that were the mainstay of their early sets, getting those songs locked and loaded. At this point, the covers – referencing bands like the Small Faces, The Who, and The Stooges – served an important purpose. As Matlock says, 'People didn't know what to make of it till we did a cover version like 'Substitute' [or] 'Whatcha Gonna Do About It'. [They would] recognise the tune, and [maybe] understood what we were trying to do.'

Not that your average 1976 gig-goer could be expected to know either '(Don't Give Me) No Lip' or 'Understanding', which came second and third at the Marquee, after the Swankers original, 'Did You No Wrong'. They were obscure B-sides by Dave Berry and The Small Faces respectively. It was another of McLaren's tests, one Rob Symmons – who had snuck into the Marquee with his mate, Vic Godard – passed with flying colours:

Rob Symmons: When they did 'No Lip', 'Understanding' [&c.], those were all my songs – I had all those singles ... That was it for me. They were doing better versions – [because] they were destroying those songs.

McLaren had taken steps to ensure the Pistols brought along their own apostles for the sermon at the Marquee. Nils Stevenson, brother of photographer Ray, got his first sight of the band he would road-manage for the remainder of 1976 after 'Malcolm said, "You've got to come and see the Pistols." Vivienne, Chrissie Hynde and Malcolm came to pick me up in the old Mini.'

And while Steve and Siouxsie made their own way from Bromley, Simon Barker went 'with Jordan and Valerie [from the shop] ... There was three rows of chairs in front of the stage, and Jordan and Valerie jumped up on stage, dancing, and taking her top off and everything.' Evidently, orders had been received and understood.

At some prior point McLaren had decided to make Jordan part of the act, if only for tonight. He probably hoped the invitation he'd extended to photographer Joe Stevens would be accepted, and another leading snapper could capture the visual side of Sex *and* the Pistols. Unfortunately, Stevens misunderstood the nature of the performance to which he had been invited:

Joe Stevens: I wasn't paying any attention. I was sure what he was talking about was ... some sort of a dildo show ... 'cause he said something about 'Sex Pistols'. I said [Kate and I] were busy ... So we didn't go to the Marquee gig, but [my colleague] Neil Spencer did ... He said there were bodies all over, people [were] going bananas ... [and] to go [see them] if you want some good snaps.

Spencer's unexpected presence was proof that all of McLaren's previous networking was paying off. He had actually invited *NME*'s Tony Tyler to come and see the band he missed back in November. Once again, though, Tyler turned up late, accompanied not by his girlfriend Kate Phillips, but by Spencer. They promptly discovered they had missed part of the spectacle when Spencer was informed he had 'missed the cavortings with the two scantily clad (plastic thigh boots and bodices) pieces dancing up front. In fact, I only caught the last few numbers; [but it was] enough ... to get the idea.'

In lieu of semi-naked women, the two writers were greeted by the sight of a chair sailing through the air. And much to Spencer's surprise, the deed was met with 'obvious nonchalance [by] the bass, drums and guitar'. His initial thought, that the chair had been directed *at* the band, was soon shown to be erroneous: 'I saw it was the singer who'd done the throwing. He was stalking round the front rows (sic)... baring his teeth at the audience and stopping to chat to members of the group's retinue.' Even without a glimpse of Jordan's boots'n'bodice, the visuals were proving an arresting point of entry into the punk aesthetic:

Neil Spencer: The Pistols looked completely unique. Big mohair sweaters and spiky hair – absolutely nobody looked like that. People were shouting abuse, but what was novel was that the band screamed right back ...[Yes,] the Pistols were musically derivative, but what they had was a lot of guts – very immediate ... John was very verbal, which meant there was a lot of interaction with the audience.

Someone else found himself responding to the visuals first and the music second:

Nils Stevenson: The band were all over the place, not playing very well, not being sure of what songs they were playing, [but in] the chaos Rotten [started] saying, 'I've always wanted to watch this group play,' and just walked offstage with this long microphone lead, and sits in the audience, sing[ing] along when he wants to, and throw[ing] Jordan across the floor, throw[ing] chairs about ... [It] reminded me very much of Iggy Pop ... He had the same sort of irreverence and craziness. He was running across the stage, spitting in girls' faces and pulling them by the hair. ... I knew I just had to be involved.

Once again, the audience quickly divided, though not down the middle – rather, between the many neophobes and the few neophytes. Steve Severin loved the whole thing, 'They threw a few chairs around, and Jordan got on stage and wiggled about, and they upset everybody, including the Hot Rods, [which was] the first schism between the old and the new ... We suddenly felt this enormous allegiance to the Pistols.'

Rob Symmons and Vic Godard, having happened on the gig by chance, were also immediate converts; Symmons for the reason already given, Godard, because 'it sounded so shambolic that it didn't sound good enough to be professional'. The germ of the idea for Subway Sect was planted that night – a band 'so shambolic that it didn't sound good enough to be professional'.

Despite the unequal division between those for and against, the Pistols announced they were going to do an encore, their version of The Who classic 'Substitute'. It was the final straw for one Gallic fan, who heckled, 'You can't play.' This time it was Matlock, not Rotten, who stepped up to the mike, 'So what!' before launching into a blistering blast of maximum punk rock.

Immediately after the set Tony Tyler took Spencer to meet the band, at which point the latter recalls, 'They gave me that famous quote, "We're not into music, we're into chaos," which had obviously been primed by Malcolm.'

The two *NME* scriveners were not the only ones venturing backstage to have a word with the band. The headliners wanted to know who was going to pay for the damage to their stage monitors and microphones. According to Matlock's account, 'It was the first time we'd had proper monitors onstage – which meant it was the first time John heard his own voice. And he didn't like what he heard. So he trashed the monitors.'

'Eddie', aka Barrie Masters, later claimed, in an authorized account of the largely-forgotten band, that he 'gave [Rotten] a little kiddy slap. Nothing hefty. So he starts whingeing like a little girl, and told McLaren, [who] sent him back with some other guy. I went to give him a slap and he ran away.'

Actually, none of the Rods got their hands on the Pistols, as evidenced by a bellyaching interview they gave *NME* just six weeks after the incident, in which guitarist Dave Higgs complained, 'They can't play or nuffink, they just insult the audience. We wouldn't mind, 'cept they wrecked our gear, destroyed it, so we had no PA or monitors. We waited for them to apologize, but they fucked off.' At this point tough guy Masters interjected, 'Lucky for them. If we see them in the streets, we'll kill 'em.'

(And yet, they never did. Instead, they attempted to jump aboard the new wave bandwagon a year too late, now calling themselves The Rods, prepared to do anything they needed to do to pass themselves off as punks.)

The incident would only serve the Pistols' purpose, giving them a ready target for future bile as well as a physical manifestation of all that they hated about pub rock. For McLaren, though, there was one minor headache. The gig had been secured through the personal intervention of Marc Zermati, who was understandably appalled when he heard 'Rotten [had] destroyed all the equipment, and … Barrie and the guys from the Hot Rods [ended up] threatening to punch them'.

Before word could get back to his friend, McLaren suggested to Zermati he come and check them out himself, at a private party on the Thames two days later, to which he was cordially invited. He arrived to find 'it was pretty weird, the place – this big gay party'. Not his kind of scene at all, and his companion was equally unimpressed. McLaren had suggested Marc bring along Sean Tyla, of the Tyla Gang, perhaps already thinking of getting his band of 'musical incompetents' a production deal:

Sean Tyla: [Marc Zermati] took me to a party once, near the Thames to meet Malcolm McLaren and watch the Sex Pistols. Malcolm wanted Marc to sign the band and me to produce them. McLaren started talking in telephone numbers and I told him the band was shit anyway. And that was that.

Tyla would be one of the many invited to Andrew Logan's annual Valentine's Party at his Butler's Wharf loft who was non-plussed by the Pistols in all their audio-visual glory. The host, who revelled in his outre image, concurred. He later claimed the Pistols were never intended to be 'the main attraction, they were just a group that played', and that he had only ever booked them as a favour to Malcolm, who had told him 'he had these boys – he called them "the boys" – he wanted to launch somewhere … interesting. And an Andrew Logan party was interesting.' Not that is how one Bromley boy remembers an evening when the McLaren guest list threatened to outnumber the host's:

Simon Barker: All that [Logan] crowd loved Vivienne and them for what they were doing, but they were really scared of them, 'cause Vivienne and Malcolm held them rather in contempt … So Malcolm used that, got them to play at Andrew Logan's party, then he freaked out. [Because] Malcolm … invited everyone and anyone. Logan was freaking out 'cause he had this nice flat and there were all these people … John Rotten was shut outside, and finally he persuaded them to open the door and let him in, and he was so mad … he said to Vivienne, 'Where's our fucking drink?' And she said, 'I think its all gone.'

If Vivienne reasoned an angry Rotten was a lively Rotten – which would have been oh so Situationist of her – Barker recalls her receiving 'the biggest black eye she ever had in her life' for her pains. As for Logan, Jordan witnessed him 'freaking out because it was like anarchy had been transported into his little paradise and he hadn't realized what was going on'. Meanwhile, McLaren was having a meltdown of his own, rushing up to his favourite fetish model to beseech her to join the band onstage:

Jordan: Someone from *NME* arrived – it might have been Nick Kent ... [Malcolm] was really excited. 'The *NME* are actually here. Do something, Jords! They've actually turned up! We've got to do something that will create a scuffle, a story.' ... He wanted them to get a bit of outrageous publicity. He said, 'Take your clothes off, girl.' And I said, 'Naw, I'm not going to.' He said, 'Go on, we haven't got much time.' I said, 'I'll [only] do it if John knows ... I'll do it if John rips them off!' [So] in the middle of 'No Fun', John [did it and] broke all the zips on my leotard, which was a real piss-off. It was all for publicity! ... The Andrew Logan crowd were pretty unshockable, so we were in good company to do it.

If the stunt was intended to be for Nick Kent's benefit, it was actually Joe Stevens who ultimately benefited, snapping the famous shot of Rotten grappling with Jordan's bra and mammaries which McLaren later used 'as a poster' while he filed it with the *NME*, just in case. Stevens was impressed, not only by the band but by the way McLaren had mustered a crowd of movers and mavericks to witness the mayhem:

Joe Stevens: Mark Zermati was there, Chrissie was there, Katie and I were there. Janet Street Porter ... We couldn't figure out what the hell it was ... I think the gig was two short sets ... I remember Janet Street Porter saying it was her all-time favourite show, [because] it was tits and ass, and a bit of nastiness.

Kent, no longer an item with Hynde, was required to make his first outing to see the Pistols under his own steam, but cruise along he did – just not on *NME*'s behalf. He was simply a curious bystander, as he would be for much of the year of Punk, after playing such a central part in its genesis as a critical champion of the likes of Beefheart and The Stooges and guitarist-singer in early incarnations of both the Pistols and The Damned. His version of that night in February he only articulated when required to write a brief profile of McLaren the following November, when the Pistols' brand of mayhem was about to go national:

> The Sex Pistols must have played three sets that night. They sounded rough, shambling, like young kids who're still self-conscious and a bit disorientated by it all but who were drunk so it didn't much matter anyways. They kept playing the same numbers – The Stooges' 'No Fun' kept coming up and Johnny Rotten, who prior to this performance I'd always considered a pretty shy, neurotic young kid, delivered the sort of performance that would later capture the hearts of Caroline Coon *et al*, even though a certain Iggy Pop would've been more than a little amused(?) to witness some of the tyke's audience assault tactics.

McLaren's underlying motive, in putting the Pistols on at a private party attended by people who, as Jordan says, 'were pretty unshockable', would be duly debated ad infinitum. Lydon would even claim, 'That sort of nonsense was what [Malcolm] grovelled and hankered for, hanging around with all these fake socialites.' Steve Severin, standing at the sideline, retained a better grasp of what happened that night, 'By the end of the evening … the art crowd got the message that they were being pissed on from a great height.'

If further proof were needed that McLaren's primary concern remained 'showing young people, eighteen, nineteen years of age, [a way] to find expression in what they are doing', he had encouraged Bernie Rhodes to bring his own would-be prodigies.

Tony James and Brian James both seized the opportunity for a night out (and free booze). For the latter James – already a proficient lead guitarist in the James Williamson mould – it was his first glimpse of the future and (like many an early Pistols convert) what most impressed him was the sheer front the band displayed onstage: 'I thought, "Oh, they're not very good players but they ain't half got a lot of attitude." It was between the numbers when John used to come into his own, when he'd be talking. It was just like a stand-up comic … He did put over this air of not giving a fuck.'

Mick Jones also agreed to tag along. It would be the last time the London SS trio would appear in public as members of the same band. Jones emerged from the party with the same kind of strange light in his eyes that shone from girlfriend Viv Albertine after the Chelsea School of Art gig. As he told *The Word*, 'You just knew straight away, as soon as you'd seen them: you ain't seen nothing like this.' He also realized, with similar immediacy, that London SS were not of the same genus; and it was time to put together a band that was.

If Kent's memory serves him well, the night ended on an appropriate – though not perhaps a high – note. After the nth version of 'No Fun' wound down to its cacophonic conclusion, 'a seriously disturbed-looking Lydon began smashing up his mike stand. At this point Logan swanned over and suggested that maybe their set had reached its fitting conclusion.'

A good time was had, if not by all, by those for whom the Pistols' set/s were the evening's abiding memory. McLaren returned to his nice apartment with his slightly-bruised girlfriend, nursing thoughts of a Nick Kent review and a series of Joe Stevens snaps across the centre-pages of the UK's premier music weekly, *New Musical Express*, circulation two hundred thousand-plus and counting.

But when he opened the paper, the following Thursday, he scoured in vain for such a spread. Instead, much to his surprise, there was a half-page review of the Marquee show, penned by Neil Spencer with a headline that was suggested by Tony Tyler – 'Don't look over your shoulder, but the Sex Pistols are coming'. He couldn't have said it better himself. It had taken him just three months from a standing start to turn London's rock scene on its head and transform the Pistols into something more than tomorrow's fish and chip papers. Next stop: Nashville.

2. THE NEW NASHVILLE TEENS

[February 19th – April 29th]

THE BEAT GOES ON

Joseph Stevens

Sex Pistols Squirt the Issue

THE MARQUEE, LONDON —"Hurry up, they're having an orgy on stage," said the bloke at the door as he tore the tickets up.

I waded to the front and straightway sighted a chair arcing gracefully through the air, skidding across the stage and thudding contentedly into the PA system, to the obvious nonchalance of the bass drums and guitar.

Well I didn't think they sounded *that* bad on first earful — then I saw it was the singer who'd done the throwing.

He was stalking round the front rows, apparently scuffing over the litter on the floor between baring his teeth at the audience and stopping to chat with members of the group's retinue. He's called Johnny Rotten and the monicker fits.

Sex Pistols? Seems I'd missed the cavortings with the two scantily clad (plastic thigh boots and bodices) pieces dancing up front. In fact, I only caught the last few numbers; enough, as it happens, to get the idea. Which is...a quartet of spiky teenage misfits from the

Joseph Stevens

wrong end of various London roads, playing 60's styled white punk rock as unselfconsciously as it's possible to play it these days i.e. selfconsciously.

Punks? Springsteen Bruce and the rest of 'em would get shredded if they went up against these boys. They've played less than a dozen gigs as yet, have a small but fanatic following, and don't get asked back. Next month they play the Institute of Contemporary Arts if that's a clue.

I'm told the Pistols repertoire includes lesser known Dave Berry and Small Faces numbers (check out early Kinks' B sides leads), besides an Iggy and the Stooges item and several self-penned numbers like the moronic "I'm Pretty Vacant," a meandering power-chord job that produced the chair-throwing incident.

No-one asked for an encore but they did one anyway: "We're going to play 'Substitute.'"

"You can't play," heckled an irate French punter.

"So what?" countered the bassman, jutting his chin in the direction of the bewildered Frog.

That's how it is with the Pistols — a musical experience with the emphasis on Experience.

"Actually, we're not into music," one of the Pistols confided afterwards.

Wot then?

"We're into chaos."

Neil Spencer (NME)

2

'Hurry up, they're having an orgy on stage,' said the bloke at the door ... I waded to the front and straightaway sighted a chair arcing gracefully through the air, skidding across the stage and thudding contentedly into the PA system ... I only caught the last few numbers; enough, as it happens, to get the idea. Which is ... a quartet of spiky teenage misfits from the wrong end of various London roads, playing 60's styled white punk rock as unself-consciously as it's possible to play it these days, i.e. self-consciously ... They've played less than a dozen gigs as yet, have a small but fanatic following, and don't get asked back ... I'm told the Pistols' repertoire includes lesser known Dave Berry and Small Faces numbers besides an Iggy and the Stooges item and several self-penned numbers like the moronic 'I'm Pretty Vacant', a meandering power-chord job that produced the chair-throwing incident. No one asked for an encore, but they did one anyway.

– Neil Spencer,* NME *February 21st, 1976

There are reviews and there are moments the world tilts. History has rightly categorized Spencer's depiction of the Marquee gig as the latter. Lines like 'they're having an orgy on stage', and 'a quartet of spiky teenage misfits from the wrong end of various London roads, playing 60's styled white punk rock' leapt off of the page, confirming the link between the Pistols and punk rock from the outset.

Taken in tandem with Tyler's attention-grabbing headline, and a snap of a toothsome bug-eyed Rotten from the Rock collection, its effect was as ripples on the pop culture pond. These reached even unto the other side of the pond, thanks to America's rock monthly *Creem*, where Lester Bangs' proto-punk prose had resided since 1970. The Detroit-based 'zine reused the review minus the headline, but with an even more atmospheric snap of Rotten from the Pistols' March 100 Club debut.

It couldn't have come at a better time, or in a better place. *NME* by 1976 was the music weekly of record, the one newspaper music fans from Sydney to Stranraer bought religiously, in Britain on the Thursday it came out. Other papers trawled it for news (as London's *Evening Standard* did that week, paraphrasing Spencer's prose to make 'semi-nude girls' the phrase that leapt out). It was publicity money couldn't buy. But it came at a price. The Pistols were immediately banned from the Marquee, proving how prophetic Spencer had been when he wrote they 'don't get asked back'.

NME's gossip column the following week went so far as to claim the incident had led to the Pistols being 'dismissed as support band to Eddie and the Hot Rods on the Rods' current tour after only one gig'. If that had been a genuine carrot, dangled in front of them in the hope they'd behave, it was now public knowledge that this was a band who bit any hand which fed them, or indeed lent them their monitors.

Where the *NME* really came into its own was out in the provinces, beyond the satellite towns, north of Watford Gap, west of Westway. It was there where music fans scoured its pages for the next big thing, convinced anything and everything that was about to shake the foundations came from London, New York or L.A., and *NME* was their weekly window into that world. Two such souls were Howard Trafford (aka Devoto) and Pete McNeish (aka Shelley), students at the Bolton Institute of Technology. They were sat in the refectory that Thursday lunchtime for their weekly ritual, jointly reading their communal copy of that week's *NME*, when Pete gave Howard the Spencer review to read:

Howard Devoto: I was reading [*NME*] but I completely missed his review, and Pete handed it back to me and said, 'Did you read this?' It was that 'We're not into music, we're into chaos' line, and the fact they played a Stooges song. It was like, 'Who the fuck in Britain plays Stooges songs?' … And it was [so] obviously confrontational.

Trafford and McNeish had been trying to put together a band for a few months after Trafford grabbed McNeish's attention with an ad pinned on the college bulletin board requesting like-minded 'musicians … to do version of Sister Ray'. Between them, they were probably the only pair of students within a ten-mile radius who knew the title of this sixteen-minute slice of metal machine music on the Velvets' least accessible album; and they soon forged a close, artistic union. But it was proving hard-going working up arrangements of Stooges and Eno songs with a drummer from the local tub-thumpers union. As Devoto admits, 'It was really not happening.' And it was starting to get under his skin:

Howard Devoto: I was reading about what was going on in New York, with the emergence of groups like Ramones and Television, and thinking, 'God, that sounds so much more interesting and fresh than anything that is happening here.' Really, I just wanted to put a group together to do something different – and my feelings at the time couldn't have been too uncommon; there must've been a lot of people similarly pissed off with the current music scene. They only needed a bit of direction to go off and do it themselves … [to] create another generation of music.

Perhaps a trip to see this English incarnation of The Stooges might serve to recharge their batteries and refocus their energies. And it just so happened there was a National Union of Students conference in London that weekend – and McNeish was the Bolton Institute's NUS rep. Two birds, one stone. By a further stroke of good fortune, the Pistols *were* playing that weekend – in fact they had shows in St Albans, High Wycombe and Welwyn Garden City, Thursday through Saturday, at colleges where an NUS badge would always get you in.

After weeks of relative inactivity, the Pistols were revving to go. Indeed, the night before Trafford and McNeish borrowed a car to drive to High Wycombe via Reading and London, the Pistols made their long-awaited return to Hertfordshire College of Art and Design, scene of their third-ever gig. McLaren had used his powers of persuasion to convince the well-known photographer Ray Stevenson to come out of self-imposed retirement from Rock to check 'his' new band out.

After painting the Pistols as neo-revolutionaries, he inserted one small caveat, 'They can't play very well. But that's not what's important. It's their attitude!' His interest piqued, Stevenson ventured out to St Albans where he found the Pistols charity-shop chic already taking root, and enough visual cues to keep him on an unpaid retainer for the remainder of 1976.

Shanne Hasler was again in attendance, as were Simon, Steve and Siouxsie from Bromley, venturing north of London for the first time. Hasler was unimpressed by this 'rival' clique, 'I thought they were posers in the worst sense.' But she fully acknowledged that the trio stood out from the crowd, 'Siouxsie, very tall and glamorous, like a model, [standing with] this bloke with dungarees and red hair.' The whole effect was rather striking.

But if the St Albans gig (which passed off without incident) was almost a homecoming for a band who rarely if ever 'get asked back', the following night at High Wycombe they were back to being 'bad boys', wrecking the equipment of the headliner and generally being as brattish as sociopathic lab brats. And if Hasler made her presence felt again, two art students from 'Manchester' and one from Reading (Howard Trafford's friend, Richard Boon) also garnered an invite after turning up at the Sex shop in the afternoon with a copy of *Time Out*, hoping to meet the band but having to make do with their manager. McLaren was secretly bowled over to discover these lads had driven two hundred miles to see a band they had only just read about, with no real idea what to expect.

Hasler, who knew what to expect, was impressed by Trafford's (and McNeish's) dedication – but just as stunned that 'there was a bloke in a leather jacket who'd come all the way down from Manchester' as she was by the Pistols' response to an audience who, unlike those at her own college, were not content to sit idly by and barrack the newbies:

Shanne Hasler: The place was packed with people sitting cross-legged on the floor, students with long hair and joss sticks, shouting abuse at them. It was great. I remember [Rotten] just lay down on the stage, and some bloke leapt out and started thumping him, and there was a great big punch-up.

Perhaps they were angry at the lack of semi-naked girls. Or perhaps the audience simply couldn't hear what Rotten was saying – or singing. Because things had started to get out of hand earlier that evening. As Matlock recalls, 'A couple of our mates got very plastered and [then] insisted on doing our sound. So we locked them in the van, but they punched the window out and did the sound anyway.'

The High Wycombe set soon declined into farce. One eye-witness remembers, 'Rotten leering over the stage; someone grabbed his mike and pulled him into the audience. The power was then cut off.' If so, it was not before Rotten had again beaten the microphone within an inch of its flexed cord. And this time he was actually confronted by the headliners, a standoff indelible enough to be recalled by McLaren and Matlock long after the band blew up in both their faces:

Glen Matlock: After[wards], the guy from the Screaming Lord Sutch band comes and says, 'You broke our microphones.' John … swore blind that he hadn't broken them. But I'd seen him a minute before really pummelling them into the ground.

Malcolm McLaren: We were supporting Screaming Lord Sutch and the microphone which Rotten was using suddenly went dead … He got hold of the microphone and smashed it to the ground, jumping on it. The PA guys and roadies swarmed on stage from every direction but Big Jim, Steve's mate, was there, very pissed, and … he was holding them back.

The pair from Bolton Institute stood in a semi-euphoric state of shock. Spencer's review, for all its purple prose, had not prepared them for anything like this. Trafford first and foremost was in awe of the sheer gall of the Pistols' frontman, whom he well remembered 'smashing their microphone down and stalking off the stage', though he later learnt the latter action was because Rotten was nursing a cold and was 'going off to be sick in the toilets after a number and returning ten minutes later – very unusual'. His friend, Peter responded more to the underlying humour and the way they sent up the audience's expectations, which struck a chord, or three:

Pete Shelley: At High Wycombe … there were a lot of people who didn't like what was going on – [these] louts playing loud, unkempt music. The important thing about the Sex Pistols was … they weren't like everybody else … They looked very coordinated – a proper band – but they also got down to what me and Howard thought was the basis of exciting music – fast, loud, no kowtowing to the audience … Somebody telling the audience to fuck off was revolutionary in those days … It was also hilarious – the comedy part of punk always got lost in the translation. It was Theatre of the Absurd in some respects, making a Godawful noise to get a reaction. They were hanging together by a thread – there was this sense that it could fall apart at any minute.

McNeish went outside after the Pistols' set for some air, where he noticed that someone 'had put a brick through their van window'. He naturally attributed it to either one of Sutch's roadies or a punter who had been caught up in the 'great big punch up'. It never occurred to him that it was the Pistols' own 'soundmen' who had done the damage.

Fortunately for the band, all was well that ended well. When Rotten once again brazenly refused to own up to his act of mike-destruction, Screaming Lord Sutch, a man who had seen enough madness to turn anyone into a raving loony, 'just burst out laughing at the bare-faced cheek of it all' – much to Matlock's amazement. Meanwhile, the owner of another local venue, watching from the wings, wanted to introduce himself to McLaren. Ron Watts found himself thinking, 'Yes, they're wild enough, they've got enough anarchy in them.'

The Pistols were just what he had been looking for, but not for his Nag's Head pub, a High Wycombe hostelry he owned. He instead intended to unveil these young urban guerrillas at his 'other' venue, the 100 Club, a famous r'n'b club since the days of skiffle, located at 100 Oxford Street, WC1, a pebble's throw from the Marquee at the epicentre of the West End. A support slot there on March 30th, the first available, would allow him to gauge their peformance-art fully while giving the Pistols an unexpected re-entry into the heart of the city.

Meanwhile, Trafford, McNeish and Boon were anxious to know if the Pistols were playing anywhere the following evening. They were playing down the road in Welwyn Garden City, a place that was the very epitome of 'suburbia dream', and as such another perfect place for Rotten to rile the local students as the Pistols continued bringing their unique pox down upon the colleges of South East England.

Again, Rotten insisted on pushing the audience's buttons until they responded in kind, demanding a reaction, positive or negative, to the tidal surge of sound the other Pistols produced:

Richard Boon: Welwyn Garden City the following night they were opening for Mr Big, and it was a horrible student union venue. All these horrible students didn't like [the Pistols] at all, sat at the front of the stage with their back to the band, making mocking gestures to the back [of the hall], so when they started 'No Fun', Johnny ran along the front of the stage and tousled all these guys' hair. So their mates … picked Johnny up, threw him on the floor and there was a big melee. … The band kept playing [as] Johnny crawled out from this scrum, got back on the stage, and said, 'Well, that was no fun.'

This was hardly the first time Rotten employed such a tactic to trigger the requisite response. Drummer Paul Cook would look on in amazement whenever Rotten 'would stand at the edge of the stage and mess up the people's hair in the audience. It's lucky he didn't get killed because he wouldn't back down … There were fights at all of the [early] gigs. John used to instigate them. He'd get that attitude from the crowd; an aggressive attitude that worked both ways.'

This time, though, the band finished their set without further incident and packed away their PA. Afterwards, they talked to Bolton's wandering NUS rep/s, one of whom recalls, 'They were very tickled that people from Manchester had come to see them.' The pair even secured an audio memento, the northern lads deciding to record the occasion, a necessity because, as Devoto says, 'We thought, we will go and do something like this in Manchester.'

So, for the first time tape rolled on a Pistols performance, proof positive that the 'can't play' camp were full of it. The covers were still in the majority, and 'Pretty Vacant' still lacked its latterday lilting intro, but otherwise it is all there; in need of refinement, but containing 'the basis of exciting music – [medium-]fast, loud, no kowtowing to the audience'. The sound of the city, captured before its rough edges could be pruned.

The spiky Hasler also rounded out her weekend with a trip to High Wycombe, and was duly informed the band would be returning to the Central School of Art the following week, on the off-chance any word of mouth was starting to foam forth from WC2. It was not.

Hasler arrived at CSA with a friend, to find 'six people, maybe more, [standing] around the outside ... [But] they did a really good set ... They just used to take the piss, annoy people cos they were so apathetic. At the Central [gig], Lydon chucked the microphone at me, trying to get me to join in. Nobody did that sort of thing.' And for those more into the visuals, there was the usual off-stage distractions. Film student Julien Temple, catching the Pistols for the first time, felt, 'The impact wasn't just to do with the band; there were [also] the few fans that they had: Jordan, Siouxsie, Sid, John Grey.'

* * *

If such a visual adjunct was important in turning the Pistols from band into movement, McLaren still felt he needed a sister band, literally. As such, through the late winter of 1976 he endeavoured to put Chrissie Hynde in front of just such a band.

While she was still prepared to show her face (and backside) at Sex, the brassy gal from Akron, Ohio – the home of Devo and assorted Dead Boys – found herself pushed into auditioning for Mick Jones' first post-London SS combo at the Pistols' Denmark Street rehearsal room, with Matlock on bass and Steve Jones on drums. When that plan faltered, McLaren put her in the ill-conceived Masters of the Backside with Dave Zero, backed by Brian James, Rat Scabies and Ray Burns, i.e. three-quarters of the future Damned. At the same time, Hynde continued witnessing the Pistols' musical momentum building inexorably gig on gig, and it was driving her – and her friends – nuts.

Kate Simon: Chrissie was always coming over, and saying to me, 'I gotta find my band! I gotta find my band!' And I thought to myself, 'If I hear that one more time, I'm gonna kill this chick.'

The Hynde Project was not McLaren's only headache that spring. Once again, he was struggling to maintain the Pistols' forward momentum, necessary simply to preserve their tenuous internal equilibrium. Without a booking agent, and with his art college directory already well-thumbed, McLaren was struggling to come up with enough onstage action to ward off the notoriously low boredom thresholds of his young tykes. Rotten in particular was growing disaffected.

The quarrelsome quartet's sense of frustration was stoked by the cancellation, at the last minute, of a scheduled gig at the Institute of Contemporary Arts in March, plugged by Spencer in his *NME* review. Around forty to fifty people had turned up, only to find the band standing around minus any equipment. When one curious onlooker approached Steve Jones, skulking with the rest of the Pistols in one of the ICA alcoves, he responded, 'How do you know we're the band?' All it really took was one look.

Jones turned hospitable once he recognised his interrogator, 'Aren't you the guitarist from Over The Hill?' It was indeed John Perry – who was just about to start a long-standing partnership with McLaren's old buddy, Peter Perrett. But for the past eighteen months he had been in the very rock band Jones grew to appreciate during their monthly residency at The Kensington pub. Perry's own curiosity had been piqued by Spencer's *NME* review – ripple two.

Ripple three came when said review inspired a young couple from Ferryhill, Co. Durham, to drive three-hundred-plus miles to London for the weekend to play spot the Sex Pistol. (They may even have had the ICA gig in mind.) Unfortunately, they enjoyed nothing like the same good fortune as Trafford and McNeish; and had to content themselves with a trip to the Nashville to see The Stranglers, a band from Guildford who, unlike the Pistols, had the Albion Agency behind them and a regular residency at the West Kensington pub, where they soon started to attract fans from the punkier end of the pub-rock spectrum.

Like their fellow northerners Trafford and McNeish, Pauline Murray and Peter Lloyd already somehow knew that Sex was the Chelsea headquarters of the Pistols' empire. In fact, they were making their way there when they saw a familiar figure heading the same way, a face they had already seen in the pages of *NME*:

Peter Lloyd: Pauline was my girlfriend from thirteen. We were obsessed with music. She went to the grammar school and I went to a secondary … We saw that Neil Spencer review; the name just jumped out at you, the picture [of Rotten] and the name of the band. It was like, 'Wow, I've got to check this out.' So I said to Pauline, 'We've got to get to London.' We'd come [in] to Sloane Square and Johnny Rotten was on the Tube – we couldn't believe it! So we followed him up the street [to Sex] … I go in, [went] straight up to Malcolm and said, 'I like the Television pictures.' … The wall was plastered with pictures of Richard Hell and Television. I'm sure he [already] had photos of Hell with The Heartbreakers … and all he wanted to talk about were these Television demos that he had … The Pistols were all there, sitting in the corner … As I left Sex, Malcolm said, 'Whatever you do, don't go and see Eddie & The Hot Rods – nothing to do with us!' … [I later found out] when [I] left the shop Vivienne started running around, going, 'They've come all the way from Newcastle to see us.'

Lloyd's vivid memory of Sex is confirmed by another teenage visitor to the fetish emporium with the great jukebox. Simon Barker remembers, 'They had a noticeboard [at Sex], and it was the first time I ever saw pictures of Richard Hell and Tom Verlaine, on this noticeboard where Malcolm had pinned them up. It was the first time I saw pictures of people with torn t-shirts and safety pins.' Sex also had a copy of 'Little Johnny Jewel', Television's indie debut 45, on the jukebox.

The link between London and New York was firmly planted in all those who visited. Lloyd remembers talking to Matlock at one point, and being told, 'Malcolm's got this Television tape – there's this great song on there, called "Blank Generation".' Which is why Lloyd remains convinced, 'Malcolm told them to write a song like "Blank Generation" and they came up with "Pretty Vacant".'[12]

[12] The accepted version of the story is that Matlock took the song title from the Television poster that hung in the Sex shop. If McLaren had an actual copy of the Television version, then Matlock probably heard it before he wrote 'Pretty Vacant'.

Visitors from near and far continued to feed McLaren's 'fantasy' of a movement that could combine fashion, music and social politics. Pauline Murray's abiding memory of that first time she visited Sex was 'talking to him about the Pistols. He said … there would be a scene in England, and it'd be massive. We couldn't imagine it. We wanted to go to New York – that's where we thought it was happening.'

Jordan, who was the shop's focal point for all first-timers, remembers one music fan with a broad Scouse accent who was equally taken with the fetish side, 'Pete Burns used to buy loads of stuff. He'd come down from Liverpool with wads of money, and buy a load of stuff in one go … A couple of people from Manchester who'd latched onto [us] would come down, a couple of people from Liverpool … Newcastle. I couldn't even understand the people from Newcastle, it was another world.' Indeed it was – even if Peter and Pauline were from Ferryhill, thirty miles south of the Tyne Bridge.

Of course, what spiritual tourists like Burns, Lloyd and Murray really wanted was to see the Sex Pistols in action. McLaren already knew any revolutionary reverberations would need to travel beyond London and its suburban satellites to make the movement truly national. Indeed, he rang Lloyd up the following week and asked him, 'Any chance of getting a gig in Durham?' Lloyd made a few suggestions, which McLaren said he would follow up. But for now, he had more immediate concerns.

Even he knew that without a residency like the one The Stranglers had secured for themselves, the Pistols would remain an art project, nothing more. It was residencies at the Elgin and the Red Cow that had almost made Joe Strummer's 101'ers and Declan MacManus (aka Elvis Costello)'s Flip City legends in their own pub lunchtimes.

Getting mildly desperate, McLaren was on the verge of agreeing to a support slot at one of The Stranglers' Tuesday Nashville nights, if that's what it took to get a foot in the door – a means to an end. The Nashville, or The Nashville Rooms to give it its full title, was a murkily capacious pub situated next to West Kensington Tube station; generally considered the first port-of-call for pub-rockers after graduating from 'one man and a dog' residencies elsewhere.

Fortunately, just three days before their scheduled date with the ex-Guildford Stranglers, the Pistols were offered a more palatable alternative: a Saturday bill with the notoriously eccentric, chronically unreliable ex-Bonzo, Vivian Stanshall. If it was meant as a more understated entry into The Nashville Rooms' annals, it didn't stay that way for long. As subscriber Jan Behrendtz reported in a posting on the God Save the Sex Pistols website:

> Viv Stanshall cancelled his appearance very late and [so] his good friend Roger Ruskin Spear ... did his one-man-show with his robots act onstage (aka The Giant Kinetic Wardrobe). The Pistols were supposed to be the support band but in the end the playing order was reversed, i.e. Ruskin Spear went on first and then the Pistols. Mr Ruskin Spear decided this was the only way of rescuing his robots from damage as the Pistols entourage ... were all over the place both on and off the stage and the atmosphere got quite hostile. Mr Ruskin Spear basically did his show ... handed the stage over to the Pistols and fled the place.

This 'previously undocumented' Nashville Pistols show on March 20th was actually reported the following week in the world's best-selling music weekly; said mention in *NME*'s 'Teazers' confirming another night of mutual antipathy: 'The Pistols had all sorts of listed buildings thrown at them at the Nashville on Saturday night (ask for it really, don't they?).'

Evidently, their brand of raw punk offended the weekend regulars for whom pub and rock went together like steak and kidney. Possibly one of those lobbing 'listed buildings' at the band went by the name Martin Fieber. This particular man of letters felt compelled to write to the *NME* the following week – from the West London SW6 postcode – with what would soon become a familiar complaint:

> I recently saw Sex Pistols, and I'm afraid I have to say that they were not even indicative of what's wrong with the youth of today. If this generation can't illustrate what is wrong with it through the medium of music then there must be something wrong with it. P.S. They weren't even the worst band I've ever seen.

If Fieber and fellow fibbers' first clash with the Pistols confirmed that communication was only possible between the like-minded, others embraced the aesthetic with alacrity. One of McLaren's little helpers at Sex, Alan Jones, had finally convinced Caroline Coon, sixties radical turned *Melody Maker* journalist, to enter the lion's den; and 'almost immediately, she started promoting it quite heavily'. She seemed to have found what she had been looking for since the sixties dream died:

Caroline Coon: There was an immediate recognition [on my part], seeing these 19-year-olds deconstruct pub rock and take rock'n'roll back to its basics, but with a genuine anger. Standing at the back … you could see the pub audience turning their noses up, but the kids in the crowd knew what was going on … What impressed me most, however, was their total disinterest in *pleasing* anybody except themselves. Instead, they engaged the audience, trying to provoke a reaction which forced people to express what they felt about the music. Quite apart from being very funny, their arrogance was a sure indication that they knew what they were doing and why.

Coon, an ideal apostle for any youth movement going, would become a key proselytizer. Just not yet. A few days later, she went to her editor Ray Coleman 'dead keen to write a feature about the band'. She was shot down in flames, 'To say my suggestion was considered premature, if not ludicrous, would be an understatement.'

At the same time, McLaren continued to cajole others on her paper and the other potentially receptive music weeklies – *NME* and *Sounds* – to experience the band for themselves at one of three London gigs he'd finally lined up after a month of inactivity to demonstrate that the Pistols remained wholly 'indicative of what's wrong with the youth of today'.

One of those he attempted to contact, *Sounds*' in-house reggae 'rep', Vivien Goldman, was a close friend of Coon's. However, when he phoned the office, Jonh Ingham intercepted the call, informing Vivien, 'You're not gonna like this band.' Unbeknownst to McLaren, Ingham, who had arrived on these shores from his native New Zealand via America's less-than-happening west coast, was as anxious to champion the next big thing as the manager. In fact, he had been looking out for the next Pistols gig ever since he read Spencer's review. Ripple number four:

Jonh Ingham: When I read Neil Spencer's review in the *NME*, it wasn't so much what he wrote. It was the name itself ... I really wanted to find out more about [them]. I was well into hatred by that time.

Although McLaren was delighted to chance upon another like-minded journo, before Ingham would be allowed to meet the band, he'd have to meet the manager, to 'pass some test ... He gave me the Malcolm Manifesto. His music was Gene Vincent, Jerry Lee [Lewis] and Eddie Cochran ... [He] was wanting to start something new, and how do you start something new? You do the opposite of what's going on. If everyone's got long hair, you have short hair; if everyone has flared trousers, you have straight trousers. He went on and on, for like forty-five minutes.'

Perhaps surprisingly, the most frequent point of reference in 'the Malcolm Manifesto' was the Rolling Stones, specifically the pre-Decca Stones, whom McLaren claimed 'no one [had] wanted to know, but when they saw a lot of bands sounding like that, with a huge following, they had to sign them'. Ingham was intrigued. Now he just needed to see the band *perform* – assuming there was still a band left to see.

Cracks had already started to appear in the McLaren-Rotten relationship; cracks which threatened to become a gaping chasm by the end-of-March night the band made their 100 Club debut. Rotten, both disillusioned and empowered by his time with the Pistols, increasingly felt he was being manipulated (which he was), and was becoming strangely resentful of the once-in-a-lifetime opportunity he'd been given. Did he really want to slide back into the sink estate he had come from? It seems a part of him really did.

Matters came to a head at the Oxford Street club, mid-set. Rotten had invited his little clique of like-minded yobs, the 'three Johns' – John Wardle (aka Jah Wobble), John Beverley (aka Sid Vicious) and the more mild-mannered John Grey – who generally preferred central London gigs. Well, the 100 Club was certainly that; and so, as Matlock told Fred Vermorel, 'John was with his mates that night and it was all like: I'm in charge of the group and I do exactly what I want to do. So he stayed in the 100 Club and he got well pissed with his mates. By the time he got on the stage he was falling arse over tit, couldn't sing the words of the songs properly and kept coming in at the wrong time.'

The rest of the band were not amused. In fact, this is almost certainly the occasion Jordan described when, 'Steve smashed the [100 Club] sign at the back … Then Steve started to do all the singing, which got John even madder.' The reason Jones intervened is that Rotten was singing the wrong words 'at the wrong time'. When Matlock confronted him, Rotten challenged the bassist to a fight. When that didn't work he decided to quit the band mid-gig:

Chrissie Hynde: While they were playing, Johnny kept picking up his mike stand, over his shoulder, trying to spear Glen Matlock. There was always this tension … [Anyway], he not only left the stage, he left the club … The band were so frustrated, Steve Jones … ripped his guitar strings off with one hand.

It was when Rotten 'left the club' that things got really heated; and it was McLaren who took Rotten to task. Accounts vary as to who won the slanging match, but that there was a verbal confrontation between vocalist and manager is not in dispute. Hynde thinks, 'Malcolm McLaren went running out into the street to try and retrieve him.' Nils Stevenson believed he never got that far, 'John … started to leave, he got off the stage and walked up the stairs, and Malcolm … shouted, "You get back on that stage or you're over." [He was] really furious.'

Rotten had been goading McLaren throughout the set. University of Sussex student Billy Broad (aka Idol) – who was there that night because of a four-word postcard sent by his Bromley friend Steve Bailey: 'Get back to London!' – recalls how 'John kept haranguing Malcolm. He would say, "Get me a beer, Malcolm, you cunt." Nobody was in the audience, and Malcolm was standing off stage saying, "Fuck it, get it yourself."' One presumes McLaren – who was not adverse to giving the whole band a little Dutch courage in a glass before a gig – realized the singer had already had quite enough.

Whatever words were exchanged on the stairs, Rotten did return to the club and the stage, only to begin taking it out on the audience. As Idol writes, 'I remember [Rotten] noticing a few people in the audience with long hair and flares, then haranguing them for being out-of-date hippies, demanding they go back to their Melanie records.' But far from repelling the broad-minded, slightly wild youth, 'The Pistols' don't-give-a-shit attitude … spoke to me. Steve Bailey was right. We had found what we were looking for.' And it wasn't just Rotten who spoke to him: 'The Pistols onstage were unlike anything we'd ever seen before … Even at this early stage, the Pistols had their signature sound – tight and aggressive, with lots of blistering guitar riffs from Jones.'

The future Idol – who perhaps thought Rotten's stage-departure was staged – was bowled over. For Hynde, though, the spectacle was slightly embarrassing. A champion of the band to the many contacts she had developed in her time as Nick Kent's girlfriend, she had invited guitarist-producer Chris Spedding and his girlfriend Nora (later to become Mrs Rotten) to check them out. Nora was distinctly unimpressed, 'I thought they were awful … It was so bang-bang, rock'n'roll.' Spedding, though, heard enough to take it upon himself to stop Rotten from committing career-suicide:

Chris Spedding: Chrissie … took me to the 100 Club the night they almost broke up. That was quite an experience: Johnny Rotten was either pushed or jumped off the stage in disgust and McLaren screamed at him that he wouldn't get his taxi fare home if he didn't get back on stage, so at the end of the gig, I took Rotten under my wing and we went out with Chrissie, Chris Miller and my girlfriend at the time, Nora Forster … Rotten was very upset and said he wanted to leave the group. I told him not to because I believed there was really something there.

Spedding's presence at the 100 Club – deemed worthy of a mention in the *Sounds*' gossip column, 'Jaws' – suggested there was already a buzz around the band, even if it had yet to translate into packed clubs. It certainly wasn't hard to pick the guitarist out in the 'crowd'. As he admits himself, 'There was hardly anybody there. They'd frighten audiences away in those days. There'd be twenty people in the club at the beginning and about two by the time they finished playing.'

One of those who did not stick around for the whole set was John Curd, a powerful London promoter who booked the Roundhouse, Chalk Farm's striking architectural monstrosity and a major rock venue since the birth of psychedelia ten years earlier. Curd thought the Pistols were beyond awful, and swore he would never let them play his place/s. He proved a man of his word.

Fortunately for the band, the night's performance had only further convinced 100 Club owner Ron Watts that they had 'enough anarchy in them'. Even the Rotten exit, pursued by a bearish McLaren, failed to faze him. He proffered the possibility of a brief residency in May. But McLaren wasn't sure he needed Watts. Of the two gigs scheduled that week, he was convinced the one he'd organized in the land of Sex shops and strip shows would become a home away from home for the band.

But first they had a return date at the Nashville, and this time they were propping up one of London pub-rock's most frenetic revivalists, The 101'ers. And it seems their rabble-rousing reputation was already sending ripples of fear through Pubrockland. The girlfriend of 101'ers frontman Joe Strummer, Paloma Romero, who was away visiting friends that week, remembers Joe telling her how the Sex Pistols 'went in and smashed the gear of the [Count] Bishops, which was the rival group of The 101'ers. [Now] it was The 101'ers turn.'[13]

* * *

In fact, the only thing the Pistols would smash that night were Strummer's preconceptions about how a band should sound and look, starting with the latter. Having 'walked out on stage while they were getting their soundcheck together', he 'heard Malcolm going to John … "What sweater do you want?" I thought, blimey, they've got a manager, and he's offering them clothes!'

[13] Paloma has almost certainly confused The Count Bishops with Eddie & The Hot Rods.

Another person privy to the soundcheck was Dave Goodman, the soundman McLaren had hired for the night, on the cheap, at the recommendation of the Albion Agency. Goodman remembered them being 'incredibly loud during the soundcheck'. Having done all that he could soundwise in the pub's dank confines, Goodman grabbed a beer and retired backstage to await the night's revelries. It was there he 'found Malcolm winding the band up – telling them how the audience were a bunch of apathetic old farts who needed shocking into some sort of response'.

McLaren may not have known for sure whether his campaign of badgering the music papers, and/or a general buzz forming around the band post-Spencer's review, was about to pay dividends but he was taking no chances. He was clearly banking on another night of mutual antipathy, even inviting photographer Ray Stevenson again on the off-chance some visual record was required.

In fact, both *Melody Maker* and *NME* had sent reviewers to report on this battle of the bands, although neither assignee seemed on the cusp of conversion to McLaren's cause. *NME*'s Geoff Hutt admitted attending the gig, 'gleefully anticipating a shambles of massive proportions,' and seemed more than a little put out when the Pistols failed to deliver said 'shambles', prompting the miffed man to conclude:

> Real lovers of Attitude may find the stance of singer Johnny Rotten rather contrived. He has the makings of a good punk, looking genuinely untogether, bored and contemptuous and using his whole body as a sneer, but his between numbers jibes at the audience … are too rehearsed, as is the half-hearted heckling which seems to emanate mainly from the group's followers … The trouble is that the Pistols are too good for anyone to really hate them. The occasionally touted assertion that they 'can't play' is far from the truth. They try nothing flash but play hard and sharp within limitations which act as a positive discipline. Vocally, they are strong, Johnny Rotten's impeccable sense of dynamics being complemented by more orthodox back-ups from his bassist. Their own songs are intelligent punk rock (if that's not a contradiction) and … they go down well, perhaps to their disappointment, but perhaps not.

At least *NME* again devoted most of what was a lead gig review to the Pistols, along with another nice shot of the whole band in visual harmony (Mick Rock again), barely mentioning the actual headliners. By contrast, *Melody Maker*'s Allan Jones was firmly in The 101'ers corner before a note was played, having previously attended Newport Art College with Strummer and being responsible for the first notable feature on the band the previous July. As such, he neither opened his mind nor his ears when the Pistols made their grand entrance, obliging him to digest a large portion of humble pie, between lame excuses, when punk came to pass:

Allan Jones: John Rotten stumbled to the front of the stage … his dark eyes alive with venom. 'I bet,' he screamed at the bewildered audience, few of whom were at all familiar with the group or its nascent attitude, 'that YOU don't hate US as much as WE hate You!' He was quite mistaken: the audience responded to Rotten's jeering abuse with extrovert disdain and made clear their instinctive dislike for the Pistols' leering aggression and crude music.

Jones was appalled. Appalled enough to feel a need to unburden himself. Rather than spending every column-inch on his beloved 101'ers, he spent the first half of his column and a half review – which duly ran in the following week's *MM* – taking these unctuous usurpers down a peg or two:

> The whole contrived and misguided aesthetic of 'they're so bad, they're great' has, with the Sex Pistols – a recently much-vaunted four-piece band of total incompetents from West London – been taken to unprecedented levels. Their dreadfully inept attempts to zero in on the kind of viciously blank intensity previously epitomised by The Stooges was endearing at first: the predictably moronic vocalist was cheerfully idiotic, and the lead guitarist, another surrogate punk suffering from a surfeit of Sterling Morrison, played with a determined disregard for taste or intelligence. The novelty of this retarded spectacle was, however, soon erased by their tiresome repetition of punk cliches. They do as much for music as World War II did for the cause of peace.

Predictably, having damned the Pistols with not even faint praise, Mr Jones proceeded to laud The 101'ers to the rafters: 'The 101'ers were, by comparison, perfectly glorious ... Joe Strummer [being] one of the most vivid and exciting figures currently treading the boards.' He had failed to notice Strummer's own reaction to the support act, or he would have realized just why his friend was so pumped up when he finally hit the stage:

Joe Strummer: I went out front to watch [the Pistols], and there was hardly any audience ... Five seconds into their first song I knew we were like yesterday's papers ... As soon as I saw them, I knew that rhythm'n'blues was dead – that the future was here somehow ... [That night] they were firing on all cylinders – Steve Jones was one of the best guitar players I'd ever seen. He could sound like ten men ... It was a mind-blowing package – they had the attitude, the songs and the ability ... Even the name was fantastic ... [And] there was a comedy in what they did – [which] wasn't inadvertent, it was something they used ... [Whereas] we played 'Route 66', ... going, 'Please like us,' ... this quartet were standing there going, 'We don't give a toss what you think, you pricks, this is what we like to play, and this is the way we're going to play it.'

In fact, so profound was Joe's conversion that the minute The 101'ers singer took to the stage, he started acting like Johnny Rotten. As soundman Dave Goodman later recalled, 'Strummer kicked in one of the monitors after he [had] sat there gobsmacked, watching the Pistols,' about which Goodman himself was not best pleased – even if he felt similarly 'gobsmacked' by the Pistols:

Dave Goodman: [Their appearance] on stage [was] accompanied by much jeering from the audience, who seemed to take great exception to their age and appearance. The band ... told the audience if they 'didn't like it, they could fuck off!' They were loud, manic and loose. When they performed 'Substitute', it was as if they played it as badly as they possibly could, just to annoy people. [After which,] Rotten said, 'That's an improvement, ain't it?' ... They even did an encore, just because no one asked for it.

Afterwards, Goodman approached McLaren, 'You got any more gigs? We like what you're doing.' Malcolm's response said it all, 'Fucking hell, someone's offering us some help.' Goodman and his sidekick Kim Thraves would forthwith be an integral part of the Pistols live set-up, and a great many of the sonic problems that had plagued the band early on would start to recede. Perhaps Goodman's presence even had a bearing on the number of people that night who thought they had come to West Kensington but found themselves on the road to Damascus.

Although Strummer would later insist, 'The rest of my group hated them – they didn't want to watch it or hear anything about it,' the response from his fellow squat city rockers was not so clear-cut. 101'ers guitarist Clive Langer, who up to this point had thought his own band 'were really fashionable and up-to-date', had a similar response to Strummer, 'Fuck, we're nowhere.' But he didn't agree that this was a good thing. Their drummer also felt the Pistols rocked the bar but took umbrage at certain extraneous elements already surrounding them:

Richard Dudanski: Musically I liked them. I liked the songs they played and I liked the sound they generated. I also liked the feeling they put in and the attitude they had, which wasn't so dissimilar to the early days of our band … But there were two aspects … that didn't impress me at all … The first was the guy who was orchestrating everything that they would do. Looking at them with arched eyebrows like a schoolmaster with his pupils; asking if they wanted this, telling them to do that. There was no disputing who was boss in that outfit, at least at this early stage … Second, was the crew of fans that they brought down with them.

Strummer could barely contain himself and the minute he got back he called his girlfriend Paloma in Scotland, 'He was all excited about it. He got totally converted by them. I remember him telling me about his ambition, saying that he really wanted to make it.' It was a telling remark, and something of a parting of the ways for him and Paloma, who simply could not conceive of 'making it' as one of life's primary goals.

It was not the only separation Strummer would have to endure concurrent with his birth pangs as a punk. For, unbeknownst to him, there were already others who wanted to get to know the born-again Strummer, eyeing him up as a potential frontman for their own proto-Pistols outfit. Three of them – t-shirt salesman Bernie Rhodes and twin guitarists, Mick Jones and Keith Levene – shared in the magic suffusing the Nashville that night:

Keith Levene: There was nothing [happening at the time]. Just some terrible pub-rock bands like Eddie & The Hot Rods and The Stranglers … Then you had the Pistols at the Nashville. They just wiped the slate clean. I'd never seen anything like it … I just walked into the Nashville … [and immediately] I knew this was fucking It. Nothing could ever be quite the same again … I knew where I was standing was the right place for me to be in the world, and [from] what I heard that night … no one could touch the Pistols.

Levene, a former Yes roadie (really!) and an accomplished guitarist in his own right, had gone to the gig with Rhodes, who seemed most impressed that Steve Jones had been entrusted with one of New York Doll Sylvain Sylvain's guitars by McLaren. It seemed like both an expression of faith and a passing of the baton.

For Mick Jones, the Pistols' performance merely reaffirmed what he had witnessed at the Logan farrago. As for Strummer, he was someone already on this Rock'n'Roll Mick's radar: 'I would go and see bands, check groups out, looking for people. [Even] before the Pistols there was Bazooka Joe and The 101'ers … a few groups like that.'

After the Nashville gig, Rhodes, Jones and Levene were all agreed: Strummer was the man for them. All they needed now was a drummer and they might just be able to rival the boy-band from the Bush – that is, assuming they could convince Strummer to quit an established band, with a first single due out soon, to join a band formed on a wing and a punk prayer and managed by a motormouth with no off-switch.

For Rhodes, the race was now on. Further motivation was perhaps provided when he saw 'other' remnants of London SS – those who had decided they had no need of his punk John Sinclair routine – scoping out the same audience for a frontman of their own. Brian James, Chris Miller (aka Rat Scabies) and Ray Burns (aka Captain Sensible) had been a unit for a few weeks now, having carried on rehearsing together even after McLaren failed to persuade them to back Hynde in her lust for some received glory.

Miller, who attended a few early Pistols shows at the invitation of McLaren, who hoped to find him a place in his own schemata, remembers them fondly, 'They were fun gigs, people would boo and throw things at them. They'd never get an encore, but there'd always be half a dozen spiky-headed oiks.' Among those 'oiks' was Sid Vicious, who on this auspicious night caught the attention of Miller's companion, Brian James:

Rat Scabies: On the 3rd April '76, me and Brian were in the bar at the Nashville for a Pistols show – hanging out, looking for singers. John Beverley came in wearing this amazing gold lame jacket and looking every inch a star. Brian said, 'He's a singer' – so I went up and asked him to come along and audition for us. Twenty minutes later the same night, Dave Letts walked in and Brian said, 'Fuck me, there's another one.' I told Brian I already knew him … [Back then,] he looked like one of the New York Dolls, a Thunders haircut, back-combed and sticky-uppy. He wore a black leather jacket and drainpipe jeans.

They invited Letts [aka Vanian] to audition as well. It seemed like the Kensington pub was positively overflowing with potential punk poster-boys that evening. The future frontmen of three more futurist punk bands were also checking things out, having already been exposed to the same virus.

Stuart Goddard, no longer part of Bazooka Joe, caught the Pistols at 'both' April Nashville shows and realized the seeds planted at St Martin's were bearing fruit, 'They were in a class of their own … [They] chugged along … but they sounded real good.'

Vic Godard and Rob Symmons also returned for a second look after religiously scanning *NME* hoping to replicate their Marquee moment and finding something even better. In just six weeks Godard noticed a discernible raising of the bar, 'The Nashville concerts were brilliant. Fantastic. But every time they played they got a bit better. Glen Matlock added a lot to them with his backing vocals and his bass lines.' A show 'few' attended was teeming with would-be movers and shakers. Yet another maverick artist was starting to see a musical career as an alternative to large-scale drug dealing:

Peter Perrett: [At] the Nashville there was more people. [Rotten was] more abusive towards the audience … it wasn't as chaotic [as the Chelsea gig]. It seemed like they were trying to make it into a proper gig. The songs had beginnings and endings, better musicianship. There were people in the audience shouting fuck off. There was definitely more verbals, something about 'you hippies', a marking out of lines from the old guard.

And yet, on a night that represented something of a turning point for seventies rock, Rotten was weighing up his options. In fact, in his (first) autobiography, he claimed that he and Cook got into a serious argument before their set, 'We were really yelling and screaming at each other. Then the curtain went up, and we stopped fighting and went on with it … [But] when the curtain went down, I went over to Malcolm and said, "I quit. I've had enough".'

Whatever Lydon's therapist might read into the curtain as visual symbol, there was never any such concession to theatricality at the Nashville. But Rotten's dissatisfaction was real. Thankfully, after the show he bumped into Don Letts and his china-doll girlfriend, Jeannette Lee, rival King's Road clothiers who ran Acme Attractions. Though this was not really his kind of music, and he remembered the PA being 'really bad', Letts had been blown backwards by the Pistols, 'It was [all] this fucking energy – it was a revelation.' So he invited Rotten back to their Forest Hills home and they stayed up all night 'rapping on about reggae'.

What Lydon didn't tell Letts (or Lee) was that he was increasingly 'frustrated and getting ready to quit the Pistols'. Once again, though, time spent with someone poleaxed by a Pistols performance enabled him to see (more of) the big picture.

★ ★ ★

Before he had the chance to deliver on that end-of-set threat, Rotten found himself soundchecking at the seediest shop in Soho. It was a day later and the opening night of the Pistols' new Sunday residency, arranged by McLaren a couple of weeks earlier.

El Paradise was McLaren's overly optimistic attempt to create a CBGBs in London's Soho – a place where like-minded outsiders could come together but where no self-respecting pub-rocker would be caught dead. Jonh Ingham captured the vibe of opening night perfectly in his first feature on the band:

> The small, sleazoid El Paradise Club in Soho is not one of the more obvious places for English rock to finally get to grips with the seventies, but when trying to create the atmosphere of anarchy, rebellion and exclusiveness that's necessary as a breeding ground, what better place? … One expects to go down a hall or some stairs, but the minute you turn the corner you're there. A small room twenty or thirty feet long, bare concrete floor, a bar at one end, three and a half rows of broken down cinema seats.

The place really was tiny – smaller (and scuzzier) than even CBGBs – but McLaren, as per, had grand plans. The week before, he told *NME*'s 'Teazers' all about his 'new Sunday venue at Brewer Street's old Paradise Club in darkest Dirtymackshire … The Sex Pistols will be resident, [but] Mal [also] hopes to promote other "young off the wall bands who can't get gigs at established rock venues".'

The auguries seemed propitious. Despite being advertised largely 'by word of mouth and leaflets, the 4th April was a night with a memorable sense of occasion', or so Caroline Coon later wrote. While insiders and outsiders gathered as one, Kate Simon, Joe Stevens and Ray Stevenson were all invited to provide a visual record. Unfortunately, lighting was in short supply. As Stevens ruefully notes, 'Ray Stevenson had his strobes set up, and they were radio strobes, so he had them in the back of the band … [But] his lights were the only lights they had for the show … I had trouble focussing, cos I couldn't see the band.'

Simon seemed more interested in what the friend she'd brought,

Paul Getty III, thought about the whole circus. If Getty was a fish out of water, he was a whole lot hipper than Caroline Coon's companions, members of The Arrows, a great punk name but actually a pop factory product. Their reaction has gone unrecorded – and was probably unprintable.

Coon herself ended up engrossed in conversation with her rival scribe, Jonh Ingham, who remembers, 'She got very peeved that she was going to be scooped … [and all because] she had Ray Coleman to deal with.' The presence of Ingham, even before Allan Jones filed his wide-of-the-mark Nashville review, confirmed her worst fears. The very fact that McLaren had invited Ingham to this show, and *not* the previous night's, suggested he believed Jonh was already on the programme. Ingham's review of El Paradise – which actually ran a day before Jones' slam – confirmed the perspicacity of McLaren's judgement:

> If you hate Patti Smith for all that noise and rock and roll energy at the expense of technique and sounding pretty, then you'll really hate the Sex Pistols. Their aesthetic is Shepherd's Bush Who and speed-era Small Faces – they play it fast and they play it loud. The guitarist doesn't bother too much with solos, just powering his way through whatever passes for a middle-eight. But this isn't to say they're sloppy, far from it … Unfortunately, you couldn't hear any lyrics, a fact which annoyed the singer just as much [as me]. In the second song he rammed the mike stand back and the cymbals went over. At the end of the third he berated the audience: 'Clap you fuckers, because I'm wasting my time not hearing myself.'

Two weeks later, Ingham would rewrite his review as part of a full profile of the Pistols, taking the opportunity to recall how Rotten in his frustration, 'begins a slow handclap; about three people join in. John is a man who likes to confront his audience, not to mention the rest of the band.' It was an astute observation, especially at a time when he knew nothing of the internal friction that was tearing at the band's seams, to which he unwittingly applied sticky plaster in the form of a two-page spread in a national music weekly.

For tonight, at least, Rotten was obliged to keep himself in check, as he was quickly reminded when, in keeping with his usual response to equipment failure, he started taking it out on the nearest inanimate object/s:

Glen Matlock: When it came to show time, John … started smashing the footlights one by one. As he did this, a Maltese fella started striding purposefully towards us from the back of the club. We knew he was the owner of the club … He was built like a brick shithouse and he plonked himself down right in front of the stage. He put one elbow on the stage itself and stared straight at John … For three numbers John looked everywhere but him.

Wisely, Rotten decided to rein in his propensity for destruction. To quote Nils Stevenson's diary, '[Having been] really manic when they eventually get on the small stage, … Rotten calms down when Vincent and his henchmen arrive to check on the proceedings.' This left the singer to concentrate on other aspects of his performance-art. One of those there that night who was watching the man-at-the-mike for the first time, Ingham was delighted by this more verbal persona, 'There was some stuff between the songs where John was trying to be Johnny Rotten, [which] was funny to me. It was like a comic book. It wasn't the madman we all saw nine months later.'

There might be another possible explanation for Rotten's demeanour that night. For the first time, he was largely preaching to the converted. Ingham's description of the audience that night provides a prosaic freeze-frame: 'Flared jeans were *out*. Leather helped. All black was better. Folks in their late twenties, chopped and channelled teenagers, people who frequent Sex … People sick of nostalgia. People wanting forward motion. People wanting rock and roll that is relevant to 1976.'

One of these 'chopped and channelled teenagers' was Marco Pirroni, who had been a Sex regular for a year or more when he finally caught up with Malcolm's band:

Marco Pirroni: [The place] was disgusting. I thought it'd be like a little theatre, it was just a shop, the side of a shop. There was a partition and there it was … I picked up a flyer [at Sex]. They were on the counter. That whole hand-out thing came from Television.

I remember he had a Television hand-out when he came back from New York, with the song 'Venus De Milo' [on it]. Putting the names of the songs on the poster was an amazing idea … I'd never been to see a band *not* at a theatre or arena – it was the first club gig I'd [ever] been to. You know that thing where people say it changed my life – it didn't change my life. I already thought what they thought, that just cemented it. Because no matter how brilliant you think this is, there's also the thought: I could do that … I came out thinking, 'Yes I'm right. I'll carry on along this path – [but] more determinedly.' I [just] didn't have any flares or Yes albums to throw away, or any hair to cut.

Pirroni was wholly unfazed by the setting, or the sight of Alan Jones (the Sex worker, not the rock critic) with a Cambridge Rapist mask on, taking the money at the door. Jones would certainly have recognized him from the shop, as would Jordan, who was supplying the refreshments.

Fortunately, the sixteen-year-old Pirroni refrained from sampling the 'punch' Jordan concocted, which consisted 'of all this booze [put] together. We found people were disappearing through the night. They were just collapsing basically … We had the best night ever.'

All in all, the evening proved a great success. They even made a profit after the £90 rental (although McLaren told Nils Stevenson 'we haven't'). Perhaps McLaren had really found a place 'for English rock to finally get to grips with the seventies'. Yet he continued pursuing a twin-strategy: finding a residency where the band could bond with their true demographic all the while making frenetic forays into London clubland to spark controversy and further a burgeoning reputation as bad boys determined to piss on Pop.

Secretly proud of the Pistols' progress to date, McLaren of all people should have known pride cometh before the fall. In his case it would prove literally true. The week after the El Paradise, with Jones and Ingham's reviews in that week's music papers, he paid a call on John Curd to see if he could get the Pistols added to the bill for a two-nighter at the Roundhouse in May. Patti Smith was due to become the first CBGBs act to cross that lonesome ocean. Curd did not candy-coat his response, 'Forget it, you're not playing in this town. It's a terrible band. You can't play. I don't like you.' When

McLaren told him not to be such an ass, Curd kicked the effete Svengali down a set of Camden Lock stairs.

Nor did Curd change his mind later on. He continued his spat with McLaren, and by proxy the Pistols, even barring the band from backstage after a Runaways show in October.[14] Meanwhile, he happily doled out a two-nighter at the Roundhouse for The 101'ers, who by their own admission were 'fucking nowhere'.

On April 17-18th, Strummer's current band propped up a bill that otherwise constituted Van Der Graff Generator (a favourite band of Rotten) and Bowie's ex-backing band, The Spiders From Mars. Even though the frontman would have considered Curd's critique of the Pistols as cretinous as Allan Jones's, Strummer had yet to hand in his notice or call time on pub rock. But internal tensions spilled over the second night in Chalk Farm, when his closest friend nearly punched his lights out:

Richard Dudanski: We were in the final throes of the mega ending at the end of 'Gloria', where Joe and I would use up literally every last bit of energy before I would crash out the song and the set. Joe was ready to stop a bar or two before me, and hit one of my cymbals as a sign to 'stop now' … I didn't take at all kindly to someone bashing my kit, and leapt up from my drum stool with a fist poised to strike. We looked angrily at each other for a split second, and then realized what the hell, and finished off the song with an even more violent demolition of the kit than usual.

By the time Strummer and 'Snakehips' nearly came to blows, the Pistols' El Paradise residency had gone 'tits up'. No one can seemingly agree on whether there was a second Soho show. However, 'Jaws' reported the following week that the 'Sex Pistols *keep* [my italics] going down a storm at their regular venue, Soho's Burlesque Strip Club, but sadly, the venue is already proving to be too small and gigs are about to be deferred until a suitably raunchy but larger dive can be found' – which rather suggests Paradise was not yet lost.

[14] The Runaways' show at the Roundhouse was on October 1st, and was attended by all of the Pistols, save Rotten, thus precluding any possibility of them performing at Didsbury College on the same night.

Descriptions of an El Paradise show from Shanne Hasler and Bertie Marshall (aka Berlin Bromley) proves hard to tally with opening-night reports by reliable eye-witnesses. Berlin's curious account in his own punk memoir of 'Little Debbie, looking adoringly at Jones, who at one point whipped out his cock and pissed into the audience', suggests someone with his watersports confused. But his description of trouble in Brewer Street – 'The gig fell apart [after] a stripper tried to do a striptease on stage and got booted off ... Discord and violence filled the room, bottles sailed through the air ... someone pulled a knife ... chaos ruled' – tallies with Shanne Hasler's memory of 'that bloke Wobble ... throwing glasses. I don't know what that was about'.

If there was trouble, it provides a likelier explanation for why the Pistols were kicked out of El Paradise than the one McLaren gave 'Jaws', 'The promoters upped the rent in the middle of the second week.' The loss was keenly felt by fans like Billy Broad, who was thoroughly enjoying an Easter vacation away from his fellow south coast students, as he became part of an 'audience [which] was made up of people like us ... [as] week by week we saw them get better'.

* * *

Thankfully, the Pistols' expulsion from their own private Eden was not so keenly felt by the band. By the time they were ready for a return match with The 101'ers on April 23rd, Ron Watts had agreed to a Tuesday residency at the 100 Club through May, and McLaren finally accepted that this would be their real home away from home. There would be no more talk of promoting other 'young off the wall bands who can't get gigs at established rock venues'.

As another plus, the Pistols would be entering The Nashville Rooms as The 101'ers equals, having had two major plugs in the papers in the past few days. Leana Pooley's round-up of the weekend's entertainment in the *Evening Standard*, the leading London daily, had given them the big build-up:

> With any luck, we're in for a dirty weekend. Sex Pistols are a vulgar, raunchy, loud band. 'A rough and ready version of The Who,' says the manager of the Nashville. Sex Pistols will be playing there tonight from about 9pm to 10pm, and they should end the week

> with a bang ... Johnny Rotten, the lead singer, will be pounding out 'I'm Pretty Vacant' while the rest of the group swear at the audience. All good clean fun.

But what really packed the Nashville out that night was a cover-story in the music weekly, *Sounds*, which appeared two days earlier, penned by Mr Ingham, who had not only passed the McLaren test but also Rotten's withering examination.

Granted an audience in their local pub after something of a Mexican standoff between Rotten and the other Pistols, when Ingham asked, 'How come you're doing it, John?' the safety-catch came off and the gimlet-eyed Rotten unleashed both barrels, 'I'm against people who just complain about *Top of the Pops* and don't do anything. I want people to go out and start something, to see us and start something, or else I'm just wasting my time.'

The journalist knew he was getting the sort of verbal blast which would hold up in the light of print: 'Johnny was so focused. Later on, he slowed it all down, once he figured out the press. [At this stage] that sarcasm was just coming at you ... But he didn't treat it like it was a manifesto, it was a conversation.'

When a more measured articulation of the manifesto was required, Ingham could rely on the savvy McLaren, who contributed as much to the finished article as Rotten, and was in no doubt where the real problem lay – the venues: 'The trouble with pubs is that they're bigger than the bands. They're all full of people playing what a crowd wants rather than what they want because they can make a reasonable living from it. If you want to change things you can't play pubs. You don't have the freedom.' So it is doubly ironic that the next time Ingham, Rotten and McLaren said hello, it was in a pub where the Sex Pistols were packing 'em in at Pub-Rock Central.

Ex-101'er Richard Dudanski may still believe that 'the majority in the [Nashville] Rooms' had 'come to see us', but the only thing that had changed in the twenty days since the two bands last shared a bill was the notoriety of the 'support act'. It also failed to occur to Ingham, who had missed the previous showdown, 'that it was probably full because of this two-page piece' he had written. But full it was.

For some Nashville regulars used to seeing bands 'playing what a crowd wants', this was the first time face to face with a band who made no concessions. It was a shock to the system even for someone destined to become The Stranglers' publicist:

Alan Edwards: When I went to see the Pistols, it made me feel like a really old man. I was only twenty at the time, [but] it made me feel like I was fifty … I just hid in the corner, literally, drinking Double Diamond, wondering what was going on – all these people with amazing make-up, fights and God knows what.

Graham Lewis, not yet wired for sound, was currently booking bands at Rotten's old stomping ground, Hornsey College. He loved the fact that 'people were expecting pub rock, and [instead] they got this group that was playing really funny versions of Small Faces songs … The singer kept asking people questions, and they weren't used to that.'

Lewis found it 'hilarious – [which] it was'. And inspirational. Before seeing the Pistols, he had 'almost given up the idea that I'd get to play in a group that I liked'. Within five months, he would be organizing group-trips to see the Pistols.

The fact that the majority of paying punters came to the Nashville to see Rotten, not Strummer, probably drove a further nail into the coffin Joe was commissioning for his band. Like Rotten, he loved being the centre of attention – even if it meant his self-worth fed on it till his ego consumed all vestiges of his former self. But still he hesitated, even as he invited along an old friend harbouring ambitions as a rock journalist for a second opinion, the two of them standing side by side during the Pistols, caught in the moment:

Pete Silverton: The Pistols played in the large back bar which had a real stage and a proscenium arch and curtains. As they played, Joe stood in the crowd, eyes locked on the stage, staring into his future. He told me he'd seen them before and that they'd changed his life … I stared with him, listening to the gleeful racket, feeling a bit lost and unsure, till they played a Small Faces song which helped me start to make sense of it … Later, when Joe had finished his own show and was recovering, sweatily, in the cubby-hole of a dressing room, he told me that he'd broken up his band.

What Strummer failed to inform Silverton was that he had been tapped up by Bernie Rhodes, after exhausting all other alternatives. If the proto-Damned could find 'two' potential vocalists, in Sid Vicious and Dave Vanian, at the previous Pistols show, Rhodes reasoned he could surely find one. Richard Boon, still in exile at Reading Art College, was sat behind Bernie that night, and saw 'Caroline [Coon] bringing these pretty boys to [him]. Bernie was obviously looking for a vocalist ... And Caroline was, like, "This is Toby."'

But Coon had no more clue than Rhodes, who had despaired of ever finding a frontman for Mick Jones's ensemble when Strummer nudged him in his righteous direction. He finally gathered up the nerve to approach Joe. By then, the Pistols' set had ended and so, to Strummer's mind, had The 101'ers. Yet the others endured another month of prevarication before he dealt the final blow.

In just three weeks, with no more than two further gigs under their belt, the Pistols had taken the twin-reverb of insistence and intensity that was the veritable hub of their sound, and turned it up another notch. Those who had seen them already spotted it straight away. Dudanski puts it down to a noticeable improvement in sound – 'The first night the sound was awful, but the second time it was really good and you could hear Steve Jones' guitar' – which he attributes to 'a good PA and ... Dave Goodman on the mixing desk'.

Nils Stevenson didn't think it was simply down to the sound. Rather, he sensed 'things really started coming together ... around the time of the Nashville [shows] ... Steve [was] getting a bit more dexterous, and Rotten [was] learning some discipline – cos [before that] he'd just go, fuck it in the middle of a song, and stop singing'. Others who were there that night concur:

Joe Stevens: It [had] started to flesh out a bit. I didn't mind them playing more than about thirty-five minutes. I regretted when they'd play fifteen minutes and then stand around, get further drunk and sweaty, and [have to] put up with all the bullshit, and then they'd come back and do another set.

The longer set also gave Rotten more opportunities to wind up the crowd. This night, though, even he couldn't get a rise out of them, hence him audibly berating them, 'Wake up fuckers, you're still standing still!' As the tempo rose, so did the ever-present tension. It was, as Stevens notes, 'the first time [in a while] you had an element of real danger and fear [in rock]. The opening chords to "Pretty Vacant" always [seemed to] start a riot.'

Sure enough, one non-paying punter took that unmistakable intro – Matlock's mischievous homage to the pop sensibility of Abba – as a cue for ensuring someone got their head kicked in tonight. It devolved to McLaren's missus, Vivienne, ever willing to make a spectacle of herself, as she had six months earlier at Empire Pool, to start a ruckus. Which is exactly what she did, telling Caroline Coon after, 'I was bored and decided to liven things up.'[15]

Matlock, who had perhaps the best view, saw nothing Situationist about the ensuing fight: 'Vivienne was pissed. She went to get a drink and somebody nicked her seat, so she took a swing at this bloke. Sid ... used this as an excuse to lay into her.' Nils Stevenson has also cast doubt on her post-fight explanation, 'Later, Vivienne claimed she'd done it on purpose to get publicity, but I don't believe that.' Once the incident was written up in *NME*, within a fortnight, it mattered not. The writer in question, a future Pet Shop Boy angling to be a pop critic, firmly placed the blame on Westwood's bleached head:

Neil Tennant: One of their coterie of fag hags picks a fight with the girl sitting next to her. The girl isn't interested but the fag hag succeeds in getting a reaction from her boyfriend. He ain't really an aggressive type, but Ms. Hag perseveres ... and seven or eight of the band's chums leap over to the scene of the crime from all over the Nashville and proceed to beat the shit out of this bloke. Fists aren't the only weapons.

For most of those at the show, the incident – at least in the moment – seemed like something and nothing. Even on the audio tape it isn't

[15] Westwood, with her revisionist blinkers on, denies this version of events in her recent as-told-to memoir, insisting she would never instigate violence. Dame Westwood, let me introduce you to the young firebrand Vivienne.

clear why the song has come to a lurching halt as one by one the band stop playing, before Matlock informs the audience, 'Leave it out. We've got another number yet,' and they pick up the beat, Rotten improvising lines like, 'Ah, rock and roll – like it should be,' until he finds a suitable point back into the song.[16] Howard Thompson, there checking them out in his A&R role at Island, didn't even recall the fight specifically, though as he says:

Howard Thompson: As far as the Pistols are concerned ... it was always pretty chaotic and the crowd was often a distraction. The sound mix usually did them no favours. There was always shit going on and you had to keep aware of what was going on around you, so things like proficiency, stage-craft, material (kind of) took a back seat to the event itself. Nobody in the audience (or band, for that matter) seemed to care if someone was out of tune, or if the band taunted the audience for being boring.

Thompson does remember, 'The show itself veered between shambolic (with a handful of people at the front causing a small ruckus) and quite good.' For Pete Silverton, standing at the back with Strummer, the fight was also barely worth mentioning, being simply 'a fight [that] broke out amongst the people in the front row ... It looked real enough, but like most pub fights it erupted in incomprehensible flurries. It was impossible to tell who was hitting who and why – except that, as in most pub fights, women seemed to be involved somehow.'

But what made this fight different, and ultimately newsworthy, was the willingness of McLaren's *enfants terrible* to get involved themselves. Indeed, according to Tennant, it is only at this point in the set that 'Johnny Rotten comes alive. While the reaction of the rest of the band is a little confused, Mr Rotten joins in the fight and has a few kicks at the victim. He cackles, he leers, the amps are turned up ... [as] The Pistols finish another unforgettable act.'

Once he had been on the receiving end of a proper kicking

[16] The following week's 'Jaws' column in *Sounds* quotes Matlock's request, confirming that this is the tape which has long been misassigned to April 3rd.

himself, Rotten distanced himself from any such intent, claiming in 1978, 'My only contribution to that was to kick 'em off the stage because they were getting in the way.' Not so. As the pictures – and several reliable eye-witnesses – make plain, Rotten got thoroughly caught up in the moment:

Jonh Ingham: Paul keeps playing. Glen tries to stop it. Steve gets off on it, but carries on playing, and John leans down into it and throws a punch or two. There's the band personality in one snapshot.

A series of snapshots were taken by Joe Stevens. The real reason the likes of Stevens, Simon and Stevenson happily took up McLaren's invites to those Nashville nights was because the unexpected was becoming the norm at Sex Pistols shows; and for now McLaren, a bona fide Situationist, seemed content to let things play out.

Stevens' girlfriend Kate Simon puts the whole thing down to the speed, not of the band but in the audience, 'Everyone was really hopped up on sulphate … That sulphate was really good for listening to this stuff.' The young Rotten, something of a speed-king himself, was wired to the national grid that night – maybe because, as the Velvets' Sterling Morrison once said, it 'braced you for hostile audiences', while also making one uncharacteristically aggressive.

If Ingham was mildly taken aback when the singer threw himself into the fray, 'with this look of glee, immediately div[ing] off the front of the stage and … throwing punches,' his companion that night, promoter Brian Morrison, was appalled. He turned to the *Sounds*man to counsel him, 'You got to drop this band. You're gonna ruin your career.'

Meanwhile, McLaren thought in for a penny in for a pound, and coming from the school that believed no publicity was bad publicity, threw a few punches himself. For those still onstage the whole thing was an annoying distraction at a time when they no longer needed Rotten's between-song antics to grab an audience's attention.

The music now said it all – as two prescient professionals realized. Howard Thompson admits he 'didn't really know what to make of [them], … [but] there was a palpable buzz in the air … Clearly, something was going on.' And Kate Simon remembers, 'There was a lot of creative energy and buzz around these gigs ... You could feel it growing.'

Matlock and Jones tried to rein things in. Matlock knew, from prior experience, 'A fight is always more interesting to watch than the band. So we jumped off stage – not to join in, but to stop it. At least I did ... [even if] it was Vivienne who really deserved a sock in the mouth.' To Jones's mind, it 'seemed normal ... for something to go wrong at that point'.

But the really worrying aspect of the incident was the role of Rotten's mate, Sid Vicious, who took it upon himself to dispense justice to *both* Westwood and the boyfriend. As Joe Stevens says, 'You could see the look in his eye. He wanted to get into that one. But I don't think he liked Vivienne ... He would have liked to have seen Vivienne getting killed.'

Simon Barker also realized for the first time that Sid just wanted some action, 'That was the first time there had been violence. [If] Vivienne caused the problem, [it was] Sid [who] whipped off his belt and started beating this bloke up, who was just trying to defend his girlfriend ... Glen was trying to pull them apart.' Barker even thinks, 'They might even have known that person.' Richard Boon is pretty sure 'the guy who had the shoulder-length hair was at lots of the Pistols gigs. [But] Vivienne started slapping [him], [she] liked that kinda risk.' Maybe now he would take the hint and either go back to his Melanie records or cut his hair.

For the headliners, the incident soured the whole evening. Richard Dudanski was left in no doubt it was all pre-arranged: 'By the second time ... it was more a question of them goading the punter[s] and actually looking for a confrontation. Even at the time it seemed a pretty blatant tactic to create a stir in the music press.' Convinced it was 'Malcolm [who] was manipulating the press, to the extent of creating fights', Dudanski admits, 'It worked a treat.'

Once again, the Pistols had made their message manifest – two days after McLaren had warned the world in print that pubs and the Pistols went together like oil and water. For Strummer, it only added to the excitement. He too had had enough of playing the Nashville – for all the reasons McLaren had previously cited. When he took to the stage that night he made a special point of asking the audience to 'give it up for the Sex Pistols!' before launching into a gloriously ironic 'Too Much Monkey Business'.

As for the Pistols, they were not immediately banned from the Nashville – the following week the owner hired the place out to the band, who played 'a private party' to which they brought their own sound system. This time they got to play their whole set without interruption, as well as two encores, and as Paul Cook says, 'the crowd really liked us', something the tape of the show – oft-bootlegged as the night of the punch-up – bears out.

But at this juncture the media storm had yet to break and, crucially, the Pistols' own part in the pummelling of a punter had not been written into the public record. When that happened, the Nashville – and all like-minded pub-rock venues – closed their doors to the Pistols for good. Rotten, for one, couldn't care less. According to his second memoir, it was a decision the Pistols had already made for themselves: 'We banned ourselves from the Nashville by sheer choice [because of that] back-to-the-pubs thing.'

After all, as he had just informed *Sounds'* 60,000+ readers, 'I hate shit. I hate hippies … I hate long hair. [And] I hate pub bands.'

3. PROVINCIAL GAINS

[May 5th – July 3rd]

3

The sound is a mean cacophony, not unreminiscent of Bowie's early Spiders, the material a mixture of Anglo-American teen punk classics – The Stooges 'No Fun', 'Substitute' and a naively-perverted rerun of the Small Faces 'Watcha Gonna Do About It' – and furious originals. The bulk of attention centres on lead singer Johnny Rotten, mod/skinhead in appearance and demeanour, peer of the sneer and all-round bad kid. Unfortunately the Sex Pistols seem unable at present to sustain their grubby villainy through more than two consecutive gigs, still slipping over the razor-line that divides genuine menace from self-consciously petulant attitude-copying. On a good night, though, they're the nastiest little cluster of individuals to have boarded a London stage in years.

– Giovanni Dadomo,* Time Out*, May 7th, 1976

It had been almost a fortnight since the showdown at the Nashville and, disappointingly, none of the rock journalists whom McLaren had encouraged to attend had penned a piece for the following week's papers. Even Giovanni Dadomo – angling for a full-time job at *Sounds* but currently a part-time reviewer for London's weekly 'what's on' magazine, *Time Out* – skirted the controversy when previewing the Pistols' first residency at the 100 Club. Yet he had certainly been at the infamous April 23rd show (and probably the 29th, going by his comments about not maintaining 'their grubby villainy through more than two consecutive gigs'), as had his wife, Eve, one of at least four photographers to capture the moment.

McLaren need not have worried: Providence was still rooting for the Pistols. She was just taking a week-long mini-break. As Malcolm strolled out one May morn, he found his local newsagent teeming with reports of the Pistols' latest shenanigans in West Kensington.

In a weird twist of happenstance, *NME* ran as a news feature – at the front of the weekly, not as a gig review at the rear – a letter from would-be pop journalist Neil Tennant, recently recruited by Marvel Comics as a UK editor (on his way to *Smash Hits*, Pet Shop Boys and a house in the country). The letter began:

> As you know, the Pistols are composed of three nice clean, middle-class, art students and a real live dementoid, Johnny Rotten. Now on Friday night El Dementoid wasn't really on top form, although the rest of the band were doing their best to compensate. Johnny's heart wasn't in the music. His lack of interest was naturally reflected by the audience, who, disappointed, weren't reacting sufficiently to the band. So how do the Pistols create their atmosphere when their music has failed? By beating up a member of the audience. How else?…

Evidently, Tennant was already attuned to the Pistols since he compares the Nashville fight night to previous shows. He may even have had his own personal reason for describing Vivienne Westwood as 'one of their coterie of fag hags'. But he surely cannot have expected the *NME* to take his 'reader's letter' and make it an article in 'Thrills'. What probably tipped the balance was the fact that Joe Stevens had the photo to go with this tale of music and violence: 'I had all of the Sex Pistols in the shot, and they were fighting with the audience. Rotten was throwing punches … Steve Jones, I think, whacked someone with the guitar.'

If Spencer's *NME* review had registered with UK members of the _____ generation, Stevens' snapshot and Tennant's story reinforced the Pistols burgeoning reputation for blending 'music and violence'. Tim (aka TV) Smith, then at college in Torquay, remembers reading 'a small piece on the Pistols at the Nashville in the *NME* … This seemed like a band who had the danger and real life you were looking for.' He made a note to check the band out, though it would be September before he would.

In Manchester, the story also made music fan Terry Mason sit up and take notice. He immediately told his friend Bernard Sumner, who later recalled that the reason Mason 'dragged' Peter Hook and him 'down to see them' at the Lesser Free Trade Hall was because 'he'd read somewhere about the Sex Pistols having a fight onstage'. Here, then, was a band who had found a way to combine the Salford trio's two great passions, 'music and violence'. But if Smith and Sumner were both loyal *NME* readers, it was *Sounds* who carried the story first, beating all their rivals to the punch with a report that came out on Wednesday, May 5th:

> The Sex Pistols ran into suitably heavy weather last Friday night at London's Nashville Rooms, where fisticuffs broke out between cuddly Vivienne of the Sex Shop and a punter. Manager Malcolm McLaren attempted to staunch the considerable flow of blood … while voice-man John Rotten (sic) quipped, 'Ease up, we haven't finished the song yet.' The song in question was 'Pretty Vacant'.

If McLaren's plan was to engender an Us and Them mentality among the music weeklies' readership, he was succeeding. Even the press was shouting, 'Which Side Are You On?' after James Johnson of the London *Evening Standard* predictably picked up on the story a day after the *NME*, and two days after *Sounds*, informing all Londoners about a gig he did not attend but was able to report 'involved … a free-for-all … after a Pistol associate became involved in a fight with a stray and apparently innocent member of the audience'.

McLaren knew he needed all the help he could to ignite interest where apathy still ruled. The night the *Sounds* story ran, the Pistols played a one-off gig at a disco club on the Finchley Road, but despite placing ads on London's one commercial radio station, Capital Radio, Matlock remembers, 'There was only about eleven people there – including the band.' (Among the others were keeper of the visual record Ray Stevenson and Marco Pirroni.)

The gig circuit was still the gig circuit, and going off-piste made for a long, hard climb. The following night the Pistols returned to familiar turf, North East London Poly, for what soundman Goodman described as 'a happening gig with loads of sweat and encores'.

But most London gig-goers had other things on their mind that May. Two (once) great British acts – David Bowie and the Rolling Stones – were back in Blighty for the first time in three long years.

Even though they were both playing cavernous cattle barns with ping-pong acoustics – Bowie was at Wembley and the Stones were at Earl's Court, scene of a catastrophic Bowie gig back in 1973 – they remained for now magnets, attracting sonic youths of all ages.

It seems McLaren couldn't even persuade his northern correspondent, Howard Trafford, to see the Pistols when he came to London that week. He was going to see Bowie instead, a decision which apparently brought a verbal volley from Vivienne, her contempt for the '76 Bowie being almost as great as for the '75 Ferry. At least Trafford made one concession to the changing ways. As Richard Boon recalls, when his friend turned up for the unveiling of the Thin White Duke, 'Howard was totally seditious. He had his peg-leg jeans' on and for the first time looked like he belonged at Sex.

The gig itself – one of four at the Empire Pool – was both a musical landmark and a sign of Bowie's increasing alienation from his sundered self and loyal fans, many of whom began searching for something else in the immediate aftermath. For McLaren, it was a case of, I told you so:

Malcolm McLaren: When we played the 100 Club, half the audience we were attracting were kids who normally would've been over the road at the Crackers disco. These were young kids – mostly in the 16-17-18 bracket – who'd been into Bowie and Roxy Music but who'd been left behind...who'd left *them* behind because those acts had just got too big, too distant, and who'd ended up going to discotheques just for something to do, where there was this excuse for a scene. [1976]

A group of devout Bowie fans from Bromley, Kent, had already found the Pistols and although their Bowie fixation remained strong, given a choice between multiple nights at Wembley Arena or a return to the 100 Club, there was no contest. The prospect of a weekly residency for the Pistols across three consecutive Tuesdays (11th, 18th and 25th) finally gave these suburbanites the chance to bring along like-minded souls. As Steve Severin says, 'I just got everybody to come along at some point. Some came back, some didn't, but each week there seemed to be twice as many people there.' For one friend with a Bowie/Velvets fixation, Berlin, that first 100 Club gig was a life-changing experience:

> I couldn't take my eyes off the Pistols' singer/screamer Johnny Rotten who was crouching onstage in a sweater full of holes and safety pins, a white Peter Pan collar shirt, the kind schoolboys wear, torn and hanging, orange crop, he was screaming into the microphone ... all the violent energy spewing out of Johnny's mouth, now blowing his nose into a handkerchief, then spitting ... Each song seemed to start then disintegrate immediately, their aggression coming mainly from Rotten was amphetamine-fuelled, something I felt viscerally ... Something had changed in my brain. What, I wasn't exactly sure.[17]

At one point he turned to his friend and shouted, 'Where is all this energy coming from?', not quite convinced just four men onstage could send out such pulsating power. But even after they secured a reliable soundman who resolved some residual sonic issues, other factors would interfere with the experience, meaning not everyone responded positively. Siouxsie, fast becoming punk's premier peacock, insists that those who took a more hostile view still outnumbered the apostles of anarchy:

Siouxsie Sioux: As opposed to people trying to get close to the stage, people were actually backing off, like clinging to the walls, saying, 'Let me out of here.' [But] it was great the way the band, and Lydon at the time, fed off of that.

Some fled the scene almost immediately. These included one singer-songwriter signed to Ray Davies' Konk label and fronting Cafe Society, for whom the May 11th gig made him fear for the very future of (his kind of) music:

Tom Robinson: The 100 Club was half-empty, and the audience was still mixed between kids in flared denims and long hair, and a

[17] Which show Berlin is describing in his largely-forgettable memoir is unclear. The fact that Berlin makes no mention of a fight onstage or Rotten storming off makes me inclined to go with one of the May shows.

smattering of do-it-yourself punk types … After the support band, Krakatoa, there was a huge gap before the Pistols came on. They didn't tune up, and Rotten's first words were, 'Who's gonna buy me a drink then?' … They shambled on, played diabolical versions of oldies like 'Whatcha Gonna Do 'Bout It'. It was totally anti-showbiz and anti-musical, very negative, with these overtones of violence. After fifteen minutes, I couldn't take it any longer. I had to leave but … I knew something was going on and I'd have to get to grips with it.

Like Adam Ant and Joe Strummer before him, seeing the Pistols live served to put Robinson's musical values in a blender. What he initially found hard to stomach, he soon realized was the way to health and happiness. As Robinson turned his back on Cafe Society, he would revisit the Pistols, eventually finding The Clash, with whom he would form the more solid bond until the Tom Robinson Band learnt to put the angst in earnest.

Quite what Robinson found so 'anti-musical' about the Pistols at this juncture is unclear. But it was hardly an uncommon reaction, especially among those who professed to be Music Biz pros. Indeed, it was with precisely the intention of debunking such preconceptions that Chris Spedding now volunteered to take the Pistols into a recording studio:

Chris Spedding: I found it very weird, all that [in the press] about them not playing music. If they were notable for one thing it was that. They were always in time and in tune. I couldn't understand why some … had chosen to attack them on the very thing that was their strength. Obviously, they've got cloth ears. [1976]

Getting someone as well-respected as Spedding on board at such an early stage was quite a coup for McLaren. It was almost as if he knew what he was doing, using his carefully cultivated contacts to make something happen – just as soon as the band began to justify his carefully-tailored hype. Well, by now they did. Marco Pirroni, who also came back to the 100 Club that May, recalls discussing precisely this point with McLaren:

Marco Pirroni: Malcolm used to spout [about] anarchy all the time. [But] he did care about the music … He said, 'They've got to get tight, they've got to get good.' … He went to proper people, [like] Chris Spedding … He didn't just bung 'em into any ol' studio. They weren't trying to make them the worst they could be. And they *were* good.

Spedding was to some extent putting his reputation on the line. Which is why he was determined to capture their muscular musicianship, prepping them at their rehearsal space: 'I went to a couple of rehearsals … and got them to go through their whole repertoire and I took notes, [then] I chose … the three best songs … they had at the time.'

The gang of studio novices duly assembled outside Majestic Studios, a state-of-the-art sixteen-track facility, the morning after they blew Krakatoa all the way down Oxford Street. McLaren, never one to miss a trick, invited Ray Stevenson down to capture the moment on his candid camera. The three tracks Spedding had chosen were 'No Feelings', 'Problems' and 'Pretty Vacant':

Chris Spedding: I didn't want to go in and just have total anarchy. I knew enough about presenting something to record companies to know that they usually wanted three songs. I'd used [Majestic] when I did the *Here Come The Warm Jets* album with Eno. And we got the same engineer, Derek Chandler. I got them to go in there at ten o'clock in the morning [and when] I got there about quarter to eleven they were all set up. We started recording about eleven, about one o'clock we finished and I mixed them … There was two guitar overdubs, that was about it … They'd not been in the studio before … I had [brought] my amps and I stood over the drums while he tuned the drums to get out all the buzzes. Fortunately, his drums sounded pretty good anyway, so there was hardly anything for me to do [except to make] sure that they had a headphone balance and that the singer in his isolation booth could hear all the instruments properly. I asked them to do a rehearsal for me and I switched on the [tape] recorder. So they thought they were doing a rehearsal and they were actually doing their first take … I never really got them to hear themselves back and get all nervous about it ... They were [all] more or less first takes, first time in the studio ... Rotten sung live, but ... in an isolation booth ... You can actually hear the way the band played together. It's not like [the] guitar-overdub soup [found on later recordings].

(Hearing the trio of tracks on a bootleg E.P., in the early eighties, post-*Spunk*, post-*Bollocks,* was quite a shock to the system. As Spedding says, there is no 'guitar-overdub soup', though there is at least one obvious guitar overdub on 'No Feelings'. What the guitarist-producer captured does not sound like a demo tape – as Goodman's July tracks do – but like the first three tracks of a potent debut album the original Pistols never completed before transitioning into a more musical orthodoxy.)

For the band it had been an eye-opening experience. Rotten, in particular, felt going 'to a proper recording studio ... opened our mind[s] to the possibilities'. Predictably, he gave all the credit to Spedding and none to McLaren. It was McLaren, though, who immediately put the demos to use. Two of the initial recipients were Jonh Ingham at *Sounds* – whose entire playlist the following week was these three songs[18] – and Howard Trafford, who dubbed a cassette-copy and sent it to Tony Wilson at *Granada Reports*, a nightly local TV show with musical content, who promptly lost it, though not before making a note in his diary, 'Sex Pistols – June 4.'

Tellingly, Malcolm did not send a copy to Nick Kent, though he surely heard Zermati's dub. It seems the *NME* scribe no longer figured in McLaren's plans. And it was too late to send cast-iron proof the Pistols could play to promoter John Curd. Patti Smith was already in town preparing for her two sell-out shows at the Chalk Farm Roundhouse, with The Stranglers confirmed as the audio aperitif both nights.

If the Pistols intended to attend either gig (16-17th May) they would have to do so surreptitiously. Maybe they did. Rotten's verbal

[18] A weekly list of the three albums/singles *Sounds* journalists were most listening to appeared alongside the album and singles charts. Ingham devoting his entire list to the three Spedding demos was quite a statement.

blast at the New York poetess during a particularly ferocious 'New York' two weeks later in Manchester suggests if he was there, he had not left impressed.

For everyone else, Jonh Ingham included, the shows were an epiphany; and the audience was full to the brim with potential punk apostles and assorted loose cannons. Neither Mark Perry (later of Alternative TV) nor Robert Lloyd (of The Prefects) had yet seen the Pistols, but both had been counting the days since *Horses,* the previous autumn, for punk's androgynous angel to appear at their side of the pond. Subway Sect's Vic Godard and Rob Symmons – who had begun discordantly jamming in each other's bedrooms – also eagerly awaited auguries from across the ocean, as did Steve Morrissey, who travelled up from Manchester to pledge his allegiance.

Also in attendance (possibly both nights) was Joe Strummer, still deciding whether to piss on the past or not. According to his best friend, Richard Dudanski, the experience was as transformative as seeing the Pistols the first time, 'He was to rave about that gig of Smith's for the following weeks, even incorporating a commentary on it into the long middle section of "Gloria".'

Unlike the Pistols, Patti Smith's message was overtly redemptive – the kids taking things over, not kicking things over. Her belief in rock & roll was not yet couched in apocalyptic terms. As a result, there were times on both nights when the band nearly drowned in her sea of possibilities as tight, terse punk rock gave way to long, indulgent jams. A particularly painful 'Land' on the second night simply ignored Air Traffic Control as Patti preached her hippyish homilies to the crowd. 1976 was no Year Zero for this sinner.

If fans flooded to see the second future of rock & roll incarnate to come out of New Jersey in the past six months, it was her guitarist, Lenny Kaye, who got a glimpse of the Rotten Book of Revelation. When his old friend, Greg Shaw, from *Bomp!* magazine, suggested they visit the 100 Club the night after the Roundhouse, he was willing and able.

Shaw was in London managing the Flamin' Groovies and writing the odd piece for *Phonograph* magazine. He had already established a bond with the Sex Pistols' singer founded on a mutual disenchantment. As he later said, 'I had long talks with Rotten.

From the beginning, his agenda was that he hated … the whole rock culture … We had that in common.' Shaw's lengthy review of the Pistols' May 18th 100 Club gig suggested he got most points of reference. He even noted the similarities to early Television and prophesized that London's young werewolves could soon overtake the dilettantes of New York punk:

> In music and sheer energy, New York is far away the new Mecca … [However,] London's big advantage is a circuit of clubs and pubs where bands can work their way up, plus vastly influential music papers like *New Musical Express* that will support the scene. All that's lacking is bands … [But] The Sex Pistols [are] a new band that is causing considerable controversy. Early shows featuring girls in leather fetish gear brought them nothing but trouble, so they've dropped that bit. Now it's just them … They think of themselves as the only true 70s band, and in a way they could be right … [Yet] their brand of revolt, though far from spontaneous (most of the heckling in the audience – and there's a lot, some of it quite vicious – seems to come from their supporters) has much in common with the 1964 Mods … They remind me very much of Television, when Richard Hell was with them and they still did 'Psychotic Reaction' … Their sound is a straight blast of tortured punk rock. They are tighter and more dynamic than any New York band I've seen since the Dolls, and their original songs (with titles like 'Pretty Vacant', 'Only Seventeen', 'Submission' and 'No Feelings') are potentially strong … Guitarist Steve Jones … plays no solos, relying on rapid chording, spurts of feedback and a fevered assault on his instrument … They also do a fine version of The Stooges' classic 'No Fun'. There's a lot of Iggy in Johnny Rotten, as he taunts the audience into a violent mood that seems to come more naturally to the English working class. The night I saw them the violence was relatively contained, but in previous appearances chairs have been known to fly across the room.

This remarkably prescient review appeared Stateside the following month, where its contents were duly noted by Tommy Ramone, who until now thought *his* band had the patent on 'tortured punk rock'. For companion Kaye, it reinforced an abiding conviction that rock was an endlessly renewable resource. In the relatively controlled environment in which he witnessed the Pistols he saw a band updating rock, not sweeping the past away. But if Rotten had his way, all bands of retro-rockers – Shaw's included – would be drowned by the tide of change.

* * *

McLaren had seen first-hand just how parochial the New York scene could be and how reluctant the CBGBs bands were to leave their Bowery lofts and Alphabet City apartments. He knew that if the Pistols were really going to crack rock's glass ceiling, they were going to have to turn their back on London's 'circuit of clubs and pubs' and venture into the hinterlands.

He thus began to plot a break out from London's cosy circuit. Unfortunately, this is pretty much where his contacts gave out – as he discovered the minute he tried to construct a mini-tour of the northern marches around a support slot to the Doctors of Madness at Middlesbrough Town Hall and an unconfirmed show at Manchester University Union (which, though listed in *NME,* fell through).

Despite his best efforts – and Peter Lloyd's input – the week-long tour ended up looking like it had been stuck together with sticky paper and sniffin' glue. A couple of 'pub' gigs east of the Pennines, in Northallerton – the backside of beyond – and Scarborough would preface the Middlesbrough show; hairy gigs in Barnsley and Hull would be the other part of the shoestring sojourn.[19] It meant six days on the road for six guys in a van – the band, road manager Nils Stevenson and soundman Dave Goodman. If the band expected to live out some rock & roll fantasy, it was them, not England, that was dreaming. McLaren wisely stayed at Sex:

Nils Stevenson: If you were in some dodgy place like Hull or Scarborough, you'd get the money up front ... There was a lot of pubs on that tour and they were the really dodgy ones ... We'd have the cheapest, cheapest vans – we had one to go to Scarborough that wouldn't go up hills ... We had to call the police in at Barnsley,

[19] The dates for the Barnsley and Hull gigs have never been confirmed, but both Nils Stevenson and Johnny Rotten have referred to them independently. On the other hand, no reliable first-hand testimony has ever been produced for the so-called Lincoln college gig on that first northern sojourn.

this awful place out in the sticks, there was no buildings about or anything, just this pub in the middle of nowhere. But the place filled up and things got a bit hairy … [Rotten would] get quite lippy, put them down and things like that, but … it was just the look of the group and their lack of professionalism [that] used to incense these people. They wanted a hippy group with long hair – they could accept that. But these kids really pissed them off.

Opening night in Northallerton, the band were just happy to see a pair of familiar faces. Peter Lloyd and Pauline Murray had made the thirty-mile hike from Ferryhill and after a great deal of searching finally found the 'club', which as Murray remembered, 'was literally like a row of garages, and the end one was a night club. The people in there were like your regular crowd. No stairs, just a few tables around, small PA.' Goodman dismissively described it as 'a right chicken-in-a-basket place'. And just to add to the sense they had entered the Twilight Zone, the compere acted like he'd come direct from seventies TV show, *The Wheeltappers and Shunters Social Club*: 'Tonight ladies and gentlemen, in cabaret, all the way from the Big Smoke, the amazing Sex Pistols!' When the Pistols plugged in, though, it was as if Dickens' street-urchins had come back to life and learnt to play:

Peter Lloyd: Rotten was mesmerising, even with a tiny audience to perform to, and already [he] looked a star in a pink drape jacket and drainpipes. Glen Matlock was very sharply dressed [in] a Vivienne Westwood t-shirt … It was rock music, but [not really].

Pauline Murray: They came on and it was like nothing we'd seen before … [They] did their blistering type of stuff through a tiny PA and the people were gobsmacked. People forget how funny the Pistols [sounded] to people who had never seen anything like it.

Once again, in the netherlands of Northallerton the lightning-conductor did its job. Pauline Murray was another bored teenager with a vague hankering to be a singer. As her then-boyfriend says, 'We were obsessed with music … [and] just before punk broke [Pauline] was doing a few folk clubs. There was a folk club at Sedgefield and she went with her acoustic guitar and did some Cockney Rebel songs, [and some] Bowie and the Velvets.' But it took the Pistols' 'blistering type of stuff' to turn Pauline's miasma of musical ambition into a laser powerful enough to penetrate Punk's upper echelons.

Murray was very lucky she caught them when and where she did. Because the Pistols, whether they realized it or not, were back in their element – pissed off and ready to piss off the punters who didn't like what they had to say. A handful of London gigs to audiences comprising either apostles or those too cowed to complain was not what the band at its best – and particularly Rotten – feasted upon. As Jordan astutely observes, 'They did to some extent feed off other people's aggression … In a way [Rotten] didn't really like people liking him, because it meant he wasn't doing it right.' The boy couldn't help it, and nor could the audiences:

Dave Goodman: Every time the Pistols played they got some reaction from the audience. They created a lot of violence. Their gigs used to stir up this venom inside people. Like the bouncer, for no reason at all, beats up one of the audience. The music got [to] them.

Sometimes, though, Rotten liked to go too far – as he did in Scarborough on their second night 'up north', when he seemed determined to wind up some very leery-looking longshoremen. The spliffed-up soundman looked on in a cloud of wonder so disorienting he thought he was in Blackburn:[20]

Dave Goodman: The Pistols managed to upset everyone before even playing a note – by taking a helluva long time to start, so when they wandered on there were only a few people at the front of the stage. Anyway, once the stage light – singular – had gone on, the crowd had to take notice. The stage was only about two feet off the floor so the punters were right up against it, eye to eye with the

[20] Goodman describes a number of gigs in his (as-told-to-Phil-Strongman) memoir which fail to tally with the known facts. Blackburn (15th September 1976) is one of them. His description of that gig – and Dave was a lovely guy and a great talker – is almost certainly the confused recollection of another gig 'up north', across the Pennines.

Pistols. 'Come on! Bloody get on with it! Show us what you can do!' ... Rotten just stared back sinisterly. Steve, who seemed paralytic, spent over ten minutes [sic] tuning his guitar at ear-splitting volume. The crowd grew more and more uneasy. 'Get off, if you can't play!' The mob was turning ugly.

Peter Lloyd, who had travelled with the band in the van, was promptly identified as 'one of them' by the pissed-off punters. He began to fear for his life. To his recollection, the problem was that 'Steve Jones kept breaking guitar strings and leaving the stage to change them, giving Johnny the opportunity to announce, "Steve has just gone for a quick wank!" This was not going down well with the few punters and glasses were thrown.'

Fortunately for Lloyd – and the band – 'there was only about twenty people there. It was an afterhours place – all these guys come in [already] drunk.' For all of his taunting, Rotten remembers 'standing onstage and challenging them, but they wouldn't come up to the stage'. They did, however, come backstage, where Lloyd found himself targeted before 'Johnny and Steve jumped in'. Jones, a little worse for wear, was always up for a scrap but even he was taken aback by the level of hostility directed at them: 'Travelling up north to play for people whose first reaction was to hate us ... It was like we were from fucking Mars.'

At this point keeping a dozen drunks at bay may have been par for the course. But what if the audience reacted the same way the following night in Middlesbrough? There was sure to be a respectable crowd there to see the Doctors of Madness; in which case, even a van full of Pistols might have a problem, problem, problem...

When the band arrived at Middlesbrough Town Hall, Matlock was concerned to discover it 'held about two thousand people'. Not quite, but even at close to a thousand, it was their biggest gig to date; and they were expected to make an impression with just the 'pub' PA they'd brought in the van. The Doctors of Madness were refusing to lend them theirs, possibly because they'd heard stories of what might happen if they did. Resident Doctor Richard Strange recalls being profoundly annoyed that the Pistols had 'turned up with virtually no gear and assumed they could borrow ours'.

Matlock notes, 'All we had was these two Eliminator cabinets … and two HH 200 watt amps … But it was great. We just blew them off the stage, just with sheer enthusiasm.' Peter Lloyd is not so sure, 'They never went down well anywhere. People didn't know what to make of them.' But if they made only minimal impact on the Doctors' audience, they had maximum effect on the headliner. Richard Strange was supposedly overheard in the dressing room afterwards, muttering, 'How do we follow *that*?!'

Pauline Murray, who had seen the Doctors a few times and was a fan, says she saw the energy draining from them, which was fast becoming the Pistols' party trick: 'They wiped a lot of bands out. It sounds a cliche but I saw it happen. They lost all their confidence, those bands, when the Pistols came along.' Lloyd stood watching the Doctors with Matlock, who proceeded to critique everything that was wrong with them while Steve Jones rifled through their belongings backstage. The Doctors had been done over, in more ways than one.

After a dark night in deepest Teeside, it was the long and winding road home in a van with no torque. Along the way, they stopped off near Barnsley for 'a Teddy boy reunion' in 'a Teddy boy pub, of all places, in the middle of nowhere', where, according to Rotten, they had to play their 45-minute set twice. Welcome to the Star Club, Johnny! At the end of the night, Rotten remembers there being 'some very angry middle-aged Teddy boys' and Nils Stevenson had to make 'the landlord call the police so we could be escorted out'. A gig in Hull, the night before or after, was equally hairy, though this time the local college of fishermen preferred to fight each other, while the band played on.

So there was a communal sense of relief when this van deposited its human wares on the doorsteps of the 100 Club the evening of the twenty-fifth, for their third consecutive Tuesday at this Oxford Street hostelry. McLaren was on hand to greet them, and to half-listen to Nils's account of a week in hell.

As soon as the Pistols started soundchecking, he knew it had all been worthwhile. They had gone up another notch, musically. When Pirroni ran into him later that night, McLaren told him, 'They've just been up north, and now they're really tight.' When their favourite rock journalist, Jonh Ingham, asked Rotten how it went he put on a brave face, 'We went down really well. I thought they'd hate us.' For the foursome, getting back in one piece qualified as success.

Both Ingham and Pirroni noted the improvement McLaren had already heard for himself. In fact, for Pirroni there was a moment that night when he 'realized how good they were ... [It was] that telepathy, tension thing, where Rotten would be slagging off the audience, and Steve and Paul would be doing something, and they would just go into a number at the perfect moment.'

Ingham, reviewing them for the first time in nearly two months, simply noted, 'The music continues to improve. "Whatcha Gonna Do About It" was properly insolent, and The Stooges' "No Fun" is beginning to hit just the right note – the band sound really bored playing it. Their originals also sounded properly full of broken glass and rusty razor blades ... What next in their plan for world domination?'

Another fan, there that night for a third helping, realized the bar had been raised again. Joe Strummer, a month on from the Nashville, sensed an affirmation: 'You couldn't compare the Pistols to any other group on the island, they were so far ahead.' Still high on rebellion from Patti at the Roundhouse, Joe had arranged a pow-pow with Bernie Rhodes at the 100 Club. He wasn't the only one who feared time was passing, or that those who didn't jump onboard the punk bandwagon would be left behind. Rhodes let the Pistols wash over him and then gave Joe an ultimatum: In or Out. The singer jumped onboard the Clash Express that night.

A distinctly different gig, a couple of nights earlier, had probably helped to make Strummer's mind up for him – and given him the idea for a song. If Patti Smith and the Pistols were performing the kind of music he wanted to make, he no longer wanted to play sixties Britbeat covers.

The Rolling Stones had just shown him they needed no help massacring their extensive back catalogue. While the Pistols were trundling around the northern reaches of Albion, the Stones had settled in at the 17,000-seater Earl's Court for a week of shows that showed they were hopelessly out of touch if they thought Billy Preston's enormous organ and a fifty-foot inflatable phallus (on which Jagger bounced up and down during 'Starfucker') was any kind of substitute for the soulful musicianship of Mick Taylor, Bobby Keys and Jim Price, the core musical components last time they played their homeland.

For someone like Strummer, who had just caught a glimpse of the future, the Stones circa '76 sounded like a band of graverobbers. Peter Lloyd was just as appalled, '[When] I saw the Stones … I'd just seen the Sex Pistols, and there was no comparison. I was on such a high from the Pistols, and this new amazing thing.' He penned a letter to *Sounds*, calling the Stones yesterday's papers. It never ran. The reviews in the UK press, though, were mixed at best and the Stones retired to lick their wounds. (They would not be heard from again until 1978, by which time the Pistols had come and gone and Strummer's prophecy had come true – no 'Rolling Stones *in 1977*'.)

Meanwhile, The Pistols continued their mission. A return north already beckoned, for a show in Manchester originally intended as part of their first northern tour but which ended up being a one-off gig in every sense of the word. Even the choice of venue was symbolic – the Lesser Free Trade Hall was this exclusive little 425-seater venue built above the Free Trade Hall, the two-thousand capacity home to the Hallé Orchestra and scene of the most apocalyptic confrontation in rock history to date: Dylan's 1966 'Judas' concert.[21]

McLaren may have been only dimly aware of that momentous confrontation, but he knew enough to reject the first two suggestions Howard Devoto and Pete Shelley had made when a provisional booking at Manchester University's Union fell through. Their own college, in outer Bolton, was not an option; nor was the Commercial Hotel in Stalybridge, a popular pub-rock venue for headbangers and inbreds. So, as Shelley says, 'We went to the Lesser Free Trade Hall and found that it was thirty-two pounds [sic] to hire.'

With the venue sorted, McLaren pushed the pair to spread the word at the Pistols' behest, even providing them with some A3 posters for the gig, and placing a display ad in the *NME*. Devoto responded in kind, placing an ad in the *Manchester Evening News* and

[21] Dylan's even more famous confrontation at the Free Trade Hall took place a decade earlier, almost to the day, on 17th May, 1966, and like the Pistols' set was recorded for posterity, being finally released officially in 1998.

handing out leaflets before two gigs the previous week at the spacious Free Trade Hall and its rival, the Palace Theatre.

Quite how many Kiss and John Miles fans took up his offer has never been confirmed, but it wasn't many. However, there were a few who *were* prompted to attend the party after reading Howard Trafford's preview in the *New Manchester Review*. Unaware that the writer had a vested interest in shifting tickets, the attuned responded to Howard's hard-sell:

> On June 4 the Sex Pistols board a Manchester stage for the first time at the Lesser Free Trade Hall. If you haven't read any of the articles on them in the music press recently then you've missed some of the juiciest print in months – fans beaten up, abuse, strippers ... The Sex Pistols are the foremost punk outfit in the country. Every song is so mean, tight, fast and offensive you'll probably be too engrossed to notice the mike stand John 'Le Demented' Rotten just hurled your way. The element of real danger gives them the edge on any performing band around. If you actually go to hear the music you won't be disappointed either. They're plenty proficient.

One reluctant absentee, though, was Devoto's close friend and fellow Pistols convert, Richard Boon. Knowing he couldn't make the Manchester gig he arranged a 'warm-up' show at his own art college in Reading the week before, at which the Pistols were once again 'blistering'. If the Reading 'Art Exchange' were expecting something more Exploding Plastic Inevitable than Iggy & the Stooges, they got two for the price of one: anarchy *and* performance-art:

Richard Boon: I persuaded the woman who held the purse strings that this band would be really fantastic to put on. They had as a support act a performance-act called the Kipper Kids who [would] sit and work their way through a bottle of whisky each and tell each other a few stories and then punch each other up. Good opening. Then Johnny comes on and does the classic, 'We've seen your paintings – we pay our taxes for this rubbish?!' And then they were just blistering. There weren't many people there despite me doing cut and paste flyers, but it spread the virus ... Steve was throwing more rock guitar shapes onstage and Johnny was getting wittier and more ironic. [Yet] he was … constantly surprised that the audience found them at all interesting.

★ ★ ★

When the Pistols rented the van overnight for their second jaunt north, they had no reason to think they were about to play to the most receptive audience they ever encountered. Given that Barnsley and Hull shared roughly the same latitude as Manchester, they expected pretty much the same latitude they had received from Yorkshire's Teddy boys and Humberside's fishermen a fortnight earlier, i.e. none.

For McLaren, the whole exercise was a loss-leader. Having already advanced Trafford the £26 hall-rental when he visited Sex in May, and with no other shows to off-set the four-hundred mile round trip, he was taking quite a punt. It was one he sought to minimize by tagging along and overseeing the evening's entertainment.

He arrived that afternoon to find Trafford and McNeish had switched support-acts, realizing that their own band were nowhere near ready to rock,[22] and that they had sold less than fifty tickets at 50p a pop. He must have feared the worst. But he was determined to make the best of a bad job, and went looking for as many likely lads as he could to bolster the numbers. After a quick 'recce' of the environs, he discovered the Free Trade Hall had its own pub tagged onto the rear. It seemed as good a place to start as any. A group of lads (and one ladette) in the corner looked promising:

Malcolm McLaren: I ended up drifting around the local pubs before the band went on, seeing if I could talk any likely looking people into coming down to the gig. I saw the guy who later started The Fall – Mark E. Smith – I said, 'There's this group playing over the road you really ought to see.' He said, 'Why the fuck would I wanna do that?' I said, 'They're really good.' … I told him they were the Sex Pistols and he said, 'Oh yeah, I've heard a bit about them. [Pause] They sound fucking shite.'

[22] The prescient few who had bought tickets in advance were given ones which listed 'Buzzcocks' as the support act, as reproduced in *I Swear I Was There*.

Ever the charmer, Smith duly admitted he was impressed by McLaren's nerve, walking into Cox's Bar with 'this leather suit on … [and] winkle pickers. Pretty unusual in those days.' It didn't mean he was about tell McLaren that all four of them were there specifically to see the Sex Pistols, even girlfriend Una Baines, who admits she 'was [initially] put off by the name, being a feminist'. Smith, Baines, Martin Bramah and Tony Friel had already had long conversations about forming a band, both Bramah and Friel being already competent guitarists. Convinced they knew it all, they had come not to praise the Pistols but to bury them:

Martin Bramah: There was a little article in *NME* or *Sounds*, a review of a London gig that the Sex Pistols had done, in which they described this band doing a couple of Stooges songs and there was a picture of Johnny Rotten … Seeing a kid with short hair doing Stooges songs didn't add up, so we went with the idea that we were gonna heckle.

In fact, the Lesser Free Trade Hall that night was positively teeming with wannabe musicians. It had even been picked as a place to meet a prospective guitarist responding to a 'musician wanted' ad in the *New Manchester Review*. Standing outside early evening was a young Steve Diggle, in the right place at the wrong time when McLaren, who was 'hustling kids in off the street', began to give him the spiel:

Steve Diggle: I was just there to meet the guitar player from the ad [I'd placed] … I asked him who was on and he said the Sex Pistols. 'Oh, what are they like?' I asked. 'They're like The Who.' Fucking hell, really? 'Yes, they do "Substitute." Are you coming in?' I told him I couldn't because I was waiting for this guitarist to turn up from an advert in the *[New] Manchester Review*, and suddenly he seemed to know all about it, 'Oh, are you the bass player, then? The guitarist is inside collecting tickets.' I followed him inside. I'm thinking, We were [supposed to be] meeting outside and going down the pub. It transpires [Pete] had also arranged to meet another bass player who had answered his [own] ad in the paper and Malcolm was keeping an eye out for him … Malcolm introduces me … in the ticket box and we agree to meet in the bar a bit later. I wait to see the Pistols. The place is really empty. Lucky if there were fifty people in.

Having done his own stint on the steps, McLaren sent first Goodman, then Kim Thraves, outside to 'hustle up some punters: "It's only 50p, mate, come on in, they're the future of rock & roll."' This meant there really were less than fifty souls inside when Solstice burst onto the stage in all their bedenimed glory – and McLaren wasn't helping, actively dissuading another local guitarist, Iain Gray, from entering early, saying, 'The support act are on at the moment and they're crap – come back in half an hour.' Those who had the pre-printed tickets which read 'Sex Pistols + Buzzcocks' must have been baffled by this bunch of long-haired Luddites. As soon as these musical throwbacks started playing, at least one punter there to see 'the future of rock & roll' began fuming:

Ian Moss: I'd read the little pieces that [had] appeared in the music press and the fact that it mentioned The Stooges sealed it … There'd been that build-up that hinted at things going in [this] direction. You just felt sooner or later there's gonna be something not nearly It, not pastiching It, but really It … [Being] on my own, I sat right-hand side, halfway along. I saw all of the support act and I thought this is diabolical. I couldn't believe the people clapped, I was that affronted by it. They were that bad and that orthodox, it worried me … I distinctly remember thinking, 'Are the Pistols just going to be a kinda short-haired fancy dress version of this? Just another rock band … I'll give it three or four songs and if it's crap, I'll get to the pub.'

Meanwhile Martin Sinclair, who worked at the same Stockport Bookshop as a young Paul Morley, had been tipped off that the Pistols were coming to town. Sinclair went along because he 'was always looking for something new and the name of the band was interesting', only to be equally perplexed to discover 'the support was a hippy band who played long, long songs with long solos'.

When Solstice 'climaxed' their set with a tediously over-extended cover of Mountain's 'Nantucket Sleighride', Moss and Sinclair were ready to call it a night. Thankfully, both decided to give themselves a chance to be convinced. That moment when the Pistols plugged in and began to play – absent from the only audio document we have – is frozen in the memories of almost everyone there that night. It was a 'fuck me' moment for one and all:

Ian Moss: They came on and just looking at them, there's a surge of electricity, a jolt – they started playing and for me it was absolute euphoria. I'm not one of those people who thinks they were so bad, they were good. I thought, 'Wow, they're my age, they look great, [and] they're untamed.' And then they start playing the covers … and [I think], 'These people are me, I'm not alone.'

Martin Sinclair: If you stayed in on a Friday night you were a stiff, so I went with a lad called Ian Taylor … When they came on, they were just so different … Johnny was wearing a mohair jumper which he ripped to shreds during the course of the concert. I certainly remember 'No Fun', 'I'm Not Your Steppin' Stone' … great choice of material. He introduced each song … They worked hard. There was a lot of bemusement [but] they had a good reception … We didn't think they were very good [musically] but the style, the brevity of the songs, the whole package, we *knew* … We actually counted [the audience] … It was well under a hundred, but we definitely counted them. We said at the time, 'This is gonna be really massive.' … For me, not knowing the New York Dolls or The Stooges, it was so different from what had come before.

Iain Gray: Johnny Rotten ambled on … and that was just a shock. He was one of the most frightening people I'd ever seen at that time … It was just so exciting, the sheer presence of the band with Rotten. Everything I believed in about music up to that point was destroyed, and rightfully so.

Steve Diggle: All of a sudden the Pistols just ambled on. There was Rotten with [his] bright yellow teeth … Steve Jones is thrashing his guitar. Matlock and Cook were so fucking loud but just brilliant together; honestly, forget any of those stories about the Pistols not being able to play. I hadn't seen or heard anything like it in my life. This was fast and furious. I was totally transfixed and knew there wasn't anything like them in the whole country.

Peter Hook: Rotten had on this torn-open yellow sweater and he glared out into the audience like he wanted to kill each and every one of us, one at a time, before the band struck up into 'Did You No Wrong' … I remember feeling as though I'd been sitting in a darkened room all of my life … This even more intense noise [was] showing me another world, another life, a way out … It wasn't just me feeling it, either – we were all like that. We just stood there, stock still, watching the Pistols. Absolutely, utterly, gobsmacked.

Bernard Sumner: Once the band came on and started playing, I was too blown away to worry about who was in the crowd. From the moment they swaggered on to the stage … and launched into 'Did You No Wrong', I knew that this was something different. It was their attitude that hit me; there was a real spite in their performance, sheer aggression combined with an indifference to the audience that occasionally bordered on outright contempt … For the first time at a live performance I found I could truly identify with and relate to the people on the stage.

All the above would take from the experience a belief they could make music themselves – leaving Morrissey languishing in the shadows.[23] If Moss took a while turning his drinking pals into a punk band, Iain Gray, a guitarist from Wythenshawe, would be among the first to take his cue from the Pistols, responding to a *Melody Maker* ad placed by someone who called himself 'Rusty'. 'Rusty' turned out to be a Macclesfield ex-public school boy, Ian Curtis.

(Though it's impossible to confirm, one would like to think his was the anonymous display-advert placed in the 12th June issue,

[23] Both Ian Moss and Iain Gray would be identified in David Nolan's *I Swear I Was There* – an oral history of the Pistols' Manchester gigs – as mere 'audience members' but his shorthand designation rather insults Ian Moss, frontman for The Hamsters and Kill Pretty, two latterday punk bands with at least as significant a pedigree as post-punk art-rockers Crispy Ambulance (whose frontman, Alan Hempsall, was another 4th June attendee).

which read, 'Vocalist With Powerful Emotive Voice Seeks Creative Innovative Band.')

For the next six months the 'two Ians' would be inseparable. Six weeks later, Gray brought Curtis and his recent bride to see the band that had changed his life; before Curtis was approached by a rival gang of LFTH converts – Peter Hook, Bernard Sumner and Terry Mason – at the Pistols' *third* Manchester gig and whisked away to Warsaw.

Martin Sinclair would be co-opted into a band formed by Stockport's set of June converts, playing guitar in the short-lived original line-up of The Negatives, a performance-art combo founded by writer-friend Paul Morley and local photographer Kevin Cummins. Everybody, it seemed, who attended that show ended up part of a band, although not everyone was destined to change what Nolan, in his oral history, portentously calls 'the shape of rock'. Epiphany after epiphany, convert after convert, almost the whole audience that night felt the tide of history rush over them.

Although nothing can ever replicate that experience, the tape of the show – bootlegged to death but never officially, or even semi-officially, released – audibly carries its DNA. There is something utterly compelling lodged within that iconic ferric tape; a surge of sound that demands a response. (That crackling code also resides in less archetypal guise on both Nashville tapes from April and the 100 Club recording from three and a half weeks later.)

All one needed to do was tune to that frequency to sense the power and feel galvanized to respond in kind. And at the Lesser Free Trade Hall, respond they did, initially with their bodies – after Rotten sarcastically inserted into the 'Seventeen' bridge, 'I like the way you all sit down' – but soon enough with their re-tuned minds:

Ian Moss: By halfway through, I couldn't contain myself. Everyone's seated and I got up and went to the front and danced … McLaren and the London posse were beside me, to the left-hand side of the stage, and I was just going for it … By the time they played the encores pretty much everybody was stood up; and there's more banter between the audience and John. I remember John the Postman shouting out Shadows of Knight, Thirteenth Floor Elevators, and

John was [nodding] alright, alright; and then he says Eddie & the Hot Rods, and John [snaps], 'Our imitators!' ... [Afterwards] I got on the 210 bus, and there was two guys, the only other guys upstairs, who I recognised [from] the gig, and we were just like, 'Wasn't that incredible?!'

Ian Taylor: Johnny Rotten made the biggest impression on me ... He just grabbed the microphone and went, 'Fuck Off', which was a refreshing change from 'Hello Manchester'. The set was short, but they were *good*. They were quite tight, [but] the energy they produced was something else – particularly the guitarist. They did an encore, but I remember they had to play something again because Johnny Rotten said we don't know any more ... They were very well received. People liked it ... Everybody I spoke to [thought the] band was amazing ... It was something you'd never seen [or] heard before.

Martin Bramah: Suddenly you realized, 'Oh, we can do that ourselves.' ... It's hard to say which part of the puzzle slotted into place, but it was ... [probably] the energy that was coming up. Music meant everything to us. Just that thought – 'We can do that' – had so much momentum it carried us through to actually gig together.

Una Baines: Everybody in [music] had become very precious. The Prog Rock people were very aloof. [So] it was a real revelation. I remember Johnny Rotten having a red jumper on, with holes in it, which I thought was very cool. It was just brilliant ... I think it gave [us] the confidence to think we really could do it. Because it was simple. That's not in any way derogatory to the Sex Pistols. It was very refreshing. I can still hear that excitement, when something comes on from that era.

That excitement is also conveyed in the four published 'reviews', two of them letters to *NME* and *Sounds* by inveterate letter-writer 'Steve Morrissey, King's Road, Stretford'. The other overviews were more measured, penned by a pair of Pauline fanzine editors from Stockport, Welsh and Morley. Though neither ever seems to be cited by those who argue for the importance of June 4th, they provide the best portal – the bootleg tape excepted – into what being there was really like.

Morrissey was first out of the traps, penning a letter to *NME* the following week, congratulating 'the bumptious Pistols, in [their] jumble sale attire', for leaving 'those few that attended dancing in the aisles'. He also noted that, 'despite their discordant music and barely audible audacious lyrics, they were called back for two encores. The Pistols boast [of] having no inspiration from the New York rock scene, yet … the Pistols' vocalist/ exhibitionist Johnny Rotten's attitude and self-asserted "love us or leave us" approach can be compared to both Iggy Pop and David Johansen … I'd love to see the Pistols make it. Maybe then, they will be able to afford clothes which don't look as if they've been slept in.'

A week later, he had tweaked his prose but not lost his passion for the performance, encapsulating his enthusiasm for *Sounds'* readers: 'I attended the Sex Pistols onslaught … out of curiosity, and although they have no manners and don't use their instruments in the traditional way, they should make it for their enthusiasm alone. Their concert terminated after two encores and over an hour of dancing in the aisles. Musically, like many newcomers to this field, they owe a lot to the New York Dolls and, of course, The Stooges … Now, the Sex Pistols are within arms reach and those that have seen them live will agree that their presence is cause to rejoice. At last, rock'n'roll.'

This Stretford 'scallie' had few friends and attended the gig alone. He would later suggest his own enthusiasm was not matched by fellow attendees, 'The first Sex Pistols appearance was quite difficult, there weren't any instructions. Being northern, we didn't know how to react … People were very rigid … unwilling to respond to the Sex Pistols. The audience was very slim anyway, it was a front parlour affair. If somebody spoke three rows back you could hear what they said, … flares were not entirely taboo at that point, … and as I say, nobody stood up.'

The photos taken by Paul Welsh, whose contemporary review ran in the eighth issue of his mimeographed fanzine, *Penetration,* contradicts Morrissey's memory, with most fans standing by the encores. Although Welsh heard much the same reference-points in the music as Morrissey, he for one left feeling distinctly blitzed:

> Well, at last our prayers have been answered with the 'Sex Pistols'. They are musically everything that a Velvet Underground, Stooges, New York Dolls freak could wish for, while visually they look like poor customers at a jumble sale, tacky, sleazy, distasteful and yet somewhat natural. They attack their numbers as if they were attacking a gang of thugs in a street fight … They blitz the audience with power chords and vocals set in a different key to the music. When I saw them, they whipped the audience to a frenzy with ease, and when responded to Johnny Rotten actually smiled! 'Sex Pistols' are, at the moment, unique and they're amazing live … See them soon.

Having had the wit and wherewithal to snap photos, Welsh passed them onto Stretford Steve; and they somehow ended up in *New York Rocker* that summer, credited to a 'Steven Morrissey'. Welsh's Stockport-based 'zine had been running since 1973 and, as its title suggests, heavily championed The Stooges, along with The Velvet Underground, the Pink Fairies and Hawkwind. In the issue with the Pistols review, the cover was devoted to Kiss, still considered cousins of the New York Dolls, who they so obviously set out to emulate.

The other local 'zine editor in attendance that night was another Stockport boy. Paul Morley had been planning his inaugural 'zine for some time, having already penned most of the content. He also had a drawing of Dylan for the cover, and a largely apocryphal article on Marc Bolan and Patti Smith when he visited the Lesser Free Trade Hall and realized an about-face was required:

Paul Morley: [Rotten] meant it, man … and you felt that more than anything you'd ever come across before … The funny thing is, they could play really well … It wasn't a shambles at all. They were very powerful and they had all the right moves … When you came out, you knew something had happened … But it never occurred to you that maybe every single person in that room would go on and form bands … I was doing a fanzine at that time. I'd started to put it together before I'd seen the Pistols ... I had to change very quickly in mid-flow ... I rammed in a little bit about the [gig].

Morley's half-page, last-minute review of the LFTH gig in *Out There #1* showed this potentially gifted writer had accidentally swallowed a thesuarus, while his ill-advised comparisons with 'Verlaine's New York' was based solely on press cuttings. Nonetheless, as a contemporary account of the evening he conveys the right punk spirit and a great sense of urgency:[24]

> So there we were. Priding ourselves on attractive elitism, upwards of seventy or so cross-sectioned furry freaks and plastic poseurs politely settled in the quaintly draped hitherto mysterious Lesser Free Trade Hall. There to see a youthful contemporary quartet play the street avant garde music of the sixties in its properly repressed seventies setting ... Acceptably stylised, thankfully few traces of commonplace modern ill posturing, the sound owes not a little to two of the few genuine geniuses in rock, Iggy Pop and Ray Davies ... The rough, raw tidal surge transforms the quartet into one neat unit of aloof intimidating punks. Guitar, bass, adopt suitable respectable easy-split stances. Rotten plays Frankenstein playing Lionel Blair with a hint of the forced mechanism of Bowie, Ferry ... Technically they're accomplished. Defined limits, but they're disciplined and don't stray. Hard, loud, clean, brisk and as relentless and as guiltless as a zipless fuck. Their harmonies are spot off. If one of their songs ventures past the 200 second mark, they contentedly sustain the nifty moronic monotonous peak they initially attained. They plagiarise admirably. The Stooges 'No Fun', The Monkees 'I'm Not Your Stepping Stone', 'Substitute' by The Who ... [while] The Pistols' own songs are London mirror takes of Verlaine's New York violent rejections and sexual rebuttals. They're excellent. Aggression through Repression. Get on with it.

Inevitably, the ripples set in motion by the Pistols' performance to these 'seventy or so ... freaks and plastic poseurs' would take a while to reach the edge of an entrenched pop pool, even as Dave Bentley's

[24] Unfortunately, his printer did not follow suit, and the 'zine only appeared in October when the musical world had already tilted off its axis and the homemade punk 'zine scene beckoned.

audio verite document of the Sex Pistols' brand of good time music began to discreetly disseminate.

By the time Morley's cogent words found a limited local audience, another solitary bystander who came that night had succeeded in getting the Pistols on TV, receiving a royal bollocking for his troubles. Tony Wilson, the well-known local TV presenter, had received the package from Devoto containing a cassette of the Spedding demos and a complimentary ticket for the event.

Wilson stumbled into the hall just in time to catch their opening salvo. By his own admission, he 'didn't know what the fuck was going on, until they played "Steppin' Stone".' With that reference in place, he began to realize they were 'fabulously exciting' and 'absolutely real'.

At the time Wilson was on the look-out for potential 'guests' to put on a late-night music show he was down to compere, *So It Goes*, and was thinking no further than that. But within a few days he had started to doubt his own memory of that Mancunian moment and decided he needed positive reinforcement to persuade both himself and the powers-that-be at Granada that the Pistols were as good as he half-remembered. In fact, he later claimed, 'My producer told me I had to see the Pistols again before we could book them,' a common tactic employed whenever Chris Pye wanted to deflect one of Wilson's gushing enthusiasms.

As such, Wilson was convinced – or probably instructed – to take Granada researcher Malcolm Clarke to the northern tip of London, Walthamstow, less than a fortnight later, to catch the Pistols at its Assembly Hall. Possibly, he was looking to kill two bands with one stone. The headliners that night were Ian Dury's Kilburns, with whom he was equally taken.

Dury, who in mock response to any supposed threat the Pistols posed, musical or physical, had already 'polish[ed] the razor-blade ear-piece, oil[ed] the knife, and primp[ed] the barnet', thought the Pistols set was 'smashing', as did Wilson. What no one, certainly not Wilson, knew was that he was calling time on the Kilburns. The Walthamstow event, also the one and only time the Pistols shared a bill with The Stranglers, would be Ian Dury & The Kilburns' swansong. Whether Dury sensed the swelling tide we'll never know, but by the start of 1977 he would have come up with the requisite components for the first Blockheads and was ready to be Stiff.

If Wilson just wanted to see the Pistols again, he could simply have waited for their imminent return to Manchester. Barely had the June gig finished before Devoto, Shelley, McLaren and the band headed for Tommy Duck's to talk about a return date. Even though no one had made any money from the show – contrary to what Shelley later claimed – everyone, Devoto included, felt the experience alone 'was worth it to come back again'.

One Pistol, in particular, had been blown away by the reaction. As Devoto recalls, 'I remember John being quite … chuffed … At the end he said something like, "Where do you all come from?"' And the singer was smiling when he said it. He later accounted for such an uncharacteristic display of bonhomie, 'They liked us for what we were. They hooked on to the energy instead of the *NME, Sounds* and *Melody Maker* gossip angle.'

⋆ ⋆ ⋆

Even by early June, Rotten had it in for the music weeklies – who had been nothing but supportive of the Sex Pistols. Writers at *Sounds* and *NME* in particular had embraced McLaren's plan to shake up the industry. And yet Rotten, having beamed his beneficence on Manchester, turned up at the 100 Club eleven days later seemingly intent on giving *NME* and its rivals something other than the music to gossip about.

On June 15th, at Rotten's behest, the Pistols crossed the line between cartoon violence and the real thing. It was as if he was determined to sabotage the band's upward trajectory now that the music no longer resembled 'Rubbish Rock'. The pantomime aspect in previous 'incidents' turned genuinely nasty in the blink of a blade; and it was Sid Vicious and Jah Wobble doing their friend's dirty work. Their target was Nick Kent who had unselfishly helped shape the Pistols' musical direction. The 'two Johns' waited until one of Kent's chunkier companions, Island A&R Howard Thompson, went to the bar to buy a round before leaping into action:

Howard Thompson: Before the band came on, I noticed a guy leaning against the side of the stage facing us. He looked a little menacing and seemed to be staring specifically at us. When the band came out, he came over and stood directly in front of Nick and started acting all tough, kicking Nick's ankles. Then he pulled out what looked like a small knife with a 2" or 3" blade and just held it under Nick's nose ... It was intense and very quick, but he returned the knife to his pocket and, as the band started to play, the situation quietened down. I thought this might be a good time to get the drinks in so I made my way to the bar, which now had no queue waiting to be served. When I got back, Michael [Beale] was clutching his arm and Nick was holding his head, dazed and bleeding.

Both Vicious and Wobble already had form from incidents at the Nashville and El Paradise. The harmless Nils Stevenson had also been on the receiving end of a bottle from Wobble at a party held by Andy Czezowski. But this was the first time they were seemingly 'obeying orders'. Roger Armstrong, who was standing 'right beside them', noticed that 'Johnny was basically winding Sid up, in a half-joking sort of way, to go and get the hippy'.

The 'hippy' in question had almost single-handedly espoused the punk aesthetic in the premier music weekly for the past two years. Quite why Rotten targetted Nick Kent has never been clear. His later explanation – 'Nick Kent would constantly slag me off in the press' – is an out-and-out lie. Yet it is one he has stuck to, in his latest memoir claiming that 'a lot of people had a lot of issues with Nick Kent. You can't go around just being spiteful and inaccurate in what you write, and think that somebody isn't going to do something about it.' Kent hadn't written a word – good or bad – about the band. Maybe *that* was the problem.

Whatever the motivation, it was *Rotten's* henchmen who carried out the orchestrated assault on Kent just as the Pistols were mounting the stage for their eagerly-awaited Oxford Street rematch. The following November Kent even hinted it was not a solitary incident, and that 'Rotten's personal involvement in [such] incidents ... [which] "set up" unsuspecting patrons, using the likes of Vicious to create the tensions' as the band began their set, was not unknown.

When it came to violence, Sid Vicious was very easily led. He certainly knew there were elements among the (other) Sex employees who had it in for Kent. If, as Brian James suggests, there was 'a lot of gossip at the time that Vivienne spurred Sid into doing it', Sex shopworker Alan Jones informed *Mojo*'s Mark Paytress, 'We all hated [Kent]. And what Sid did, we were all cheering, believe me. The way he looked – leather trousers, leather jacket, scarf round his neck.' In other words, people who wore the 'wrong' clothes had become a target.

Kent took the assault badly, but the person he still primarily blames is McLaren, whom he felt 'turned on me. We were real friends before that – we'd sit down and talk. But … that was just vicious – [as if] you are now an enemy. I knew what was going to happen … Vicious pointed in my direction, and McLaren was nodding his head … It was all timed.' Yet it was not Vicious who put the fear of God in the scribe: 'What I was frightened about was when his mate Jah Wobble pulled a knife and stuck it two inches from my eyes. That's what fucking scared me, 'cause that guy had a look on his face like he really wanted to hurt me.'

Whoever gave the two lanky louts the nod, a stunned Kent returned to a friend's flat in Maida Vale. That friend was Marc Zermati, another former confidant of McLaren, who recalls, 'He was covered in blood. He told me Malcolm at the time needed more press. That's all. We [had] worked together on the concept [of the band] and suddenly Malcolm decides it [would be] easy to get press if something like that happens to Nick Kent. He was trying to be a Situationist.' If he was the instigator – which I doubt – McLaren realized soon enough he had made a serious mistake, issuing a press release disclaiming any role:

> Contrary to the rumours and to put the record straight, the fight at the 100 Club between Sex Pistols fan Sid Vicious and Nick Kent, Michael Beale (Eddie & The Hot Rods management), and an employee from Island Records [Howard Thompson] was not premeditated. It was an individual's spontaneous reaction that fortunately did not spoil the gig. The Sex Pistols and most of the people there were not even aware of the fight until after the gig

ended. No one was seriously hurt, only slightly bruised and cut. It all adds up to a rock & roll event in the traditions of London's clubland.

Not surprisingly, Kent's own paper refrained from reporting the incident, feeling that it gave McLaren's band the oxygen of publicity. Indeed, for the next two months there was barely a mention of the Pistols in the weekly music paper. *NME* did, however, review the show that night, even mentioning in passing 'the fight which one hears is essential to any Sex Pistols gig'. But reviewer Phil McNeil was more concerned by the threat the Pistols posed to the future of Rock than to his fellow IPC employee, coming up with perhaps the most off-target sign-off in the history of this esteemed journal:

> The Sex Pistols' version of 'Whatcha Gonna Do 'Bout It' starts with the words 'I wantchoo ta know that I hate you, baby,' and sitting in the 100 Club surrounded by sullen Pistol lookalikes, as a despised hippy who hasn't had a haircut since … my brief flirtation with skinheadness five years ago … the 'vibes', as we hippies say, are a bit heavy. The fight which one hears is essential to any Sex Pistols gig has just been waged rather too close for comfort, and onstage singer Johnny Rotten looks vicious as he raps out 'Get me a drink!' in an exasperated monotone and waves the glass menacingly. Any band that does 'Stepping Stone' (that and 'Substitute' were the only other songs I recognized through the wall of sound) is okay by me, but … the Pistols are actually a bit boring. There's no question of so-bad-it's-good; they are tight and energetic. Rotten's not a great singer, but that's no problem, Glen Matlock is fine on bass and Paul Cook is an excellent, fierce drummer. What spoils them is Steve Jones' guitar, and really it's an insoluble problem. He's a good player, ideally suited to the Pistols' belligerent high energy; violent chords and no lead work whatsoever. But his sound is too modern, too electric … [So] although the Pistols have an admirable physical energy … it will take a far better band than them to create a raw music for their generation.

Any expletive-strewn response to McNeil's dismissive review from Denmark Place has gone unrecorded but when the Pistols returned to the 100 Club a fortnight later they had added two new songs to their repertoire. Well, one new song and one anti-song, with which they proceeded to open the show. Though it went unintroduced, the latter was called 'Flowers of Romance' and as Rotten explained the following year, it was a 'song we used to start with in the early days – just noise, no music – just to confuse the people who said we couldn't play'. It was the closest to Rotten's beloved Beefheart that the Pistols ever came.

Thankfully, their other new song had words and a tune and both were corkers. It even had a false stop-start ending in mid-song, proof that the Pistols really could play. The song in question, 'I Wanna Be Me', was widely interpreted as a(nother) dig at Nick Kent, but lines like 'down in the crypt, where the typewriter fits … with your pen and pad, ready to kill … you wanna be someone, you wanna be meee' suggest Rotten looked to cut a swathe through the press at large. And yet, maybe it was another of McLaren's wind-ups. Writing an anti-press song sure sounds like one of McLaren's ideas. As Lydon says, 'Malcolm couldn't stand the good reviews: "That's not what we want! We need these old farts to hate us!"'

In which case he must have loved McNeil's piece, which appeared in the July 3rd *NME* – too late to be incorporated into a cut'n'paste flyer the manager had sent to the promoter of the Pistols' next provincial assault: a reenactment of the Battle of Hastings. The rematch was scheduled to take place at the Pavilion on Hastings Pier on the Saturday after McNeil's review ran.

For years, everyone who ever cared wondered how in the hell the Pistols ended up on the same bill as Budgie, a band of earnest mid-seventies Britrockers and another of those outfits about to be blown to kingdom come by all the Pistols wrought. It took an article in a local paper to prompt promoter Barry Taylor to come clean:

> I'd heard reports of London gigs involving the Sex Pistols, and it was evident that something unusual was happening. I'd not seen or heard them before, but was intrigued and decided to try and book them … They looked like a bunch of Martians arriving from outer space, complete with safety pins holding their clothes together. I'd never seen anything like it. I am not sure what the Budgie fans made of the Pistols shambolic, yet exciting set. It was an incongruous pairing of bands, to put it mildly. [But] there was an unpleasant scene after

> the gig. John Lydon was not impressed with the PA, provided by a local musician, and expressed his displeasure. I appreciated Glen Matlock's intervention … as a fracas loomed.

Once again, the usual problem reared its head. The headliner, in all their prog-infused pomposity, had refused to lend the Pistols their PA. As a result, promoter Taylor had to ring a local musician 'with about three hours to spare', to ask if he could help:

Joe Rytlewski: Luckily I was able to take along my own PA, complete with a battery powered mixing desk. You can probably guess what happened next. Come the Sex Pistols soundcheck and the mixing desk wouldn't work, the battery was flat! Thankfully, Budgie then relented, and the Sex Pistols were able to use their PA after all.

What may have got Budgie's backs up was their first sight of the promotional flyers McLaren had forwarded to Taylor, which gave precious little indication it was a Budgie gig. Even their name was partly obscured by a review of the Pistols, one of several McLaren cut 'n' pasted, all of them negative and/or provocative, Tony Tyler's 'The Sex Pistols are coming' headline taking pride of place. He had also somehow arranged for the gig to be advertised in both *NME*'s and *Sounds*' Gig Guides as featuring *only* the Sex Pistols.[25]

But despite McLaren's endeavours, few who attended were there to see the Pistols. Indeed, two confirmed Budgie fans wrote to the *NME* to complain at the coverage the Pistols were receiving at the expense of, well, bands like Budgie, who could be relied on to play recycled footstompfs until the Normans went home:

> You seem to be running features nearly every week on the Sex Pistols, portraying them as a high-energy violent group, with cheap thrills thrown in. However, when they supported Budgie at Hastings, we found that none of this to be true. We saw no sex and no violence. The Pistols certainly did not strike fear into even

[25] In *Sounds'* case, the Pistols' Hastings Pier gig was highlighted with a photo of the band in the Gig Guide section, which must have really annoyed the actual headliner. It also confirms McLaren was on the ball when it came to getting the band listed in the two music papers that mattered most in 1976.

> the younger hearts of the audience, simply because they looked physically incapable of it, and in no way was the music high-energy or liable to incite violence. Practically nobody got off on them. Meanwhile, the same thing was not true of the headliners … [who] produced a true high-energy set.

The partially deaf DJ at the Pavilion, Nigel Ford, who had been used to warming up a crowd for The Glitter Band or Curved Air, was another attendee unable to 'detect any likeable or memorable hooks/ riffs in any of what [the Pistols] were throwing together. However, their followers seemed to greet each track with great enthusiasm. Each time I thought, "Ah! perhaps that'll be a good one then," only for it to sound as uncoordinated and tuneless as those before!'

Another 'music fan' who was there to see Budgie has provided an equally fanciful account of proceedings. Bobby Walker convinced himself, 'They were onstage for less than 20 minutes. They couldn't play. They played "(I'm Not Your) Stepping Stone" three times [sic] and … The Stooges "No Fun" … There was only one punk in the audience. A really nice bloke who called himself Sid Vicious.'

Even Walker's last sentence is wrong. The unmissable Jordan, whose parents lived nearby, had also arrived at the pavilion, only to find that most of those attending were fans of neither band, 'Nearly the whole audience were German, Italian and Swedish tourists all down there for their summer hols. It was absolutely bizarre.'

If Walker failed to notice Jordan, he did run into a former school friend, Marion Elliott, who was there because it was her birthday and she was tired of seeing the same ol' bands. She, at least, got the point of the Pistols. Indeed, just about the only thing Walker recollected right was that 'Marianne [sic] was so impressed with the Pistols at that gig she changed her name and formed her own band':

Poly Styrene: I'd seen this tacky Day-Glo sign with 'Sex Pistols' all over it and thought, Gosh, I wonder what that's about … I'd always been singing, just knocking around, not with a band or anything. But then I saw the Sex Pistols … [It was] on my 18th birthday, in Hastings on the pier … They stood out from all the hippy bands I'd seen before. They were incredibly young and fresh … They couldn't play their instruments very well [and] the sound was terrible, but they had a certain charm.

Actually, the problems with the sound seem to have been largely down to the soaring temperatures. It was another balmy evening in a record-breaking summer at the coastal resort, and the effect it was having on Jones' guitar was to send it perpetually out-of-tune. Indeed, so pronounced was the effect that local guitarist Mick Mepham convinced himself it was deliberate: 'When the Sex Pistols started up they sounded really rather good, powerful and tight. After a few songs though, they started de-tuning their instruments and started taking the piss out of the audience, which didn't go down too well!'

By now Rotten's default response when there were sound problems was to take 'the piss out of the audience'. It led to a fractious end to proceedings and words being exchanged with the soundman. The Pistols did not stick around to find out whether the headliner had anything to say (they didn't), but packed up their gear and headed back to London, leaving yet another would-be punk-rocker gazing at the future through her mail order x-ray spex.

The Pistols had to be in Sheffield the following evening for what they hoped might be another Manchester-like experience. And this time they were taking no chances with an unsuitable support-act. They were bringing their own – four lads who had all seen the Pistols at the Nashville in April, fronted by a man with worse dentalwork than Rotten and almost as much stage-presence, ex-101'er Joe Strummer. Having said a not-so-fond farewell to his former bandmates at a fraught gig in Hayward's Heath four weeks earlier, Strummer was raring to go.

However, he was not exactly keen to advertise his new band's debut. A passing remark of his, which found its way into *Sounds*' 'Jaws' column the day before the Sheffield gig, noted, 'Ex 101'ers person Joe Strummer asks for five weeks grace before new band The Heartdrops take to the road.'

As if this wasn't smokescreen enough, when 'his' band turned up at the Black Swan with the Pistols, he informed an already-unhappy landlord they were no longer called The Heartdrops. They were

Clash, as in a clash of cultures – like the one between pub rock and punk. For those who thought the latter four-letter word held a New York patent, events over the next six months would necessitate a wholesale rethink.[26]

[26] The 'The' in Clash was only adopted a couple of months later, seemingly at the 100 Club punk festival.

THE SPARK

4. THE JULY REVOLUTION

[July 4th – August 6th]

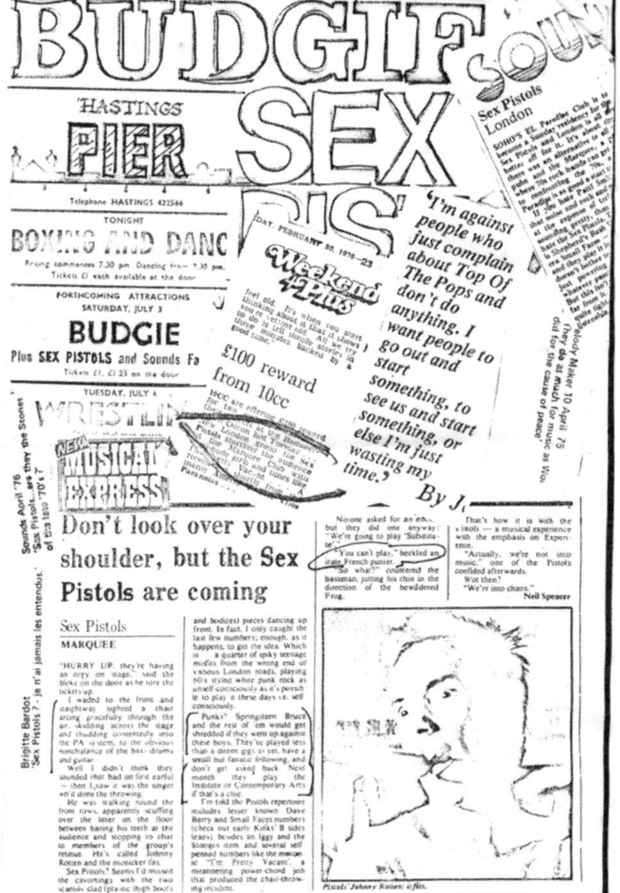

BUDGIE

SEX PISTOLS

HASTINGS PIER

Telephone HASTINGS 422566

TONIGHT

BOXING AND DANC

Boxing commences 7.30 pm. Dancing from 7.30 pm.

Tickets £1 each available at the door

FORTHCOMING ATTRACTIONS

SATURDAY, JULY 3

BUDGIE

Plus SEX PISTOLS and Sounds Fa

Tickets £1, £1.25 on the door

TUESDAY, JULY 6

WRESTLIN

NEW MUSICAL EXPRESS

Sex Pistols

London

'I'm against people who just complain about Top Of The Pops and don't do anything. I want people to go out and start something, to see us and start something, or else I'm just wasting my time.'

By J

Weekend Plus

£100 reward from 10cc

Sounds April '76

'Sex Pistols... are they the Stones of the late '70's?'

Brigitte Bardot

'Sex Pistols ? - je n'ai jamais les entendus.'

Melody Maker 10 April '76

'They do as much for music as Wo... did for the cause of peace'

Don't look over your shoulder, but the Sex Pistols are coming

Sex Pistols

MARQUEE

"HURRY UP, they're having an orgy on stage," said the bloke on the door as he tore the tickets up.

I waded to the front and straightway sighted a chair arcing gracefully through the air, skidding across the stage and thudding contentedly into the PA system, to the obvious nonchalance of the bass, drums and guitar.

Well I didn't think they sounded that bad on first earful — then I saw it was the singer who'd done the throwing.

He was walking round the front rows, apparently scuffing over the litter on the floor between baring his teeth at the audience and stopping to chat to members of the group's retinue. He's called Johnny Rotten and the monicker fits.

Sex Pistols? Seems I'd missed the cavortings with the two scantily clad (plastic thigh boots and bodices) pieces dancing up front. In fact, I only caught the last few numbers; enough, as it happens, to get the idea. Which is ... a quarter of spiky teenage misfits from the wrong end of various London roads, playing 60's styled white punk rock as unself-consciously as it's possible to play it these days i.e. self-consciously.

Punks? Springsteen Bruce and the rest of 'em would get shredded if they went up against these boys. They've played less than a dozen gigs as yet, have a small but fanatic following, and don't get asked back. Next month they play the Institute of Contemporary Arts if that's a clue.

I'm told the Pistols repertoire includes lesser known Dave Berry and Small Faces numbers (check out early Kinks' B sides lately), besides an Iggy and the Stooges item and several self-penned numbers like the mutant-ic "I'm Pretty Vacant", a meandering power-chord job that produced the chair-throwing incident.

No-one asked for an encore, but they did one anyway: "We're going to play 'Substitute'."

"You can't play," heckled an irate French punter.

"So what?" countered the bassman, jutting his chin in the direction of the bewildered Frog.

That's how it is with the Pistols — a musical experience with the emphasis on Experience.

"Actually, we're not into music," one of the Pistols confided afterwards.

Wot then?

"We're into chaos."

Neil Spencer

Pistols' Johnny Rotten: it fits.

4

Screw you critics. It's your fault entirely and you'll never be forgiven. What's with this trekking across the Atlantic every time you need a new cult band to discover? Ever try looking in your own backyard? Of course not. Sure the Ramones were a lot of fun – but so are the Sex Pistols, so why the 'here they come, here they come' publicity for the New York foursome, whilst the Pistols only get a mench if some punter gets his face modified during their set? No doubt the next phenomenon will be the visit to these shores of Television, whilst The 101'ers shuffled off this mortal coil with barely a postscript.

– *'And Now, the Sex Pistols controversy'*
letter by 'Tony',* NME *17th July 1976

What had evidently upset 'Tony' was the blanket music-press coverage which greeted the Ramones' UK debut at the Roundhouse, North London's most circular rock venue, on July 4th, where they had been playing *support* to the Flamin' Groovies, six weeks after Patti Smith's band stormed the same building for two nights, changing the face of British rock. Independence Day or not, Ramones had nothing like the same pulling power as Patti, despite a glowing review of their (at the time import-only) debut LP by Nick Kent in *NME*. And yet, it is the Ramones at the Roundhouse which has been cast – at least by Legs 'Print The Legend' McNeil – as the day the English punks paid homage to New York's travelling band of blitzkrieg boppers:

Arturo Vega: All the London bands were hanging out in the alleyway, trying to get into the Roundhouse to see the Ramones. Johnny Rotten asked me if he could come through the back door and meet the band.

Danny Fields: Mick Jones and Paul Simonon of The Clash were there [that night] … Paul and Mick weren't in The Clash yet, but they were starting it. They were afraid to play until they saw the Ramones. I mean, Paul and Mick [actually] told the Ramones, 'Now that we've seen you, we're gonna be in a band.'

All of which seems rather odd, because on the same letters page as Tony's tirade (above) was another contribution to the 'Sex Pistols controversy'. It was a letter from a 'real music lover', who had just seen Johnny Rotten, Mick Jones and Paul Simonon hanging out at the Black Swan in Sheffield the very same night they were 'trying to get into the Roundhouse to see the Ramones', a patent impossibility. They had even brought equipment with them. Not that the letter-writer – who also sent the same letter to *Sounds* – was greatly impressed by what he heard:

> Last night I went to see the Sex Pistols and Clash (formerly 101'ers) for the first time. I was very, very disappointed. Both bands were crap. It's enough to turn you on to Demi Roussos. There is currently far too much publicity being given to [these] pub bands by the music press. Clash were just a cacophonous barrage of noise. The bass guitarist had no idea how to play the instrument and even had to get another member of the band to tune it for him. They tried to play early 60s r'n'b and failed dismally … The Sex Pistols, despite having the weirdest bunch of followers in the audience (and what a set of freaks they were), were even worse. John Rotten really lived up to his name. I've heard Mickey Mouse sing better. The rest of the band are average musicians, but all the material they played was the same. At the end, Rotten stayed on the stage and shouted at the audience … Pathetic, just pathetic.

The disgruntled gentleman – who identified himself as Reg Cliff on the *Sounds* letters page – was not imagining things. That sultry summer evening neither the Pistols nor Clash were anywhere near Chalk Farm. They were four hours away as the van flies.

If Clash were mere novices, Strummer excepted, the Pistols were playing their forty-third gig since they exploded onto the London music-scene with all the force of a full-blown hurricane the previous

November. In less than eight months they had honed themselves into a band tighter than one of Westwood's fetish corsets. If Mr Cliff was immune to their tensile charms, he may have been in the minority, for once. The support-act's singer certainly loved their performance:

Joe Strummer: They were brilliant. They were firing on all strokes. We had a sort of Roxy Music audience. The Pistols had had a few ... articles, right, that one in *Sounds*, but it wasn't a lot for people to go on ... I remember being amazed that at least two or three hundred people turned up. Girls in leopard-skin overcoats ... sharkskin suits, that type of thing – they were very receptive.

Another person surprised by the encouraging turnout was the Pistols' soundman. Goodman's admittedly shaky memory, ever prone to hyperbole, has the Pistols playing 'with all the windows open – you could hear them from miles away ... [And] by the end of the evening, Rotten's dry wit had well and truly won over most of the audience and the joint was rocking. Five hundred punters squeezed inside, and another two hundred outside still able to ... hear the show.'

If the Pistols really did win over the sweaty majority that night, it was again against the odds. This was a pub-rock crowd. Many of those there undoubtedly came to see the support act. Because, whatever name they were using on the flyer – and it was probably The Heartdrops – Strummer and co. were apparently 'ex-101'ers' – which counted for something at the Black Swan.

At least two students had been nagging the landlord for weeks to re-book The 101'ers, unaware that they had 'shuffled off this mortal coil with barely a postscript'. Ges Tessier and his friend Andy had first seen Strummer's former band 'on a Sunday night in the spring ... Loved the group. I can [even] remember them doing "Gloria" and "I Saw Her Standing There" as encores. As Andy and I went to see a gig at the Black Swan most Sundays, we ... asked the Landlord to re-book The 101'ers as soon as possible. We asked him virtually every week.' Just before the end of term, Tessier saw 'a sign saying that on the first Sunday in July, two bands were booked. The second band were sub-texted, (ex-101'ers).'

The 101'ers had developed quite a reputation playing pub-rock outposts like the Black Swan and Derby's Cleopatra's thanks to their barnstorming shows and recognisable covers, and presumably their 'next' incarnation would sound much the same.

Imagine, then, the reaction when Clash took to the stage and began to play, and it became immediately apparent that bass player Paul Simonon's deficiencies – highlighted by Mr Cliff in his letter – weren't confined to an inability to tune his instrument. He couldn't even play the simple up/down bass intro to their first song, an instrumental called (appropriately) 'Listen'. The audience might have done so if the instrumental in question hadn't broke down before it got going, forcing the quintet to start again – after everyone on and off stage stopped laughing, ex-101'er singer included:

Joe Strummer: We had a song called 'Listen' which had a bass line that went up in scale and then down a note to start, and Paul was so nervous that he just kept going up the scale and we all fell over laughing, 'cause we didn't know when to come in.

The landlord was not amused. Mickey Foote, an ex-101'ers roadie now entrenched in the Clash camp, remembers him berating Strummer, 'I booked the fucking 101'ers,' which clearly wasn't the case. But he sure as purgatory had expected a band *like* The 101'ers. Even Foote admits, 'There were sixty or seventy 101'ers fans who were a bit disappointed ... But there were [also] at least half a dozen people there who looked a bit punky. [So] word had got up there.' These were the same punters the open-minded Mr Cliff dismissed as 'a set of freaks'.

Another pair of 'real music' lovers were left underwhelmed by Clash gig #1. Pistols bassist Glen Matlock, who 'really wanted it to work, because Mick [Jones] was my mate and I was keen for something to happen', asked for a second opinion from his own band's opinionated vocalist. Rotten's understated critique cut to the quick, 'They're not very good, are they?'

Soundman Goodman recalled 'a chaotic discordant set. [Yet] considering it was their first public airing, [they] managed to hold their own despite shouts of disapproval from the crowd.' Strummer did his best to make concessions to the disapproving crowd, their 'discordant set' containing very little of the future Clash in it – probably only 'Listen', 'Protex Blue' and '1-2 Crush on You' (a revamp of a 101'ers original). For the first and last time Strummer tried to meet a Clash audience halfway, performing 101'ers favourites like 'I Can't Control Myself', 'Too Much Monkey Business', 'Junco Partner' and 'Keys To Your Heart', their solitary 45.

According to Mick Jones, Clash were also all 'dressed in black and white. A couple of us had ties on, black and white shirts,' hardly the visual statement manager Bernie Rhodes was looking to make. After all, he had insisted Simonon should be part of the band based solely on how he looked, a mentality that draws Marc Zermati's ire. The most damning thing he can say about both McLaren and Rhodes is that, 'right from the beginning, they're people from fashion, so they had no [real] idea. They were more into fashion. They thought they were managing boy bands.'

McLaren certainly did know about music, even if his ex-car dealer friend thought he was shuffling a pack of cards. It was one of Rhodes' mantras, overheard by Rat Scabies during his stint in London SS, that, 'Three bands are a movement'; which makes London SS a one-band movement, spawning as it did The Clash, The Damned, Generation X and The Boys without ever producing three of a kind, let alone a full house. But he was immediately convinced Clash was his royal flush.

Even Rhodes, though, knew they would have to defer to the Pistols, because as all K-Tel albums used to insist, 'The original is best.' Yet Clash 'stand-in' drummer Terry Chimes always 'felt like the Pistols were the opposition. The others … were saying, "No, they're our comrades in arms."' If so, they were doing their best not to let it show in Sheffield. Rotten insists, 'Strummer and the rest of them had a horrible attitude at that gig. Keith Levene … was the only one who could actually hold a decent conversation with us.'

Nor would Rotten warm to them in time. In the years to come, he would all but blame them for the death of the movement: 'There was no sense of competition in that environment at all, before … the cliches started to arise, of every song at a hundred miles an hour, screamed. All that came from The Clash.'

For now, a false camaraderie would prevail even as Clash retired to lick their wounds, rework their retro-repertoire and further tutor their bassist in the basics. The main problem with Paul Simonon, who had been playing less than six months and had to mark up his bass to know where to place his hand, was his inclination to focus on unimportant matters, 'I just wanted to jump around, but Mick wanted it to be in tune.' (It was a battle Jones would have to wage for some months before a victory of sorts was finally secured.)

In fact, the whole band needed work. The twin-guitar thing was visually arresting – Levene and Jones in tandem, thrashing out rudimentary rhythms – but as one witness to their second public performance notes, 'The Clash with Keith Levene was like two Ramones out of phase with each other.'

Having joined just five weeks earlier, Strummer had failed to allow himself enough time to whip the others into shape. Hence their collective decision to ride shotgun to Sheffield for their out-of-town preview and then all but disappear from view for the next six weeks. If it hadn't been for Mr Cliff's note to the overground press, said debut would have passed without mention – as Strummer presumably intended.

Their next performance to paying punters would not be until August 29th, when they would again be obliged to the Pistols for receiving a supporting role. Also on the bill that night would be Buzzcocks, who were McLaren's 'other' great white hope and a direct threat to Rhodes' imagined hierarchy of punk.

★ ★ ★

At least Clash had managed to get through their whole set in Sheffield. The same could not be said of the Buzzcocks' April Fools' debut. Like Clash, Buzzcocks had felt a 'dry run' was necessary before their public unveiling as ostensible support to the Pistols that June. Their 'dry run', though, made the Black Swan song seem like *Yesssongs* as their technical limitations were made manifest at their very own technical college.

For starters, their April 1st set at the Bolton Institute where Shelley and Devoto were students was so poorly attended and truncated that, as Devoto wrote to Boon the day after, 'It was [more like] our first rehearsal, live.' The brief busk was a Buzzcocks gig in name only, comprising as it did covers of Bowie's 'Diamond Dogs', Eno's 'The True Wheel' and one other song. After which, Devoto informed Boon, 'The management switched off the PA and started up the disco.' The singer still insisted, 'We were great,' even if he had to admit any actual 'music was pretty awful'.

The ten-song set they had intended to perform was supposed to include two of Shelley's early songs, 'Get On Our Own' and 'No Reply', but those songs' debuts would have to wait until they found a new rhythm-section. The drummer was the first to quit, straight after the plug was pulled. As Devoto wryly recalls, 'At the end of the [Institute] gig we just sat there and the drummer Dennis raised one hand high and said, "I'm at this level," and held the other hand low and said, "You're at this level."' Dennis would not be seen for dust; and Garth Davies was soon sent packing for sharing Simonon's minimal chops as a bassist, minus the model looks and punk attitude.[27]

Undeterred, the northern duo shrugged off this false start and kept their eye on the prize. There was just one problem: having booked themselves to support the Pistols in Manchester, time was not on their side. In the end, that summer support slot went to Solstice.

Only after that fateful night and a chance meeting with Steve Diggle – all due to a misunderstanding from McLaren – did a new four-piece Buzzcocks emerge. It still took an ad in the local paper to recruit sixteen-year-old drummer John Maher just in time. The new D-Day for Buzzcocks Mk.2 was July 20th, the Pistols' now-scheduled return to the Lesser Free Trade Hall. They had better be ready *this* time around because by the end of the first week in July Buzzcocks were fourth in line. Devoto and Shelley, bent on creating a fully functioning punk band ever since their crash-course in the Pistols aesthetic back in February, were no longer alone.

While Simon Wright and friends in Weybridge, and Vic Godard and Rob Symmons in South London, continued rehearsing their roles in the end of Rock, some loose ends left dangling by Rhodes' and McLaren's attempts to muster a movement from the ragbag of

[27] Garth would make a more enduring return to Buzzcocks on Devoto's departure in February 1977, as the rest of the band decided to play musical chairs.

musicians who made up London SS and Masters of the Backside had been rehearsing in earnest. And leading from the front was guitarist Brian James, who had spent several frustrating months in London SS trying to get Mick Jones to drop the attitude. He eventually took the hump, his amps and the band's part-time drummer, Chris Miller, through the exit door:

Brian James: Mick had a lot of arty ideas, which personally I didn't think had much to do with music – or what I wanted to put into music. He was into concepts and I just like to get up and play and let whatever happens, happen.

When McLaren offered Miller a slot in another (part of the) grand scheme, staring at the backside of Chrissie Hynde, it only served to renew his acquaintance with Ray Burns, a fellow former cleaner at Croydon's Fairfield Halls, now the bassist in Johnny Moped's band. After their brief experiment with Hynde, Miller and Burns hooked up with James and began rehearsals for a band who played fast and loose with barre chords. Meanwhile, Miller and James were making regular checks on the Pistols' progress which convinced them they had better get a move on.

But it was only after the recruitment of vocalist Dave Vanian – spotted at the Pistols' second Nashville gig in April – that The Damned (named after the cult black and white film, *Village of The Damned*) made rapid progress. Like Buzzcocks, they already had a set of largely original songs. Brian James, the band's main songwriter, had been stockpiling teen-anthems for a while – in fact, ever since he formed Bastard in Belgium back in 1974 (who later mutated into Plastic Bertrand's backing band).

In the interim, James's most famous song would receive its world premiere as part of another weird, out-of-town preview for punk, at the end of May 1976 – but not with Vanian on vocals. The other three Damned souls had been befriended by Nick Kent during the long months spent looking for a vocalist, and had been asked to accompany him on two shows at Cardiff's Chapter Arts Centre under Kent's chosen nom de plume, The Subterraneans, a reflection of his Kerouac fixation.

These gigs, booked weeks earlier, ostensibly represented the launch of Nick Kent's own band, though it was a girlfriend of his, Hermine Demoriane, who took most of the vocal duties, backed by the unfamiliar Damned trio. According to an advert in the local paper, they were due to play 'songs of random passion'. Three possible candidates would be performed solely by James, Burns and Miller, who steamed through a trio of James originals: 'Fan Club', 'I Fall' and 'New Rose'.

The reaction of the Welsh audience on hearing their very first punk anthem, 'New Rose', has gone unrecorded but the trio returned to London convinced they were onto something. They resumed rehearsing with Dave Vanian, leaving Kent to his own devices and band name.[28] Another false dawn had passed.

At this stage, Malcolm McLaren was still taking an interest in the Miller's new tale. After all, according to Bernie's rudimentary arithmetic, they were still a band shy of a movement. It was McLaren who found The Damned a church on Lisson Grove where they could rehearse during the day without interruption, and it had the added bonus of being 'really cheap'. Miller also persuaded him to give the new band a much needed break by letting them support the Pistols at the 100 Club on July 6th, the final night of another colourful West End residency.

But after McLaren heard them rehearsing, he realized they were not what he had in mind. All parties concerned agreed they should find another manager – and find one they did: McLaren's own accountant, Andy Czezowski. Seeing two of his King's Road clients, McLaren and John Krevine at Acme, branching out into rock, had convinced Czezowski he could, too.

The ex-accountant even footed the bill for the now-named Damned to record a three-song demo in the basement studio of James's friend from London SS days, Matt Dangerfield. Dangerfield was already in the process of forming Powerpop's almost instantaneous answer to punk, The Boys. Czezowski's recollection of the recording suggests even 'basement' is something of a euphemism, 'The basement of this

[28] Nick Kent would subsequently release a single as The Subterraneans, backed by most of The Only Ones. It was to prove the extent of his rock ambitions.

house … was the coal cellar beneath the street – a squat basically. [Vanian] did the singing in the corridor to get the echoes, and the drums were put in the coal cellar.'

Perhaps surprisingly, 'New Rose' was not among those tracks laid down by Dangerfield. Instead, the quartet hastily captured 'I Fall', 'See Her Tonite' and 'Feel The Pain'. Even though they had yet to gig as an entity, the sprightly sound of The Damned, especially on 'See Her Tonite', resounded round the room and down the years. If they could work up some more like-minded material they could yet surprise the Pistols' WC1 crowd, previously driven to distraction by support acts who looked and sounded nothing like English punk's paradigm.

But before this potentially auspicious gathering of the clan, there was the return of the Ramones to navigate; and this time the Pistols and Clash, fresh from their joint northern excursion, were prepared to show their faces. For a band like the Ramones, this July 5th show at the hot'n'sweaty Dingwall's, a cramped Camden Lock club that was usually home to regular r'n'b, was the perfect antidote to the impersonal and slightly imposing Roundhouse. Used to playing another spit'n'sawdust shithole, CBGBs, they were quite looking forward to the experience as they mounted the stage, only to be greeted by a hail of plastic beer glasses, a couple of them lobbed by English punk's vanguard:

Glen Matlock: I got the Pistols banned from every gig in London 'cause [when] the Ramones came on [at Dingwall's], all leather-jacketed up, I thought, 'Let's see how tough [you] are.' And only because it was a plastic glass, I threw a glass at 'em. And they stormed off stage. [The] promoter saw me do it, and we got banned from everywhere.

Mark Perry: There [still] wasn't a feeling of a scene – it was just another gig … [but it was] at Dingwall's I first met … Brian James of The Damned, [who] told me about his band. So in the first issue [of *Sniffin' Glue*] I put, 'The Damned are great.' I hadn't seen them … I got chucked out [after] I threw a glass, it was a hard plastic glass. I'd finished my glass and it was such a crush of people I wanted to get rid of my glass. I just threw it to the front, where I thought it'd be out of harm's way. I got spotted by a bouncer and I was straight out. It was only two songs into the set.

Matlock and Perry weren't the only rebels without a cause who misbehaved that night. At the end of the night, Stranglers bassist Jean-Jacques Burnel was 'walking Indian file through the crowd, leaving the venue. Steve and Paul from the Pistols were with Paul Simonon … [who] had this nervous tick where he used to spit. He did it as I walked past and I thought he was spitting at me, so I thumped him.'

Just eighteen days after sharing a stage with the Pistols, The Stranglers found themselves ostracised from London's private punk club as the comrades-in-alms closed ranks. At the same time, the Pistols found themselves banned from Dingwall's and the Rock Garden, two venues they had been scheduled to play later that month, adding to a growing list of central London clubs that considered them personae non gratae.

So the real impact of the Ramones had nothing to do with their brand of music and a lot to do with the presence of so many proto-punks in a confined, sweaty space. Punk revisionists like Generation X's Tony James later claimed hearing them live meant 'everybody doubled speed overnight', but if so, it must have been *literally* overnight. Exactly twenty-four hours later The Damned made their live debut playing at the exact same hundred-miles-an-hour.

Brian James wholly rejects his namesake's thesis, insisting, 'On the stuff we were playing already, the speed I was getting [came] from the MC5.' In fact, by sending up The Beatles with a pell-mell cover of 'Help', The Damned were really driving a stake through the parodic heart of the Ramones' rah-rah brand of rock & roll.

Ron Watts, punk's most important cheerleader at this juncture, called the July 6th Damned/ Sex Pistols bill 'a watershed of a gig'. It is hard to argue, especially after a surprisingly fine tape of The Damned's debut set emerged in 2009, which throws cold water on the notion propagated by Caroline Coon, writing in October 1976, that when The Damned 'played their first gig … not that they actually played together that night. Each one of them did his own number in a private daze. Out of time, out of key, the cacophony was terrible enough to be great.'

Jonh Ingham, who caught The Damned's fourth gig nine days later, concurs with Coon, 'It was like four different bands playing together at 78 rpm.' Yet his review in *Sounds* the following week gave them an unequivocal thumb's up as a revved-up version of Rubbish Rock, the ol' Pistols 'Can't Play, Can Play' mantra receiving a highly positive spin:

> Describing The Damned is pretty hard … They're beyond good or bad, beyond comparisons, beyond even being ultimately offensive … The Damned just are, and if you don't like it, piss off … I assume that with one exception the songs were [all] original. This was because the stun setting of the music made the lyrics inaudible – they were into the chorus before it was obvious they were radically redefining the Beatles' 'Help' … What really made it unique, though, was their concept of timing. God knows who was making the mistakes, but not once did they make tempo changes in unison. Since all this took place at Mach 5, the resulting melange sounded positively avant-garde. In fact, The Damned's troubles may start when they learn how to play.

Actually, the band that turned up on July 6th, less than three months after their first rehearsal and with no experience of playing live, sound remarkably together and wholly prepped (even if Scabies told Ingham afterwards they never rehearsed because doing so would 'spoil the excitement'). What *was* avant-garde was the way they blurred any and all division between guitar, bass and drums, making a sound that was a buzzsaw to the Pistols' sledgehammer.

The Pistols, who that night opened with a rip-roaring 'I Wanna Be Me', were still somewhere off in the distance but it was immediately clear that The Damned had stripped rock bare and, in England at least, stolen the Ramones' thunder.

For the next six months they would pull in the same direction. So when McLaren dismissed an offer from Shanne Hasler to play a return gig at her art college the following week – saying, 'St Albans? No, not gonna do that, waste of time.' – The Damned leapt at the chance to take the Pistols' place. Just as Hasler found the Pistols funny first time around, she fully embraced the humour in The Damned, 'I thought they were hilarious … [Captain Sensible was] in a white suit and white square shades … just stood there, didn't move the whole time.'

★ ★ ★

However, McLaren seems to have taken an instant dislike to his friend Chris Miller's new band. It wasn't yet personal, they simply offended his musical sensibility. For all his talk of anarchy, the man liked his medium-paced rockers with a recognisable riff and a rudimentary sense of time.

He may even have secretly begun to fear that the Pistols themselves were becoming too good to be a scam. At a New York conference on 'Punk and History' in September 1988 he would go as far as to suggest, 'The Sex Pistols were [meant to be] part of breaking [pop culture] down and saying that there was no point any longer in playing well … I probably sold that better than anyone, often to the detriment of those working with me, who ultimately really did want to be good.'

If he really did fear such a transformation – and I don't imagine for one second that he did – the fourteen days after The Damned's debut would have made him rethink his strategy. Because in that time the Pistols became not merely good, but genuinely great. And it was all his fault as he lined up two shows designed to demonstrate what was required if they were to make the transition to larger venues and play with the big boys; after which, he set aside a whole week for them to work on a second set of demos. And this time they would directly reflect the live set and the live sound. McLaren's chosen producer would be Dave Goodman.

The next event in the Pistols' July punkathon – after Hastings, Sheffield and the 100 Club – saw them play a Lyceum 'all-nighter' on July 9th, alongside The Pretty Things. And for once, they were in awe of the headliner. Jonh Ingham remembers them being 'absolutely petrified before they went on … It was the first time they'd played in [such] a big space,' and because of the way such all-nighters worked, they had to follow the Pretties, a band who had been there, fucked it up and were still standing tall. Once the best r&b band in London, they still had it, as the Pistols witnessed first-hand:

Jonh Ingham: The Pistols played after The Pretty Things – and here's a band doing it in their sleep … They'd never shared a stage with a professional [outfit]. They saw how high the bar really is. [But] the Pretties were real friendly.

In fact, the Pretties were led by a confirmed fan of the Pistols. Phil May had already 'been to see them at the 100 Club … For me it was a breath of fresh air … I loved seeing the Pistols and the anarchy coming through again … [even if] a few of the older members of our audience felt it was threatening to them, their lifestyle and their music.'

Fellow Pretty Jon Povey agreed that 'the Pistols were incredibly energized' and that 'it was a very powerful performance'. But he also considered them to be 'the most chronically out-of-tune band I'd ever heard', perhaps because the heat again played havoc with Jones' guitar. Or not.

Ingham vehemently disagrees with the Pretties guitarist. In fact he described this set at the time as the moment Jones found his muse onstage: 'He takes off in shuddering, blasting experimentation, face screwed up in concentration as he searches for unheard notes.'

An even more impressed witness that evening was a young musician from the Surrey sticks. Paul Weller from Woking had his own band, The Jam, a derivative three-piece who had been playing the occasional local gig for the past couple of years awaiting a mod revival. Weller remembers the Pistols 'were the last band on … and we were all speeding out of our heads'. But he stayed to see them, and he was glad he did. At the end of it, he had but one thought, 'I've got to be part of this.' And he would be. Just not the inner circle.

Predictably, not everyone at the Lyceum that night was attuned enough to hear the Pistols' sonic transubstantiation. *Melody Maker*'s Allan Jones, there to review the Pretties, remained on their case. Warming up by damning the Pretties, Jones put the boot in for a second time in the pages of the former youth bible: 'For the first ten minutes of their set, the Sex Pistols, who followed [The Pretty Things] and closed the event, were almost tolerable. They've improved since I saw them last, but their stance as Dead End Kids of the Terminal Zone is really quite wearisome.'

Jones would later claim that this was the night 'the penny dropped with a very loud clang and I thought, "Fuck, this is brilliant."' Methinks not. He would continue to cast himself in the role of Cnut for a while longer, even as the Pistols demonstrated that they were not merely a force to be reckoned with, they were the rising tide of change, and were fast approaching the height of their considerable powers.

Ingham was there again the following night, when the Pistols played the Sundown on Charing Cross Road (their first show on that arterial thoroughfare since St Martin's). He remembers thinking it 'was a[nother] quantum leap in ability from previously. Up until this point, they were getting better at it, but it was still the same kind of noise … But suddenly there was this major step up in musical ability … in one night.'

Others who knew them well made this their one time at Sundown, and largely concur with Ingham – even if Goodman seemed to remember 'some prat of a DJ wanted them off after only two numbers, [so] the set degenerated into a barrage of abuse between the band and DJ'. The generally reliable Marco Pirroni suggests, 'They were getting better, but staying the same,' while Siouxsie Sioux was delighted by the Sundown show simply because 'it was different, a bigger stage and you could see Rotten move for the first time'.

Sid Vicious, who went along with Siouxsie and Steve, didn't care what they sounded like. He couldn't see his friend John and so began to jump up and down to get a better view. When his friends joined in, he found he had invented a new dance, one that suited him down to the ground because it allowed him to bounce into people and instigate trouble, his favourite pastime. It was duly christened the Pogo, after the stick his mum refused to buy him as a child.

After five gigs in eight days, now was the perfect time to take the Pistols into the studio – as long as Rotten's voice held up. The presence of A&R men at recent gigs was a reminder to McLaren that industry interest was growing almost as fast as the band were improving. Just as he had predicted.

For some reason he had come to feel the Spedding demos didn't capture their essence. Or perhaps he simply decided to call their soundman's bluff. Goodman had been claiming that he could capture the band's live sound with just a portable four-track reel-to-reel rigged up in their usual rehearsal space. What did he have to lose?

Dave Goodman: I listened to the [Spedding] tape and I thought I could do better on my four-track … So I was challenged to bring it over to their Denmark Street rehearsal room … and run the cable upstairs and put the mixing-desk on Steve's bed … We spent a week recording the first six tracks that [later] went on the *Spunk* album … When they were relaxed and all in tune with one another, the spirit of what they were expressing really came through in the music. Terms like 'turgid' and 'terse' were used to describe their music. It was a question of capturing that.

If the Spedding session was one Majestic afternoon, Goodman was determined to put the boys in the band to work, 'We spent a week, Monday to Friday, recording those demos, but that was just recording the backing tracks.' For Rotten, the pressure was off as he believed he was only there to provide guide vocals – not that he had the slightest idea what that meant. He still sang everything full throttle. Indeed, as Goodman informed me, 'One or two of the vocals that were done at Denmark Street ended up on the finished master, but when [John] went home we [usually] overdubbed his vocal track with some guitar overdubs, knowing that we were going into [an eight-track] studio.[29]

For Goodman, this was the first real opportunity to demonstrate he was more than just a 24/7 'stoner' and soundman, meaning he was perpetually trying different things. On 'I Wanna Be Me' f'rinstance, as he explained, 'We just turned it up full – you get this real square wave distortion [by] overloading the line inputs on the mixer … and you just blend it with the guitar sound … Engineers would tell us you couldn't do it 'cause you might blow up the desk, but we never did.'

[29] The quasi-legit CD, *Wanted: The Dave Goodman Tapes*, contains three of the raw four-track versions in their pre-overdub state; the only indication of how the demos originally sounded. They are: 'Satellite', 'Pretty Vacant' and 'Submission'.

If the original four-track tape was a real beggars banquet, Goodman made it a moveable feast by taking the seven tracks they'd recorded that week – 'Anarchy In The UK', 'I Wanna Be Me', 'Seventeen', 'No Feelings', 'Pretty Vacant', 'Satellite' and 'Submission' – into Hammersmith's Riverside Studios, where he 'transferred it onto eight-track and put on lead vocals and a couple of extra overdubs. And then we went to Decibel Studios and mixed it, and ... put on a last few overdubs, like [the] kettle on "Submission". There's also [other] ideas [there], like put[ting] a third track with a whisper over it [on "Satellite"] and putting a long reverb on his voice on "Submission".' Everything Goodman tried seemed to enhance the experience.

All in all, it had proven a real labour of love; one which McLaren agreed to fund further once he heard the raw four-track tape from Demark Street. He was in complete agreement with Goodman that this was how the Pistols were meant to sound.[30]

(McLaren went further, some might say beyond the pale. When the 'majors' didn't work out, and the guitarist began to develop a little too much studio craft, he put out a bootleg album of the Goodman demos – the legendary *Spunk* – the week before Virgin issued their own official artefact, which was *Bollocks*. He even managed to reconcile with Marc Zermati long enough to 'work [together] to do the bootleg record all over Europe. He was [always] asking, can we do more?' This was both an inspired subversion of The Official Product – whilst rubbing Branson's face in *la merde* – and a way for McLaren to let the punk cognoscenti know what the Pistols sounded like when they were the most subversive band since Elvis, Scotty and Bill.)

★ ★ ★

But before McLaren and the band had the chance to review Goodman's four-track tape, they had another date with destiny at Manchester's Lesser Free Trade Hall. And this time, advance sales were quite encouraging. In fact, he decided to take a chance and

[30] After McLaren made EMI put 'I Wanna Be Me' on the 'Anarchy' B-side, the Goodman version of 'No Feelings' was scheduled to be flipside to A&M's 'God Save The Queen'.

invite the London music press to join them on the overnight trip, or at least those elements most inclined to champion their common cause. This meant Jonh Ingham, who still had a long leash at *Sounds*, and Caroline Coon, who continued to push Ray Coleman to let her explicate the punk aesthetic to *Melody Maker*'s innately conservative readers:

Richard Boon: Malcolm had shrewdly brought some press up, to demonstrate that it wasn't just this little cocoon[ish] 'London' thing. Malcolm always had this riff, 'Bands are springing up all over the country.' Actually, they weren't springing up, but he had his riff … 'There's all these kids: they're bored, they're disaffected, they've got short hair,' and he'd make up [band] names. He was a big propagandist for this whole putative movement … Bringing up Jonh and Caroline was his way of showing that this stuff is [really] happening.

It was another fluke disguised as a masterstroke. Buzzcocks were for now just a name on a ticket stub or concert poster; whilst the most punk thing about Slaughter & The Dogs – the other act on the bill, already a known quantity to gig-goers in South Manchester – was the name. (In reality, a crass twin allusion to Mick Ronson's *Slaughter On Tenth Avenue* and Bowie's *Diamond Dogs*.) Fortunately for the Pistols' manager, Buzzcocks were everything Devoto and Shelley had promised they would be, opening the night's proceedings with a set that put the buzz in Manchester punk. Ingham was impressed enough to devote a generous wedge of his full-page review to the Mancunian band's premier performance:

> Devoto stands and sings a lot like Johnny Rotten, and indeed the band sounds a lot like the Pistols, perhaps because Howard hauled guitarist Pete Shelley down to a London Pistols gig so that the light could be seen and the course charted. Whatever their inspiration, they're promising. Howard, wearing sneakers, pencil thin Levis, t-shirt and baggy blue jacket, is singing … the strangest love songs you've ever heard … [with] titles like 'Breakout', 'You're Shit', 'Put 'Em Down', 'I Love You Big Dummy' … It's the Boston Strangler

> singing the dance of romance, his face getting redder, eyes popping, kicking and punching the air. At first they are rhythmic to the point of rigidity. Shelley – who is wearing tight salmon pink levis, sleeveless 'Buzzcocks' t-shirt, shades and short hair – [is] not even bothering with the concept of a middle-eight, let alone a solo … But soon he begins to open out. By the time they fire up a high rev version of the Troggs' 'I Can't Control Myself', he's pulling out all manner of interesting riffs and changes … The climax came with a wild feedback solo, Shelley throwing his axe at the amp. When he went on a little too long, Devoto came out of the wings and pulled the guitar from him. He pulled it back. Devoto grabbed all six strings and yanked, ripping them asunder. Shelley propped the now screaming guitar against the speaker and left via the audience. Thus finished the set.[31]

Call Jonh impressed. And he was not alone. Others in the hall – which this time was three-quarters full – were delighted by Manchester's riposte to retro-rock. Even the classically-trained Richard Witts, a percussionist in the world-famous Hallé Orchestra and therefore inclined to attend any gig at the Free Trade Hall, found Buzzcocks 'musically, very interesting … [in the way] they negotiated their technical limitations between them, to make something that really was exciting and did communicate'.

Witts, who was there because he had heard John Peel describe the Pistols as 'something new', was impressed by both exemplars of the punk paradigm and delighted to discover each knew the difference between 'repetition' and 'insistence'. The experience convinced him that what he was 'hearing was more exciting than what was being done … [in the] contemporary [classical] music scene'. Tired of technique without forward direction, he was inspired to co-found and develop The Manchester Collective, from which bands like The Fall and The Frantic Elevators would spring forth, before forming his own avant-garde post-punk combo, The Passage, with the now-Fallen Tony Friel.

The Frantic Elevators would be another band formulated as a result of the second Pistols sortie, but not because its singer, the

[31] Devoto confirmed in conversation that the whole grabbing-the-guitar finale was agreed in advance and not the spontaneous act many witnesses thought it was.

violently red Mick Hucknall, was among the attendant. It was his friend, guitarist Neil Moss – the co-author of 'Holding Back The Years' – who embarked on this spiritual journey, agreeing to tag along with his brother Ian, to see what all the fuss was about. Ian, suffice to say, had not lost the religious-like fervour imbued in him six weeks earlier. But it was to Buzzcocks that his brother responded more:

Ian Moss: It was Buzzcocks that transformed [Neil's] way of thinking – the way the Pistols transformed mine. At that point he decided he wanted to make his own music. He was probably [already] in a band at that point, maybe with Mick Hucknall, but it was all that 'Freebird' crap … Neil got it as an idea, and saw that the shackles were off and that you didn't have to be a virtuoso. And that was liberating for him.

Another person who felt liberated by the Buzzcocks' set was Steve Morrissey, still an inveterate reader of (and letter-writer to) the music papers. Morrissey later suggested that 'between the first and the second appearances [the Pistols] had changed, and become a lot more nauseating (in the attractive sense)'.

It seems Stretford Steve was already looking to qualify his initial adulation. Although he still considered himself a Pistols fan, seeing Buzzcocks and getting 'to know Richard Boon and Linder and the group … was the beginning of something … [which] was less to do with the Sex Pistols, and more to do with the Buzzcocks … [Buzzcocks] were of major importance to me … I liked the intellectual edge the Shelley-Devoto Buzzcocks [had]. I liked the fact that somebody like Devoto could survive in that atmosphere … [and] that Shelley had steeped himself in *Hunky Dory*, which I found quite fascinating. I couldn't see it in other punk groups.'

The 'Linder' to whom Morrissey refers was Linder Sterling, a student in visual arts at the university who, like her future man-friend, had come to see the Pistols, having been waiting for a bus at Southern Cemetery when she 'saw a van going past, [which] had the [gig] poster tacked to the side, The Sex Pistols. Not knowing anything … I went along that evening with a friend who was a kitchen designer.' Having paid her money 'to a male in a gold lurex jacket' she found herself entering 'a totally different world':

Linder Sterling: With both Pistols and Buzzcocks that night [there] was some sense of being rushed towards a destination. Playing very badly, very quickly, but it was very, very exciting; a real sense of never having seen this before: the whole [sense of] disintegration, [yet] being very focused at the same time.

By the time the Pistols came on, Devoto and Shelley had noticed the two pretty girls sitting by themselves at what was almost exclusively a male gathering and, as Sterling notes, 'came to sit next to myself and the kitchen designer, [who] being very northern, starts talking to them.' When they found out Sterling was a designer, they set about exchanging numbers. After all, provincial punk was bound to need designers almost as much as penmen. Word of mouth only got one so far, though it had already ensured a turnout which was more than triple its predecessor.

Playing his part in that oral process had been Paul Morley, even as he began to suspect that the pen might be mightier than the (spoken) word. With *Out There* still at the printers, caught between typesetter and printing press, he was inspired by the Buzzcocks' union with the Pistols to audition for northern correspondent at *NME*, a position otherwise unoccupied. He would use his first *NME* piece in early October to re-review Buzzcocks' live debut as a way of affirming both his and their punk credentials:

> The audacious spontaneity of it all was overwhelming. They walloped the audience hard in the stomach. And the audience, for the most part, just stared blankly. Buzzcocks' thick lumpy rock was in parts hysterical, and at times it was amazing the whole thing didn't fall apart. The drumming, though, was precise and pinned down any wildly flailing noise whilst the spongy bass soaked up the taut bland vocals, leaving a cruel trebly Woolworth guitar to knock shape into each distinctively similar tune. All guitar solos were unwanted, unorthodox and very, very funny. The end of the set was also very funny. Guitarist Peter, prompted by over-enthusiastic reaction from some cocky members of the front rows, extended a teetering

> almost whimsical solo into a loose limbed scuffle between himself, the guitar and the floor. Howard, temple-throbbing lead vocalist, sensing the pending destruction of a key piece of sound-producing equipment, mimed pleads to Peter to calm down. Peter responded by assaulting his fragile amplifier. He then laid his guitar alongside the amp, producing some fine feedback that duelled happily with the courageous bass and drums which had all this time been quizzically pumping along. Then he bounded off stage, followed by Howard. The rhythm section systematically disintegrated and the anonymous members followed suit – tearing out of the back of the theatre.

Sounds already had a 'northern correspondent', Ian Wood, who also attended the July show, though with Ingham in situ he was obliged to keep his counsel, which is fortunate, since his oft-expressed judgement was that the Pistols were 'a bad, out-of-tune heavy metal band who seemed devoid of any real ideas other than performing a weak copy of Alice Cooper'.[32]

The Buzzcocks were just delighted to get through the set. For Devoto, 'It was just doing that extraordinary thing of going out in front of people and opening your mouth,' while for Steve Diggle it was a case of 'all this energy just pour[ing] out of us and into the crowd – to such an extent that it seemed the gig lasted all of two minutes. We spat our heads off for ten songs, or however many we did ... Shelley smashed his guitar to bits and the audience went crazy. The atmosphere was electric.' The Pistols and their manager were all delighted by what they heard. Now this is what Rotten had meant when he asked for 'more bands like us'.

As with all those early Pistols performances, the sense that this was something *anyone* could emulate was palpable. It was just as McLaren – and now by proxy Devoto and Shelley – intended. It was an idea Malcolm articulated to Nick Kent, this time on the record, later that year, 'The Pistols don't play great and as such, a kid in the audience can relate to that. He can think, "Yeah, I can possibly play that." There's that proximity. A kid can visualise himself being up there onstage.'

[32] Wood was soon replaced, for a short time by Steve Morris, on his way to Joy Division, and then by early punk fanzine editor, Mick Middles.

Just as the Pistols were starting to become a little too good for the collective good of punk, Buzzcocks had carried the punk chromosome north, having been fully briefed by the man in the bondage trousers. In the process, they inspired the first Manchester punk fanzine to spring up from the pen and ink-cartridge of Steve Burke, aka Steve Shy. *Shy Talk* even 'employed' a moonlighting Morley. Ironically, Shy's presence at the Pistols' July 20th appearance came about because of his friendship with the 'other' lead singer that night, Slaughter & The Dogs' Wayne Barrett:

Steve Burke: Before punk, I never read the *NME* or *Sounds.* I just wasn't really into that kind of music. I knew Wayne Barrett though ... It was Wayne who persuaded me to go to the second Lesser Free Trade Hall gig ... I fell madly in love with Buzzcocks. They just seemed wonderfully original. I had never seen anything like them before. The Pistols also looked incredible. Johnny Rotten looked like an alien ... For the first time it seemed to bring the rock audience and the younger glam fans together. There was a unifying aspect ... When the suggestion of writing a fanzine came up, [I saw it as] just a case of writing about ... the things happening around us.

However, before everyone – Shy included – could enjoy the Pistols, they would have to stomach the band Burke had been brought to see. Slaughter & The Dogs, for all their high energy, produced a far more virulent reaction than the straight-laced Solstice had received six weeks earlier. Despite the Dogs being the main draw for a significant percentage of the audience, Ingham spoke for the majority when he suggested they were on the outside looking in:

> Anyway you slice it, it is rapidly apparent that the Dogs are well outside the boundaries drawn by the Pistols ... On a local radio show they defined 'punk' as being a cross between David Bowie and the Rolling Stones. But fuck definitions. Pete Shelley reckons they're an offence just to the word itself ... They should also learn to differentiate between genuine demand for an encore and a huge scream of relief at their exit. It would save their outnumbered fans a lot of bother.

Wholly unwittingly, the Wythenshawe outfit ended up serving the greater good by audibly and visibly delineating what punk was *not*, just as cogently as Buzzcocks had defined what it could be. Una Baines, part of a gang otherwise composed of Fall guys, still remembers just how retro they looked, 'Slaughter & The Dogs hadn't quite punked up yet. The singer was wearing green lurex [trousers]. Very Bowie-esque. [But] I loved Buzzcocks – instant love. There were sides [being] drawn.'

The other attendant female presence destined to be central to Manchester punk, Linder Sterling, was even more dismissive, 'I remember the green satin sorta-Bowie look of Slaughter & The Dogs, and thinking that didn't seem right – it didn't seem *new* ... Slaughter & The Dogs ... still had one foot very firmly in the past, [whereas] the Buzzcocks had one foot in the future.'

Dick Witts, as impartial an observer as any there that night, also took an instant dislike, 'I thought Slaughter & The Dogs were kids out for glory – and it showed up in their repertory.' Ian Moss, who managed to miss Buzzcocks, 'walked in and saw Slaughter & The Dogs, and was appalled ... 'cause they were trying to pretend to be something else and I absolutely loathed them, from that moment.'

Martin Sinclair, who had also returned for a second helping of the Pistols, had already had his fill of the Dogs 'at a club in Stockport, a really rough place, on a Saturday night ... the winter before'. He shared with all of his mates – Morley included – an instinctive dislike for this band of unregenerate wannabes, but already feared that 'what was below was now [coming to] the surface'. A dumbing down seemed inevitable, and with it, would come a place for a hastily-reconstructed Slaughter & The Dogs in the pantheon of punk. But for now they remained on the other side of the fence, behind a sign that read, 'Beware the Dogs'.

With an almost-full hall and tensions between the two factions already running high, a kerfuffle was probably inevitable. It came towards the end of the Dogs' glam-metal set, possibly instigated by Paul Morley, who reverted to soccer-hooligan long enough to start 'flinging peanuts at Wayne Barrett, the singer of Slaughter & The Dogs ... because I thought he looked like a really dodgy copy of Bryan Ferry'.

The local lad – minus his usual crew – was asking for trouble. As Iain Gray points out, the Dogs had 'brought along a load of David Bowie, Roxy Music fans' from the same infamous council estate – once the largest in Europe – as Gray himself. Fortunately for Morley, when the trouble started, he found a host of allies of whom he had not previously been aware, thus guaranteeing the future Fall nothing but glowing reviews from this quarter:

Martin Bramah: We were part of the big fight at the front of the stage when Slaughter & The Dogs came on. We didn't like them at all, so were heckling them. We didn't know they had a huge following on the other side of the hall … There was a lot more of them, but they were younger than us.

Barely had the tumult died down than it was time for the Pistols to mount the stage, and this time they would not have to work the audience up into a fevered pitch. As Ingham wrote, 'The notorious Sex Pistols, the band the promoters of the French Punk Rock festival claim are going too far, … were greeted with a wild ovation. John stood there and beamed. Then Steve jumped to the front of the stage and started ripping off the opening to "I Want To Be You" [sic], legs apart, swinging his hips from side to side.'

Much of the underlying tension duly dissipated, but the energy did not. As Morley recalls, 'I remember the second one being much more of a charge in the atmosphere and a much more exciting place to be.' For Peter Hook, another football hooligan on sabbatical, the very fact that 'it was all going off' made it 'a lot more exciting than the first gig'. Yet some of those who had witnessed the birth of northern punk six weeks earlier felt something had been lost:

Ian Moss: I was slightly disappointed [by the Pistols] at that [second] one, perhaps because it wasn't mine. Now there were all these distractions. It was more orthodox. The Pistols went on, and they're all stood up. There's a ready-made audience this time. It's not like there's something to prove. [That said,] the Pistols were better, because they were still on an upward trajectory.

Martin Sinclair: By the second gig there was more of a scene going, and it was full up, [though] not with the nicest people I'd ever met. It was a different looking clientele – these were not the people you'd see at a Frankie Miller gig … And when the Pistols came on, Rotten was annoyed that the audience didn't recognize [some of] the songs, 'Don't you recognize "No Fun"?' … It had lost some of its charm already, [even if] there was a bit more stage-craft.

That stage-craft was still not entirely down to Rotten. In response to some jeering, Richard Boon remembered, 'Johnny [started] doing some slow handclapping above his head, and I look back at the mixing desk and there's Malcolm making the same gesture.' Steve Jones needed no such coaching as he set about, in Ingham's words, 'piling on the energy through the solos … while … rewriting the whole Guitar Hero's Stances textbook … rocking out on the beat with precise, soaring feedback endings.'

For a fair few who had missed out on the earlier Mancunian epiphany, this second stab at spreading the word more than sufficed. It certainly still had that edge of direct inspiration. Martin Fry, later of ABC, who already knew his alphabet of Rock, thought 'they were incredible: a brand-new entity that nobody had ever seen before, yet their existence made perfect sense. John, [who] had a polythene bag with beers in it, between songs … would glug the beer and just stare at the audience, calling us a bunch of "fucking statues".' And for a young couple brought there by Iain Gray, Ian and Deborah Curtis, the inspiration had even more immediacy, as if one of them was already running out of time:

Deborah Curtis: Four small waifs strutted across the stage dressed like cronies of Oliver Twist. I wondered who was the mastermind behind this plan, but Ian was ecstatic. Seeing the Sex Pistols was confirmation that there was something out there for him, other than a career in the Civil Service. Their musical ability was dubious that night, which reaffirmed Ian's belief that anyone could become a rock star.

The Pistols not only let the cat out of the bag that night by revealing 'that anyone could become a rock star', they once again unleashed the dogs of war. A second series of scuffles marred the Mancunian mania for a brief moment. And this time someone onstage took one for the team.

Eddie Garrity, aka Ed Banger, a friend of Slaughter, was at the side of the stage 'looking after the beer' and stuck his head round the curtain just in time for 'a bottle [to go] ping right on my head. The Pistols came off, and … I'm there with blood pouring down my head. My mate Pete had been punched on the nose. Someone says, "You're a right bloody mob, aren't you? Headbanger here, and him with a nosebleed."'

Manchester punk band Ed Banger & The Nosebleeds were thus christened in a pool of Ed's blood.[33] Meanwhile, the audience had become a ravening horde of punk-rockers before Eddie's – and Ingham's – eyes:

> Pretty soon a guy was doing the Wilko Johnson robot zigzag at high speed up and down the aisle. People near the front began to jump about more. As the band blasted into 'New York', a guy came leaping down the aisle … At John's encouragement, the front rapidly filled with wildly bopping people. One enthusiastic couple pushed each other back and forth in time to the express-train rhythm, and God help anyone in the way. By the time 'Problems' had blasted to a close the joint was screaming.

The mayhem had been sparked by a brand-new song the Pistols had decided to debut that night after demoing it with Goodman the previous week. If 'Anarchy In The UK' was the summation of all that the band had been edging towards in the last few months, for once McLaren the erstwhile anarchist had not been prepped:

Jonh Ingham: In those sixteen days [in July] the Pistols *really* learned how to play … Steve is doing all that feedback and noise, and suddenly everything's clean. And the Manchester gig is where he put the whole damn thing together. The way that space really filled up with people was the first time [that happened]. Malcolm's

[33] The legendary Nosebleeds, up and running by early 1977, broke up barely a year later, having released one Rabid 45, 'Ain't Bin To No Music School'.

standing at the very back and he's not ready for 'Anarchy', that's for sure. They haven't told him about it ... When they went into the UDA, IRA [bit], his mouth dropped. Just non-plussed. Caroline and I are going, 'Can you believe this?'

Even Slaughter & The Dogs got to hear 'Anarchy' before McLaren. Their guitarist, Mick Rossi, admits that 'seeing the Sex Pistols soundcheck had a profound effect on me. We'd done our soundcheck ... then the Pistols had their[s], and Steve Jones started the chords of "Anarchy" ... I [just] thought, "That sounds fucking good."'

There was still no prospect of Buzzcocks or the Pistols inviting them to join their gang, nor of a return date at the same venue. Their own set of fans had put the kibosh on that. As Devoto soon learnt, 'The Lesser Free Trade Hall weren't prepared to take any more bookings.' But in the afterglow of another extraordinary night on Peter Street – the site of the 1819 Peterloo Massacre, when another disenfranchised group confronted the powers-that-be armed only with their own anger, and a yearning for a voice – anything seemed possible. For now, all forms of forward-thinking music remained permissible:

Steve Diggle: I walked from the Free Trade Hall and stood in the bus queue with all the kids I'd been at the gig with ... They were all saying, 'This is amazing,' and patting me on the back. I could tell that they had all got it, they understood what it was all about and what we and the Pistols were trying to do. The message was DO IT YOURSELF.

The Pistols returned to London, Ingham and Coon in tow, now prepped to put the finishing touches to their latest set of demos – cast-iron proof they could really play. The latter pair, suitably shocked and awed, jointly agreed to browbeat their editors into letting them tell the world what was happening beneath rock's radar, under their very noses.

* * *

Across the first three weeks of July, an English punk scene formed around its undisputed originators and instigators, the Sex Pistols. Clash, The Damned and Buzzcocks had all ridden bumper to bumper with McLaren's pile-drivin' crew, each creating enough of a stir to warrant mentions in the music weeklies, Ingham doing both The Damned and Buzzcocks proud with highly favourable reviews before month's end. (Clash for now had to make do with Cliff's unenthused epistle to *NME* and *Sounds*.) Readers of *Sounds* were for now the ones clued-in, thanks largely to Ingham, but 'his' music weekly still lagged some way behind in its unceasing circulation war with *NME* and *Melody Maker*.

McLaren needed *Melody Maker*, in particular, to come on board. It was they, after all, who had given Roxy Music and David Bowie the big push and first championed the New York Dolls. Hence his assiduous cultivation of Caroline Coon, who finally broke cover on August 5th, 1976, when Ray Coleman finally gave punk a front-page splash – 'Punk rock: crucial or phoney?' – and allocated most of a two-page centre-spread to Coon's own 3,000-word 'think piece', 'Punk rock: rebels against the system', in the hope it might shut her up at editorial meetings.

Coon, who had been following the Pistols since March, was determined to find (or found) the punk movement McLaren had been talking about for the past year. Hence, she included Clash, who were only 'recently formed [and] currently rehearsing'. And she mentioned Slaughter & The Dogs, mainly in order to talk up her trip to Manchester: 'All doubts that the British Punk scene was well under way was blitzed two weeks ago in Manchester, when the Sex Pistols headlined a triple, third-generation punk-rock concert before an ecstatic, capacity audience.' Yet she excluded The Damned from her 'Who's Who of Punk', though she had already caught them in the act at the Nashville.

When she still came up short, she decided to include – or so the headline suggested – 'bands like Eddie & the Hot Rods, The Stranglers and Slaughter & The Dogs'. Dear, oh dear. For all the careful coaching Coon had received from Malcolm, she had missed the mark by a mile. Her decision to lump in The Stranglers and Eddie & The Hot Rods, the last vestiges of pub rock, drove McLaren to despair.

Other bands she mentioned in passing – The Jam and the Suburban Bolts – she knew only by name, not necessarily the right one (the 'Bolts' were actually a Birmingham glam-metal band, the Suburban Studs). None of these constituted part of McLaren's carefully cultivated scene, and to make things worse, she prematurely typecast 'punk rock' as usually 'played faster than the speed of light', patently not the case in August 1976.

Coon opened a further can of worms by suggesting there was an ongoing debate between those who, by their own admission, 'saw Johnny Rotten and he CHANGED our attitude to music (Clash, Buzzcocks)' and those who insisted they 'played like this AGES before the Sex Pistols (Slaughter and the Dogs)'. Not at the 100 Club and the Lesser Free Trade Hall there wasn't. For them, Year Zero was in full swing.

Equally worrying was Coon's determined use of the term 'new wave' while harping back to 1964, when 'the Beatles, Stones, Kinks, Who, Them, Animals and The Yardbirds – in effect, a new wave – blasted out of the national charts'. Was she simply wrapping a nostalgic yearning for the music of her youth in a pseudo-radical mantle? Or had she simply not noticed a small but cohesive movement coalescing in front of her?[34]

As if all this was not problematic enough, Ray Coleman wasn't about to let Coon have her say without providing 'balance', i.e. allowing one of the paper's 'voices of reason' cast doubt on her critical judgement. As such, spread across the lower half of the centrespread was a rebuttal by none other than Allan Jones, under the headline, 'But does nihilism constitute revolt?'

Not that Jones was exactly a modern Cicero. Any argument he could muster was somewhat undermined by the fact that much of what he attacked, he hadn't even heard. Thus, for him, 'it is this irresponsible emphasis on violence and mundane nihilism – perfectly expressed through the Sex Pistols' "Anarchy In The UK" – that is so objectionable.'

His premature dismissal of one of punk's greatest anthems was based solely on the title. He wasn't in Manchester, and he wasn't on McLaren's list of potential recipients for the recent demo of that very

[34] The redacted version of her original article on the *Rock's Backpages* website rather suggests Ms Coon might like to disown large chunks of it.

song. So he couldn't have heard it – as one highly informed *Melody Maker* reader pointed out in the letters page three weeks later, going on to suggest, 'I haven't seen Allan Jones at a Sex Pistols gig since you could start hearing the words, so how does he know what *any* of their songs say?'

Even those who did want to hear the words of 'Anarchy' were having to wait. The Pistols were not due back at the 100 Club till the Tuesday after Coon's controversial cover-story, the response to which soon spilled across *Melody Maker*'s letters page. Not that those readers who considered punk to be 'a stagnant pool of one-chord wonders, generated by a lot of morons who feel inadequate' were awaiting their West End return with bated breath.

No one outside the inner circle – save a couple of engineers at Riverside and Decibel – were yet privy to the Pistols' latest anthem for the new age. The band were taking a breather, letting the dust settle, and waiting to see if those who 'saw Johnny Rotten and CHANGED our attitude to music' could yet muster a riotous retort to the pretenders Coon seemed to think should be admitted to their exclusive club. McLaren remained adamant: without the benediction of him and *his* band, no one, but no one, could be a punk-rocker. Maybe it was high time he considered expanding the membership.

COMBUSTION

5. LET THE FESTIVITIES BEGIN

[10th August – 21st September]

5

We wanted to ... become part of what we thought was going to change the face of rock music. Then we found out that wasn't the aim of other groups. When we first saw the Sex Pistols, we thought that was their aim, but then we found all the other groups, such as The Clash, just wanted to put the life back into rock ... and the Sex Pistols ... start[ed] becoming a real good *rock* band. We wanted to finish rock & roll.

– Vic Godard, in conversation with the author

If the Pistols' own media battle for the right to exist had largely been won by the end of July 1976, the future direction of punk was no longer solely in their hands. It could not even be taken for granted that their goal was the same as those – like Godard – they'd first inspired to pick up unfamiliar instruments and make a racket. If, as McLaren claimed at that 1988 conference on 'Punk and History', 'The Sex Pistols and their lyrics and content ... was [supposed to be] an acknowledgment of the fact that rock & roll as a popular culture had finally ceased to be,' then he had got it badly wrong.

Instead, night after night, the Pistols were providing a much-needed shot in the arm for the moribund musical genre, which meant that those who followed in their wake could no longer agree whether to follow their lead or stay as primitive as the primordial Pistols had been. As if that was not worrying enough, the lines were fast becoming blurred as to what a punk band looked and sounded like. If for the Pistols, the underground American sound pioneered by The Stooges and the Velvets had always been second string to their Britbeat bow, other bands who had been playing a brand of *Nuggets*-style garagerock since at least 1974 seemed keen to tie their flag to the punk mast now that Coon had made the name a tad more inclusive.

A couple of these more gig-hardened pretenders – The Stranglers and The Vibrators – at least had punky monikers. If The Stranglers had already been excommunicated, The Vibrators – who had evolved out of an outfit called Despair, and now included Bazooka Joe's ex-drummer John 'Eddie' Edwards – were given an opportunity to state their punk credentials on August 10th, as the Pistols returned to the 100 Club after a five-week gap. This time the place was almost full, and Oxfam chic was most definitely In.

Knox, frontman for The Vibrators, insists he saw the funny side, 'When we were playing with the Pistols, the audience had torn jackets ... [but] it hadn't really polarized. We had friends of ours turning up wearing funny clothes.' However, any feeling of camaraderie was not mutual. As Mark Perry wrote in the third issue of *Sniffin' Glue*, 'The Vibrators seemed lost against all those stares from the Pistols audience. All they could muster was, "We all know you're so cool."'

If they didn't quite know where all the hostility was coming from, the Pistols and their singer, nursing a Rotten cold, duly amplified it. Knox later said he was 'electrified, the music was so aggressive', but as far as McLaren was concerned, Knox and co. had fallen at the first hurdle.

While Knox came to consider his first Pistols gig a transformative experience, his reaction was as nothing to the one that sideswiped a young Mark Perry. He had been brought to the club that night by Caroline Coon, who had taken a shine to the punk virgin. Coon had already been leading the boy astray, taking him under her wing after a trip to Hastings – two weeks to the day after the Pistols' own visitation – in the back of a van with Eddie & the Hot Rods, each seemingly under the impression these guys had something to do with punk rock. When he was introduced to the Pistols by Coon at the 100 Club – carrying copies of the latest *Sniffin' Glue* with Eddie & the Hot Rods on the cover – he was quickly disabused of that notion:

Mark Perry: It was Caroline who took me – and she did take me! One of the places where I sold the fanzine was the Rock On stall, and through them Eddie & the Hot Rods' manager [asked] how would I like to go on a trip with [the band]. So I ended up in the back with two other journalists – Jonh Ingham and Caroline Coon – on the way to Hastings. And they said, 'Oh, we've seen your fanzine.' I still had hair down to my shoulders. And they told me about this scene, blah blah blah … Caroline started taking me places … It was very, very exciting. I met the Pistols and their entourage. They were all sitting at a table, Caroline took me over and said, 'This is Mark. He's done a fanzine.' I handed the fanzine over. They were all looking at it, and they were all being very cool, a bit sneery. Sid Vicious actually chucked it on the floor … [I'm sure] they despised Eddie & the Hot Rods.

If Coon was not sure herself what the diktats of punk were, Perry had wandered into the 100 Club convinced cool meant 'long hair down to my shoulders, [and] a brown satin jacket … Then when the band came on … I had my suit ripped off 'cause of the pogoing … Within a week, the hair had come off, just cut it all off.' The experience did wonders for Perry's prose too, his brief review of the Pistols (in *SG* issue three) capturing the zeitgeist for the first time:

> The Sex Pistols are a force, you get that feeling from their audience and it sticks in your mind. The clothes, the hair and even the attitude of the audience has a direct link to the band … Even I've got cropped hair now, you just can't help getting into it! As the Pistols pounded out their 'music' the image was in every corner of the club. Their sound is pure energy … You've got to experience [it] to understand.

Perry felt the full force of the Pistols in flight. Although a later convert than most other futurist punk contemporaries, he felt a familiar desire to emulate that energy, first in the prose of his famous fanzine and then on record, as the man behind Alternative TV, who for a short while in 1977–78 were one of a select few cutting-edge bands looking to 'finish rock & roll'. For him, just seeing a singer 'say, "Fuck off, if you don't like it piss off out," to be that confrontational, was really exciting … I'd never seen anything like that.' Again, it made what had seemed 'some unattainable thing' become not just possible, but directly achievable:

IGGY

Marshall

NO

Mark Perry: [For] someone like myself who was well into his rock music, you did feel like this music scene was … a closed shop, and there was no way you were going to batter down that barrier. But once you saw the Pistols, kids like you up onstage bashing away on guitars, you did feel you could have a go yourself … I didn't [do] it straight away, because I went round the other way and tried to have a go at being a writer, but [I was] inspired by that same thing.

Perry had arrived at Punk Central just in time. Attendees at the 100 Club were no longer Us and Them. In fact, according to the 'Jaws' account of this night down at the rock & roll club, the 'audience looked as if they'd just stepped off a Hipgnosis album sleeve. Among the stars and studs [there] to sample a taste of the Pistols' anarchistic rock were the following liggers: Chris Spedding … Papa John Phillips and his model wife Geneviève Waïte, and John Paul Getty. Half of Chrysalis Records [also] came to check the band out.' It seemed only a matter of time before the levee broke.

And when the flood came, there were plenty prepared to rush in where pub-rockers feared to tread. In the four days before the next potentially earth-shattering Pistols performance in Birmingham, Buzzcocks and Clash would both make moves designed to ensure they had the right gear when the punk tsunami hit.

In Buzzcocks' case, this meant the cross-weave of glam, disco and Oxfam chic adopted by the kids from Pips disco who had recently made the switch to The Ranch, an after hours bar run by the locally-legendary drag queen, Foo Foo Lammar. Devoto and the band had 'started hanging out there [with] the Bowie kids', attempting to cultivate a northern Louise's, the preferred after hours London hang-out for the Pistols (and many of London's prostitutes).

Devoto eventually summoned up the nerve to approach Frank (aka Foo Foo) hoping to persuade him to let Buzzcocks play a couple of shows at The Ranch and maybe establish their own weekly residency. Flyers advertising shows on August 12th and 19th were handed around, and a small crowd made the short trip to Piccadilly from Pips. All well and good.

Richard Boon, now back north, remembers, 'There was no stage and there were all those kinda Bowie people, some people who were getting It, the early adopters like … Steve [Shy], who used to go to Pips [and] turned their style around.' Unfortunately for Buzzcocks, The Ranch was not so much a club as an annex to a club:

Howard Devoto: The Ranch was the kids' bar at Foo Foo's … It was a small bar. [But] there was a hatch, and his club [was] through there. So we start up and [we're] fucking up his act in there. So this heavy started walking in … between us. Between numbers, he says to me, 'You the boss then? Foo Foo says you'll have to stop.' We only played about four numbers.

Like the Pistols' own Soho adventure, Buzzcocks' foray into clubland had been cruelly and rather abruptly terminated by an angry club-owner. It was back to Piccadilly Square, aka square one. But at least Devoto had again managed to do 'that extraordinary thing of going out in front of people and opening your mouth'.[35]

Clash were not quite ready to do the same. And yet a semi-formal unveiling finally took place the day after Buzzcocks' Ranch dressing-down, at Rehearsal Rehearsals, the semi-derelict Camden Lock rehearsal room Rhodes rented so that they could live, breathe and eat wallpaper paste together. It was his own little indoctrination camp and he expected the world to come to It. Their first London performance would be an invite-only affair, an idea he perhaps gleaned from conversing with one or more Ramone after Dingwall's. Their first 'public' performance had been as a three-piece at their own Performance Studio, i.e. rehearsal space.

Clash had hunkered down all summer long, avoiding contact with 'the scene'. Inside their NW1 bubble, they built a repertoire that owed almost nothing to The 101'ers or Chuck Berry, at least not overtly. If Strummer occasionally ventured out, Jonh Ingham had 'never even seen [the rest of] them before – even at the Nashville. Which was really full. And they weren't at the 100 Club.'

As punk's main press advocate, Ingham was invited to the grand unveiling along with fellow *Sounds* correspondent, Giovanni

[35] There is some dispute about whether there was one or two Ranch gigs. There were certainly two gigs advertised, but the 'residency' appears to have been terminated after just one truncated performance.

Dadomo. Even Rhodes realized he needed Ingham on board. indeed, it was probably honest Jonh who penned the first positive review the band ever received – a paragraph in 'Jaws' the following week:

> If you think the H-Bomb's hot, wait till you see The Clash. Risen from the ashes of The 101'ers, King Joe Strummer and his cohorts … unveiled the results of two months intensive rehearsal at an exotic soiree in their swank rehearsal studio before an exclusive assembly of hard Mach-Rock fans … From looks to movements to playing, it was blindingly obvious that the world will soon be at their feet (the survivors anyway).

The small pro-punk element in the music press wanted cultures clashing and, following McLaren's lead, they wanted it to seem somehow preordained. Once Coon announced there was a punk movement, the search was on for leaders to load up with as much ideological baggage as they could bear. Coon had already done her bit, writing about Clash in her 'punk special' as if they were already a living, breathing, gigging entity. Abandoning any pretence she was a dispassionate commentator, she volunteered to introduce Clash to the twenty or so invitees, including the overseer of The 101'ers' label, Chiswick:

Roger Armstrong: They actually did it like they were doing a show. They were hiding behind a curtain … Somebody got up, it might [well] have been Caroline, and made an announcement – 'The CLASH!' – and they ran on with their painted jackets, gave it everything, and there's like ten of us there.

The Dadomos, Eve and Giovanni, were two of the 'ten'. For both it was a career opportunity. While Eve snapped away, visually fixing the band in all their stencilled, paint-splattered glory, Giovanni convinced himself he was witnessing 'the first band to come along who'll really frighten the Sex Pistols shitless … It's like the gleaming and totally unstoppable bastard son of the Pistols and the Ramones with the firepower of Status Quo.'

What he really witnessed was a punk band he could call his own – and thus make a name for himself. And as Ingham says, 'I certainly didn't want to hog it.' Dadomo's half-page *Sounds* review, which ran alongside one of his wife's snappy freeze-frames, was a masterclass in 'never mind the quality, feel the hype' journalism. It was exactly what Rhodes had been hoping for:

> The Clash were unveiled last Friday evening in a small but rather splendidly decorated – by the lad themselves, no less – rehearsal room in darkest Chalk Farm, London … The invite was for nine … Five striking looking gentlemen strolled in. The four who carried guitars plugged them into the waiting amplifiers, the fifth took his place at the drum-kit. The gentleman on the extreme left ([who] looked not unlike a slightly more vicious Keith Richards …) gave a hoarse count-in … and for the next forty-odd minutes it was like being hit by a runaway fire engine – not once, but again, and again … and again … The Clash could make it on looks alone practically. They all have that cropped hair, skintight trousers look … [but] what hits first is the gut-curdling power of them … I mean to dispel any notion that the music is one relentless semi-cacophony, because in all that nuclear glare there are incandescent gems of solos and references to everything from 'You Really Got Me' to younameit … There were one or two little cock-ups, but considering the nature of the event The Clash still managed to come up with one of the most memorable debuts of the year so far.

Unlike Ingham and Coon, Dadomo had no real barometer with which to measure 'one of the most memorable debuts' of a punk band, having yet to catch either Buzzcocks or The Damned in the act. But even punk's main proselytizers were impressed by what they witnessed at Rehearsal Rehearsals. For Ingham, though, the first hint of a preordained agenda did not take long to manifest itself. After the performance he was talking to Mick Jones and 'started to see that … it was like, "This is a career opportunity, there is no alternative, we are going for it."'

Having seen first-hand the ever-present tension between McLaren and the four Pistols when it came to their respective goals, Rhodes was determined to ensure that when it came to Clash such concerns had been ironed out before they even played a note. In fact, two of the five were already thinking this ain't for me, and Rhodes' endless indoctrination only served to convince them they were right.

At this juncture the A&R man most impressed by the early Clash had other priorities. Polydor's Chris Parry was a hundred and twenty miles away the following night, trekking all the way to Birmingham to see the Sex Pistols' Midlands debut. And he liked what he saw: 'What appealed to me was their stripped-down garage sound. I liked the mix of energy, sex appeal, nastiness, rebellion and short, to-the-point rock & roll. The attitude was also remarkable.'

None of which explains why Parry felt the need to drive all the way to the Midlands to see a band who played London three times that month. In all likelihood, he did so because he didn't want the competition to think he was a player for the Pistols' signature. At least, not for now. It also afforded him the opportunity of witnessing them in an environment where they had to win over an audience of the curious, not a prepped coterie of like-minded fans.

They did so by first alienating most attendees with an extended 'Flowers of Romance', before dispelling any and all concerns by unleashing 'I Wanna Be Me' and their latest lyrical offering, 'Liar', in stun-gun succession. One belligerent Brummie had been waiting six months to see exactly this:

Robert Lloyd: I was a fan already of The Stooges, the Velvets, the MC5 – the usual suspects … But as soon as I read the [Spencer] review of the Sex Pistols in *NME* I knew I wanted to see them … Somehow you knew. [So] when I went to see the Sex Pistols – it would have been Barbarella's – it was like, 'This is the kind of stuff I want to do.'

Also there that night was Toyah Willcox, who says she 'accidentally saw the Sex Pistols at a gig in Birmingham and it changed my life forever … Suddenly I was in a room of spitting, shouting, angry people. I thought, right, I belong. I've found my voice.' Unlike Lloyd, she may well have ended up there 'accidentally'. Barbarella's was not only Birmingham's primary outlet for heavy metal, but also almost its only outlet for new live music, and many young tykes made a weekly pilgrimage there irrespective of the headliner.

In a sense, that willingness to take what they were given explains why Barbarella's was a perfect breeding ground for the punk revolution, even if Birmingham punk bands would remain in short supply for the foreseeable. The Pistols certainly appreciated the positive reception, having learnt the hard way that all provincial gigs – Manchester excepted – were a crap-shoot, and that the shit hit the fans as often as it hit the band.

Their next provincial performance, five days later, saw them lob a sonic grenade at the audience only for it to come back a damp squib. According to both bassist and soundman it was probably their most surreal gig ever. The West Runton Pavilion in Norfolk catered to a demographic starved of good music, and as soon as the Pistols began their soundcheck it became clear why.

As Goodman later recalled, 'The manager started freaking out about the volume. He threatened not to pay us unless we turned it down … We did the deed. "Still too loud!" shouted the manager. We turned down again. "Too loud!"' According to Matlock, 'In the end we were just larking about, pretending we were miming, like you'd do on [*Opportunity Knocks*]; and this bloke [still] comes up and says, "No lads, it's no good, we'll pay you what you're due, but we just can't hear the bingo in the other room."' (It would not be the last time the bingo-crowd would win the day.)

Unfazed by yet another weird provincial experience, the Pistols packed up their equipment and drove to Nottingham's Boat Club, where they were again met by a crowd who, 'apart from some blokes at the lip of the stage in black sequinned t-shirts and braces … expressed, at best, complete apathy and, at worst, downright abuse.' Or so 'Zob the Tuffdart' alleged in a letter to *Sounds*.

Zob had become 'very angry [when] they demolished "Substitute"', evidently a capital crime in Zob's eyes. Accordingly, they became the only band Zob had ever 'witnessed at the Nottingham Boat Club who did not receive an encore'. And Nottingham became a place the Pistols learned to loathe a full year before they were required to return there to defend themselves against an obscenity charge for using that venerable Anglo-Saxon word, bollocks.[36]

[36] The 'obscenity' trial after the release of *Never Mind The Bollocks* centred on a Virgin store in Nottingham. The case for the defence was made by John Mortimer QC, of Rumpole fame, and the Pistols won their case; a result about which newspapers who print the word as b******s in 2015 seem blithely unaware.

And to think the Pistols could have been sunning themselves in the south of France. Instead, on their evening off between Cromer and Nottingham, it was The Damned who found themselves 'headlining' the first French Punk Festival at Mont-de-Marsan, an event at which the Pistols were originally supposed to share with Richard Hell's new band.

However, as *Sounds* reported in late July, the promoters had cancelled their appearance because they had gone 'too far'. How they had gone too far has never been explained but Ingham suggested at the time that going 'into the intricacies of why the Sex Pistols weren't booked is asking for libel suits'. Given that the promoter was Marc Zermati, it was probably the incident with Nick Kent which cost them an all-expenses trip to Toulouse's medieval neighbour.

The Algerian promoter then proceeded to book Clash as co-headliners to Hell, only for Hell to admit that his new band – the nascent Voidoids – was not ready. And ultimately, neither were Clash. So a bill of pub-rock acts was hastily assembled, with the help of pub-rock impressario Jake Riviera, to which The Damned were tagged on as token exemplars of punk:

Marc Zermati: The Clash were supposed to be on, but they were not really ready, so they did not come. People pretend they were supporting the Sex Pistols, because I refuse the Sex Pistols, but it's a lot of bullshit, a Malcolm story again. Jake [Riviera] didn't know The Damned at all, nor did Nick [Lowe]. They did not like them at all. But the guys from The Damned … were the only punk band [there].

Perhaps feeling a certain obligation to live up to the Pistols' anarchic reputation in absentia, The Damned proceeded to give the French a quickfire musical lesson in legerdemain, playing at a tempo that should have turned every song into a blur but merely intensified a groove the other bands couldn't even maintain at half their speed. Of course, this may not have been their actual intention. As their manager Andy Czezowski says, 'They were totally fucked out of their heads. They just wanted to get on and make as much noise as possible.' If that was indeed their goal, they fully succeeded, garnering a glowing review from Caroline Coon into the bargain:

> As The Damned stand ready to walk the plank onto the stage, the other musicians don't exactly rush to catch their set. The interest is more subtly expressed. All at once, a whole lot of backstage people appear nonchalantly in front of the stage. It takes one number for The Damned's guitars to be mixed high enough, and then they make a valiant attempt to hang together. Rat is attacking his drum kit with the guts of a demolition expert, but he's finding it difficult to whip up the usual speed since the scorching sun is evaporating his energy as fast as his sweat. The first three numbers couldn't have been better in the circumstances. The crowd spread out in the stands; all 350 of them … The French are ardent Iggy fans and they leap skywards when Vampire Vanian … crawls and jumps satanic and crablike across the stage, the very essence of Iggy … They were ten times better than many expected, even though Nick Lowe said, 'They are the worst band I've seen since the Sex Pistols.' … [Indeed,] as far as punk rock goes, there was no contest. The Damned wiped up.

It helped that they had precious little competition when it came to playing with passion. The bulk of the bill – Nick Lowe, The Gorillas, the Tyla Gang &c. – would have struggled to make up a single band energetic enough to brook comparison, a point Coon made herself, calling The Damned, 'a refreshing change from bands who have been onstage so often that they have everything down pat and have forgotten the most fundamental quality needed to make anything creative transcend the ordinary – the element of risk.'

A few days in the company of Jonh Ingham, covering the event for *Sounds*, had served to concentrate Coon's critical faculties and get her back on message. The Damned, though, seemed strangely determined to distance themselves from punk – and the Pistols – suggesting there was already some bad blood between these former partisans in punk; or The Damned simply thought the best way to get noticed was to bad-mouth their betters.

On the coach from France The Damned were at pains to let Coon know they were 'unhappy with the punk label, [but] accept the need for a term to distinguish their music from other styles of rock … As Rat Scabies, their loudmouth drummer, announces with punk logic, "If we had formed six months ago, they'd be writing about us like they are the Sex Pistols." Yes, Rat Scabies believes The Damned are a thousand times better than the Sex Pistols.'[37]

Whatever twisted tale this Miller had to tell, he was not about to be given a voice by his old friend, Malcolm McLaren. While The Damned were gallivanting around France, McLaren announced a gathering of the nascent punk clan to which Rat and friends were pointedly *not* invited: 'A Mid-Nite Special' on August Bank Holiday Sunday at The Screen On The Green, featuring Sex Pistols, Clash and Buzzcocks – 'Midnite Till Dawn'. No Hot Rods, Vibrators or Damned fans need apply.

★ ★ ★

The Screen On The Green was McLaren's big play – his first opportunity to show that three bands was indeed a movement. And once again he made sure everything slotted neatly into place. The venue, an art cinema in Islington, had been on his radar since May, when a Pistols gig was scheduled then cancelled. He even arranged to screen arthouse movies while the bands set up, which took a while. In fact, they had to build a stage from scratch as the cinema insisted on screening its regular fare, only turning the place over to the Pistols at the end of the night.

(Strummer later insisted, 'We didn't play very well that night because we'd built the stage … By the time the gig came up I was completely worn out,' one of a number of excuses used to explain the less than incendiary performance.)

Equally importantly, the gig was well advertised and coming on a Bank Holiday weekend, people could travel up to London and back before their more straight-laced friends had noticed they were missing. Peter Lloyd and Pauline Murray again made the 300-mile hike from Ferryhill and immediately on arrival ran into Caroline Coon who told them, 'I knew you'd be here.' (Lloyd 'used to write her these long letters before punk'.) The Durham double-act also met Buzzcocks' one-woman cheerleader Linder Sterling standing outside. Sterling, who had come up from Manchester with Buzzcocks, already

[37] The Damned's Mont-de-Marsan set was officially released in 2005 – three years after the release of the Sex Pistols' August Screen On The Green set – and in tandem rather scuppered Scabies' assertion.

looked the part. When Vivienne Westwood came up and asked her who she was a fan of, she replied, 'Me.'

Lloyd thought Linder 'looked amazing'. But then, who didn't that night? As Marco Pirroni astutely observes, 'It was the first time you thought there was something happening ... Everyone [there] thought like me, everyone liked the same things as me and, more importantly, everyone hated the same things.' Gaye Advert (née Black), in full undertaker make-up, had come up from Torquay to check the Pistols out and was made to feel right at home by the Bromley Contingent, who had decided to treat the event as something of a 'coming-out ball'.

For *NME*'s Charles Shaar Murray (and his wife) it all came as something of a shock, 'All kinds of folks in bizarre costumes ... are milling around the foyer playing wild mutation ... A bunch of people including a chick in SM drag with tits out ... [are] dancing around [onstage] to a barrage of Ferry and Bowie records ... The area near me'n'the missis reeks of amyl nitrate.'

The 'chick in SM drag with tits out' was, of course, Siouxsie Sioux, whose appearance proved so provocative that CSM's resultant review carried a photo of her which received equal prominence to one of an enraged Rotten. That photo would come back to haunt the lady, as her attempt to cross *The Night Porter* with *Cabaret* extended to a very visible swastika armband. For now, it helped put her at the visual fore of this amorphous movement in the months before she realized she could add sound to the vision.

Buzzcocks, who were not so inclined to strike the same pose of studied boredom as those from Bromley, had warmed up for this important showcase by toying with the enemy, pub rock, at a one-off show in Stalybridge the night before. The Commercial Hotel regulars were not amused. As Devoto recalled, 'They did not go for us in Stalybridge. They just lined the doors and looked at us, surlily.' Shelley suggests they *were* allowed to play two sets, flanked by 'all these bikers and their girlfriends [who] came along, and ... sat there with their helmets on the table beside them'.

It meant Buzzcocks were fully primed when the doors of The Screen On The Green finally opened, beckoning all-comers in. For Steve Diggle, 'It suddenly started to make a lot more sense to me: this was where we belonged.' They had already warmed up the crowd by busking on a few proto-punk classics, building a sense of common purpose that would come in handy when their fellow support-act started to get all competitive:

Richard Boon: We pull up in a van to The Screen On The Green, and it's still shut, but there's already a small queue and Pete gets his guitar, gets out the van, and gets the small queue to sing along to 'Roadrunner'. When we did get in, there was The Clash down an alley putting on their painted clothes and skinny ties; and they were, like, 'Who are you lot from the north?'

The excitement was palpable as the vibe coming from Clash that this was a battle of the bands contest. Their divide and rule tactics would ultimately change the whole dynamic of punk, but for now it just left a bad taste in Mancunian mouths. As Diggle points out in his punk memoir, 'We had no fucking idea who the Clash were but the name fit perfectly. One of those band names that always looks good written down … [But] I caught on from the very start that the Clash … were pure show business.'

Buzzcocks were cut from different cloth – as Stalybridge's bikers knew only too well. Their early live sound caught most unawares as staccato bursts of feedback were crowbarred into even their poppiest paeans – meaning at this stage 'Friends of Mine', 'Orgasm Addict' and 'Love Battery'. Wrapping up proceedings with an extended traducing of The Troggs' 'I Can't Control Myself' and Beefheart's 'I Love You Big Dummy', their eleven-song set suggested the garage-band hall of fame awaited.[38]

For all of Buzzcocks' hard work in preparation, though, Diggle found the response from The Screen On The Green throng disappointing: 'The London crowd wasn't interested in a bunch of northern oiks and they let us know it. They weren't all standing there, demanding to be entertained. Some got into it, but it was a frosty reception nonetheless.'

[38] Anyone marked absent from The Screen On The Green didn't know that sound until 1994, when a 2-CD bootleg appeared in Scorpio's Punk Vault series that captured all three 'Mid-Nite Special' proto-punk bands in audio amber.

Someone who should have known better gave them almost no chance to win him over. Giovanni Dadomo, having adopted Clash as his meal-ticket to critical kudos, allowed himself 'two and a half numbers to convince [myself] that [Buzzcocks] were a boring and highly unimaginative quartet and rougher … than a bear's arse.'

Dadomo's rave review of Clash's Rehearsal Rehearsals 'preview', which ran in the previous *Sounds,* had almost single-handedly ensured they would play after Buzzcocks, even though The Screen On The Green was only their second public performance. Not surprisingly, when Clash took the stage they sounded not merely more ragged than a northern cock but patently unready. It inspired one reviewer, dragged there by a photographer friend, to write his most famous paragraph in a quarter-century of rock journalism:

> Sooner or later – later, actually – a group called Clash take the stage. They are the kind of garage band who should be speedily returned to their garage, preferably with the motor running, which would undoubtedly be more of a loss to their friends and families than to either rock or roll … Joe Strummer has good moves but he and the band are a little shaky on ground that involves starting, stopping and changing chord at approximately the same time.

Having arrived too late to catch Buzzcocks, Shaar Murray was unable to draw any point of comparison, but his prominent review let Rhodes know orchestrating a media hype might not be such a breeze unless his band developed some chops. The band themselves responded the way Rhodes had taught them to: writing a righteous riposte in song (the magnificent 'Garageland'), and suggesting it was all a conspiracy to deny Clash what was rightfully theirs.

Both Strummer and Simonon would later claim the sound had been sabotaged. As late as 2008 the latter was insisting he 'couldn't understand why we sounded so awful onstage that night, and then the Pistols came on and sounded fantastic. It was that old trick of giving us a bit of the PA and not all of it. I suppose they were a bit scared of us.' This from a man who could barely hold his instrument, let alone play it, about a band who at their blistering best (as they were that night) had no peers, punk or otherwise.

Appropriately, they opened with 'Deny', a song about self-delusion. But Dave Goodman was not amused to find himself accused of 'sabotaging their sound ... That's bollocks. I loved the Clash and worked hard at making them sound good.' It wasn't his fault they didn't sound like they did in a rehearsal room the size of a public convenience.

However, excuses needed to be made when even Clash's chief cheerleader, Giovanni Dadomo, noticed 'their equipment was to do the band a grave disservice tonight, losing Joe Strummer's hard-to-mix vocals until they became an unintelligible mumble and generally poleaxing the band's nuclear potential.' Of course, he still 'thought they were amazingly good' – to his mind, they had to be.

Dadomo's review convinced Clash it wasn't their competence, but rather Goodman's, that remained in doubt. The tape made by one of 'the two Bills', legendary Portobello record-dealers, ultimately demonstrated the opposite was true. After a great deal of tuning up, the Screen sound was meaty, beaty, big and bouncy from the minute they ripped into their punch-drunk opener. But even after they found their equilibrium, lengthy between-song tune-ups dissipated momentum. Only the triple-whammy finale – 'I'm So Bored With You', 'London's Burning' and their one true punk anthem, '1977' – hinted at a conveyor-belt of Clash clarion calls to come.

Some of those without recourse to said recording – preferring their memories and previous Pistols performances as a point of comparison – remember the Clash set that night without any fondness. Boon thought, 'They were awful – they [still] had Keith, and it sounded really like the Pistols to my ears,' while Peter Lloyd's own description of Levene and Jones that night is hard to beat, 'Like two Ramones out of phase with each other – one'd start and [then] another'd start, with [the] other guitar.' The one longtime Pistols fan who actually appreciated the Clash set was ironically the person most determined to 'finish rock'n'roll' for good:

Vic Godard: I used to like The Clash when they played the same speed as bands on *Nuggets* ... I got a brilliant tape of them at The Screen On The Green ... All the Clash songs are so much slower than on the album, and there are some good tunes that never made it onto their album. Keith Levene in that era was great … I liked that sixties garage sound they had.

One can't help wondering whether the order of acts at The Screen On The Green represented another sub-section of McLaren's masterplan. Putting on Clash – a band who 'sounded really like the Pistols' – immediately before the real McCoy was bound to make the Pistols stand out like a golden shaft in the darkness. Already he felt a greater affinity with the Mancunian outfit, musically and aesthetically.

Indeed, the one abiding memory Devoto has of that performance is 'wandering back to the sound desk after the set and McLaren saying to me, "You know, your songs have got real content."' High praise indeed from a man credited with only having eyes (and ears) for the Pistols. Sensing a common bond, he even expressed his fears for the future to Richard Boon that night, 'I remember talking to Malcolm at the [gig] and he was desperate to get a record out, [thinking] it was all gonna fade away.'

He need not have worried. The place was positively teeming with A&R men – and on a Bank Holiday weekend, well past curfew. He clearly had got under the industry's skin with his scheme to make the Pistols 'the Next Big Thing'. What was slightly dispiriting was the continuing inability of most of these musical arbiters to *relate* to the next sound of the city – even when it was staring them bug-eyed in the face.

Producer Chris Thomas, invited there by fellow producer Chris Spedding, 'thought The Clash were better. With the Pistols, it was just shell-shock. I don't remember any great musical merit coming out of it.' EMI's Nick Mobbs says it reminded him 'of when I was a fan, not having anything to do with the business. And yet, at the same time, my head was saying, "They're not very good."' Evidently, Mr Mobbs had no head for rock music.

Yet the most non-plussed head-hunter to attend was Dave Dee, head of A&R at Atlantic Records, who was already becoming exasperated by McLaren's brinksmanship: 'As a musical thing I found them very unmusical – perhaps the fact that it wasn't disciplined prevented me from liking it … It's right for now because they have an image, but I can't see it going anywhere … We'd be interested in signing them for a single or an E.P. … if their manager was sensible and didn't want the world.'

McLaren *did* want the world – and he wanted it *now*. And he had marshalled his forces well, even encouraging those contacts he could call up to bring (reluctant) scenesters to the party. If Spedding had told Thomas to check them out, he arrived not in the company of Roxy Music's producer, but of their favourite support act. 'Sadistic Mike', aka Japanese guitarist Kazuhiko Kato from Sadistic Mika Band, who had supported Roxy Music's 1975 tour as a result of McLaren personally giving their 1974 album, *Kurofune*, to Bryan Ferry. Here was a chance to return the favour. Mike liked what he heard.

Photographer Joe Stevens was also inspired, or prompted, to call Charles Shaar Murray and suggest, 'You want to see something good?' CSM knew what was coming: 'He said, you're going to ask me to come and see the Pistols. Isn't it a bit violent? I said, Yeah, but you'll get through it.' In the end, Murray had to admit Stevens had done him a favour. The Pistols' performance persuaded this eminent music critic to endorse what was still beyond the ken of A&R men:

> The Pistols slope on stage and Johnny Rotten lays some ritual abuse on the audience and then they start to play. Any reports that I had heard and that you may have heard about the Pistols being lame and sloppy are completely and utterly full of shit … The first thirty seconds of their set blew out all the boring amateurish artsy-fartsy mock-decadence that preceded it purely by virtue of its tautness, directness and utter realism. They did songs with titles like 'I'm A Lazy Sod' and 'I'm Pretty Vacant', they did blasts-from-the-past like 'I'm Not Your Steppin' Stone' and 'Substitute' (a Shepherd's Bush special, that) and they kept on rockin' … Believe it: this ain't the summer of love. They ain't quite the full-tilt crazies they'd like to be, though: Johnny Rotten knocked his false tooth out on the mike and … he kept bitching about it all the way through the gig. Iggy wouldn't even have noticed. Still, they got more energy and more real than any new British act to emerge this year … And if Elton ever sees them I swear he'll never be able to sing 'Saturday Night's Alright For Fighting' again without choking on his Dr Pepper.

The Pistols had put their best feet forward, blasting straight into 'Anarchy In The UK', prefaced by the briefest snatch of a 'Flowers of Romance' feedback-fest. Just as the 'Anarchy' riff announced it was anthem-time, Goodman set off 'a blaze of smoke bombs', inspiring what Ingham described, the following month, as 'their best gig yet, Steve raging away in simultaneous feedback, noise and ringing, crystal clear rhythms. Paul and Glen thundering like a stampeding herd of cattle.' The band, though, were not amused by Goodman's stunt. Who did he think they were – The Who at Monterey?!

Glen Matlock: When we were getting ready for the [Screen On The Green] show, Dave Goodman turned up with a surprise for us. Here, he said, I've got these bombs for you, they'll go off during the set, big flash, big bang, be great. Get out of it, we told him, that's fucking hippy shit … we don't want to know … On we went. Halfway through 'Anarchy' – our first number – and BANG! Wallop. What the fuck's that? Dave had broken his promise.

For those who had travelled the length of the country, 'Anarchy In The UK' was everything they had hoped for. Peter Lloyd was again inspired to make his point to the *Sounds* readership, informing them, '"Anarchy In The UK" says everything, for teenage rebellion – the 70s answer to "My Generation". Older rock fans and critics find it hard to associate with it and understand it – [yet] could this be the start of a new generation?' He also informed its readers, 'They've improved 100% since the last time I saw them in May,' and expressed amazement 'that no record company has taken a chance and signed them up'.

He couldn't have said it better if McLaren had been leaning over his shoulder as he put pen to paper. Even Dadomo had to admit, the Pistols' leap in standard in the last two months had been quantum:

> You simply wouldn't believe how this band have changed, from an amiably aggressive but ultimately sloppy bunch into bona fide rock'n'rolling mothers. The most common criticism of course is 'they can't play' … Bullshit, they can play – the rhythm section would sound great if they were with Status Quo, the Flamin'

> Groovies or Val Doonican, and I wish Pete Townshend would check out their guitar player for a few hints on how to handle an axe like it was a dangerous weapon. A lot of the change is, I'm sure, down to the solution of that age old bastard problem of [the] PA. Suffice it to say that the Pistols seem to have leapt that major hurdle in the time since I caught them last and it's made a world of difference ... There were no lengthy breakdowns so that [Rotten] would have to waste time making inane attempts at annoying his audience. Rather than pouring beer over his head and making a general asshole of himself for a third of the set [he] is now able to concentrate on his singing.

If a chagrined Rotten spent much of the gig bellyaching about his tooth – 'it fucking hurts!' – he had never sung better. The last four songs: 'Pretty Vacant', 'Problems', 'Did You No Wrong' and 'No Fun' – absent from all circulating tapes until 1994, when some sage soul fast-forwarded through the cassette-master and found the last twenty minutes had been on there all along – were more smoking than anything Goodman secreted in his private pouch.

When proceedings finally came to an end and the crowd filed out into foggy London town, McLaren ensured their parting glass runneth over by playing Goodman's July demo of 'Submission' over the PA. If that didn't convince the bleary-eyed members of the Biz they were in the presence of a potential phenomenon, nothing would.

★ ★ ★

And yet no matter how much they continued to raise the bar on themselves the Pistols kept clearing it next time around – The Screen On The Green being no exception. Two days later, they returned to the 100 Club for their penultimate appearance and they were again on fire. This time they slipped a snatch of 'Flowers' into their oldest teen-anthem, 'Pretty Vacant', and encored with reprises of both 'Anarchy In The UK' and 'I Wanna Be Me', as if prepping for their first TV recording the following day.

(A 1979 Japanese bootleg LP of the show was for some, myself included, the first audio evidence of what a night down the 100 Club with the Pistols sounded like, and it has still to be bettered.)

They were enjoying the moment. As were the crowd, which

was now ample enough to fill the rectangular cellar to the rafters. The crush was such that various regulars decided to take their cue from Vicious, pogoing above the crowd to catch sight of the band. It prompted a hilarious account of the phenomenon in *Sounds* from 'Claudio Magnani (nice Italian waiter), Kettner Restaurant, Soho':

> Many bands can claim to have had abuse, stones, beer glasses etc. hurled at them but how many bands can claim to have had people – yes people! – hurled at them. This honour was bestowed upon the Sex Pistols last Tuesday when they played the 100 Club … The main figures in the incident which followed were four notable punks under the names of Shanne Skratch [aka Hasler], Chaotic Bass, Ray Pissolt, [and] Mark P[erry]. The Pistols had just started playing The Stooges' 'No Fun' when these four punks decided it was time to move from out of the wings (bar), so they forced their way to the front in true punk manner. They proceeded to let loose by dancing and jumping up and down. Due to the effects of the tankard, their movements were awkward and bumps into people were replied to with pushes. Being good punks they pushed back, and with greater force … Before you could shout 'Johnny Rotten can't sing' about thirty people became involved in the pushing and the shoving. The area around front stage was like a battle ground. People were pushing and shoving whoever was nearest to them … Bodies were being pushed around the stage front like sacks, knocking microphones and people over. The end result was one pinched mike, broken glasses and watches and some bruised people. It's a pity the chaos didn't occur earlier on, during the appropriate song, 'Pushing and Shoving' [i.e. 'No Lip'].

For now, a general good humour prevailed. But there was no guarantee it would carry over to another time and place, and fans unversed in early punk etiquette. If Claudio was there simply to enjoy the show, two scribes had come to check out Clash, playing their third public gig and third Sex Pistols support slot. If Giovanni Dadomo was just keeping tabs on them, Nick Kent returned slightly reluctantly to this old stamping ground. He thought the Clash set 'impressive without being particularly musical; and it was clear that they'd [now] heard the Ramones … and Mick Jones [had] said, "Okay, let's play these songs at three times the speed we normally play them."' In doing so, he was creating a problem, going against the wishes of fellow guitarist, Keith Levene.

For the Pistols, problems were a day-to-day occurrence, but so was a common determination to turn Rock on its head. And what better place to really shake 'em up than Manchester, second home to the band and the movement, and the first home of Granada TV studios. Because, after much toing and froing, the Pistols had been booked to close the last show in the first series of Granada's late-night music show, *So It Goes*, compered by none other than Tony Wilson.

Although the show would not be going out live – they weren't *that* stupid! – it was going to be recorded live to tape and with Tony Wilson on their side the Pistols hoped it might even be broadcast pretty much 'as is'. Wilson's producer was happy to go along with the majority of Wilson's madcap ideas for the show, even if he hadn't as yet realized that the Pistols closing the series might be a political statement on Wilson's part:

Chris Pye: The remarkable thing about Granada then [was] ... there was no barrier between enthusiasm and getting it done. Nobody said how much is it gonna cost. Once they checked you weren't bonkers, away you went. So that Granada music thread came about because there were individuals inside Granada who had obsessions, and management didn't stop them. They just left you alone. Tony did [the early evening] *What's On* because there was no one else. Tony was always in your face ... [Then] *So It Goes* came about because I persuaded [David] Plowright we needed to have a more hip music programme and I decided early on that Tony was crucial ... Tony and I, mainly Tony, was the inspiration for who we should book. I said, let's get Clive James, let's get Peter Cook – the quirky things were me – [but] the musical thrust was all Tony. I didn't know who the Sex Pistols were. There was some mainstream stuff Tony and I both understood, but [with] some stuff Tony just walked in the door and said, 'You know what, we should put this guy on.' ... The whole thing was done a bit on the fly. We didn't sit around for months thinking about this. He probably said to me on a Monday, 'We should have Malcolm McLaren['s band on].' ... [Some] of it was responsive to record companies but there was still a taste issue. We wouldn't put it on unless Tony thought it was worth doing.

Once the Pistols had heard the good news, everyone agreed they should perform 'Anarchy In The UK', their most apocalyptic anthem, and do it The Screen On The Green way prefaced by feedback and caterwauling before segueing into that pummelling piston of a riff. But when they turned up at Granada, the song the Pistols ran down for the assembled few was 'Problems', a prophetic choice:

Jordan: The Pistols did quite a tame rehearsal in the afternoon. I'm not even sure if it was the same song … So it wasn't anything like the final product. The crew were led to believe it was going to be peachy and nice.

'Peachy and nice' it would not be. To put this slice of the apocalyptic in context one needs to recall just how unlikely it was that a band as notorious (and *unsigned*) as the Sex Pistols would be on British television in 1976, and allowed to play live into the bargain. For the past half-decade there was only one weekly programme that had *live* music – BBC2's *Old Grey Whistle Test* – but it only booked signed acts and its presenter was still getting over the New York Dolls' appearance three years earlier. *Top of the Pops* and teatime teen shows like *Magpie* were mimed, and anyway only well-behaved chart acts were invited. So a show like *So It Goes* – and a compere like Wilson, who enjoyed upsetting the apple cart – was a Godsend:

Chris Pye: Tony was a very manipulative figure, and it is probably true that he was manipulating me [by putting the Pistols in that last slot]. If we'd had them for show three we'd have had time to discuss it, but because it was a late booking and he slipped it in, and it was the last of the series, [my attitude was], 'Oh, that's fine.' For which he gets bonus points.

If Wilson really had been in charge, it could have been called *Anything Goes*. But he wasn't. Granada owner Sidney Bernstein was. The Pistols were fine and dandy as far as he was concerned, but when

Jordan joined them onstage – after 'Malcolm asked me … to see if I could lend a bit of ambience' – the gates of hell came off their hinges. The Nazi armband she was wearing was *verboten* as far as Bernstein was concerned. As the producer of a feature-length 1945 film called *German Concentration Camps Factual Survey*, the footage of which was so harrowing the British government decided it could not be shown – and it wasn't, until 1984 – Bernstein wasn't merely affronted by Jordan's fashion statement, he was incandescent:

Chris Pye: Bernstein owned Granada and inside Granada there was an internal TV service. In everyone's office there was a TV set and a button that went 1-2-3-4-5-6 and any time of the day you could turn your button and it would show you what was going on in Studio Two, Studio Three [&c.]. And when we were in rehearsal with the Sex Pistols I got a phonecall from Sidney Bernstein, who [had] looked at [us in] Studio Six and said, 'These people who are wearing Nazi armbands cannot go on my television channel!' He was very insistent about this. So I had to take Malcolm McLaren into the back dining room … and I said, 'Malcolm, we can't have [anyone] wearing Nazi armbands.' And Malcolm's view was, 'Fuck off.' That was his starting position. But … ultimately we got there. And they took the Nazi armbands off … [after] I explained, 'It's quite simple. This guy owns the studio, the building, the TV channel and we have things on the shelf that Peter Walker has filmed that we can put on instead.'

McLaren wisely decided not to push it. But that didn't mean he was just gonna cave in. Instead, he used the underlying tension to his – and the Pistols' – advantage. A dispute about what equipment they could use further stoked a fire under the Pistols, and when Clive James made his distaste for them plain, they seemed about to blow. As Jordan rightly states, 'Our backs were up. That's why the [final] performance was so good.' At this point McLaren stepped in, not to tell them to tone it down, but rather to issue them their instructions:

Dave Goodman: Malcolm started giving the band one of his little pep talks in his usual 'undogmatic' way … He thought that it was a good idea for the band not to stop playing after their allotted time, but to carry on regardless … There was no way they wanted Wilson coming up after their number and standing in front of them while he signed off the series … The band stuck to their scheme of leaping all over the shop and the cameras were bumping into each other … trying to focus on the boys. Nils followed instructions and threw a chair on stage, towards Jordan, who was dancing on the side. Steve kicked it off, hitting a camera after John had given it 'the finger'. When their three minutes were up, they carried on playing regardless. Glen kicked the mikes over and Steve smashed up his guitar. Glen threw his bass down and it started feedbacking loudly. 'What the fuck are they doing?' mouthed an engineer in the control room … Rotten just stood there, surrounded by demolished equipment, giving a piercing stare at the frozen audience.

As per their instructions, the band kept going. As Jordan glanced at Johnny, he clearly 'wasn't ready to stop. He was giving quite a lot of verbal to the audience and knocking the stuff around.'

Amid the maelstrom, despite their best endeavours, the cameramen failed to keep Jordan out of shot as they had been instructed to do. The perfect shock trooper, Jordan loved the reaction she garnered, 'Those were the days when you could actually take advantage of that situation. Nils Stevenson ripped all the buttons on my Anarchy shirt open. The band were just really pissed off … You can see it in that shot of John at the end; he was feeding off the negativity.' In fact, that famous shot of Rotten staring into the camera as the song went supernova was *So It Goes* director Peter Walker's solution to the problem of how to edit a song that refused to end:

Peter Walker: The end of the number was totally different to what you see now. They started to kick the microphone stand around, kick the drums apart, kick the amplifiers over. They were doing a big job on their own kit on the stage. The young lady who was at the side with the armband on joined in … The whole thing ended with all the chaos and all the gear falling apart, with [Rotten] just staring into the lens … The audience … didn't know whether to applaud or not. That look saved it, because I could go back and edit that look … so it looked like the song was coming to an end. When in actual fact it never did.

Wilson later claimed, 'As they came off the stage there was complete silence, except for the footsteps of the producer coming down from the box to try to hit somebody.' Pye dismisses that frankly incredible version as 'nonsense'. He does, however, admit 'we all sat around the following day going, "Fucking hell, what happened last night? What is David Plowright going to say?"'

The performance of 'Anarchy In The UK' on *So It Goes* is still probably the most alive rock performance ever shown on British TV. Even the point at which Matlock leans into the mike to sing the harmony line, realizes the mike doesn't work and kicks it off the stage, works perfectly in the context of the order-from-chaos being caught on camera.

For the band, it was simply business as usual. But they still decided to make themselves scarce. As Matlock put it, 'A few mike stands went over at the end of "Anarchy", nothing more.' Even if Wilson was later reprimanded, he remained the compere for *So It Goes* when Granada commissioned a second series, the following year. And this time the staid Mr Walker was nowhere to be seen.

The emphasis of the show would now be mostly, if not entirely, the wave of bands following in the Pistols' wake. And to kick things into gear, Wilson decided a repeat broadcast of 'Anarchy In The UK' was in order. After all, only two regions had ever seen the show first time around – Granada (covering the North West) and London Weekend – coincidentally the two hubs on the punk machine. It also gave the Pistols an opportunity to catch it themselves, since the original broadcast went out on September 4th, while they were in Paris doing a number on the French disco scene.

★ ★ ★

The small but proactive French punk scene had been keeping tabs on them ever since the French punk 'zine, *Rock News*, had featured the band on the front cover of its fourth issue back in May. Promoter Pierre Benain – an old friend of McLaren's who was trying (unsuccessfully) to set up a Paris branch of Sex – had recently invested heavily in a new disco club on the outskirts of Paris, Le Club de Châlet du Lac. He now agreed to showcase the Pistols on opening night. As with many of Malcolm's schemes, it seemed like a good idea at the time:

John Lydon: Malcolm loved to paint himself as the orchestrator of this burgeoning movement, but it was [now] all happening above and beyond his control. His every move was clueless. That September he took us to France for the first time and we ended up playing to a packed crowd in a Parisian discothèque, for a diehard disco-dancing crowd.

Clueless or not, it was another situation which no one could fully control, in the very home of Situationism. And if Jordan had offended Sid Bernstein with her Nazi regalia, it was as nothing to the reaction which now greeted the Bromley Contingent – fronted, in every sense of the word, by the imperturbable Siouxsie Sioux. Having convinced the entire Contingent to take a day-trip to Paris, what she and her fashion-conscious friends did not quite realize was just how big French disco had become; or that if there was one thing Parisians loved more than free admission to a club, it was a riot.

As Pistols road manager Nils Stevenson wrote in his diary, the band and the Bromleys arrived at the gig – after an afternoon soaking up café society while drawing more stares than the Mona Lisa – to find 'a massive crowd congregat[ing] outside the club ... Inside there's plenty of aggro directed at Siouxsie, whose swastika and pert bare breasts provoke a furore from French patriots.' Caroline Coon, who had managed to blag another French trip out of her long-suffering editor, captured the tension borne of mutual incomprehension in another instalment from her chronicle of the children of this revolution:

> The Pistols own myth, far more outrageous than anything Paris has heard in years, had preceded them. The club was scared to advertise their presence, so the 3,000-strong audience was largely ... there because of the free admission. Johnny Rotten presented Paris with his most far-out outfit yet – a black bondage suit, strapped and chained at the knees and elbows, crucifixes, swastikas and safety pins dangling in profusion. Jerking mechanically and ... shouting

> 'Destroy! Chaos! Anarchy!' in appropriate moments at each song, half the audience were immediately reduced to shocked submission. But as the band leapt about the illuminated glass stage, red laser beams burning the air around them, powering through 'Anarchy In The UK', 'I Wanna Be Me', 'I'm A Lazy Sod', the London fans in their winkle pickers, two-toned hair and near-naked rubber and plastic fetish wear, were being aggressively punched and near-knifed for their sartorial audacity.

Coon claimed the music did finally get to the Gauls, with 'most of the audience [once it] recovered from their shock … explod[ing] into a wild display of rock'n'roll dancing [while] the band, encouraged by this show of approval, took off'. But in his diary Stevenson states, 'The Pistols' performance itself is greeted with bewilderment,' and he later informed Jon Savage, 'The punters had no idea what the group was actually like, and they were … really pissed off when the group played.'

Another member of the Pistols crew, Dave Goodman, dismissed the performance as 'fairly average. No one was struck by lightning or burst into flames,' while Billy Idol describes 'the French audience watch[ing] the show impassively, while scowling at us' English fans. Either way, Siouxsie was lucky to escape with her life – as was Rotten, who 'almost broke [his] neck because the stage was lit from underneath, and as you trotted out you couldn't see anything':

Billy Idol: All we wanted to do was shock, because that was all we felt was left to us. During those early days, within our little universe, an understanding of other people's interpretations of our actions was beyond us. On this night … this Paris audience was getting increasingly incensed at us. Obviously, *The Night Porter* wasn't very big in France. As the band thundered to the end of the set, things started to get even uglier … Siouxsie was glaring and giving back as good as she got. Soon, a whole section of fans started throwing stuff at us … We managed to run across the stage and find refuge with the band in their tiny dressing room. We later found out it was the anniversary of the day France declared war on Germany in 1939.

According to Simon Barker, the aggro did not simply fade away: 'There were so many people waiting outside that we just waited in the dressing rooms till the promoter said it was safe for us to go.' The Pistols were due to return to the club in two days time, this time to a paying audience of young Parisian punks but the Bromley Contingent decided they'd had enough of Gallic hospitality and high-tailed it back to Kent.

For the Pistols, the second show was almost a return to normality. As Zermati says, 'There was not a lot of people ... [and] they were playing at the back.' But at least the small crowd responded the minute the first chords of 'Anarchy' replaced the dying embers of 'Flowers of Romance'. Encores of 'Did You No Wrong' and a reprise of 'Anarchy' proved a fitting finale to their French adventure.

In years to come, both gigs would pass into legend – where they blurred into one – as French punks belatedly realized this had been their one opportunity to engage directly with the punk revolution across the Channel, in its infant infamy. Riton Angel Face, from Detroit-style garage band Angel Face, had turned up expecting something more like the MC5, but 'the show impressed me a lot. The sound, the look, etc... All was perfect – and even I hated French punks! After a few songs I was closer to the bartender than the band, but what a fucking show! The sound was incredible: loud and clear. The exact opposite of the French bands.'

It was presumably this second show that Rotten himself fondly described to the first New York punk emissary, Mary Harron, the following month: '[Paris] was really good, they loved us ... Instead of sitting down and thinking about it, they just knew they liked it and got up and danced, and done what they wanted, which is how it should be. It's hard to get people to react like that when they've been dullened most of their lives.'

It seems they made more of a splash than they had reason to expect. Certainly, by 1977 the punk look – minus the Nazi iconography – had taken a firm hold in Paris and the number of people claiming to have been at either show had swelled to Lesser Free Trade Hall-like proportions.

★ ★ ★

While the Pistols were away the five-piece Clash came out to play, in what for Strummer was a familiar setting – the Roundhouse – to an unfamiliar response: absolute apathy. Quite what they were doing on a bill with the Kursaal Flyers, Joe alone knew. He may even have called in a favour to get his new band this support slot, but the minute they got there they knew they were in the wrong place. It was the Black Swan all over again, but no longer with any concessions in the material on offer. They weren't even prepared to trim a fifteen-song set, which ran for fifty minutes, to Screen On The Green-like proportions. All the headliner could do was look on in wonder at what the future held:

Will Birch: We were soundchecking … and they turned up. They came through one of the doors and I saw them, and I looked at the guys around me and said, 'Boys, this is over, what we're doing. Forget it. Just look at this.' Didn't matter what they sounded like. They just looked fantastic.

Fortunately, there is ample evidence of 'what they sounded like' that night because one audio chef had a cassette-recorder with condenser mikes and tape. John Cooke, who had already seen the Pistols at Barbarella's, continued paying attention as the summer heated up and the punk soundtrack became ever more insistent. He remembers 'reading Giovanni Dadomo in *Sounds*. I think it was a rehearsal or press showcase he was writing about. But he made them sound like the greatest band ever … We were there to see the Kursaal Flyers, but as Will Birch said, as soon as the Clash walked in the room, [w]e knew it was all over. I just thought they were stunning.'

The tape – Clash's second such – supports Cooke's assertion. In a single week the punk quintet had come of age. The addition of 'I Can't Understand The Flies' and 'Deadly Serious' to the set and a revamped '1-2 Crush on You' all helped, but what was markedly different was Strummer's vocals. He came through loud and clear on the Roundhouse PA, both in the songs and between the songs, as he took the audience to task for being boring.

At one point he asked the audience, 'What exactly are you doing here?' Rather than answer the question, he was met with shouts of 'Get off!' Strummer played dumb, 'Get off what?' To which more raised voices retorted, 'The stage!!' Strummer, though, was not about to concede ground, preferring to lay into the hecklers for paying 'your one pound-fifty and [you] just come in here and sit down like it was a fucking TV set'. He chose to ignore the obvious: they had neither come to see him, nor to be insulted. They were there to see the Kursaal Flyers, who looked on patiently waiting their turn:

Will Birch: They didn't go down very well … Joe was a bit vocal between the numbers. He made some comment [directed at us] – he didn't slag off the Kursaal Flyers particularly, but he more or less said that's all a load of old rubbish and this is the new thing … 98% of the audience didn't give a shit. The place was full of 27-year-old hippies.

Among those '27-year-old hippies' was 22-year-old Eric Goulden, who had come up to London from Hull, nursing an ill-advised plan to be a singer and a cassette demo of a single song, 'Whole Wide World'. Wreckless Eric – as he became a few weeks later, when he ventured into the Stiff Records office and announced, 'I'm one of those cunts who has a demo tape' – agreed with Birch and Cooke that Clash on this occasion stood for not-so-much a step sideways from pub rock as a full frontal attack on all it stood for:

> The Clash was a life-changing experience. Most of the bands I saw around that time were totally harmless, but not The Clash … Keith Levene was still in the band, so there were three guitar players. They were the most confrontational thing I'd ever seen. They looked like stick insects – tight, straight-legged jeans; short, homemade haircuts. Strummer wore a black shirt with Chuck Berry Is Dead bleached into the back of it. From the moment they came on there were adverse comments and snide remarks about the regular Sunday At The Roundhouse audience … Their sound was an aggressive cacophony of out-of-tune guitars and ragged vocal chants. I wasn't sure that I liked it but I found it very attractive. They weren't going down at all well … I almost felt that I should make some pledge of

> allegiance – there was something going on. I wasn't sure what it was, but this air of dissatisfaction was something I could identify with.

An 'air of dissatisfaction' was certainly emanating from stage-left where Levene was slowly stewing in his own bile. Much as he had tried he simply wasn't on the same programme as the others, and when Strummer appeared at the next rehearsal with a song called 'White Riot' – ostensibly his askew answer to the Notting Hill Gate riot – it was the last straw. It drew the response, 'I'm not fucking singing "White Riot" – you're joking!'

At the following rehearsal, Levene turned up late. When he plugged in and started to play, Strummer started 'poking me in the arm and going, "Look Keith, just what is wrong with you, man, are you into this or not?" I'm not into it so I just leave my guitar up against the amp, feedback howling back like mad, like white noise, and I just walk out.' And then there were four.

(Levene had 'realized then just how much [he] resented rock & roll,' and began his search for a band who could finish it, not redeem it. It would take him a further eighteen months, but he would eventually join forces with the former vocalist of the Sex Pistols, who once again was calling himself John Lydon and looking to sound like Can, not the can-can.)

For *The* Clash, it was both a setback and a clarification. The departure of Levene allowed the band to run the Ramones close in the speed stakes, as Jones no longer needed to concern himself with playing in the same key as the one decent musician in the band. They had less than a fortnight before their next gig – their fifth to paying customers and a fourth support slot to the Pistols – but it was an important one. In the interim, five songs disappeared from the set – four of them never to be seen or heard of again[39] – while 'Deny' was retired as set-opener, perhaps because of its close proximity to the Pistols' 'Liar'. 'White Riot' got to set the tone instead. They really weren't joking.

The four-piece Pistols, meanwhile, having managed to return

[39] The four songs in question are 'I Know What To Do About It', 'All About', 'Fireway' and 'Bernie's Shakedown'.

from France in one piece, almost immediately embarked on another tour of duty up north: a four-date, five-day stint either side of the Pennines, beginning in Whitby and ending in Blackburn for a gig at the Lodestar, rearranged from the previous month. Once again, while Lancashire welcomed them with something approximating to open arms, Yorkshire decided they sucked and spat 'em out. In Whitby, it seemed the first cousin of the Cromer club-owner was running the place, if one future theatre director remembers right:

Bob Eaton: It was in a sort of country and western bar attached to the hotel … called the White Horse Bar or Inn, but that might be memory warp. I had seen a poster in town a few days before and, never having heard of the Pistols, asked my mate Terry, who shared a house with me, who they were. 'Punk, mate,' he said. 'What the fuck's that?' I said. So we went along. There were probably less than ten people in the place and it was really bizarre, with cow horns and pictures of Nevada on the walls … I do remember a couple of kids in front of us looking suitably energised. I was almost 28, so really too old to know what was going on, but they seemed okay. Then the guy who ran the place got some complaints from the neighbours and asked the band if they could turn it down a bit. Obviously they couldn't, so they spent the rest of the evening sitting on their amplifiers in silence.

If the rest of the country was slowly waking up from its dreaming, on the Yorkshire coast time continued to stand still – as did most of the audience, the Pistols' second disco crowd in eight days. As one internet postee wrote about this infamous occasion, 'It was a Saturday night disco night and my wife and I were the only people there to see the Pistols. Everyone else was there for a Saturday disco, and were totally fazed by the Pistols … After around 30 minutes, the DJ started the disco up again and asked them to leave the stage.' A subsequent posting, on the Vintage-rock blog, filled in a few more blanks about the night the ____ generation lost its argument to the Whitby dancing queens:

> I persuaded [my girlfriend] that we should go along and see what this punk thing was all about … When we arrived in Whitby we

> went straight to the Royal Hotel, which is the splendid white hotel which overlooks the harbour. We went into the bar and asked where the Sex Pistols were playing. The staff gave us strange looks and didn't seem to know anything about the gig, but suggested it might be in the disco which was … around the back … We saw a poster advertising 'Saturday Disco Night featuring Top Band The Sex Pistols' on a gate, which led us into a pub, or [maybe] the back room of the hotel … We soon spotted the Pistols who were sitting at a table in the corner, so we knew that we had arrived at the right place. John was wearing a tam, a pair of bondage trousers and a Teddy boy jacket … The place started to fill up around nine-ish with a regular Saturday night crowd of young people, all dressed up for their normal disco … There were no punks there at all (except the Pistols, that is). The DJ started to play some seventies charts music … and a small group of girls took to the dance floor. After a little time, the DJ introduced tonight's 'group': The Sex Pistols. The girls dancing at the front didn't know what was happening. The Pistols were deafening and started with 'Anarchy in the UK' … By the time they were into 'Stepping Stone' the crowd were getting restless, and couldn't believe their eyes or ears. John was staring at them, snarling the lyrics. The DJ sensed that the Pistols weren't going down too well … and between songs he turned their sound off, said, 'Thank you for tonight's band the Sex Pistols, now its back to the disco,' and started his disco up again. And that was it. The Pistols had played for around 20 minutes.

Four months after the Pistols had played down the road in Scarborough, and were greeted with anger and incomprehension, they failed to even get a rise out of the young folk of Whitby, who just wanted to indulge in some Saturday night boogie. So much for making the requisite provincial gains.

The next night the Pistols visited Leeds for the very first time; and again, according to Peter Lloyd, who travelled down from Durham, 'It wasn't massively packed.' It seemed the apathy might be getting to Rotten, who Lloyd remembers sitting 'in the dressing room afterwards, burning his arm' with lit cigarettes, a practise he had adopted since the July Lyceum show.

For all his onstage intensity, Lydon was already struggling to cope with the adulation and infamy his adopted name inspired in wholly unequal measures. Steve Jones, meanwhile, took Lloyd back into the Fforde Grene to play him the Goodman demos through the sound system. He was rightly proud of how they had come out, still hoping the Pistols could become punk's Faces.

The next day the Pistols crossed the Pennines, and their mood started to improve. That night's show was in Chester, the county town of leafy Cheshire, just thirty miles from Manchester, and when they arrived at Quaintways they were relieved to find it was a proper rock club. But with the exception of Paul Morley, the token Mancunian present, the locals looked like they expected something metallic. What they got did not fit the bill, unless they meant *Metallic K.O.*

There remained too many vestiges of a band looking to 'finish rock'n'roll' for the locals' liking, even though a few embraced the sound of rock fracturing. Amateur musician Steve Allan Jones 'couldn't believe you could get on stage with not much more than raw energy … The crowd (mainly heavy rock fans) didn't like them much, but they were great, really meaty sound, great attitude.' So not a complete loss; rather another loss leader in the Pistols' ongoing attempt to transmit their subterranean signals above ground and into the mainstream. Yes, they were still making converts in the most unlikely places – just not any game-changers tonight.

After a night off recharging the (hire van) batteries, they pulled up at the Lodestar in Blackburn expecting another hard day's night. Instead, club owner Margaret Grimshaw informed them it was a sell-out. In fact, she was wondering if they might do 'an extra show', such was the demand. Perhaps the trick was to price the entertainment right. As Maggie told *Mojo*, 'It was 30p to get in, and we cleared out all the furniture. But they went down really well.' Though she had been warned 'about the violence and the spitting', she had not been warned about the volume. The Pistols' motto was PLAY IT LOUD, and that night in particular they seemed determined to subdue any dissenting voices – and there were always some – by blowing out eardrums:

Dave Goodman: The band eventually steamed into 'Anarchy'. Fuck me – they were loud! … They stood their ground against the crowd and gave as good as they got. Crashing from song to song, their energy seemed endless. They started to win over … the audience

... although there was still ... shouting from those opposed to the band ... They left the stage with Rotten advising the audience that if they wanted more, they could ask for it. There was a certain amount of conflict as to whether they did or not ... John said that as they'd liked them so much, they would do the entire set again. This almost caused a riot.

They didn't actually play a second set, but they did play an extended encore which culminated in a reprise for 'Anarchy In The UK' and a now-rare live performance of 'Did You No Wrong', their original crowd-pleaser. By then, Jones's guitar had gone seriously out-of-tune but no one cared, least of all the soundman, who continued running tape – as he often did – expecting to erase over it with the next performance. As it happened, the Blackburn encore survived at the end of the first reel from the next show.[40]

Those in Blackburn who didn't like the band or the volume they played at were, of course, entirely free to leave. Which was not the case two nights later. For the first and last time, the Pistols were playing to a truly captive audience – at Chelmsford Maximum Security Prison. When John taunted the prisoners at one point, 'Why don't you go home if you don't like it then?' the guard standing next to the mixing desk jabbed Dave Goodman with his elbow, 'Is he bloody kidding or what?'

The very idea of doing a prison gig smacks of the sort of Situationist who, envisaging a riot, ensured he got a tame reporter on-site to witness the surely-inevitable conflagration. And in September 1976 there was no reporter more attuned than Jonh Ingham, who was delighted to be cast in the role of the Granada TV producer in this punk remake of *Johnny Cash at San Quentin*.

Unfortunately for McLaren, there was no riot and there were only so many Pistols reviews even Ingham could get away with. When he submitted his eye-witness account to the *Sounds* review editor, it got the veto, perhaps because no one quite believed such a showdown took place. Ingham did what any seventies rock scribe

[40] The original Goodman soundboard tape of the Chelmsford Security Prison gig includes two versions of 'Anarchy In The UK'. One of the versions is screamingly out of tune, this is the one included on the quasi-official release. The real Chelmsford version remains unreleased.

would, and passed it to a punk fanzine to publish anonymously. There it languished in xerox limbo until some time after Goodman released the audio evidence which confirmed the *Sounds*man had not been making it up after all:

> Chelmsford maximum security prison isn't no council tenancy, but it is in the suburbs right next to some office buildings and a service station on the corner (quick getaway) … Any band that cares to can play, except for Hawkwind. Everyone was on acid … I mean, the prisoners … and there was a minor riot … Tonight it's the Pistols … [and] John has dressed for the occasion: NO FUTURE FUTURE FUTURE down the front of his shirt, ANARCHY dripping across the back. … At a table at the other end of the room a group of screws have afternoon tea … It really needs [Jean-Luc] Godard, camera slowly tracking from one end of the room to the other, from Pistols to police, to get the full effect … [At the soundcheck] the small theatre echoes a lot … [as] the band warm up with a diamond hard 'Wham Bam Thank You Ma'am', then a few of their own. When the soundcheck finishes everyone except sound wizards Dave and Kim have to go backstage, and the audience are let in … Six blacks stroll in; five of them walk out after ten minutes. Some guys have sewn flares into their Levis … [The Pistols] walk on one by one. … [Rotten] welcomes them with a greeting from the Queen (cheers and whistles) and a message from the recently released Ron, who would have loved to come, but he's been banned. Dead silence. John enunciates 'Anarchy' very clearly. There is wild applause … They are playing great. In the short breaks between songs John taunts them: 'You're like a bunch of fucking statues! I bet you've all got a good case of piles! Move!' 'We're not allowed to.' 'I don't care – tear the fucking place apart!' The audience loves it, yelling back with no hesitation. They even warm to some of the songs: 'Submission', 'No Fun', 'Stepping Stone', 'Problems', 'Liar', all get heavy cheers and whistles. Steve is exploring clean country, lots of clear, precise notes. Middles and ends have been altered, tidied up. John is enunciating what he considers the important lyrics very clearly … As the intro to 'Seventeen' winds up, Paul leans back, both arms in the air. Only instead of crashing down into his skins, he just keeps on going over backwards, stool and all. 'Pissed!' yells John, pointing an accusing finger at the culprit lying on the floor helpless with laughter … The prison hippie – long hair, flares, beads, bare feet, ultra glazed

> eyes – throws his denim coat on stage. John stands on it, ignores it. The owner asks for it back. With great effort John lands it three feet short. With a nervous look around, the hippie gets up and grabs his jacket. During the last-song reprise of 'Anarchy' he leaps to his feet and starts dancing. Nobody stops him … As they walk off there's dead silence … then a sudden eruption of applause and yells for more.

Revelling in the rapport he'd rapidly established, Rotten had a ball – as did the unchained convicts. The singer duly recalled, 'We had really good fun – another receptive audience whose tastes weren't ruined by the press … "Thanks for coming," they said as they filed back to their cells.'

If another page from the McLaren masterplan was left ripped and torn, it had not been at the behest of the grateful Chelmsford 'cons', one of whom was literate (and witty) enough to pen a pseudononymous letter to *Circuit* magazine, under the nom de plume Peter Stunt, 'Secretary, Recidivists Anon, H.M. Prison Chelmsford', thanking the band personally, 'All the lads enjoyed them very much, as they seemed to be at home amongst us … [though] one or two of the guys did remark to me after the show that they did feel like punching [Rotten] in the nose for the way he spoke to them.'

And that was that, save for a passing reference from Ingham to 'John taunting the prisoners mercilessly [and them] returning the riposte with gusto', in a six-page *Sounds* punk-rock feature the following month. By then, any moratorium on the movement by the increasingly influential music weekly was officially at an end. A two-day punk festival had just put a greasy spike through the heart of London's West End, forcing even the straight press to belatedly respond to the Pistols' taunts like they had been hip to their jive all along.

* * *

There was more good news for McLaren. Punk's madame had just given birth to two noisy twins – Subway Sect and Siouxsie & The Banshees – both of whom were bent on making the most godawful racket. This was a stroke of good fortune because four bands does not a two-day punk festival make – even after he reluctantly allowed The Damned a day-pass to the revolution.

For McLaren's latest brainwave to work, he needed further entrants to the punk pantheon and if their goal was to 'finish rock'n'roll', so be it. Fortunately for him, the redemptive Clash, a necessary counterpoint, remained confident they would be ready to unveil their stripped-down sound the first evening of the 100 Club Punk Festival, September 20th; when the Pistols themselves would preside over the four-band bill.

McLaren was still unsure about Subway Sect, the band formed by Vic Godard and Rob Symmons after repeated doses of inspiration were prescribed by the Pistols. In fact, when he attended a Sect rehearsal a week before the Punk Festival they were supposed to open, he was blunt in his assessment, 'You lot are not good enough to do this thing.' But rather than ostracize the Sect for good, McLaren booked them a rehearsal room at Mano's off the King's Road – where The Only Ones were refining an all-original repertoire for a more auspicious unveiling – on a wing and a prayer, no money down.

He told them to concentrate on the four songs they already had: 'No Love Now', 'Contradiction', 'Nobody's Scared' and 'Don't Split It'. He would come down at the end of the week to see if they had improved enough to inflict the sound of the Sect on Soho. Although he decided they did pass muster, when they turned up for their 100 Club soundcheck the Pistols' guitarist couldn't quite believe his ears. It was one thing wanting to 'finish rock'n'roll', it was another matter entirely to trample on its corpse while making noises which put a banshee to shame:

Vic Godard: I was so nervous at the soundcheck. The [other bands] watched us, 'cause they wanted to know what we were like. We only got two bars into the first song and Steve Jones comes up on stage and said, 'You can't do that. If that guitar chord goes there, the bass cannot go there.' And he started taking our song apart. I said, 'Hang on a minute, our songs are a bit weird. They're not meant to sound like that.'

They were not meant to sound like *anything*. Godard now admits, 'We really *were* awful ... In our eyes, the Sex Pistols were as good as Yes.' Even their statement-song, 'Don't Split It', was at this juncture 'just a riff that I said whatever I wanted over'. And what he wanted to say (over and over) was, 'Don't wanna sing rock'n'roll.' Subway Sect's stance was avowedly atonal and anti-melody. It was a stance the head glue-sniffer and future frontman of Alternative TV appreciated from the off:

Mark Perry: Steve [Mick] and I both felt Subway Sect had the energy, but also the youthfulness, 'bloke next door' feel about them … with that anti-rock stance that they had. Made a massive impression … It was one of my major disappointments that that anti-rock thing was [soon] forgotten.

Another early punk-player looking to make his mark was Marco Pirroni. He also liked what the Sect were doing, mainly because 'they didn't seem to have any ambition at all'. They didn't even have their great punk anthem 'Ambition' yet. Pirroni was on next, even as the Sect rendered redundant the gesture he was about to be a party to: a performance-piece by the hastily-assembled, hopelessly-underrehearsed Banshees, comprising himself on guitar, Sid Vicious on drums, Steve 'Spunk' (aka Severin) on bass, and their fraulein, Siouxsie.

If the Sect did not respect the rudiments of rock & roll, they had at least spent the past week rehearsing the four songs that made up their fifteen-minute set. Siouxsie's band had met for their first rehearsal just twenty-four hours earlier, where they agreed to perform a single fifteen-minute anti-song. In fact, Pirroni had only spoken to Sioux and her boyfriend for the first time at a party the evening before, after a free concert in Hyde Park reminded him what it was he should oppose:

Marco Pirroni: They found out I could play guitar when Queen did the free gig in Hyde Park. I went to that. I've no idea why. I hated Queen. And I met Phil Salon, and then everyone else [in the Bromley Contingent], and they said, 'We're going back to Billy Broad's house.' He originally was going to play guitar for The Banshees and then he didn't want to do it. So they asked me.

Honorary Bromleyite Billy Broad was already covertly plotting his own punk passion play with Tony James, who was still without a band nine months after London SS marched into history; and probably realized the others hadn't got a clue and the laugh might be on him.

When Pirroni turned up for rehearsal the following day, it was suggested they 'just do "Sister Ray".' The others evidently thought that because this Velvet Underground vehicle rode on waves of feedback, it was just a sea of noise. It was nothing of the sort, being a carefully conceived performance-piece with a unique musical architecture. Pirroni put them straight, '[After] an aborted rehearsal … I realized they couldn't play, and there was no point [pretending]. [So] it was decided we were just going to make a noise.' Siouxsie would later claim it was a conscious statement of performance-art:

Siouxsie Sioux: All the other bands were talking about not being really able to play, and being unrehearsed and into chaos, man, and we … just wanted to take the whole thing to its logical extreme. [1978]

But far from making a radical statement about rock & roll, the Banshees simply took the easy way out, led by Sid Vicious, who after ten minutes took the view practice was for pussies and, according to Severin, told the others, 'Oh, that'll do. Let's just make a racket.' He hadn't even offered the band his latest lyrical offering, 'Belsen Was A Gas'. He still managed to show a nasty streak of anti-semitism by dedicating their performance at the Punk Festival 'to a little Jew boy called Bernie', a petulant riposte to Rhodes for his refusal to lend the Banshees Clash gear because, seventeen days after Paris's punk liberation, Siouxsie was still wearing her Nazi armband.

It mattered not. What they were about to perpetrate was never going to sound good whatever the equipment, for which Siouxsie was wholly unapologetic after the fact. They had decided, Caroline Coon explained, to do '"The Lord's Prayer" spiced up with "the most ridiculous rock songs ever written". … It's a wild improvisation, a public jam, a bizarre stage fantasy acted out for real. The sound is what you'd expect from, er, novices.'

But if, as Siouxsie later claimed, they set out to alienate the audience, they failed. According to Coon, the 'audience, enjoying the band's audacity, eggs them on, gets bored, has a laugh then wonders how much more it can take. Twenty minutes later, on a nod from Marco, Sid just stops. The enthusiastic cheering is a just recognition of their success. If the punk-rock scene has anything to offer, it's the opportunity for anyone to get up and experience the reality of their wildest stage-struck dreams.'

Siouxsie decided to cling to her dream. What had begun as a raised digit to 'the most ridiculous rock songs ever written', in twenty minutes became to Siouxsie's 'stage-struck' mind a viable way to reinvent rock & roll.

From where *NME*'s Geoff Hill was standing, he heard none of this 'enthusiastic cheering'. Instead, Siouxsie's recitation of 'her *objet trouvé* lyrics ranging from "Twist and Shout" and "Knocking On Heaven's Door" via "The Lord's Prayer"' was only 'received with politeness'. Not from Island's Howard Thompson it wasn't. Standing at the bar within earshot of Coon, he loudly exclaimed, 'God, it was awful.'

Two bands. Two gauntlets thrown down before the Rock orthodoxy. Whatever next? Fortunately for the sanity of Thompson, it was The Clash, probably the most orthodox sounding band at the whole festival. For them, the challenge was to have the same impact with a truncated set – as Coon noted, they only played 'eleven of their eighteen songs' – a single lead guitarist, Strummer's scratchy rhythm and Simonon's perfunctory bass.

While they were soundchecking, Goodman offered to tune their guitars and was shocked to discover 'they were really quite out'. This time, though, there would be no sound problems and, as Simonon later said, 'It was our event so … it was great to have everyone there on our side.' The general consensus was that they delivered the goods. Mark Perry certainly thought so: 'The Clash were really good. They seem to be getting better every time I see 'em. Their set was more loose and expressive than before … [and] the response from the audience was pretty good [even if] they're still yet to find their own audience.'

Coon, on the other hand, found 'the audience … instantly approving [and] the band … fast, tough and lyrical', the departure of Levene having 'left Joe Strummer, Mick Jones and Paul Simonon more room to move. And this they do, powering through their first number, "White Riot",' the very song that had tipped Levene over the edge.

In fact, one of a number of hacks sent to review the headliners that night used The Clash's set as a stick with which to beat the Pistols. Mystifyingly, *NME* had sent a B-list contributor to cover the festival; and although Mr Hill had come to praise The Clash – whom he thought delivered 'a powerful, tight and varied set. Their numbers are short and to the point ... and they perform as if they actually dig rock music' – he trashed the Pistols:

> At long last it's Sex Pistols time. The band strike up with the opening riff of 'Born To Be Wild' and lunge into a cacophonous 'Anarchy In The UK'. Pogoing breaks out. The band does it again. And again. And again. Johnny Rotten spits and snarls at his fans ... After the fifth or sixth 'Born To Be Wild' soundalike I am ready to split – right down the middle. Perhaps I can maintain my sanity by concentrating on just one instrument at a time, since I can't find two that are playing together ... I mean, even Alice Cooper, the shrewdest shock-rock marketing executive of them all, had to get some pretty sharp musicians around him before he could finally slice through the Gordian knot of consumer indifference. And finally, suddenly, it's over.

Again the Alice Cooper comparison I cannot for the life of me hear! One would be inclined to revoke Mr Hill's press pass had not the tide of punk washed him away anyway, along with the *Evening Standard*'s James Johnson, who after seven months of sporadically bitching about the Pistols in his weekly column, was finally sent by his editor to see what all the fuss – and, for that matter, the queue around the block – was about. His report was as balanced and nuanced as *Standard* readers had come to expect:

> 'Anarchy, anarchy, anarchy,' screams a malevolent singer called Johnny Rotten. 'See ya at the end of the world,' he declares as his group the Sex Pistols launch into an extra high-volume slice of rock music and the crowd at the foot of the stage succumb to a glazed kind

> of frenzy. The scene is a hot, crowded club in Oxford Street; which for one night a week has lately become the centre for a style of music loosely known as punk rock … Singer Johnny Rotten refuses to do interviews with the press. When approached, he responds with a terse 'Fuck off'. … [Yet] the group … have recently been attracting a great deal of interest from the music press and Britain's leading record companies. Less partisan observers are unsure whether it adds up to a new cultural phenomenon or just a giant confidence trick.

Just as the punk phenomenon was achieving critical mass, the mainstream critics were leaving their faculties in the upstairs cloakroom. In *New Society*, one uncredited critic showed he wouldn't know a new society if it hit him square in the face. He found the attitude of the audience 'no less diverting than the abusive, aggressive pose of the performers … The overall impression is of *Clockwork Orange* meets New York sado-masochism with just a hint of Weimar. Throughout the whole performance, one girl wearing a swastika armband maintains a Nazi salute.' Meanwhile, the society critic asserted, 'Johnny Rotten sneers, shouts "Go fuck!" and spits at the front row, as the band, like a steam engine in labour, begins grinding out an ear-splitting riff at breakneck speed.'

If only there was a tape of the Pistols' performance on this night to confirm said critics' recollections. Well, there is. But it does no such thing. Rather, it affirms the total recall of another top-notch guitarist who commanded Steve Jones's respect:

John Perry: The Pistols were clearly on a separate level from everyone else who played that night … There was a separation in their tightness and in their attitude … They were funny in the best sense and they were genuinely entertaining and there were bits where you laughed out loud.

The straight critics weren't just missing the point, they were missing out on a lot of fun. For all their diplomas in journalism, it took a fan like Mark P to truly capture the gung-ho spirit of what was another all-guns-blazing performance: 'The Pistols were fucking brilliant! They were really on form. There were kids on chairs, tables

... The following they've got is amazing. No one in their right mind could say they "can't play", they're getting better every gig. [And] no, there was no violence, they just played.'

And played. And played. For the weary journos, it was too much. For the numerous wild youths, it was not enough. A final blast of 'Anarchy' saw Jones wrench off all his strings during a feedback-strewn finale, signalling the end of proceedings. All the while, their soundman took note of the respective vantage points taken by those For and Against:

Dave Goodman: When the Pistols came on it was real mayhem, with the crowd jumping and gyrating in time, or not, to the music. They were surging right up to the band and spilling on to the stage ... There was [also] a line of people at the back standing on chairs, looking very out of place and uncomfortable. They were journalists and music business hacks, invited or sent down to check the band out.

Not every journalist felt this way. Ingham devoted only a paragraph to the performance – in his summary of the story to date for *Sounds* six-page '(?) Rock Special' – and managed to make Mark P's prose sound restrained: 'As the band hit the stage there is a mass epidemic of pogo-dancing. John looks at the seething crowd with a satisfied grin: "Great." As the evening progresses the band tread a thinner and thinner line between order and chaos. The encore of "Anarchy" is a blazing carnage of feedback, noise and head crushing rhythm. It is great.' For his confidant Coon, too, the leash had begun to loosen and her prose ran riot:

> The set begins. The band hit their instruments in unison. It's the fanfare intro to 'Anarchy In The UK'. SMASH – and their instantly identifiable, careering, evisceral plurge sears the air. The fans go wild. Johnny strains at his jump-suit prison. He breaks loose and burns into 'I Wanna Be Me'. The crowd sprawls at his feet, a struggling heap of excited bodies ... Steve breaks open, flinging his guitar diagonally across his chest and slicing up his fret, he leads the band with power and imagination through a breathless one hour and fifteen minutes [sic] of thunderous rock'n'roll ... They finish the set with 'Problems' and 'No Fun'. They are called back for a

> triumphant encore. The Sex Pistols were terrific. Compulsively physical. Frightening in their teenage vision of world disintegration. And refreshing in their musical directness and technical virtuosity. Whether their music will make the Top Twenty is irrelevant.

Tim 'TV' Smith, having finally made it down from Torquay to see the Pistols, spoke for the many when he recalled, 'They didn't let me down one bit: [it was] a snotty bunch of kids up on stage, giving it some, really interesting tunes … and 100% energy … There was no gulf between me and the person up there on the stage.'

Unfortunately, although the club was full of people looking to start bands, the talent pool – Tim and Gaye Advert excepted – had begun to run dry. Yes, Graham Lewis dragged the rest of Wire down to see the end of rock & roll, and Declan MacManus (aka Elvis Costello) found time to check out his fellow doomsayers waiting for the end of the world. But there is something slightly depressing – in hindsight – about Coon breathlessly reporting that 'Johnny Moped is there looking to find musicians for his band The Morons, Chaotic Bass is on the loose, Fat Steve of The Babes says he's rehearsing. Fourteen year old Roger Bullen, Rat Scabies' protégé, has just joined Eater.'

These were the very musicians who would take punk down into the (mosh) pit. It was time to cherry-pick the best of the crop before the root of the vine withered and died. Polydor's Chris Parry was in no doubt that the Pistols' brand of punk would provide the best vintage: 'The 100 Club Punk Festival remains … one of the best performances I have ever witnessed from any band. I was allowed to stand behind the mixing desk. I was transported. I imagined this was what it was like when The Beatles played The Cavern … Fans [were] going completely crazy.'

* * *

What Parry did not yet know was that he was running out of time to sign McLaren's manic street mavericks. In fact, Malcolm would start the revolution without him, fully aware that rock history was littered with bands who in their day were ranked the best live act in town, but qualify only as footnotes in Anglo-Saxon rock chronicles. The Vipers all but invented English skiffle, but Lonnie Donegan took it into the charts. The Downliners Sect were regularly packing out clubs while the Rolling Stones were mere Dartford renegades.

That afternoon, in the North London demo studio Pathway, The Damned had been recording their debut single for Stiff Records. Even without a distribution deal worth a name, 'New Rose' sounded like a hit by punk standards. The revolution in the air would soon transition to the airwaves and thus pass beyond McLaren's – and Rhodes' – control.

Already the diaspora was moving out, spreading itself thin. The same night the Pistols and The Clash put an A-bomb under Oxford Street, Buzzcocks played Holdsworth Hall on Deansgate in Manchester – a warm-up for the 'headline' slot at the second night of the 100 Club Punk Festival – sharing the bill were Eater, the first of English punk's wannabe outfits who thought the Ramones invented the form.

In fact, according to Paul Morley it was the London no-hopers who topped 'the bill because they're the ones hiring the hall'. Did Eater really think they could go on *after* Buzzcocks? Steve Diggle, with justifiable relish, relates the outcome, 'Unbelievably, they [did] end up following us [and] got canned off after three numbers: just desserts! Aside from that … it was a pretty low-key event, attracting no press.' Actually, the Buzzcocks set drew both local and national press from two figures who would continue to do their best to keep punk *and* post-punk pure. Perhaps surprisingly, it was Morley with his new *NME* hat on who took issue with the direction Buzzcocks had chosen:

> [It's] the usual kind of audience for these affairs – bizarros, curios and curious ones, plus the odd interested party. Totalling about a hundred … Buzzcocks appear to have evolved somewhat since that debut gig. Now there's nasty camp posturing, lurex jeans, nail varnish, earrings and other conditional frills associated with Mainman circa '72. It doesn't really suit them. A chubby slut in … zipped leather and tatty unsensual garters introduces the band: 'This may not be rock'n'roll. It may be rape. 'Cause Buzzcocks are gonna fuck you!' … Some kind of act has been concocted, obviously wrecking the nervous spontaneity of that legendary debut gig.

What prompted this distinctly sour review is unclear. (Morley quickly revised his critical opinion, come November.) The 'chubby slut' was actually Linder Sterling; and it took an occasional columnist at the *New Manchester Review*, who was altogether more smitten by Sterling, to out-Morley the man in the purple prose stakes and capture the essence of an occasion Morley could not. His name was Martin Hannett, who continued running his musicians' co-operative Music Force, dreaming of life at the console as the punk spirit seeped into his soul:

> The stage is set, in darkness, and generates, in contrast to the customary Cape Kennedy hardware overkill, a feeling of minimalism – guitar amplifiers, a drum kit and two microphones. Lights, and onstage oozes a demonic cherub, skintight satin and she shines with all the colours of a fresh bruise. Hand-hips stance at a microphone, she tells the audience 'Buzzcocks are gonna fuck you'. A rancid, ratlike individual scurries on stage with all the animal grace of a vole on valium – plugging in the remains of an electric guitar, Pete Shelley proceeds to explore the sounds of guitar-vomiting once beloved by Jeff Beck. His cheap equipment shudders under the impact and the man on the mixer retires to the foyer to look over Linda. She certainly does look good enough to eat. A change in the quality and texture of the rhythmic blur from the band announces the arrival of bassist Steve Diggle and drummer John Maher. A few minutes of sledgehammer on the beat braincrunching and Howard Devoto slides on stage. He looks like the witness no one wants to call. And as he spins around the stage, between delivering little staccato bursts of lyrics, he seems to be one small step away from something he can't quite handle. Buzzcocks make no concessions, with the possible exception of the inclusion of 'Stepping Stone', to the recently-established tenets of punk rock. Certainly there are the elements: the furious smashing away at every beat in the bar; the howling grind of the guitar like a football crowd dancing on cornflakes in the Grand Canyon; and three minute songs.

When Buzzcocks were finally ready to make a record, it would be Hannett to whom they turned. But for now, they had a return date with the London mob, curious to see if they had begun to defrost. Unfortunately, that mob was led by Sid Vicious and the second night of the 100 Club festival he decided to show The Damned what he thought of them, ruining it for everyone, Buzzcocks included.

Taking his cue from the way Matlock greeted the Ramones, he threw a (real) glass at his least favourite punk band as they began to desecrate The Stooges' '1970', egged on by punk partisans. As Severin informed posterity's prosecutor, 'Siouxsie and I were standing right next to him. He was aiming at The Damned, so he had my full support ... [They had] nothing to do with anything.'

Predictably, Vicious proved as inept a shot as he was a drummer and the glass shattered against one of the many pillars blocking the sight-lines at punk's premier venue, the shards hitting a girl standing next to Shanne Hasler, nearly blinding her in one eye. It had taken just twenty-four hours for the crowd to turn ugly and for the Us and Them mentality underlying punk to close ranks on The Damned. A colt reporter for the *NME* was there on his first assignment. Tony Parsons surveyed the fractious scene with growing dismay:

> The Damned were into another one of their three-minute barnstormers when the manager of the 100 [Club] jumped onto the stage and grabbed the microphone: 'We got three people outside waiting for an ambulance,' he shouted furiously as the music ground to a halt. 'If there's any more trouble I'll clear the club!' ... Such is punk rock. Earlier one of The Damned's friends in the audience had his face cut up pretty bad with what looked like a broken glass and the band screamed for the psycho who did it to come on stage so they could deal with him. Nobody showed, but all through their set they were under a constant stream of verbal abuse from a large section of the crowd who, spurred on by the taunts and putdowns coming from the stage, seemed as though they genuinely hated The Damned's guts.

Suffice to say, any antipathy was mutual. Mark P, standing at the sidelines taking it all in, saw Dave Vanian, as soon as the glass was thrown, 'jump down into the crowd to see what happened. He was soon back on stage – "Which one of you bastards hurt someone near and dear to us ... Come up here and we'll kick the shit out of you, you bastard!" No one admitted throwing [the glass].' But when the police arrived they seemed to know instinctively who was to blame, and – as *Sounds* alone reported – meted out some instant justice in the back of the police van on the way to the 'clink':

> The ambulance came, then the police. Stalking around the club looking for the aggressor, they decided to round up one Sid Vicious, a well-known figure in the Sex Pistols circles, and known to be as keen on a bit of aggro as the next Pistol-person. Ironically, Sid had done nothing on this particular night [sic]. After his sojourn in the police station, Sid looked rather the worse for wear. The resident punkess from the dull music weekly, also in attendance that night, has once again been called on to act as a kind of mini one-person Release.

The 'punkess' in question, Ms Coon, had founded the legal-aid charity Release back when the police regularly cracked skulls for the crime of having long hair. But her defence of this vicious youth was as misguided as her take on Buzzcocks, whose set she managed to catch after remonstrating with the police as they carted a cowering Sid away. Having misread the (mis)calculation behind the thrown glass, she saw calculation at every turn from Devoto and co., when all she wanted was for punk to afford 'the opportunity for anyone to get up and experience the reality of their wildest stage-struck dreams', talented or not:

> Through numbers like 'Breakdown', 'Orgasm Addict', 'Boredom' and 'Oh Shit' [Buzzcocks'] sound is quaintly compact. But their approach, though very energetic, is unnecessarily defensive and calculating. Devoto insists he is only in a rock band 'temporarily', and his self-conscious lack of commitment comes across. He doesn't laugh much and he hates being on stage. The festival ends with the Buzzcocks fluttering into the audience and Peter Shelley's guitar still on stage feeding back.

It was an appropriate end to an event that had begun with the cacophony of the Sect and the Banshees. Yet by the time Buzzcocks mounted the rickety stage almost everyone had gone home. Offered the opportunity to go on before or after The Vibrators (augmented for the occasion by Chris Spedding), Buzzcocks unwisely chose to go on last, which meant after the last Tube train left Oxford Circus.

The incident involving The Damned glass had already caused a fair few to split, leaving diehards like Mark P and Steve Mick, the *Sniffin' Glue* twins, and the ever-present Jonh Ingham to enjoy Devoto's second and last London appearance fronting Buzzcocks in relative peace. Fresh from Deansgate, they delighted both Perry and Mick. The former enthused about 'that guitar sound! Fuckin 'ell, it was a spitting, rasping monster,' leaving Mick to rhapsodize about the whole package, especially their attitude:

> On stage, the Buzzcocks, undismayed by scant audiences, don't give a shit. Their first number, 'Breakdown', showed forcefully what they're about. Devoto, with cropped orange tinted hair, stands twisted in front of the mic, his head always turned away from the audience. Pete, with a razorblade earring dangling about his head, clasps his guitar and throttles out riff after riff that proves he don't need no solos. John's drumming in 'Oh Shit' couldn't have been better, whacking away without a trace of feeling, while Steve maintains the pace on bass, rumbling away on such goodies as 'Big Dummy'. The audience don't know, the Buzzcocks don't know and even we don't know what they're about – but we all know they're good, very good!

Ingham was particularly struck by the way their music, which he found 'hard, crude and, on the Punk Festival's showing, very powerful, … succeeded in driving a large number of the audience from the room, a difficult achievement'. He was equally impressed by the imperturbable Devoto who told the writer after the set, 'It's nice for that to happen sometimes. It makes you feel like you've been there.'

Having come from their northern nowhere, they were going straight back there, leaving the London stage to the likes of Eater, Sham 69 and Chelsea, all of whom were waiting in the wings. None of these fakers were banned from the pubs and clubs of London town – unlike the Pistols, who had been in another country, literally, when Vicious elected to live up to his (originally ironic) name. As Giovanni Dadomo wrote, in place of a pukka review of the festival,

English punk's progenitors were now banned 'from ever playing the 100 [Club] again, therefore reducing the number of central London venues available by 100%'.

What had seemed like another of McLaren's masterstrokes in blueprint – a punk festival where the like-minded could come to play and preen – had turned into the last straw. The Pistols, who had always got mixed returns in the provinces, would have to spread the word there because a parliament of fools had decided they were to blame for every pillock who mistook a pillar-post for a punk band.

The next time they would play London it would be for television cameras' benefit. By then, punk had become more about front-page news and less about live reviews. And McLaren would be claiming this had always been his grand plan. Not so.

6. EVERY BAND FOR ITSELF

[September 21st – December 1st]

6

Punk rock, the latest teenage cult, has arrived in South Wales. Followers of the new craze wear chains through rings in their noses and ears and dangle razor blades from safety pins in their earlobes. Some of the punk rock boys also dress in tights and wear make-up. The girls and boys, both with short, cropped hair, emerged this week at the Stowaway Club in Newport. They were there to see punk rock's heroes – a group called Sex Pistol (sic). The group have a reputation of being unpredictable and specialise in insulting the audience. Their act has been banned in several parts of London after violent scenes. Cardiff promoter Andy Walton said many promoters refuse to handle them because of their unpredictable performances. Punk rock, he said, was music with violent visuals. The group also shouted obscenities at the audience. The manager of the Stowaway Club, Mr Martin Noone, said although there was no trouble he would definitely not be having the group back. 'I didn't believe my eyes when I saw the youngsters coming in. I had a very uneasy evening. I saw one boy pull a length of wire from his sleeve and hold it between his hands as if he was going to garotte someone.'

– South Wales Echo, ***September 24th, 1976***

While the wheels McLaren had set in motion hurtled towards their preferred destination – a record deal with a major label – those on the Pistols' van rolled west, to Wales. In the next thirty days, the band would play thirteen provincial gigs, two of which would be recorded surreptiously, and make two abortive attempts at recording 'Anarchy' for an eagerly-awaited debut 45.

The clubs of London, though, would remain out of bounds to them. By the time they played a 'secret' gig at Notre Dame Hall on November 15th, the landscape of British rock had changed out of all recognition as Buzzcocks finally gave Manchester a punk club it could call its own, just as venues in Liverpool (Eric's) and Birmingham (Barbarella's) began to change their booking policy to cater to the new sound, creating a provincial circuit of sorts.

Meanwhile, the two bands who had debuted at the 100 Club Punk Festival persevered with their anti-rock agendas. Subway Sect had come off stage that night to be confronted by Bernie the barker who offered them his version of a career opportunity: to become the co-leasees of Rehearsal Rehearsals and minority shareholders in The Clash corporation: 'Every time we play you can be the support band, until you get better.'

Siouxsie had also just left the 100 Club stage when she was approached by Kenny Morris, who offered to occupy Sid's drum stool and keep time properly. When Sioux and Steve also enlisted the services of guitarist Pete Fenton – a friend of Simone, a classically-trained violinist and Bromleyite – it seemed the Lord had heard Siouxsie & The Banshees' prayer.

Other attendees the night punk broke were connecting the dots, too. Billy Idol and his new-found friend Tony James within a fortnight had found a frontman, poster-boy Gene October, a backer in fashion-store owner John Krevene, and a band name, Chelsea. Simon Wright and Jane Wimble were just about ready to debut Trash at the same college the Pistols trashed the previous November; while Graham Lewis and friends continued refining a five-piece Wire, preparing an assault that may not 'finish rock'n'roll' but could give it a sheer heart attack.

It was more than just a scene now, it was a British movement. Relocating from their respective seaside resorts, Tim and Gaye Advert were actively seeking musicians for The Adverts while Poly Styrene was looking for like-minded souls to share her X-Ray Spex vision. Meantime in the northern marches, Pauline Murray had finally put together her own punk band, called for one gig The Point and ever after, Penetration. Peter Lloyd even secured them an October support slot at the Middlesbrough Rock Garden – after which, the drummer quit over the name change.

While these 'bands like us' made their baby-steps to punk notoriety, the Pistols continued to spread the gospel far and wide, even unto the Welsh valleys, where they were delighted to find their mission eagerly anticipated. Rotten was especially pleased by the reception in Cardiff the night after the 100 Club, telling Jonh Ingham days later, 'how much fun it was because people didn't have that London cool thing. They just took it at face value. And [so] he didn't have to do that hostile thing.' If Cardiff embraced the sound 'n' fury, the following night in Newport the band discovered the punk look had crossed the border, much to the mystification of local evening paper the *Echo*, who interviewed two of the freakier specimens:

> Devotee Mark Taylor, aged 20, of Mynachdy Road, Gabalfa, Cardiff, wears black tights, earrings in his nose and a silver collar. He said the punk rockers 'don't bother with drugs – just booze and music. Most of us are punk rock followers. My mother does not mind the way I dress but the boys down the docks where I work think I'm mad. … We don't like violence but are always ready to meet it when it comes.' … Steve Harrington, 17, of Pen-y-Caeau Court, Pantside, Newbridge, was wearing a black plastic jumpsuit with three chains suspended from rings in his nose and left ear: 'It's just the fashion. All my parents worry about is the neighbours.'

By the next time Steve Harrington caught up with the Pistols – in Caerphilly of all places – he would be calling himself Steve Strange, having stopped 'worry[ing] about … the neighbours'. He would later tell his official biographer, 'The Sex Pistols had the biggest effect on me. I saw these four lads and thought that anyone could … be in a band. They were saying, "We can't play," … but now it didn't matter.' It was a now-familiar mantra, even if it seems strange he thought the post-Punkfest Pistols couldn't play.

On one level, little had changed for the Pistols since the Marquee – they still didn't get 'asked back'. But on another, they were now blowing fans away on a regular basis, and anyone who couldn't hear it needed to invest in pipe and slippers. But while the fan base was continuing to grow, the number of young 'uns extrapolating a musical future for themselves from first-hand experience of a Pistols gig was diminishing fast.

For those into D-I-Y, there was something almost off-putting about how good McLaren's once-sloppy combo had become, as was evidenced two days after Newport when the Pistols spent a night in Burton upon Trent, as unpromising a backwater as the National Forest could offer, still playing like their lives depended on it. It was another night where 'no one was struck by lightning or burst into flames', not for want of trying. This, though, was the occasion John Cooke finally caught up with them when he had his cassette-recorder, fresh batteries and tape.

The result was a show captured with all the needles on red, and the band set to stun. Despite 'the gig being packed', our intrepid taper 'got right down the front'. So what is on the fabled *(Truly) Indecent Exposure* bootleg[41] is as in-the-face as any audio document of the Pistols in their pomp. And it was during this particular week of shows at September's end that the penny finally dropped for the soundman, in his case at a show in Stoke five days after Cooke hit record:

Dave Goodman: Tonight everything seemed perfect. I can remember sitting there behind the mixing desk thinking to myself that I was probably witnessing THE BEST FUCKING LIVE BAND IN THE WORLD … I'd seen the likes of Hendrix, Who, Stones, Floyd and Faces in smallish clubs, but none compared with this bunch. They were real – not posing. For half the set hardly any of the audience moved or spoke (we're talking seventy people at the most). They just looked on in amazement.

Not that this epiphany prompted the man at the board to start running tape nightly. Instead, he would later claim the Burton tape was one of his, 'John got me to record the gig, and took away the tape.' But that condenser-mike compression betrays its non-soundboard source. All sonic nuances go for a Burton on this front-row-centre cassette and it is all the better for it, the Pistols scattering all doubters in their path with a barrage that put the blitzkrieg in bop.

Either side of Stoke, the Pistols played Doncaster and Derby. At one of these shows, EMI's A&R chief, Nick Mobbs, caught them for a second time, after days of playing the Goodman demos to

[41] The original vinyl bootleg, *Indecent Exposure*, omitted that night's version of 'Satellite' for space reasons. The full tape, taken from a direct dub of the master cassette, was finally released on CD by the late-lamented Scorpio as *Truly Indecent Exposure*.

death, wondering if this might work commercially. It did the trick. As McLaren's new secretary, Sophie, noted in her work diary, 'EMI not at all interested at first but eventually saw them at Derby and the contract was signed within a week.'

For McLaren, it was a much-needed stroke of good fortune. Having weaved his spiel at both Polydor and EMI, these two multinational majors were now vying for the Pistols' signature, with Chrysalis on the outside rail. But for once, he read the runes wrong. Such was his determination to sign for the label he considered at the very heart of the British establishment that he threw his lot in with EMI's Nick Mobbs – a man who had taken a great deal of convincing – over Polydor's Parry, who knew he wanted to sign the Pistols the first time he saw them.

Mobbs was only finally convinced when he witnessed the Pistols as they came to the end of this rewarding road. Rotten had been at his raging best for the past week but his voice was about to pack in. A week's worth of shows now had to be cancelled, leaving the other three Pistols free to catch The Runaways at the Roundhouse. Jonh Ingham even managed to inveigle them an invite backstage, where Jones seemed particularly intent on 'meeting' Joan Jett.

By the time Rotten's throat had recovered its snarl, it was time to go in the studio – but for whom? According to Parry, when the Pistols entered Lansdowne Studios to record their first single, it was at Polydor's behest – or so he thought – 'I had put them into Lansdowne Studios, starting that Friday … I called McLaren to see how things were progressing and he said, "Chris, I have some bad news. We signed to EMI." … We threw them out on the Monday.'

Taking it on the chin, Parry went looking elsewhere for another punk pacemaker. But his memory may be playing tricks. It seems haile unlikely the Pistols ventured into Lansdowne as early as Friday. That was the day they signed to EMI. Parry and Polydor surely heard the news (oh boy) just as the champagne corks were popping in Manchester Square. It turned out they had only ever been bargaining chips in a certain canny Situationist's scheme.

McLaren may have known zip about the music industry but his days in fashion had taught him just how to drive a hard bargain. Having Polydor – and Chrysalis – waiting in the wings enabled him to put a gun to the EMI contract-department's heads and complete the whole negotiations in just twenty-four hours. He then kept EMI at arm's length by signing on behalf of the Pistols as the newly-created Glitterbest Management. It was a move straight out of the Brian Epstein Good Management Guide, leaving the label without a direct contract with the band. Smart.

McLaren also insisted on having the final say on producer, leaving EMI to pick up the tab. Finally, he reserved US rights for future dispensation, keeping EMI from the most lucrative market until they proved they could be trusted – which they could not. He had done his homework – unlike former confidant Bernie Rhodes, who would tie The Clash to the most egregious of major-label contracts in the new year.

Once McLaren had what he wanted, he gave Goodman the green light to roll into Lansdowne and roll tape at EMI's expense, hoping to capture white lightning in a set of cans. But when Jonh Ingham came to call on the Sunday evening, the band were sat around drinking beer while Goodman and the engineer fiddled with the sound. Capturing 'Anarchy' was not proving easy, partly because they were plagued by constant interruptions from their new paymasters:

Dave Goodman: EMI would send people down and we wouldn't let 'em in. The band threw water over one guy … I just thought, 'Record everything. This might be the album here.' We'd just done 'Anarchy' so many times … so we'd go down the pub and we'd come back and do a set. They had rostrums and they could all see each other.

The songs they ran down after the pub closed were exclusively 'covers', including the ones they used like 'Whatcha Gonna Do About It' and an aborted 'Through My Eyes'.[42] They even attempted to run down 'Roadrunner' but it soon deteriorated into a piss-take of 'Johnny B. Goode'. Because they 'could all see each other', they could bounce off each other.

[42] These are presumably the tapes later released, partially overdubbed, on *The Great Rock'N'Roll Swindle* soundtrack; and then complete and unadorned on Receiver Records' *Pirates of Destiny* CD, which has also been superceded by the 2002 *Sex Pistols Box*, which for all its many failings, does appear to have used the master-tape in this instance.

Despite the visual connection, the versions got more and more half-hearted until, at the end of a perfunctory 'Whatcha Gonna Do About It', Rotten suggested 'No Fun'. Suddenly, the Pistols were locked and loaded, roaring through a near seven-minute Stoogefest that made the studio walls rattle and producer and engineer hum in appreciation.

Here, at last, was the band John Cooke captured three weeks earlier at Burton; the self-same one lucky residents of Dundee, Wolverhampton, Birkenhead and Liverpool were to witness in the week separating Goodman's latest attempt to capture 'Anarchy' from his third and last, in the kingdom of Wessex.

That the Pistols' initial 'Anarchy' – their first attempt at that all-important 'vinyl quotation number one' – had come after an enforced ten-day break was perhaps part of the problem. Goodman, who had set out 'to get a rhythm track that was worth building on', felt the band were simply not firing on all cylinders.

To his ears, they never quite got it right and on the Monday gave it up as a bad job. According to Goodman, the Pistols were ostensibly expelled from Lansdowne after three days 'because John Magic-Markered the walls', but he already felt, 'it wasn't quite happening there.' What exactly was Goodman looking for? 'It was a [particular] pulse,' he later said, and it wasn't there.[43]

Perhaps it would return after four gigs in four days, even if there was a downside to this strategy. The band may have lacked match-practise, but what Rotten's punk-perfect voice really needed was the other kind of r'n'r – rest and recreation – and the high road to Scotland was not the place to find it. In fact, as Rotten said 48 hours after their October 12th gig in Dundee, 'I lost my voice and I couldn't speak, and they started throwing bottles 'cause we wouldn't go back on.' If Goodman feared for the single sessions to come he kept quiet, knowing from experience how volatile a lowland audience could be:

Dave Goodman: John put so much into this set that he almost sung himself hoarse … Everyone was very pissed. After one long amazing

[43] Nobody seems to know what has happened to the multiple attempts to record the definitive 'Anarchy In The UK', none of which have subsequently surfaced.

set, the band just wanted to collapse from exhaustion, but the crowd wouldn't have it and kept shouting for more. They bombarded the dressing room door with empty beer cans and plastic glasses until, after ten minutes of mayhem, the boys finally gave in and went back on.

A bemused Matlock felt prompted to ask a couple of backstage boys why, if they were enjoying it so much, they kept 'sling[ing] stuff at us'. They replied, 'We thought that's what you were supposed to do. We thought you'd like that.'

Already, the message was getting scrambled in transmission, even when a good time was had by all. After a rescheduled gig at Lafayette's, Wolverhampton – the same cramped club where they would open the infamous SPOTS tour ten months later – the Pistols duly arrived on Merseyside for the first of two shows either side of the Mersey, their first time in Beatleland. Surprisingly, given McLaren's and Westwood's connection with Jayne Casey's clothes stall, Aunt Twacky, and a small cabal of Scouse fetishists that included Pete Burns, this was the Pistols' first foray 'cross the Mersey.

Manchester, it was not. They arrived in Birkenhead for a 'warm-up' show at Mr Digby's to be greeted by a young female journalist from *Punk* magazine, Mary Harron, and what she later described as 'five people dressed like punks [who] all knew each other'. Despite the poor turnout, it would be a baptism of fire for the Canadian-born, Oxford-educated Harron. Contrary to the way the experience is portrayed in *Please Kill Me!*, she loved it. In fact, it made her start to doubt the less iconoclastic approach of the New York punk scene she'd been documenting until now:

Mary Harron: It was a half empty club … [and them] doing what I thought was an incredible show, although they said it wasn't, with a lot of people kind of sneering, and little clusters of fans in rubber trousers. Now I'd heard all about the Bromley Contingent, and I thought one of these girls was Siouxsie, and I went up and asked if I could interview them, and it turned out they were all local hairdressers and art students, wearing rubber clothes … who wanted to be different … There was something electrifying about the mythology that they had already brought with them. They were chaotic, which I liked, I thought they were very good, and they had this big guitar sound, Steve Jones was very good, and Glen Matlock … There was a sense of chaos, and the New York scene was not about chaos, it was anarchy, nihilism. But the Sex Pistols created a sense of, what the fuck is happening? John being really insulting to the audience, which I thought was really funny. Very obnoxious … holding the mike and saying, 'Fuck off, sunshine!' He was very sarcastic, and doing this weird kind of dance. I [really] loved it … Something *real* was happening on stage.

After the show the intrepid reporter headed backstage, to find 'the band were very amused that I was coming to interview them' for New York's *Punk*. She found Rotten, in particular, refreshingly forthright, both about the performance she had just seen and loved – 'It wasn't a good one. We can do much better than that … Travellin' around in the back of a van … fucks you up' – and the muted audience reaction ('If they don't like it, they can fuck off').

Perhaps surprisingly, Harron did not stick around for the following night's show in Liverpool One – at the opposite end of Matthew Street from The Cavern, a new club called Eric's – though in later years she seemed to think this was the show she saw; perhaps because Eric's would reinvent itself as Liverpool's premier punk venue.

In October 1976, it was nothing of the sort. In fact, Eric's was three shows into life as a one-night-a-week adjunct to a club called Gatsby's; and so hazy are the memories of the few that attended no one can seemingly agree where the Pistols played – upstairs or downstairs – or whether they even headlined. Local psychic Peter McDermott even claimed he went along because he had read about a gig 'where Shane McGowan got his ear bitten off', a reference to a Clash gig a fortnight later. In fact, almost nothing the Scouser now says about the gig stands up to scrutiny:

Peter McDermott: [The] audience were mostly hippies … It was Eric's very first ever night [sic] … No support act played before the Pistols, so they just came on cold, did their half hour or forty minutes, and then stopped – opening and closing their set with 'Anarchy'. The Pistols played in a smaller, downstairs room [sic], and then after they'd finished, they moved the whole audience upstairs to a bigger room [sic] where a local art rock band called Albert Dock … played.

If McDermott was as unimpressed as he was uninformed, he was in good company. Ken Testi, the man responsible for booking the Pistols in the first place, 'didn't enjoy it. They were trying to live up to this persona they were developing. Not friendly … The attitude of the people around them wasn't constructive in any way.' Apparently, they were not sufficiently grateful for the opportunity he had granted them.

Bill Drummond – who subsequently tried to make music Big In Japan before becoming the Bunnymen's moneyman – is even snottier about the Eric's experience, 'There were … only fifty people there and they were shit, anyway … The reason they didn't have any influence was because they were shit that night. If they'd been great, they would have had an influence.'

Given such an attitude it should come as no surprise that the famous port's contribution to punk would verge on the non-existent. They only started to catch up after certain short-haired leaders from Liverpool started travelling to Manchester to see punk in its element. By then, it was 1977 and Rafters was full to the.

The one reliable eye-witness to this inauspicious birth of 'Merseybeat punk' played bass in the support act (yes, there was one, Albert Dock and the Cod Warriors – featuring the Fishfingerettes, to give them their full name), who played a pastiche brand of powerpop which only finally left port when they became the Yachts.

Martin Dempsey and the Yachts would become Eric's regulars. But on this occasion, 'it was a weird setup at the club … the headline band played upstairs and the support played downstairs later on'. So, the Pistols played the bigger room – which suggests a reasonable size crowd – while the nascent Yachts entertained those with nothing better to do after the main fare. Dempsey found the Pistols 'quite chatty but Lydon … kinda aloof', when they shared a pint in The Grapes beforehand.

Like the rest of the Liverpool scene, it would take Albert Dock and friends some months to realize the revolution had passed them by, and that Deaf School only sounded like the future of music if one did indeed attend a college for those with hearing difficulties.

The one Scouser – actually, a Chestrian – who took something from the Eric's experience was Pete Burns, who already knew about 'Malcolm's band'. He was soon jamming with his friend, guitarist Mick Reid, a Keef clone and major Stones collector, in preparation for Nightmares In Wax, who would subsequently mutate into Dead Or Alive. The rest of Liverpool's punks stayed in The Grapes, waiting for The Cavern to reopen.

Meanwhile, the Pistols had their own appointment with destiny – a second set of sessions, this time at Wessex Studios, aiming to show EMI (and Goodman) they could produce a lethal dose of audio anarchy in the most soulless of settings. But Goodman still refused to accept anything second-rate, even after two more days at the coal-face. He later admitted his attitude drove the band to the brink of despair:

Dave Goodman: When we recorded 'Anarchy' … at Wessex the reason why it was recorded so many times is that it never captured for me what I was experiencing at a good gig. They might be playing to ten, fifty people, but it was a very clear, loud sound with a lot of psychedelic effects … In the studio, it was only a three-piece band but you could overdub the guitars so it still sounded like one guitar, but with all these high harmonies in there … EMI couldn't understand how we spent ten days trying to record 'Anarchy' … [But] no one [there] really knew what a producer did … They needed someone in there to know when to stop. That was me and it was really a case of, 'No, we still haven't cut it.'

What he wasn't getting was a lot of constructive input from the band. Rotten claims, 'We didn't know what we wanted. We each had a different idea of what it should sound like.' Cook was somewhat blunter in a 1977 assessment, 'We didn't know what the fuck we were doing!' In the end, the best musician in the band decided to take matters into his own hands. Riding roughshod over Goodman's feelings, 'upset that it wasn't sounding right, Glen went in with EMI's Mike Thorne and remixed it.'

(Whether he realized it or not, Goodman *had* captured an A-side that had 'a very clear, loud sound with a lot of psychedelic effects'.

Whereas the mix released on the 2002 Sex Pistols boxed-set, which apparently represents Thorne's idea of a hit 45, muddies the first water.)

McLaren found himself facing mutiny at the label after Thorne played *his* version at a sales meeting, sparking anarchy in the A&R dept. If there had been anything else in the can they may well have tried to use it. To his credit, McLaren stuck to his guns and used the press – in this instance, *Sounds* – to fire his own salvo: 'EMI didn't want to release "Anarchy In The UK" as a single, being worried about radio play. But with mucho arguing, hassling, and not having another finished track, the Pistols' anthem will be with us soon.'

McLaren thus headed EMI off at the pass. He had already predicted that the label would push for 'Pretty Vacant' as the first single for the usual bullshit reason – i.e. seeing anything which smacked of integrity as a front. So he instructed his preferred producer not to record that song. The soundman, a good man, willingly complied: 'EMI … had been sending down people all week to make sure that we cut a take of it. By some bizarre coincidence, that was the only song we did not manage to record.' McLaren was keeping one step ahead. Indeed, as one of Malcolm's more astute sidekicks observed after the fact:

Jordan: The most laudable thing about the Sex Pistols was that their image was formed before the record company got hold of them, and … Malcolm had that very clearly mapped out. I think they held themselves very well, when you consider the pressure of a major record company, and I know about that: how desperate a record company is to make it their idea and the Sex Pistols came out of that whole episode, of being involved with a company, really well. There's not many who do.

McLaren wanted EMI to release Goodman's 'vinyl quotation' version of 'Anarchy', backed by that sick-to-death 'No Fun' from Lansdowne – which was the single the music papers announced in their November 6th editions. Had it gone down this way, such a seven-incher would have been the summation of every development to date – which is why it was never going to be countenanced by

EMI. They knew they would have to release 'Anarchy' but not *this* maelstrom of madness.

Some of those who were party to the decision to nix Goodman's crash-course in controlled chaos would later attempt to suggest it was the manager not the label who pulled the plug. Nick Mobbs informed McLaren's first biographer, 'We were all set to release that [version] ... It was Malcolm who chickened out and said that he didn't think it was produced enough. He thought it was too raw.' But nothing about such a self-justifying statement rings true.

When McLaren issued a bootleg LP of the Pistols' studio work, *Spunk*, it comprised only Goodman's work – and the 'Anarchy' he used was the rejected one from Wessex. When he finally let Virgin release a double-album soundtrack to the Sex Pistols saga, *The Great Rock & Roll Swindle*, the 'Anarchy In The UK' was the one EMI rejected, and with the Goodman mix. All of which rather suggests it was Mobbs' lot 'who chickened out' as McLaren perhaps knew they would.[44]

With time running out for that all-important pre-Christmas release-slot, McLaren called up his old friend Chris Thomas and asked him if he'd been interested in making a pop version from Goodman's grungy template. EMI had heard of Chris Thomas – hell, he was one of theirs, having cut his teeth as engineer on the last three Beatles albums before blazing a trail with Roxy Music at Air Studios. They happily countenanced the switch. But if they thought they had won, McLaren was merely making a tactical retreat.

* * *

While the battle of Manchester Square raged, the boys in the band were sent to Birmingham for another performance that made one of those inveterate letter-writers to the music press apoplectic. In this case it was a certain Steve Horton who decided it was time he caught up with punk but ended up wondering why he'd bothered:

[44] Other actions further affirm McLaren's love of Goodman's work: when he wasn't allowed 'No Fun' on the 'Anarchy' 45, he put it on the B-side of 'Pretty Vacant'. Indeed, two of the July demos were initially selected as Pistols B-sides; and when further demos were needed in January 1977, it was to Goodman he turned.

> Last Wednesday I went to see a punk rock band for the first time: Sex Pistols and I must say they are the biggest load of crap I have ever seen. On arriving at Bogarts I was told it was 50p admission (usually 30p). When I finally got to the bar I saw that the Sex Pistols hadn't even arrived yet this was at 8.30 … To everyone's astonishment the band [did not] arrive [until] 9.00. As the place was packed and there is only one way in you can imagine the hassle of getting the gear on the stage. The band came on at 10.00 (the place closes at 10.30), and after telling the DJ to fuck off they started their first number which consisted of three chords. Played for about five minutes and that's it. I think everyone was in more of a state of shock than anything. How can a band have so much publicity and be SUCH CRAP?

In fact, the 'five minutes' was closer to forty – which was still short by the Pistols' standards. But having been unavoidably delayed, they discovered the PA was wholly inadequate for the volume they played at. A tape of the performance, made from *behind* the PA, sounds at times like the vocalist had gone for a wank. Yet there is no mistaking the surging power of the performance, even if Rotten again shredded his voice trying to project himself over the other Pistols.

Needless to say, Robert Lloyd was back in attendance, though as he remembers it, 'It was not very full – [and] fifty per cent of the crowd were biker types who would have been there any Tuesday [sic].' Also there, unbeknownst to Lloyd, were Alan and Paul Apperley, who within days placed an ad in the local *Evening Mail* for a 'Punk Bassist and Singer. Into Sex Pistols, Damned, Ramones'.

Lloyd was quick to respond, even suggesting bass-playing friend Graham Blunt be allowed to join The Prefects, as the resultant combo was soon called.[45] The Prefects were soon frantically rehearsing, aiming to be the first anti-rock outriders from Spaghetti Junction. They still had a way to go before they could contemplate gigging with their hard-up heroes, though.

Another outfit who had been actively pursuing one course, had seen the Pistols and turned left at the crossroads, were The Jam. For Woking's one-band mod revival, reinventing themselves as punks required not just a whole rethink but a relaunch. A seemingly

[45] According to legend, both Nikki Sudden and comedian Frank Skinner were among the unsuccessful auditionees for the proto-Prefects.

impromptu free gig at the Soho Market one Sunday in October served such a purpose, aligning the trio with London punk. Confirmation they had passed the audition came when Ingham and Coon duly gave them the requisite thumbs-up in print.

Five days later in Dunstable, The Jam reinforced their tenuous grip on punk by playing support to the Pistols. Weller, Foxton and Buckler came face to face with what they were up against as the Pistols blew the last few cobwebs from the punk manifesto in front of another home counties audience, seemingly ill-prepared for the coming onslaught and shuffling nervously. The Jam – who were now a four-piece, adding Bob Gray on keyboards – could only look on in wonder:

Bruce Foxton: We'd read all these things in the press about them not being able to play a note ... and they didn't have any songs. Well, they did have some songs, and they were absolutely brilliant.

Dunstable would be the last time the Pistols showed a clean pair of heels to their would-be emulators. From now on their gigs – whether carefully choreographed occasions for a once-secret brother (and sister) hood, or chaotic public gatherings – would be few and far between.

The Pistols may have blazed the trail, but the music papers needed their weekly fix and while the Pistols were ensconced in studios and personae non gratae in London, there was a void only like-minded punk combos could fill. By the time the Pistols played again, the second week of November, The Clash, The Damned and Buzzcocks were vying for lead gig reviews in the main three music papers on an almost weekly basis. And if Buzzcocks as of now had sole dominion over the miniscule Manchester scene, and The Damned were out promoting their Stiff single in the provinces, The Clash finally had the yen to play and play.

Through October and November, The Clash did their barnstorming best to fill the vacuum. Anyone expecting something akin to the early Pistols, but played at Mach nine and with slogans for lyrics, did not leave disappointed. With a fixed set, vital further weeks of Rehearsal rehearsals, a settled line-up, and a list of venues no longer open to their main rivals, they tore up everywhere they played from London to Leighton Buzzard, where Jonh Ingham caught up with them on October 9th:

> There's a carpet at the back of the stage and it goes up the wall, and they are literally running up the wall. They played the entire set in thirty minutes, so they come off and five minutes later, Joe's panicking. He grabs me and says, 'The promoter's really pissed off. We've broken our contract [to play] for sixty minutes and we got to go back on.' So I said, 'Take your four best songs and play them again.' They were amazing that night. That was the first night you knew.

Rhodes had even managed to organize gigs on four consecutive Saturday nights in October, bookended by shows at the Institute of Contemporary Art. Like the early Pistols, The Clash were sticking to art institutes and colleges in London. But times had changed and when they decided to play the University of London Union in Malet Street, a week after Leighton, they found the students in the mood to rip up cinema seats or, if none were to hand, to stomp on someone with their brothel creepers:

Mark Perry: It was extraordinary. There were no other fuckers there from the punk scene at all. It was still a bit tense with all these roughs about. I was in the dressing room and Mick had been head-butted by a Teddy boy and had a cut across his nose.

The Clash, bloodied but unbowed, returned to the ICA, where they let the Subway Sect make the first art-statement that evening, thus proving that punk's anti-rock strain was alive'n'kickin'. A stray *Melody Maker* journalist there that evening found the Sect 'so bad, so catatonically unattractive, and yet at the same time so apparently uncaring and in command, that I figured it must all be deliberate'. Indeed, it was.

Several London journalists, starved of the Pistols at the precise point awareness dawned, felt inextricably drawn to the second Clash ICA show, billed as 'A Night of Pure Energy'. *ZigZag*'s Kris Needs arrived in time to catch the Sect but dismissed them as 'a racket', even though his new friend Sid Vicious told him they were his 'favourite band ... because they're so nihilistic', a term he decided to adopt without bothering to find out what it meant. One man who knew all about nihilism was Miles, co-founder of *International Times* and a key Swinging Sixties scenester. A close friend of Caroline Coon's and early proselytizer of Patti Smith, he had returned to music journalism (for *NME*) just in time to catch The Clash (and Patti) at the ICA:

> The Clash were really good ... They are not poseurs, they are everything that *Sniffin' Glue* promised they'd be. It was as if they had crystallised the dormant energy of all the hours of crushing boredom of being an unemployed school leaver, living with your parents in a council flat, into a series of three-minute, staccato blasts, delivered like a whiplash at the audience, who were galvanized into frenzied dancing. Patti Smith was there, of course, and felt moved to climb on stage to dance.

Smith had arrived at the ICA fresh from her own gig – a triumphant sell-out at the Hammersmith Odeon, where her own onstage guest was Tapper Zukie. She had been brought to the Institute by a contingent of provincial punks, attached to Smith's support-act, The Cortinas, and anxious to show her the sound of cultures clashing.

One of these Bristolean acolytes yearned for his own pop group. Though Mark Stewart appreciated the unadulterated energy The Clash brought to the occasion, he also realized there was a lot of hectoring going on. Subway Sect, on the other hand, instantly changed Stewart's sense of what a pop group could be: 'For some reason the Subway Sect really hit a chord with me ... [because of their] really strong wall of sound and their nonchalance. When you are a kid, you notice how people stand and how people carry themselves.'

There were others at the ICA less than bowled over by Strummer's rocket-fuelled rhetoric. Without one of these there would have been no gig. John Perry had agreed to supply The Clash with The Only Ones' PA for the night, but found 'those early gigs so bad ... it wasn't possible to be enthusiastic about them'.

For Shanne Hasler, the contrast between the Pistols and The Clash was as striking as it was unsettling, 'I'd seen them all in the audience at the Pistols gigs, and I'd seen The 101'ers. It seemed funny to see them in all this gear, being a punk group.' Jordan took an even more caustic view of proceedings, 'I used to go to Clash concerts just to boo ... I hated all these old rock'n'rollers coming up and pretending they were punks ... That was the end of it.'

What The Clash needed was an audience less au fait with punk's source documents yet just as angry with the status quo. Perhaps a trip to Birmingham was in order, where a Wednesday night crowd at Barbarella's were soon won over; as was John Cooke, tape recorder in hand, and Jonh Ingham, reviewer's pen in hand. The latter, having now seen almost as many Clash gigs as Bernie Rhodes, considered it...

> The Clash's finest 45 minutes [to date] ... 'White Riot' was superb. The Clash's anthem and view of the Notting Hill Riots, it contains all The Clash's best trademarks: great hooks and chorus, a storming rhythm, and a Clash trick of everything dropping out except for Mick Jones' guitar, dropping back in two bars later ... They do [all this] with such power, speed and explosion that one assumes the lack of response from first time audiences in London is due to shock ... But in Birmingham, the audience began to applaud more and more vigorously ... It was the encore, 'I've Got A Crush On You', that clinched it.

With a fully firing Clash, it was a case of follow that. At Barbarella's, one band of local anti-heroes foolishly tried. Birmingham's answer to Slaughter & The Dogs, the Suburban Studs had shared a 100 Club bill with The Clash (and the Pistols) back in August. After further exposure to the Pistols (and The Clash) the Studs had the inspired idea of instituting a 'Punk Night at Barbarella's'. But they had not expected the same *Sounds*man who dismissed Slaughter & The Dogs to remember them from the 100 Club, or use his review to call them to account:

> [The Studs] supported the Pistols at the 100 Club during the summer, a laughable mixture of tacky jumpsuits, tacky make-up, tacky props and tacky music ... They then supported The Runaways ... [and] realized how recherché they were. Simultaneously, they

> were encouraged to check out The Clash, playing that night at the ICA [sic] … and [promptly] dropped all the make-up and props. Their hair was getting shorter. On Wednesday it took about five minutes to realize that this short-haired geezer chatting to us was actually the formerly ultra-long-haired Studs guitarist, Keef (sic). Such is progress.

In fact, the ranks of 'punk' were visibly swelling in the weeks after the Pistols' enforced abdication, as every band with even a tenuous link to them and a copy of *Raw Power* at home began to map out a path to punkdom. Bands like Eater and Slaughter & The Dogs, happy to be guilty by association if that's what it took, willingly shared bills in Manchester and London with The Damned.

On one particular November gig at Manor Hill School in Finchley, the constituency of future PM Margaret Thatcher, all three formed an unholy alliance for the night, witnessed by one appalled former acolyte:

Siouxsie Sioux: [Before] the Anarchy tour, [Eater] were doing some college dates around Ealing and Finchley, and we went to one of those, and we were looking on in horror. They were wearing these light bulbs in their ears … They looked like brickies.

The Damned seemed anxious to bring anyone into their circle of influence, even novices like The Jam whose punk status remained a tightrope walk. When booking gigs at the Nashville and the 100 Club, they were mod revivalists; when hanging out with the *Sniffin' Glue* crew and/or Shane McGowan and his girlfriend, Shanne Hasler, they were fellow punks.

It was perhaps the latter who suggested after a show upstairs at Ronnie Scott's that there was no place for an American keyboardist in an English punk band. Shanne, who was now learning to play bass in preparation for The Nipple Erectors – her and Shane's own punky outfit – had come up 'on the bus with Ray Burns; and he showed me all the Damned bass lines … We were going to see The Jam. I had this miniature bass, and Bruce Foxton broke a string, so I had to lend him this toy bass to finish the gig.'

There were now a handful of like-minded bands ready to step

into any breach at a moment's notice. When The Jam pulled out of a support slot to The Count Bishops at the 100 Club in mid-November, a band calling itself Sham 69 (as opposed to Jimmy & The Ferrets) took their place at the club and in *NME*'s review pages, where Madame Julie Burchill tried out her unformed prose style on this band who professed to be punk, but in three little words showed they were hardly of the right genus:

> Sham 69 could have got a better reception in a Chapel of Rest than in the 100 Club on Tuesday night. Fresh from the teenage wasteland of Evesham [sic], Sham 69 slashed out pure, incompetent, high voltage dole queue rock and roll to an audience of twenty, at a generous estimate … Jimmy wears a school blazer and little else. They all hate Johnny Rotten and the Pistols: 'fucking art students'.

If Jimmy Pursey was already 'dissing' the band who dissuaded him from fronting a Bay City Rollers covers band as a set of 'fucking art students', some genuine students also converted to the cause in Weybridge a year earlier were calling themselves Trash as they brought their brand of trash-rock out to suburban Surrey.

Of other outfits on the fringe of punk, The Vibrators had perhaps the most solid credentials, having supported the Pistols and Buzzcocks at the 100 Club. With energy to spare, they were natural bedfellows to The Clash (whose frontman was almost as long in the tooth as The Vibrators'). They agreed to share a bill at Fulham Town Hall the Friday after the second ICA show. And according to 'Jaws', 'You shoulda been there, [if only] to see the Sex shop underground entourage go overground.' (An unemployed Jon Savage was there, and even snuck in a cassette-recorder.)

With no Pistols performance mooted, here was a welcome excuse for a gathering of the clan. For those who couldn't make it, Giovanni Dadomo got to hail the conquering heroes with some of his usual proselytizing prose:

> Rock'n'roll devotion is exactly defined when you have to pay to get into a place like this and stick out all the sonic hassles and you still enjoy yourself. Which is what the hundred or so kids bopping frantically up-front to the sound of Clash are all about. Rock'n'roll

> devotion is what Clash vocalist Joe Strummer's all about, too. Right now he's probably the most convincing performer in the country … No shit – where other performers pose, Strummer is the very essence of the thing, at his most complete when he's actually up on the stage. Doing it. … Sure, there's still plenty of rough edges, both in the playing and equipment, and also in terms of orientation (they're definitely a post-Pistols, post-Ramones band), but even so there's something very special happening here.

For all the drum-beating the music press continued to provide, this 'very special' band was still making little impression out in pubrockland. The Clash's next powerplay was a 'bonfire night' show at another former hangout of the Pistols, the Royal College of Art, provocatively called 'A Night of Treason' on the flyers. Any art-rock was again provided by Subway Sect while the agit-rock came from Clash vocalist Strummer – aided and abetted by the Pistols' premier agitator, Sid Vicious, let off the leash for the night.

Strummer himself was revelling in all the publicity from an incident at the ICA where Shane McGowan's bloody ear lobe was bitten off in the excitement, presumably symbolizing some orgiastic response to The Clash. Never one for considering the consequences of gesture or deed, the singer decided it was time to reenact the night at the Nashville when the Pistols' frontman and his friend Sid both piled into a punter. The reaction of the students to what they considered a cacophony coming from the RCA stage now set Strummer thinking along parallel lines:

Pete Silverton: Some of the audience, when not lobbing fireworks around, take an extreme dislike to The Clash and start bunging bottles at the stage. The rest of the audience is split between Clash fans who already think their band can do no wrong and the uncommitted whose prevailing attitude is, 'Well, they are playing violent music and if you play violent, well, you know what they say about what you sow…' The band are certain how they feel about playing in a rain of bottles. Strummer lurches off stage and tries to sort out those responsible … personally.

As it happens, Strummer had form. Unlike Rotten, who preferred the verbal put-down to laying somebody out, the ex-101'er was inclined to respond to criticism with (the threat of) violence. Richard Dudanski remembers two specific incidents pre-Clash, one 'when we supported Be-Bop Deluxe at the Middlesex Poly in December '75, where Joe was at the point of jumping off the stage on to some heckler in the front rows, [but] ended up pouring a pint of bitter over him'; and 'another gig [which] almost ended up in a brawl [when] a punter [kept] insist[ing] on hearing "Route 66", which we had by then dropped.'

At the RCA Strummer was egged on by Vicious, whose period on remand after nearly blinding an innocent bystander at the Punk Festival had not served as a lesson. Standing next to Vicious was a worried Jon Savage, who noticed him straight away, 'looking like a speed demon … very leery. So I stayed out of his way. He … [then] got up on stage saying all this stuff: "Come on cunt!" and "We'll do you!"' Another attendee, Mark Perry, already knew to steer clear of Sid when he was in one of his moods: 'We knew he was a nasty git [before]. Sid was first up on the stage, [going,] "C'mon, I'll have all of you."'

Predictably, Vicious's bravado only made things worse. When another bottle sailed his way Strummer jumped down into the audience. Not for the last time, he picked out the wrong target for his (self-)righteous wrath, signing the death-warrant on a potential major-label record deal into the bargain:

Chris Parry: [A bottle] almost took [Strummer's] head off. He was really angry, and … he came running down right by where [Polydor A&R director] Jim Crook was, and obviously thought Jim had thrown it … Jim said, 'If you think I'm signing *that* fucking band, you've got another thing coming.' And he walked out.

Parry, still licking metaphorical wounds from his recent dealings with McLaren, had turned his gaze in the direction of The Clash after taking soundings from the new spokesman of all things worth a sniff, Mark Perry, who found himself 'facing up to [these bands] signing up to labels and [so] we had to have an opinion. Chris Parry [kept] asking me, "Who's the best band to sign, Mark?" doing his job as an A&R man.'

For the past few days, Parry had been pushing his immediate boss to let him take The Clash into the studio. He had just gotten the green light when Strummer decided to fight unfriendly fire with his fists. Hoping against hope, Parry contacted Guy Stevens, the former producer of Free and Mott The Hoople and all-round rock & roll maniac, to see if he would agree to record some Clash demos in-house. He leapt at the chance.

For Mick Jones, who grew up mad for Mott, it was a dream come true, 'It was great recording with Guy … He was really inciting us.' But when they started mixing the five songs Guy recorded in a single afternoon – 'Career Opportunities', 'White Riot', 'Janie Jones', 'London's Burning' and '1977' – even Jones had to admit it sounded 'a bit untogether'. Clash roadie Roadent, felt it 'didn't really capture the madness of The Clash. It was really flat, there was no dynamic in it. It was dead.' Naturally, this had to be down to Stevens, rather than the band. Strummer certainly placed the blame squarely on Stevens' shoulders: 'Guy was drinking a lot at this time … We had a very energetic unit but somehow it sounded … dull. I think Guy wasn't up to scratch.'

In truth, a stone-cold sober Stevens couldn't have resurrected these demos because all the structural deficiencies of their songs – even the cream of the crop – were stripped bare in the studio, along with Simonon's bob-bob-bob bass-playing. Some lead guitar parts from Jones wouldn't have gone amiss, either. But what was really needed were arrangements that made these songs leap off a record like Strummer leapt off the RCA stage. Only then would record companies come a-knockin' at Bernie's door.

* * *

A month earlier, Buzzcocks demonstrated how one could produce incendiary demos without a name producer and with a no-name engineer, if one carefully crafted arrangements during rehearsals. For them, the demo session on October 18th was the culmination of weeks spent rehearsing at a church youth club in Salford, St Boniface's, until they had an album's worth of material ready to record, even if at least half of it was unsuitable for pre-pubescents:

Steve Diggle: We'd agreed to play a free gig for the St. Boniface's Church youth club, by way of appreciation for all the rehearsal time they'd given us. What we didn't know was the average age of the kids that used the club was roughly eight … 'Orgasm Addict' was obviously out of the question as was 'Peking Hooligan', 'Love Battery', and as for 'Oh Shit', … I think we were down to about six numbers by the time we worked out a suitable set-list.

The eleven songs captured in a single afternoon at the four-track Revolution Studios comprised almost the entire live set, recorded with nary a pause, a smattering of feedback and their new, defining anthem ('Boredom'). They just failed to leave enough time to capture 'Peking Hooligan'. According to Richard Boon, engineer Andy McPherson 'didn't get it at all. It was like, "Is that the take then?"' But the object of the exercise, as Boon suggests, was simply to provide 'a report from up north … We ran off some cassettes – some … with xeroxed newsprint lyrics – and sent them out.'[46]

(At least one of these cassettes ended up in the wrong hands because within a couple of years it was being pressed up as the fabled *Time's Up* bootleg, enforcing the growing view that Buzzcocks Mk. 1 might have been punk's original unfired weapon. Combining elements of auto-destruction, a Velvet white-noise aesthetic, lyrics that lifted the lid on mid-seventies suburbia and Shelley's pure pop sensibility, it was the perfect companion piece to *Spunk*.)

For Devoto, it already felt a little too frenetic: 'There were bits that were a bit shambolic in a way that wasn't quite pleasing.' But this was something they could correct next time – assuming there was a next time. For now, their primary concern remained finding a Mancunian home for their buzzsaw ballads, which was proving an uphill battle. If London was now alive with opportunity, in Manchester the gulf between pubs and The Palace was a great big void.

Having played no gigs in the month since the kids' party, they agreed to another party – *in a pub!* – just for the opportunity to play. A first anniversary party for the city's 'what's up' weekly, the *New Manchester Review*, was being held at Band On The Wall, so former

[46] The 2000 CD reissue of *Time's Up* includes reproductions of these xeroxed lyrics along with other period ephemera in an expanded booklet.

NMR columnist Howard Trafford turned his personal invite into an eight-song Buzzcocks set. It was to serve as another warm-up set for a grander affair – or so they hoped, when two nights later punk came to the Electric Circus for the first time:

Richard Boon: There was a venue called the Electric Circus, which at weekends was heavy metal, and a shit-hole, but was quiet in the week. We went along [and said], 'This is a quiet night. We'll hire it. You'll get the bar. We'll get the door.' … There was an urgency about making something happen. [So] we … brought up Chelsea … Very few people came but interested people came, and interesting people came. I was doing the door for the gig. This guy came up, 'I've just come back from the Mont-de-Marsan festival.' That was Ian Curtis – he [said he] was into Iggy and bits of Krautrock.

The addition of the newly-formed Chelsea – playing their third gig in as many weeks – was an attempt to solidify the bond between Manchester and London punk, and to make this night at the Circus more of an occasion. Chelsea were the product of two distinct 'want ads' in *Melody Maker*: one placed by Tony James, who sought 'a guitarist into The Small Faces, The Who'. It introduced Billy Idol to James. The other ad was placed by Gene October, looking for 'musicians … into Television and the Ramones', which brought Idol and James into the Chelsea fold.

Yet the only information that anyone 'up north' had about Chelsea was a couple of references to a band of that name in *NME's* review of another ICA art-rock project, five days before The Clash crashed the party with pure energy. This October 18th ICA show was called Prostitution, and marked the debut of Throbbing Gristle and the public debut of Chelsea – although a thirty-minute set at the Chelsea Potter pub a couple of days earlier was the latter combo's first, unedifying contact with a 'semi-drunken' audience. According to Idol, they 'leered at us, and we leered right back'.

Genesis P. Orridge, the man sinking his teeth into the Gristle concept, didn't like the name Chelsea and billed them as LSD, intending his own TG performance-piece – part-porn, part-Prog – to drive the last nail into rock's coffin. But more folk had seemingly come to see Chelsea than his girlfriend Cossi's delightful fanny. When Tony Parsons arrived, pass in hand, he was quickly put right by Idol's suburban friends:

> I went back … to check out why so many kids decked out in punk outfits had come along to the ICA tonight. Surely they weren't interested in all this, uh, culture? 'Nah, mate,' one of them told me while adjusting the safety pin in his carefully ripped t-shirt. 'We've come to see Chelsea. They're on after the stripper.' But LSD are on after the stripper. 'Yeah, they're billed as LSD, but their real name's Chelsea. Got a great guitarist, they have. Good as Wilko, he is.' … By the end of their first number it's evident that they're coming from the same direction as the Pistols, Damned and The Clash … A good set of 1977 dole queue rock, only two of the numbers not written by the band … Billy the bass player [sic] tells me after the gig, 'We've known the Pistols for years.'

If TG would remain a throbbing presence on the periphery of punk, Bromley Billy and Mr James set their controls for the heart of punk. Initial reviews suggested they might get there with Chelsea. The group van taking the road to Manchester not only contained Siouxsie and Steve, taking a break from rehearsing another set of Banshees, but also Mark Perry, whom 'they were trying to get to write about the show'. Mark P duly penned the requisite puff-piece praising these men of good fortune, having learnt from Coon the importance of being earnest about the punk movement:

> I got a great feeling when seeing Chelsea for the first time. Before the gig (at Manchester's Electric Circus) I expected to see another bunch of Pistol/Clash imitators but of course I was wrong. They've got a whole different approach to their audience than most of the new wave. Aggression is definitely not the key word for the Chelsea guys. They want to play their music and they hope that people get something out of it … They're definitely gonna break new ground … [Billy] was one of the Bromley Contingent, but although he really likes the Pistols he has got a complete style of his own.

But barely had Chelsea established some brand-recognition when the guitarist, bassist and drummer decided they didn't like the name, the singer or their manager. Just eleven days after Mancunians got a taste of Chelsea, the short-lived outfit played their final gig at the Nashville, Billy Idol taking over on vocals for a frantic encore that served to announce the birth of Generation X.

Perry was not convinced it was the right career-move, 'I thought Gene October was a great frontman. I was never completely convinced by Generation X. I would have been quite happy for Chelsea to continue with Gene singing, and Billy and Tony writing the same songs.' But ambition was already a corrosive factor in the corridors of Chelsea. Meanwhile, Paul Morley sought to make amends for previously missing the point, writing a glowing *NME* review of Buzzcocks and a damning view of the city's response to the first punk night at the Electric Circus:

> Hey, I saw Buzzcocks a couple of times last week … They've [now] caught perfectly the groove that separates precision from chaos … coherently fusing the two hundred second pop concept with their own instinctive, distinctive idiomatic syntheses … They transcend the essentially orthodox energy adherence of the other new bands. They're trying to make accessible the avant-garde excursions of such as Beefheart, Ono, even Coleman, using at present a straight guitar/ bass/ drum/ voice line-up … They're producing the most significant musical output of any new British rock band … The demoralising aspect is that no one seems to give a damn. Punters don't care, demanding familiarity to a nauseating extent … And when the gigs do come, faulty sound equipment invariably results in the band not achieving the kind of sound they wanna for the few who 'know' and who turn up.

For many who remained stuck miles from nowhere, and preferred something solidly black to purple prose, punk was still off the Rock radar. For these potential provincial punks, the release of 'New Rose' meant they could stop guessing what punk sounded like. The Damned 45 thus caused more of a stir than all the reports The Clash and Buzzcocks garnered in places where punk was still a word with coal-black connotations.

The week Stiff Records released Britain's first punk-nugget, on October 22nd, they were rewarded for their foresight with Single of

The Week in *Sounds*, an enthused Ingham suggesting that the seven-incher was 'just the thing if your copy of *Raw Power* has worn out … [being] so hot, it's a wonder the vinyl doesn't melt'.

That week's *Sounds* also featured a page-two news story on the 'first punx on wax', and two contrasting reviews of the band in performance, one from a letter-writer in Luton who caught them at The White Swan on October 8th and felt he could 'honestly say I have never seen or heard such a load of shit in my life. The band came on, did four (pathetic) numbers, then one of the amps went up the shoot. About half hour later they performed the same four numbers all over again, followed by two more crap pieces and that was it.'

If they had unwittingly offended the Luton letter-writer, there were times when The Damned set out to alienate even their allies. At a headlining gig in High Wycombe six days later it was the Captain who drew battlelines, not the audience. Even knowing Jonh Ingham was in the crowd, and likely to write a review, did not dissuade an insensible Sensible from letting rip in a thoroughly obnoxious manner:

> The Damned never do something simply if it can be accomplished with a grand gesture. They don't ask for a beer, they scream for a blankety-blank beer. They don't tell the beard'n'denim set they're antiquated or silly looking, they scream the most abusive sewage they can dredge up … [And] at the Nag's Head last Thursday they continued on long after they had driven the objects of their contempt from the room … As one of the thirty or so people left enjoying the music, the invective got a bit tiring.

No one is sure quite why Captain Sensible singled out that night's audience, although Scabies recalls 'there were a lot of hippies [there], and [so] the Captain refused to play if there was anyone with facial hair in the audience. His tirade was so abusive that he drove the entire audience out.' Coming from a man still wearing a bomber jacket and jeans, it suggested he thought bullying those who didn't share his passion for speed was a way to assert punk credentials. But speed was no substitute for chops.

The Tuesday after Ingham's review ran, The Damned were

booked to support Graham Parker & The Rumour at the capacious Victoria Palace, and even they knew that the Rumour were no slouches when it came to turning up the heat. Warming up a crowd this large was something new for The Damned but, according to Nick Kent, they breezed it, 'The sound they achieved at the Victoria Palace was the best I've heard from them so far, and I foresee them having little difficulty adjusting to larger stages.' The headliner, though, was underwhelmed:

Graham Parker: I saw The Damned and I thought they were like a figment of the Woodstock Generation's acid trip. They were like a bad flash. They've got energy and youth and believe in what they're doing, but I don't think they're doing anything musically at all.

The Damned, having bought into the Year Zero idea hook, line and barre chord, were convinced 'no respect for one's elders' extended to those who laid the groundwork for garage bands like them – like McLaren's beloved Flamin' Groovies. The day after the Electric Circus welcomed its first punks, The Damned began what was supposed to be a joint Damned/Groovies national tour in Redcar – providing the same supporting role to the Groovies' retro-rock as the Ramones did at the Roundhouse.

If the Redcar audience divided its loyalties, The Damned were secretly delighted to find many Teeside kids were there to join *their* gang. The Groovies, who had made London their base in Britain, still didn't understand life in the provinces and Redcar was pure culture-shock:

Brian James: The Flamin' Groovies couldn't understand us. [It was, like,] 'What's all this thing with people spitting.' They were still dressed up in collarless suits. People in places like Middlesbrough [sic] wanted to see us. There was definitely a lot of [punk] attitude in the audience.

For the Groovies a tour with The Damned was a tour too far. Already riven by internal divisions, and one genuinely sick guitarist in bed, the Groovies left the tour after gig one never to return.

Perhaps the prospect of successive shows at Eric's and Barbarella's, two venues where punk already had a foothold, was the last straw.

After the next two shows were cancelled, The Damned found themselves at Chalk Farm's Roundhouse waiting for the Groovies – and their tour PA – to show up.[47] When they were still marked absent at eight pm, The Damned and The Troggs – a late addition who had a solid claim to be *the* original punk band – found a replacement PA, dropped the admission price, and went on with the show anyway.

At the same time, The Damned's spokesman decided to inform the music papers, 'We agreed to play the tour to give some modern credibility to it. But we are not interested now in supporting or bailing out living legends.' When the Groovies' Chris Wilson retorted by describing The Damned as 'the worst musicians we've ever played with', The Damned wore that epithet with pride.

Such acrimony aside, The Damned had been left well and truly in the lurch. They had a single in the shops, glowing reviews in the three main music papers but no means of promoting themselves. Three hastily rescheduled dates at Eric's, Teeside Polytechnic (presumably in reaction to Redcar) and the Electric Circus provided some faint momentum in the weeks leading up to their first John Peel session (which served as an on-air preview to their next A-side, 'Neat Neat Neat').

It was not enough, especially when their favourite music paper turned on them, sending the non-believer Ralph Whaley to Liverpool's Eric's for an on-the-road report that concluded, 'The Damned are a bunch of nobodies. They make a loud noise and expect us to pay our quids to watch them produce said din.'

When salvation came, it was from an entirely unexpected quarter. McLaren was inviting them to join the Sex Pistols on the package-tour to end all package tours – Anarchy In The UK. Perhaps they were being welcomed back into the fold. With The Clash also conscripted, could such a package tour yet be a movement?

[47] It is unclear whether The Damned played either of the two shows scheduled between Redcar and the Roundhouse, but it seems highly unlikely.

★ ★ ★

Actually, The Damned were assuredly *not* McLaren's first choice for companions on the road. While the Pistols took a well-earned rest during the first fortnight of November, the papers were filled with reports of a special one-off gig at The Talk of The Town with the Ramones and the wholly unproven Siouxsie & The Banshees Mk.2. Such a homecoming was intended as a prelude to a tour in which the only authentic English punk band billed would be the Pistols themselves. Support would be provided by a Chris Spedding-fronted Vibrators, and two Sire acts, Ramones and Talking Heads.

What all these bands had in common was not musical ideology but rather label-support. McLaren wasn't planning on picking up the tab for the whole travelling circus, despite having the smarts to include tour-support in the EMI contract. But when Phonogram – the UK distributors of Sire Records – proved unwilling to pay their way, the whole tour collapsed around McLaren's revolutionary head.

He promptly laid the blame squarely at the attention-seeking door of the Ramones' manager Danny Fields, 'The Ramones felt they weren't getting any publicity, but that's not my fault. Anyway, if the Pistols were touring America with the Ramones and we only got one line I wouldn't blow the whole thing out.'

With 'Anarchy In The UK' finally due out on November 26th, the manager was fast running out of viable alternatives. As a result he was forced to hastily construct a support bill comprising two wholly unsigned acts, The Clash and The Heartbreakers (Johnny Thunders' all-American band of full-time junkies), plus The Damned, whose indie label operated on a shoestring and a prayer. What has been widely viewed as a gesture of punk solidarity on McLaren's part was in fact a last-ditch response to being left in the lurch by the Bowery's most regular dance-partners.

Meanwhile, it seemed EMI had got their way – a polished, poppier version of 'Anarchy', courtesy of Chris Thomas. McLaren had expected more of Thomas, whom he had once put forward as a possible producer of the New York Dolls' aborted third album. But Thomas was his own man, and although McLaren suggested using Goodman's finished version as a guide, he ignored the instruction:

Chris Thomas: I certainly didn't refer to [Goodman's] version particularly. It was quite the reverse. The crime that I committed – that I got slagged off for quite a lot – was introduc[ing] them to the world of overdubbing loads of guitars. I came up with all these extra bits, like having the feedback running through the last verse.

Actually, 'the feedback running through the last verse' was Goodman's idea, except on his version it was sustained right up until the song buried itself in a tidal rush of distortion. But the Pistols themselves seemed perfectly happy with the results. It was only Goodman and McLaren who felt Thomas's take lacked ingredient X.[48]

A sanguine McLaren later confided in Richard Boon that he 'didn't really like Chris Thomas's hard rock thing, but it had to be that way for radio. He preferred the more shambolic chaos. He used to "dis" [the Thomas recording], "It sounds too polished." His smartest move was putting "I Wanna Be Me" on the B-side.' Both Boon and McLaren recognized the July demo as the real Pistols.

Almost as commercially palatable as the EMI 'Anarchy' was the performance the Pistols gave on BBC1's *Nationwide*, the week before its scheduled release. If it wasn't for the still-visceral shock the sight of Johnny Rotten on TV in ten million homes at teatime provided, one could almost believe they were just another Eddie & The Hot Rods. Thankfully, the performance they gave to an entirely different TV crew four days later, at the Notre Dame Hall, was everything the *Nationwide* runthrough was not; and *Sniffin' Glue*'s founder, for one, breathed a huge sigh of relief as he sat down to pen another glowing review:

> It was their first London gig for over a month. Some of it was filmed for TV. The Pistols were great. After a month of recording and rehearsing they were as solid as a rock. A short set was done for the cameras and they came back to play a 'real' set for the fans. Rotten was fantastic. He was breaking all the rules. What other guy would

[48]Jonh Ingham evidently agreed with McLaren, querying the sound of the single in his *Sounds* review: 'Pistols fans, I suspect, will be surprised (disappointed?) that the record isn't faster and nastier. It's just a little too smoothly produced by Chris Thomas.'

> just stand stage-centre after the set and clap for an encore with the crowd. He was saying how he wanted rock to be. No rock'n'roll cliche for him.

For much of the invited audience this word-of-mouth show was a much-needed homecoming. But for those – like Shane McGowan, Shanne Hasler, Keith Levene, Poly Styrene, Siouxsie Sioux, Steve Severin and TV Smith – now actively refining their own punk templates, it seemed more like a swansong.

Severin certainly takes the view it 'was the end of it all – that was where every suburban kid turned up in a plastic bin liner and jumped about because they thought they were supposed to … Me and Siouxsie just stood at the back and said, "It's all over."' Mark P also 'didn't see where it could go', despite feeling 'at the time [that] the Notre Dame was the best I ever saw them'.

The Pistols' pugnacious frontman was delighted to be back on the boards, Rotten quipping at the very start, 'Got boring since we've been away, hasn't it!' With all of The Clash – and their new producer, Guy Stevens – in attendance, all four Pistols were determined to put clear blue water between them and their brazenly competitive co-conspirators.

The London Weekend cameras stuck around long enough to capture 'Anarchy In The UK', 'Pretty Vacant' and a glorious 'No Fun'; but it was after they stopped rolling film that the fun really started, with the Pistols pulling out old chestnuts like 'Whatcha Gonna Do About It' and 'Did You No Wrong' as if they could somehow sense that this might be their last London show for three decades.

Almost the only song that didn't appear in the fifteen-song set was a new one they had been working on in rehearsals, 'No Future'. It was a song title that been hanging around for a while, but only now did Rotten conceive the notion it could be an alternative national anthem, even using the same opening line, 'God save the Queen'.

One can only wonder what LWT's Janet Street-Porter would have made of the song had she captured it spewing out of Finchley's least favourite hunchback at Notre Dame. Instead, she sliced up the three songs her crew had shot and intercut them with her interviews of the Pistols, The Clash and Siouxsie for a half-hour *London Weekend Show* on the new punk-rock phenomenon, aired the last weekend in November.

The Pistols bided their time, unveiling their version of 'God Save The Queen' at Hendon Polytechnic four days later at a show attended by Wire's future frontman and Subway Sect's current frontman. The crowd's reaction to this splenetic sonic screed made it seem like old times:

Colin Newman: The weirdest place I saw them was Hendon Poly. All I remember is that it was Us and Them. There were all these rugby types who hated them. They were hilariously funny, shouting at you from the stage, and they had a whole batch of the audience who looked a bit like them … [But I wondered,] 'Why are those people getting so pissed off at them?' … There was something really fantastic about the deconstruction of rock music.

Vic Godard: I liked 'God Save The Queen'. I remember the first time they did that on stage … in Hendon, and he was reading the words off a sheet of paper. It was pretty shambolic, they'd obviously only just worked the song out. It was [just] a riff with John singing over it.

If the gig was slightly shambolic, the aftermath was 'mayhem'. Goodman remembered 'the bouncers on the door threw a load of yobs out and refused entry to a load more'. But the yobs then returned with their hairy mates, and this time they would not be denied entry. For the Pistols, it was a case of exit, pursued by bears in rugby shirts. At least they had reestablished their live credentials, even if – for the very first time – they were looking over their shoulders.

Just the day before, The Clash had booked themselves a night at the Nag's Head, where they drove any memory of The Damned's bad manners from the minds of the few who managed, in the words of Kris Needs, to 'tear themselves away from Miss World to catch them … Strummer was [particularly] magnificent, screaming his words and punching the silly low ceiling in front of the stage with rage'. Needs, who had known Mick Jones since they both ran with the Mott crowd at the height of glam, was another critic reluctant to criticize The Clash with his pen.

The final sentence of Needs' *Sounds* review, which ran the week before The Clash were due to join the Pistols – and The Damned – on tour, consciously sent a shot across the bows of the other bands, informing all would-be punks to mark a date in their December diaries: 'They may be bottom of the bill on the forthcoming Sex Pistols tour but make sure you get there really early – even if it means ducking out to wash your hair during The Damned.'

If the Pistols did not yet know what they were up against, they found out when it was too late to remove The Clash from the finalized tour-bill: at a joint Lanchester Polytechnic gig on November 29th; four days from blast off.

Both bands had been sent to Coventry to test the PA they were taking on tour. While The Clash had become progressively more frenetic and hard-edged in the past six weeks, the Pistols had seemingly decided to rekindle their former gift for student confrontation in preparation for a tour that seemed to have an awful lot of dates in the halls of higher education.

A snap-happy fan remembers the dramatic contrast in styles: the speed-merchants whose harangues flew by in a flash, versus punk's original performance-artists challenging all-comers, verbally and musically. For now, the Pistols remained the champions of order-from-chaos-from-order, but only just:

Ben Browton: First on stage were The Clash, who performed their set at breakneck speed with hardly a pause between songs – they were a jangling, urgent, colourful, electric blur of anger, with Joe Strummer spitting out his shards of venomous diatribe over a wall of cacophonic metal. With scarcely a pause for breath, the Sex Pistols then shambled laconically on stage, led by Rotten in a magnificent rubber top, spiked orange hair and with cigarette burns on his arms. The Pistols set was less urgent than The Clash, and they regularly took long ironic breaks between songs, tuning up/tuning down their instruments, during which time a bug-eyed confrontational Rotten would harangue the audience with taunts like 'We know you love it!'

Such was The Clash's 'electric blur' that the student committee decided, on the basis of exactly two intelligible words, that their opening song, 'White Riot', was racist. They refused to pay either act. When it was made crystal clear that if they wanted the poly to still be standing in the morning they had better pay up, they changed their minds, but it seemed controversy and punk were by now constant bedfellows.

Two days later, at teatime, the Pistols were once again ushered into the living rooms of those hard-working Londoners glued to their TV sets, and this time they were goaded into using the language of the street in the homes of those enduring lives of quiet desperation. This was simply not done.

When Bill Grundy got a mumbled 'shit', a 'dirty bastard', a 'dirty fucker' and a 'fucking rotter' out of the working-class lads, the band who had made England rock again that summer found themselves facing a winter tour of discontent beset on every side by snipers. What had been a youth revolution of the head, set to a raucous (anti-) rock soundtrack, was now sifted through the gutter press and came out reading like the most serious threat to the English way of life since Neville Chamberlain's hollow promise of 'peace in our time'.

As for the Pistols, they were now Public Enemy No. 1. When the *Daily Mirror* labelled their performance on the Bill Grundy show, 'The Filth & The Fury', the paper cared little that the Pistols had already sussed them out on their latest B-side, 'You wanna be someone, ruin someone … you wanna ruin me.' It was time the tabloid nation rose up against their own. The last song the Pistols had penned in Year Zero was about to prove prophetic. Rotten had meant it when he sang, 'No future for you.' But it soon became clear there was no future for them, either.

7. THE CIRCUS COMES TO TOWN (B'DUM, B'DUM)

[December 1976]

7

We were sure that they would have bleeped it. Even though we were young then, it seemed obvious to us that they'd have a ten second delay or something. Then we went up to the Hope and Anchor, and people were talking about it up there as well. We couldn't believe it. That's when I realized that it had all gone out.

– Simon Barker, to Jon Savage

Everyone was really excited [about the tour]... but the day before it started, the Grundy thing went down ... The Pistols suffered quite terribly, it was really tragic, but we learnt so much from it.

– Mick Jones,* ZigZag, *June 1977

From that day on, it was different. Before then, it was just music.

– Steve Jones, 1986

Had The Sex Pistols been a play, the show could have gone on. The tabloid-generated post-Grundy outrage might even have sold a few extra tickets. Because as of September 1968 the Lord Chamberlain's censorious 231-year reign over English theatre had ceased. For the first time, the stage was a world which could encompass outlandish fashions, dirty old men and uttered profanities. Real life. When it came to music venues though, control still resided with the local councils and the councils were, and are, run by political animals. As a result, the councillors played to the gallery, and the Pistols played to (almost) no one.

Even when a college or university overrode the council's wishes – as they at least could – health and safety laws could be invoked to stop the Anarchy tour bus in its tracks. Which is precisely what happened on the opening night of the tour in Norwich, two days after Grundy. Even a threatened sit-in by the students of the University of East Anglia failed to get the gig reinstated, and the four bands had little option but to set the tour bus in the direction of Derby, the next scheduled gig.

One would like to think as all four Pistols sat in the back of the bus, idling outside Denmark Street that afternoon, waiting for their manager to get a straight answer out of the vice-chancellor of the University of East Anglia, that they caught sight of another band wheeling its equipment into the St Martin's School of Art. It was a year and 27 days since the Pistols played fast and loose with these very art students. Well, tonight – December 3rd, 1976 – one of the bands they had wittingly inspired were playing the same basement bar, to pretty much the same reception.

It was Wire's second gig; and as Pistols convert Graham Lewis recalls, 'They pulled the plugs on us after twenty minutes. Very abusive art students. Punk had now become an issue.' Though bands like Bazooka Joe were dust, fellow Wireman Bruce Gilbert was astounded to discover the St Martin's students 'were still expecting pub rock'.

Wire had unashamedly come to bury such old-school rock. If the five-piece Wire sounded nothing like the Pistols – or the four-piece Wire, who would go on to make a trio of remarkable punk and post-punk statements – they had certainly gleaned from their peer-leaders the art of confrontation.

Other musicians were left non-plussed. The night before, Wire had made their live debut at the Nashville – the locale of another infamous Pistols kerfuffle. Headliners The Derelicts came up afterwards to inform Wire they were 'the death-throes of cock-rock', after which, as Lewis dryly observes, 'They went on to play "Johnny B. Goode" and "Little Queenie" … We thought, "Too fucking right, we've got a bloody right to be there." At least we were trying to do something that nobody else was doing.'

For now, Wire had a frontman who made the pre-Nashville Rotten seem like a veritable wallflower. George Gill thought Wire were *his* band, and he brooked no argument. At the Nashville – according to drummer Robert Gotobed – 'He shouted at someone sitting near the stage, "What are you looking at? Go back to your beer!" George had this aggressive approach. At one point he threw his guitar back into the dressing room, off the stage.'

At their third gig, at the RCA, Gill's aggression was matched by at least one audience member, Shane McGowan, who, according to Colin Newman, 'smashed up a chair … [which] was meant to be telling us how good we were – because, obviously, that's what you do'. Wire were living proof, were it needed, that the punk parasite was fast invading the body politic of rock, and no amount of censorship could cure this disease of the soul.

While the Pistols, The Clash and friends were away ostensibly spreading Anarchy through the provinces, three notable new bands – Wire, Generation X and Siouxsie & The Banshees – came out to play. With a plethora of gigging possibilities unavailable a year earlier – one unexpected by-product of the Pistols' trail-blazing – the capital's punks were determined to seize the day.

Peter Perrett: [The Pistols] just changed the whole business of music. As a musician trying to make music in the London environment there was definitely a feeling it had been opened up – [just by] the fact that they were able to do more gigs after the initial ones.

Marco Pirroni: It opened up. [Before that,] nobody knew how to get a gig, you'd have to play a pub, you'd have to get an agent. Suddenly [it was like], 'I might as well ask the guy at the 100 Club. See if he'll give us a gig.'

One could even get up and play at someone else's gig. One edgy new band on the outer circle of punk, having been in rehearsals since August, decided to announce their existence with a party at their rehearsal studio, a la The Clash. The Only Ones, about to burst upon the scene with their own anthems for the new age, wanted a trial-by-friends before they made their full-frontal assault on modernity. That invited audience included Vivienne Westwood and, at her instigation, elements of the Bromley Contingent – some with a yen to play:

Peter Perrett: In December '76 we thought we'd play in front of an invited audience at the rehearsal studio in Lots Road ... It was in a basement, and we invited lots of friends that we knew, and we invited Vivienne, and Vivienne brought Siouxsie and Billy Idol and lots of her friends ... It was like the end of us rehearsing. We rehearsed solidly from August 13th, when we found Alan [Mair]. Zena put on food and stuff, and that was the first time Generation X played in front of an audience, with Billy Idol playing guitar and singing ... After our set they said, 'Is it alright if we have a go?' We just said yeah. It was a three-piece – they said, 'We don't need no lead guitarist.'

Idol was now unquestionably the frontman for this trio formed out of Chelsea's rump, but whatever his protestations to Perrett, Generation X needed a lead guitarist and their formal unveiling would have to wait.

Siouxsie, Steve and Simone were also in rehearsals, with Kenny Morris and Pete Fenton providing them with new found musicality. Performance art was out, pioneering punk rock was in. Siouxsie herself had made front-page news as the punkette Grundy tried to 'hit on' live on teatime TV, prompting the undeleted expletives fired his way by the Pistols' own sex addict.

⋆ ⋆ ⋆

If London was in musical ferment thanks to the Pistols' former deeds, the rest of the country was in tumult because these 'foul-mouthed yobs' were coming to their town. Not if its tabloid readers could help it, they weren't! The following night's gig in Newcastle had already been cancelled when the Pistols, The Heartbreakers, The Damned and The Clash rolled into Derby on December 4th, where a standoff with the councillors fast assumed comic proportions. The councillors had refused to allow the Pistols to play unless they allowed their music to be vetted first by a lot of people dead from the neck up.

McLaren never had any intention of kowtowing to the burghers of Derby but rather than telling them where to go – which he knew would afford them the moral high ground in tomorrow's tabloids – he ensured the councillors wasted their afternoon waiting for the band to arrive. He set the bus for Leeds – the fourth scheduled show, but the first one actually confirmed – while the councillors cooled their heels.

By the time they arrived in Leeds for a gig at the polytechnic on the sixth, there was already dissension in the ranks. The Damned had decided to travel separately from the rest – mainly to ensure that they didn't have to account to McLaren for their tour expenses – so had turned up at Derby's King's Hall all ready to play, a gesture which played right into McLaren's hands.

Whether they knew it or not, The Damned were already on the way out. Scabies takes the view, 'They did the Grundy show – and didn't need us anymore. And Malcolm knew it.' In truth, his former friend never really liked Miller's crew or considered them of the same genus. So any excuse would do.

Matlock remembers, 'At Leeds Poly, even before The Damned started playing, Malcolm was going, "Oh, I dunno, what do you think? I think they're bringing the whole thing down."' Even the nominal outsiders on the tour, Noo Yawk's Heartbreakers, quickly learnt to disregard The Damned. Heartbreakers guitarist Walter Lure noticing their absence from the off, 'They're not on the bus with us, so all the other guys are talking about them.'

Punk's first package tour, of necessity, closed ranks with The Damned on the outside looking in. When Peter Lloyd turned up in Leeds to see the Pistols, he remembers 'walk[ing] into the gig with Johnny, and he whispered in my ear, "The Damned are over there. Just ignore them." I had already had a lecture from Bernie Rhodes in one of the hotel rooms – the punk manifesto, for Christ's sake.' Lloyd had already found the 'people at work [had] stopped talking to me', but having decided to oversee Penetration's punk passion play, he cared not a jot. He was in Leeds to jot down one last set of notes.

At least Leeds Polytechnic's students union – in the teeth of their vice-chancellor's visible discomfort at his own impotence – were giving all four bands an opportunity to play. There was also a much larger turnout than Fforde Grene in September – even if, as Matlock asserts, 'most of the kids had come out of prurient interest, generated by the Grundy thing.' And those who did have a genuine interest were generally too scared to express themselves, as one Leeds University art student with a desire to hit things recalls:

Hugo Burnham: A lot of people were too frightened to [even] go … There was clearly a lot of off-duty police there. One kid started jumping up and down, pogoing, and these two geezers in plain clothes, the coshes were out. And we were all going, 'Fucking 'ell, I'm not gonna dance too much.' We thought we were gonna get thumped, jumped on, something's gonna go off. It was unbelievably tense – and exciting … We wanted to cheer and go mad, but it was just like, we gotta be careful.

Burnham was in a gang of three with fellow Gang of Four founder, Jon King, and future Mekon Andy Corrigan, who attracted the attention of *Yorkshire Post* photographer Steve Riding because, as Burnham recalls, he 'had a razor blade hanging out of his ear'. The reluctant Riding had been sent to snap the band/s, but seeing as 'everybody [was] jumping up and down, spitting and throwing beer and generally causing mayhem', he stayed well back – as did all the other pressmen waiting to see the Pistols get their comeuppance. At the front of the queue (but the back of the hall) was their old friend, James Johnson, whose *Evening Standard* review ran under a four-word headline, 'Sex Pistols Insult Queen', that betrayed his usual disregard for factual accuracy:

> The promise to cut out drinking and swearing quickly disintegrated when Britain's most notorious group, the Sex Pistols, were allowed to play on-stage for the first time since their controversial four-letter-word appearance on television. It was too much for some of the students at the Leeds Polytechnic gig. They walked out claiming the music was 'rubbish' and 'too crude' … As soon as the Sex Pistols hit the stage it was obvious they were determined to live up to their crude and belligerent image: 'The first number is dedicated to Bill Grundy and the Queen. It goes, Fuck ya.'

Once again, Johnson witnessed a Pistols show wholly different to the one some posterity-conscious soul taped. But this time he had travel companions to fantasyland. *Record Mirror* – the sorry excuse for a music weekly no one with pubic hair read – sent Steve Kendall who affirmed, 'They kicked off with a swipe at Bill Grundy and the

Queen, and then they broke their manager's orders [sic] by using a string of obscenities. Their music was predictably loud and crude, but alas it was also … relentless and unimaginative. When the group waited among cat-calls to do an encore, Rotten turned upon his fans and snarled, "Has the council banned you from clapping? If you don't like us, you know where the exit is!" … Scores of fans walked out, [while] … Rotten yelled at those who remained, "You're just a load of dummies."'

Rotten was actually revelling in the experience, loving every moment. He was back in his element, displaying his greatest gift as a performer – a streak of courage a mile wide. It was just like old times. According to filmmaker Julien Temple, there at McLaren's invitation, film-camera in hand, the reaction was almost medieval, 'When Rotten finally came out on the stage, it was like Agincourt. There were these massed volleys of gob flying through the air.' Photos from the poly bear out Temple's cinematic recollection, as do the reports of at least three music journalists sent there because their editors knew there was gonna be a showdown.

To a rookie like John Shearlaw (from the newly-formed *National Rockstar*), Rotten was just riveting, 'He crouched and sprang up. He stared at the cameras, at the audience. He sang with the frenzy of a committed rebel. It was brilliant … [But] the audience didn't know what to expect and weren't ready to accept what they got.' (Hence, Rotten's ad-libbed but heartfelt, 'Fuck you all!' in the middle of the final song that evening, 'Problems'.)

Caroline Coon also realized that, unlike Henry V, he was fighting a losing battle: 'Although the Sex Pistols are playing with the flood-gate release of frustration you'd expect from musicians locked in hotel bedrooms escaping the national press for four days, it takes Johnny a whole set to allay the audience's suspicion of him.'

The fullest account of proceedings, though, would come from *NME*'s Tony Parsons, the male half of the Tweedle Dee & Tweedle Dum of new wave journalism:

> The Pistols come on stage at Leeds Poly to a smattering of applause, lots of abuse and a few objects thrown at them. No way is this mob gonna be like their pogoing London supporters. Glen Matlock

> and Steve Jones plug in ... as Rotten just hangs from the mike stand, rips open a can of beer, and burns the crowd with his glassy, taunting, cynical eyes. Spiky dyed red hair, death white visage ... he looks like an amphetamine corpse from a Sunday gutter press wet dream. Something thrown from the audience hits him full in the face. Rotten glares at the person who did it, lips drawn back over decaying teeth. 'Don't give me your shit,' he snarls, 'because we don't mess ... This first number's dedicated to a Leeds councillor, Bill Grundy and the Queen – fuck ya!' And straight into a searing rendition of the Blank Generation anthem, 'Anarchy In The UK', done even better than the single which just charted at 43 ... It's a blistering start, but unfortunately for both the Pistols and the crowd it turns out to be the high point of the set. The crowd are way too restrained through 'Lazy Sod', 'No Future' and 'Pretty Vacant', failing even to see the humour in the really cocked up intro of this song. Rotten glares at them, 'You're not wrecking the place,' he says, 'The News of the World will be REALLY disappointed.' This gets a laugh, but the crowd don't seem to realize that the two things Rotten hates most are apathy and complacency, both of which are rife tonight at Leeds Poly. 'I hope you 'ate it!' he screams. 'You don't like it then you know where the EXIT door is!' ... Even with numbers that the crowd knows, like The Who's 'Substitute' or the Monkees' 'Stepping Stone', the punters never really get into it. Rotten's going crazy with angry frustration ... 'You just stand there, you don't know whether you like it or not!' ... Then they were gone and I felt for them.

Actually, the Pistols' Leeds set not only proved inspirational to the art students who were soon responsible for The Mekons and Gang of Four, but also to the other bands on the bill, all of whom had to admit they were blazing – even a begrudging Rat Scabies, 'The Pistols were fucking awesome. I'd never seen them that good: Jonesy pulled out all the shots.'

For Walter Lure, it was his first chance to see all three English bands. His verdict? 'I didn't really like The Damned ... The Clash were good guys but ... the music was a little tinny, not much balls to it. Then the Pistols sounded great ... I never heard a punk band who had as good a sound as they did.' The feeling was mutual. All the English punks stood side stage when The Heartbreakers came on. Afterwards, Peter Lloyd remembers 'the Pistols and The Clash in the dressing room [going], "My God, they can really play." They were [just] so tight.'

For one set of admiring musicians, though, it seemed like there was little point in carrying on once McLaren started messing with their heads. Scabies suggests The Damned went on at Leeds, only to find 'Malcolm [had] turned all the lights [down] on us and gave us half the PA'. Despite this, Brian James believes they 'went down a storm. [But] after the first gig, McLaren said, "It's changed now. You're going on first." I really was at the point of hitting him ... And that's it, we split.'

The next night, The Damned were down the Nashville, playing to loyal fans at a hastily arranged homecoming, a prelude to a fortnight's worth of sessions that would serve to produce a second stand-out single ('Neat Neat Neat') and a fine first album (*Damned Damned Damned*). That simple gesture – saying it on vinyl earliest, loudest and snottiest – would ultimately ensure The Damned a place at the captain's table.

And then there were three. For The Clash – now third on the bill – it was all good. Even the reviews were good, with Shearlaw coining the best line to describe their Leeds entrance, 'looking and playing as if they'd been starved for days.' Parsons, too, found them 'hard, committed, loud, brash, [playing] violent rock music, I got the impression they expected nothing from the audience or anybody else, so that they didn't have the same problems as the Pistols'.

A dyed-blond Strummer knew this was the perfect opportunity for sloganeering and rhetoric in one audio-visual package, walking on stage in 'a green sweat shirt emblazoned with the legend Social Security £9.70', and informing the audience, 'I've been goin' around for two days thinking Big Brother is really here.'

Unfortunately for him – and much to Coon's prosaic amazement – 'The students' ... collective policy is obviously when in doubt don't react at all, [and they] give him a blank. The band fight hard to stir the impassive crowd but ... there are no encores.'

With nowhere to run, nowhere to hide – a second gig in Leeds their only other option – the Anarchy tour bus duly returned to base. Manchester was next, three days later; the Pistols' third assault on the city's sensibilities. Sparing no expense, McLaren even booked the Pistols into the palatial Midland Hotel, less than fifty yards from the Free Trade Hall, where they had twice grabbed northern rock by the scruff of its brass neck.

The minute they pulled up, the manager was on the phone to Buzzcocks, inviting them to the hotel *and* the gig, offering to let them play if they were willing to replace the unlamented Damned. Buzzcocks agreed, only to find the vibe very different from previous shows:

Richard Boon: There was this very strange sense that time was running out ... The Anarchy tour was the end of *things* ... [It] was just a media rollercoaster. The first gig they come into town, they stay at the Midland, Malcolm rings, says come down ... Go up to the room, there's a TV documentary about Stalin and Malcolm is trying to explain to Steve Jones who Stalin was. We go to [the pub,] Tommy Ducks. Pete [Shelley] had gone blond, Johnny had gone blond, Joe had gone blond, and they're at the bar talking about hair-colouring ... But the gig was fantastic.

Steve Diggle: Glen said afterwards it had been the best night of the entire tour ... It was fantastic from our point of view. It was our turning point. It was sold out. We had a big home crowd in there rooting for us ... It was a turning point for music in Manchester, too. The Stiff Kittens [aka Joy Division] were apparently formed after seeing that gig ... Steven Morrissey put an ad in *Sounds* straight after, asking for musicians to form a punk band.

The Buzzcocks were indeed terrific, even if the one rock critic there from the weeklies, Pete Silverton of *Sounds*, expressed the misguided 'belief that they're a second-rate provincial Pistols copy ... the facade of the new wave with none of its substance. Their set was notable only for their mutilation of the Troggs' hoary chestnut, "I Can't Control Myself", the evening's first outbreak of pogo dancing.'

Another old friend of Strummer, Silverton was prepared to toe the party line, suggesting that The Clash were 'probably the best received band of the evening'. The audio evidence is against him –

as is Ian Moss, who remembers his third Pistols gig as clearly as his first, and who this time caught the Buzzcocks' set and heard what he had been missing:

Ian Moss: I remember watching The Clash, just walking up, and I was as close to Joe Strummer as I am to you, and being hugely impressed by the opening salvo of The Clash, how intense it all seemed. The way they looked. [But] they were [still] my least favourite act. I was more impressed by Buzzcocks.

Thankfully, the audience-taper had the good sense to record all three English bands – and record them well. What he didn't manage to capture was the tension in the air, greater even than at Leeds. But this time it was not the local constabulary or tabloid hacks who were stirring the pot. They knew better than to venture into Collyhurst on a night like this. For the poor punks on the receiving end, the evening's events merely served to underline the psychological hold these daily rags had on society's dumbest dunderheads:

Una Baines: The mentality around there was almost feudal. 'Cause that's where I grew up. If they heard anything about punks thinking they were hard, they'd be like, 'We'll show you who's hard.'

Peter Hook: It was absolutely packed, inside and out … Loads of football fans had come looking for a fight and the Pistols played under a hail of spit and bottles, with constant fights taking place in front of the stage … Once you get football fans coming – the twats who just want to spit and throw bottles – it's time to move on.

Ian Moss: It was gladiatorial the first night … At one point the local thugs stormed inside – a lot of them [were] grown men in their thirties and forties. Just angry at punk. [After all,] what else was there to do in Collyhurst in 1976? It's [that] football mentality, 'They're coming into our [turf].' They [had] come through the doors. The bouncers were incapable of stopping them. The people [inside finally] forced them out. They came in earlier, while the bands were soundchecking, and Jerry Nolan ended up fighting with them … [So] when it came to an end, there was that fear of getting out of there in one piece.

McLaren had invited New Yorkers Seymour Stein and Lisa Robinson – Sire label boss and punk hypester, respectively – to the show to see what they were missing. They had not seen anything like this since Jim Morrison whipped out his penis onstage and the Jim Morrison line now whizzing round their heads was, 'No one here gets out alive!'

EMI's Frank Brunger, who had travelled up from London with Mike Thorne, remembers the occasion as 'easily the most terrifying concert I've ever been to'. But like many of the fortunate few who caught the first two shows of the tour, Brunger had to admit the Pistols 'were great, the best band on the bill and the crowd were really into them. They were pogoing and gobbing back and beer was being thrown everywhere … It was like a war zone. We went to the back of the hall to get out of the way.'

The spitting that had never really been a feature of Sex Pistols shows before the *London Weekend Show* broadcast was again endemic. It brought a curt response from Rotten, as Silverton noted in his review:

> The kids were all gobbing at the stage … obviously believing that was the correct behaviour at a [post-]Grundy rock gig. Mr Rotten's elegant belted red jerkin and soft mulberry shirt were covered with saliva by the end. 'It's up to you. If you wanna keep gobbin', we won't play.' They stopped, and [then] it was into … the newie, 'No Future' … It seemed a good set closer: iconoclastic, demonic and rocking. The lights went down, came back up and 'Problems' blitzed us one more time. It was apparently the encore.

In the face of an audience that, to quote Glitterbest secretary Sophie's diary, 'spends all its time spitting and throwing beer over the band … [un]able to react spontaneously,' the Pistols had delivered a twelve-song set that left the ravening Mancunian hoard bawling for more. Their soundman was again impressed at the way singer and band refused to be cowed by the crowd, even after they realized the dressing rooms were at one end of the hall and the stage was at the other:

Dave Goodman: There were no side entrances onto the stage and the only way on was through the crowd. Once on stage, the band could be pinned there. Their only way off was back through the crowd ... The band refused to bottle out and bravely took to the stage and stood their ground. Missiles were thrown at them but no one was seriously hit, [while] John gave as good as he got verbally.

If Rotten seemed unperturbed by the ensuing mayhem, others in the band were starting to find it hard going. Although Paul Cook was unspecific about which Anarchy gig/s he had in mind, he later confessed to feeling 'always worried, with people throwing things on stage ... And all the gobbing, which we never started. Just general chaos surrounding all the gigs, there was no way you could concentrate on the playing.'

Ironically, Leeds Poly and the first Manchester gig not only featured the most 'general chaos', but were also the best Pistols performances. Go figure. And that night at the Circus most punk converts in the audience responded with wild enthusiasm, perhaps because, as an attendant Morrissey observes, the audience 'had to risk something ... your own safety'.

Unfortunately, at the exact moment when a large part of the national media began to lose interest in the Pistols – assuming, or praying, that punk was just another seven-day wonder – the tour came off the rails.

The cancelled shows had again begun to stack up and the tour bus had no choice but to return to the capital, where any between band on-tour camaraderie – enforced by circumstance – evaporated in the London fog. As Nils Stevenson later observed, 'On the tour it was alright, but in London the two [English] groups wouldn't hang out together or anything like that.' The exception was Matlock, who started distancing himself from his own band, developing a close kinship with Mick Jones and even thinking of a life after the Pistols.

After five further days of last-minute cancellations and rescheduled gigs that instantly fell through, they were off again, the tour bus picking up the three bands still standing and heading for Caerphilly. The minute they arrived in the Welsh valleys, though, the mood was noticeably different from Leeds and Manchester. Another large crowd was assembled outside the Castle Cinema, but this rabid throng was not planning on attending the gig. They were there to try and stop it. Brian Case, a freelance journalist writing a feature for *The Observer*, described the scene that greeted them:

> Against the improbable backdrop of the town's 13th century castle, a classic generation gap stand-off was [being] enacted. Inside the old Castle Cinema sat the Sex Pistols. In the car park opposite, bundled up against the pre-Christmas cold, stood a coalition of local councillors and Pentecostal Chapel members in a last-ditch protest … staging a carol concert as a rival attraction and a beacon.

The TV news footage of all these carol singers – exemplified by a particularly mad Welsh woman ranting and raving about a band she'd never seen or heard (neither *So It Goes* nor the Grundy show having been broadcast in Wales) – has become a visual metaphor for what Case called a 'classic generation gap standoff'. But something more important was at stake and it took Rotten to point it out, in a pre-gig interview: this was about Britain being brainwashed; which is why, when he sang 'no future', he meant it:

> **Q:** How do you feel about all this?
> **Rotten**: I'm just surprised that so many grown-up adults can behave so ludicrously childish. Don't they know their papers tell lies – I don't think they do. They live in a twilight zone.

In Caerphilly, it was the leader of these 'foul-mouthed yobs' who lucidly articulated the problem and the 'reasonable majority' who acted like a band of Salem witchhunters looking for someone to burn. Not that they were going to stop the likes of Steve Strange from attending his second Pistols gig. And, as Matlock notes, Steve had brought 'loads of mad bods' with him, to give him Dutch courage as he walked past a vicar who 'was shouting through a loudspeaker that Satan would enter the body of anyone who went in to see this vile band'. Whatever would his Newport neighbours have thought?!

Also inside the Castle Cinema, snug and warm, was Mark Stewart, and all his 'mates from the [Bristol] funk scene', slowly metamorphosing into punks. Caerphilly sped up the process, while convincing Stewart to accelerate putting together a band himself. Before tonight, he thinks, 'Everybody was unaware of each other, [but] suddenly you saw … the Sex Pistols and you thought, "This is what we are talking about."' Despite Strange and Stewart's rallying calls, the show was not well attended. Not that this dissuaded those on stage from taking the opportunity to let the protesters actually hear what they were railing against:

Dave Goodman: Only about forty or so punters managed to turn up and the bands put on a marvellous show. Our rather large PA was a bit OTT for the event but that didn't stop us from turning it up full, opening the windows and sharing our wonderful music with the world outside.

While the real freak show was outside turning to stone, the bands played with the same freedom they had when apathy, not anarchy, prevailed. And while the Pistols continued to overwhelm all-comers, The Clash again impressed Stewart with their energy. For The Heartbreakers, though, the tour was taking its toll – not because of the absence of gigs, but because of the absence of readily-available cheap heroin. By this point the only rock that interested them came from an island off China.

It was high time they got back to London and scored. That required funds. Yet every time their manager Leee Childers approached McLaren for a hand-out the former Situationist pleaded poverty. The Heartbreakers were already in everyone's bad books for racking up astronomical overseas phone bills phoning their girlfriends (or boyfriend) from the hotels they had been staying in; while McLaren had been summoned back to London to be informed EMI would be withdrawing tour-support. The Anarchy tour, it seemed, had finally hit the buffers.

★ ★ ★

Meanwhile, back at somewhere akin to a bat-cave, word-of-mouth alone had assembled a similar-size audience to the one attending Caerphilly's cinema for a punk double-header in the depths of Covent Garden which would have as great a bearing on the form's future as current events in the 'twilight zone'.

The venue was a seedy men's club called Chaguaramas, taken over for the night by Andy Czezowski who, after trying his hand at band management with The Damned, had decided being a punk-rock club owner might be less stressful. The inaugural bill was Generation X and Siouxsie & The Banshees – their third and second gigs respectively, in newly bleached incarnations.[49]

In the past few weeks the biggest challenge for both 'Bromley' bands had been finding a suitable lead guitarist, the instrumental type in shortest supply among London's punk legion. Generation X had a decent guitarist in Billy Idol but he wanted to be the band's frontman. So they scoured the youth clubs for a replacement. They found their man, Bob 'Derwood' Andrews, in Fulham, playing with a band called Paradox, with hair not quite down to his navel but nowhere near short enough for their own planned break-in – getting under the wire into the punk camp.

Given an ultimatum, shear the shag or stay paradoxical, Derwood did the deed just in time for Gen X's official unveiling at the Central College of Art – where the Pistols had once played their second gig. The ten-song set culminated in punkified renditions of 'Instant Karma' and 'Paranoid', two songs that heralded the advent of seventies cynicism by demolishing the love-is-all mantra of the sixties. Of more contemporary relevance were Gen X's own songs, which already included 'Ready Steady Go', 'Your Generation' and 'Youth Youth Youth', a solid platform for their own programme of youth betterment.

[49] In his unpublished memoir, Gen X bass-player Tony James later tried to capture this propitious moment when Chaguaramas became 'The Roxy': 'A gay disco drinking club for spade types and what looked like gangsters – night life with gin and tonics – hot chop girls – bow ties on gorilla types – we're gonna be killed ... Downstairs is a small bar ... Mirrors on all the walls – makes it look bigger. DJ box in far right corner. Right wall staircases down with railings. Posts every twenty feet ... It's small but easily big enough – a stage over there under the stairs, lick of paint, posters, our own CBGBs ... Our own place.'

The Banshees had thought they already had a lead guitarist as steeped in the Pistolean aesthetic, until Marco Pirroni explained he had no real interest in cosying up to these lapsed suburbanites. The week after the September punk festival, he had been invited to meet Nils Stevenson at the Pistols' Denmark Street studio, where he was told the Banshees were becoming an ongoing concern to which he could belong. But he had already decided he didn't 'like them as people'. Even the prospect of a proper manager, Nils Stevenson – who recognized Siouxsie's star-potential straight away – plus the (unauthorized) use of the Pistols' rehearsal room while they were on tour, failed to persuade Pirroni.

The punkified pair would have to look elsewhere. They knew they needed someone who revelled in discord and dissonance as much as them because, as Severin says, 'We were gonna do the Velvets.' This time for real. They initially co-opted classically-trained Simone on violin (a la Cale), but 'the first songs we started to write didn't sound anything like the Velvets, and the violin seemed a waste of time'.

Fortunately, before they got around to informing Simone she was surplus to requirements, she introduced them to another friend's boyfriend, Pete Fenton, a guitarist who could play a mean, slashing style of lead guitar that, aligned to Morris's metronomic drumming, gave Siouxsie and Steve the perfect staccato backdrop to early originals like 'Make Up To Break Up' and 'Love In A Void'.

At a warm-up show at The Red Deer pub, in Croydon, the short set would comprise just two of Severin's own songs, 'Scrapheap' and 'Psychic', a couple of covers (including T. Rex's 'Twentieth Century Boy'), and a more structured rendition of 'The Lord's Prayer', the finale to every show for the next two years. Siouxsie would continue nodding her jet-black, slicked-back hair to the performance-piece which gave birth to the Banshees until every element of anti-rock had departed.

The night both the Banshees and Gen X were unveiled to London's punks was the first and last time Billy, Siouxsie and Steve shared a bill. In fact, Simon Barker, who was now working for McLaren, is blunt in his assessment of what Bromleyites thought about Idol's new band, 'I still liked Billy as a person, but neither me or Steve like what he did musically … Visually, Billy looked stunning in the early days ... Shame it was let down by the music. The songs were awful.'

The Banshees, for all their technical limitations – which they would overcome in fits, starts and with further line-up changes – were undoubtedly the more challenging band. The fact that Generation X's second gig was supporting Eater; their fourth (five days later at Chaguaramas) was alongside The Heartbreakers, looking to score some much needed scratch to satisfy that itch; and their fifth was sharing an Electric Circus bill with The Drones, another band with a punk name but a dodgy pre-punk past, all suggested a band happy to sit on anybody's fence till punk defined itself. Mark P, reviewing their sixth gig at Islington's pub-rock headquarters, felt they had the songs to succeed:

> The first Chelsea gigs were good but Generation X have played killers. They sing songs about a new way of life. The way they play 'em is takin' the 'new wave' in a fresh direction. Their gig at the Hope and Anchor said it all. They broke through to a crowd who were fed up with the Pistols and The Clash being in Plymouth. The Generation X will move in a direction which can only mean more great gigs and even great records. They will make ... amazing singles.

Perry's engaging assessment would prove wide of the mark, but there was no doubting the maximum r&b coming off the Islington stage; and if Siouxsie was the most photogenic face in punk, Idol was not far behind. Where Siouxsie trumped her once like-minded friend was in blazing a trail for other Pistol apostles, specifically the more Amazonian types.

A handful of punkesses had already started two other punk bands that autumn: the short-lived Castrators – fronted by Tessa Pollitt, who at the time had 'a necklace with a little pair of scissors on it' – and The Slits, a band initially accused of being little more than (ex-) girlfriends of other punk musicians joining in on the joke. The still-born Castrators' one claim to fifteen-minute fame was a mention in a post-Grundy article on girls in (punk) rock written by Vivien Goldman for a Sunday tabloid, before Tessa left the band name behind in someone's garage, the motor running.

In fact the autumn of 1976 saw a great deal of musical chairs being played in the rehearsal rooms of the capital. Viv Albertine, inspired by the Pistols as far back as December 1975, had begun playing with another ex-Clash girlfriend Palmolive (aka Paloma Romero, Joe Strummer's ex) in the flickeringly infamous Flowers of Romance, a band with so many line-ups it made London SS look like The Who. If the Flowers' problems partly stemmed from never finding the requisite lead guitarist, the main problem was Sid Vicious. He seemed unable to make up his mind whether to be the singer or an equally ill-qualified, Ayleresque saxophonist.

For Albertine, the Flowers afforded her a first opportunity to play with like-minded souls. Punk was an idea so liberating Viv realized by October 1976 that 'all the[se] guys around me were forming bands, and they had heroes to look up to. But I didn't have anyone. I didn't want to look like or be Joni Mitchell [or] even … Fanny. Then it suddenly occurred to me that I didn't have to have a hero, I could pick up a guitar and just play.'

Vicious had even written a few songs, of a sort, which he played to Marco Pirroni when trying (unsuccessfully) to convince him to join forces: 'After that 100 Club gig, Sid said, "You should play guitar [in my band]." I had two rehearsals with him. I never met the rest of the band. [We did] "Belsen Was A Gas", then called "Postcard from Auschwitz", something about Jayne Mansfield, [and one] called "Brain On Vacation" … He could play bass a bit. I just sat down and played guitar.'

Vicious remained optimistic about whom he could entice to join forces, even trying to co-opt Keith Levene at a time when the guitarist was more interested in sex and drugs than rock & roll. When that failed he lost interest, though not before summarily dismissing both Paloma and Viv from 'his' band.

The more musical members of the band – i.e. everyone else – left like rats from the proverbial sinking ship, leaving behind his echo, his shadow and him. Vicious had already given an interview to the punk 'zine *Skum,* in which he insisted that if he ever got above his own station, musically, 'I'd consider myself to be a total cunt, and I'd blow my brains out.' No danger there.

In Palmolive's case, she took with her the songs she had already written, including 'Number One Enemy', 'New Town' and 'Shoplifting', all of which re-emerged in The Slits. And this band had legs. Drummer Palmolive had originally met Ari Up – the 15-year-old daughter of another rock 'chick', Nora Forster – 'at a Patti Smith gig. I thought [it] was great that she was so obnoxious. I had an understanding of what a front person needed to be in a band, and so I asked her to be in my band … [And there was] this other girl, Kate Khorus, I knew from the squat scene.' The pair convinced Viv Albertine to take Kate's place, while ex-Castratix Pollitt replaced the Slits' original bassist, Suzy Gutsy. It was time to get serious.

(If the Slits were soon a full-time rehearsing entity, it would be March 1977 before they summoned up the nerve to play to punters; and even then, those early Slits sets rather resembled Ingham's description of The Damned's debut, 'Like four different bands playing together at 78 rpm.')

Another female with a gift for social-commentary-in-lyrics and inspired to look afresh at the world by the Pistols in performance, was Marion Elliot (aka Poly Styrene), who had moved to London and formed a unisex band with another striking visual counterpoint, 17-year-old saxophonist, Lora Logic. The gloriously noisy X-Ray Spex would make their live debut just a week before The Slits did, with an identity already fully-formed.

Meanwhile, in one rehearsal room on the outskirts of London, another couple of refugees from the south coast – Gaye and her boyfriend Tim – were working their way through the newly-formed Adverts' first set of songs, every one a winner and a TV Smith original. 'One Chord Wonders', 'Newboys', 'Quickstep', 'We Who Wait', 'Bored Teenagers', 'Great British Mistake', 'Safety In Numbers' and 'New Church' made for quite a statement of purpose to present on their own live debut.[50]

Further along than The Slits and X-Ray Spex, The Adverts would debut at the former Chaguaramas supporting the hard-workin' Generation X. By then it would be called The Roxy, and The Adverts would become the ninth band to play the newly-christened

[50] This primal Adverts rehearsal was previously made available on the Adverts/TV Smith website as an official download.

club on January 15th, 1977; and the first to play there who had not played live during Year Zero.

Bands were now forming anyhow, anywhere, anyway. A lack of any obvious musical training (or talent) was no bar – and neither was gender. Shanne Hasler had finally 'started playing myself, cos I thought, "Anyone can do that." [Having] that attitude was good … [I wanted to do] something removed from the Sex Pistols. [So] I started playing bass.'

Likewise, Jane Wimble was a (somewhat reluctant) female vocalist in the newly formed Trash, who as Simon Wright later wrote, somehow managed in that 'six-month window … when record companies would sign any band that could manage about three chords as long as they had short hair and played fast', to secure a record deal with Polydor – at which point Ms Wimble bowed out. It was all getting a little too serious for her limited ambition. In fact, for some repeat Pistol-goers, the fun was going out of punk almost as quickly as career opportunities were coming in.

★ ★ ★

While the tabloids were prematurely preparing to draw a curtain across the nascent movement, the band who began all the trouble had returned to the provinces, popping up ten days after playing the Electric Circus at the most unlikely of venues – the Electric Circus – to start the second leg of the much-troubled Anarchy tour. This time they were gonna keep going till the wheels of the tour bus fell off and/or Babylon burned.

McLaren had managed to line up three more shows for the first punk bands leaving town. They were even on consecutive nights, like a proper tour, even if the overnight trek from Cleethorpes to Plymouth required a 345-mile drive.

It showed a commendable refusal on McLaren's part to allow his boys to be silenced. Front-page news or not, the tour they tried to kill with censorship must not be allowed to go gently into the night. With just a single date in Plymouth remaining from the original tour schedule, he decided to make the tour truly nationwide by adding two last-minute gigs that spanned England's width and breadth.

Assured of a friendly reaction at Manchester's new punk venue of choice – at least *inside* the Circus – the three bands resumed where they had pretty much left off. Or at least The Clash did, raging against the injustice of it all in a way only they could. As tight as an oil drum, they had stripped the set down to their best ten songs – beginning with 'White Riot' and ending with '1977' – after spending the last ten days ensuring that if the opportunity arose again, they were prepped to play like their lives depended on it.

And this time they didn't have to follow Buzzcocks. It had been made plain to Boon the Buzzcocks' spokesman that they 'could have gone on the tour bus after the Circus', but he realized it would be a mistake: 'It was too chaotic.' But they were all still there providing moral support and Boon, for one, was stunned by Strummer this time: 'I found the difference between The Clash [Circus] performances remarkable. They were glowing, tight. Joe Strummer was [like] Eddie Cochran!'

Also in Collyhurst that night was *NME*'s favourite satirical cartoonist, Ray Lowry, whose reaction was much the same, 'The Clash were marvellous. Other people said the same – the electricity! – they looked as though they were wired into the mains'; and Paul Morley, who summed up the general consensus in his *NME* review, 'Concentrated, intent, they look as aggressive as they sound, all of them moving just right. No perfunctory performances for these boys.'

Strummer later claimed, 'That was the night that I knew we were really going to do it, because we were better than the Pistols. They had a really hard time following us.' Yet at the time he broached no criticism of the band without whom he'd still be down the Nashville – even if that criticism came from someone who had seen the entire arc of English punk play out:

Richard Boon: Joe was very complimentary about the Pistols … At the second Anarchy Circus gig, the Pistols were being ragged and I must've said something, 'cause he said, 'Yeah, but they're still fucking great!' What was interesting about the Pistols during the Anarchy tour – they were ragged but not in a good way. Early [on], they were ragged in a good way. Then they got tight, then they fell apart, because of all the pressure.

If the pressure was getting to the Pistols, in Collyhurst it was the pressure of expectation from a very demanding audience who knew how good they could be. It seemed like everyone who had been there since June 4th had come out for one last helping. The contrast with ten days earlier was not lost on Lydon, whom Ian Moss remembers coming on stage and quipping, 'Ah, I see we've got rid of the tourists!' The thugs, too, stayed home reading page three of *The Sun*.

Moss, who had crammed seven people into his car to escape the aftermath of the first Circus gig, says that for 'the second one I went on my own, strolled up, strolled back to town after. No problem.' Those, like Una Baines, who stayed behind, even got to chat to the Face of punk, 'One thing I remember ... was Johnny Rotten just sitting on the stage, and people going up and chatting to him. None of this Us and Them, not up himself.'

Baines and Moss continued to feel inspired by what they saw, as they slowly started putting into practise the precepts of punk. In time, The Fall and The Hamsters would take the Pistols' art of confrontation to a whole other level.

For two rock reviewers who were there that night – and would be present and correct at the Circus from the first to the last – the show garnered diametrically opposite reactions. Mick Middles, a local fanzine writer who soon found a berth at *Sounds*, still felt a certain tension in the air, 'When the Pistols finally made it to the stage, a flu-ridden Rotten would cast inhuman and confrontational stares across the hall. Stares that were returned by showers of lager, spit, beer glasses and bottles. Only the stageside huddle would accept and revel in the music.' He loved every minute of it. Paul Morley, by contrast, blamed the Pistols for the crowd's, to-his-mind, muted response, accusing them of firing blanks until the final anarchic discharge, when they at last found their mojo:

> Tonight after three or four tunes they begin to bore ... Almost lackadaisical. Only volume and speed disguis[e] basic malfunctions. Each song, taken as a separate entity, is relentless, but anonymous, gut-wrenching rock & roll ... Rotten, though, was for much of the time naturally magnificent [with his] demented Pinocchio-type

> tactics ... 'All you do is stare,' he whined at one point, which is hardly surprising because all that was happening was Jones yet again tuning his guitar and Rotten himself blowing his nose – with a clean handkerchief. Hey, but they did 'Anarchy' at the very end after a churn-out version at the beginning, and it was a really great way to go, all frustrations channelled, it seemed, into this one version. It showed how ... they should have murdered us.

Evidently, the critic was already consuming the fan. Others marching the path of punk hand in hand with its creators were not so critical. Proto-Prefect Robert Lloyd, now rehearsing for the revolution in Birmingham, made it to both the Circus and Cleethorpes and thought 'the gigs were fantastic ... [All] the bands were getting better the more they played'. As for the promoter of the Cleethorpes gig, he had been steadily following the furore for the past three weeks and feared the worst, so his main feeling was one of 'great relief when it was over':

James Jackson: I knew it was likely to be lively, and by God it was. They whipped the audience up into a sort of frenzy, which was something we had to watch. Yes, we had bits of trouble, one or two scuffles, and a window broken outside, that sort of thing.

In other words, nothing one wouldn't see on your average Saturday night at closing time. Perhaps the Pistols deliberately reined things in when they saw trouble looming, curtailing their set before things got out of hand. Or maybe they were just running out of steam. The crunchy recording of this Teeside performance runs to just nine songs, ending with 'Pretty Vacant', their shortest set in months.

Another factor not to be discounted was Rotten's ever-imminent cold which had now returned with a vengeance, compounding his ill-humour – as did the seven-hour drive to Plymouth for the final show(s) of the tour. They arrived at the Woods Centre to find a queue around the block. After the Pistols had cancelled a show there the first week in October, the locals were genuinely delighted to see these grubby grockles. Or at least the local punks were. According to Steve Strange, looking for a second fix of Pistolean anarchy, 'Somebody in the audience was trying to get everybody who wasn't a punk to riot … This huge fight broke out and the punks came off better.'

It can't have been much of a contest because the Pistols' rhythm-section barely noticed. They were too busy having a ball, Matlock recalling that it 'was a great show and absolutely packed out. All the bands … played really well.' More than any other emotion, Cook was plain relieved, 'We were all really chuffed. Perhaps it was because we were at last doing what we were meant to do – play on stage … without a lot of fuss.'

In fact, as Matlock notes, 'The promoter loved it so much he decided to put us on again the following night.' This last-minute offer to play it again, son, would make for an altogether more muted conclusion to the tour to end all punk package-tours. No one was there. Matlock claims, 'The entire audience was six Hell's Angels and the other bands on tour.'

At least it gave some key instigators loitering in London one last opportunity to ride the wave; not least Jonh Ingham, who had been recovering from an operation that had laid him low for most of the Anarchy tour. He had been weighing up his options before deciding to jump onboard the bandwagon he helped set in motion by agreeing to co-manage Generation X. The very first critic to make the Pistols legends in their own lunchtime was now caught unawares by The Clash, who for the first time surpassed the power of the Pistols in performance:

Jonh Ingham: I went to the last night of the Anarchy tour and The Clash were amazing. Joe is rolling on the floor and he had a red, curly guitar cord and he got all wrapped up in it, and he had the cord across his face … The guy was a showman – he knew how to do this stuff … [But] I didn't think the Pistols were very good … They aged a lot in that year, under the pressure. [Just] look at the photos.

The headliners weren't greatly helped by the fact that their soundman – who had been making them sound good since the day he first heard 'Did You No Wrong' – was out of his head. According to Nils Stevenson – who was himself about to jump ship, all for the love of Siouxsie: 'Halfway through the set [Dave] had start[ed] singing along with the talk-back [microphone] on. He was so out of it, he thought it was hilarious.' (Sophie Richmond confirmed as much in her diary, 'SPs play well but the sound is up the creek. Dave apparently out of his head on pills.')

Goodman later admitted, 'In my drug-crazed state, they sounded brilliant.' Didn't everyone. This time he wasn't even blamed for how The Clash sounded, or how long they played. In fact, he remembered, 'The Clash put in one hell of a set and refused to end it. They only stopped when Thunders enticed them off by waving a huge joint at them from backstage.'

Eventually the plug was pulled on the Pistols. Plymouth rock would never be the same again. Nor would the Pistols. As Boon, Ingham and Morley already suspected, the tour and the attendant notoriety had begun to catch up with them. And worse was to follow. Meetings at EMI behind closed doors had reached an impasse. The dotty old dames who pressed, packed and dispatched EMI product had downed tools when presented with the Pistols' debut 45 and rather than read the ladies the riot act – or simply take the work elsewhere – the label had stopped distributing 'Anarchy', a clear breach of contract.

The label was now at war with itself, the young tykes in A&R and publishing determined to hold on to the most exciting band the label had signed in years, while the fuddy-duddies on the board were more worried what their golf partners and fellow Masons might say. One of those young tykes, the ambitious Mike Thorne, suggested the Pistols give the label a taste of the future by demoing 'No Future' and their three best potential B-sides at Manchester Square itself, in the demo studio downstairs, after digesting their Christmas pud:[51]

Mike Thorne: The Dave Goodman demos were energetic but the sound was, I thought, not very palatable to the record company crew and I wanted to gather as much [label] support for the music as I could.

[51] This fabled session is confidently dated 11th December in the unreliable notes to the *Sex Pistols Box* (2002). However, in Glitterbest secretary Sophie's contemporary diary, she clearly dates it to 27th December, which makes more sense.

If Thorne really thought that a five-minute version of the future 'God Save The Queen' was the way to solidify support – as opposed to bolstering his own credentials as a producer, prepping for *Live At The Roxy* and *Pink Flag* – he was as out of touch as Sir John Read, who would remain chairman of EMI until a similar seat at a bank opened up.

The song the Pistols had played half a dozen times was surprisingly bereft of their usual pop sensibility, as if the band's one avowed Beatlefan, Matlock, had already washed his hands of the idea. It was still just 'a riff with John singing over it'. The best of this Christmas fare was actually 'Liar', perhaps because it still sounded relatively fresh, having never been done in a studio.

(None of the Thorne tracks were deemed suitable for a second single; or even the bootleg album, *Spunk*, when McLaren got around to it. He preferred the sound Goodman got. In fact, they did not see the light of day until 2002, when a 3-CD boxed-set, low on rarities, tried – and failed – to provide an accurate record of the Pistols in their pomp.)

With troubles arriving in battalions, the one road McLaren was determined not to go down was the independent route. He demanded EMI back the band or back out of the deal and write off a substantial investment. They chose the latter, though they waited until the Pistols were safely in the Low Countries the first week in January to inform them.

Meanwhile, The Damned were back at Pathway with Nick Lowe, recording another single that screamed at ninety-mile-an-hour: If it ain't Stiff, it ain't worth a fuck. Even the B-side of 'Neat Neat Neat' had sonic thrust to spare, and perhaps a message to McLaren. It was called 'Stab Your Back'.

Similarly determined to make a sonic statement of sorts, before time was called, were Buzzcocks. The day after the Pistols laid down an E.P.'s worth of demos, Buzzcocks cut an actual E.P. at Indigo Sound Studio, where they reluctantly let their friend Martin Hannett commandeer the producer's chair. As Shelley told James Nice, 'We believed him, that he was a record producer – we were just as gullible as everybody else.' The band stood and watched as Hannett assumed control of proceedings even though he had as much of a clue as Doc Watson:

Steve Diggle: To be honest, I don't think he'd ever recorded anything in his life. He ... drove the studio's engineer mad. Every time the engineer got the sound just right, Martin would lean across and fuck it up ... until the engineer gave up and let him mix it his way. That's why we ended up with that poxy tinny sound.

'That poxy tinny sound', captured on the immortal *Spiral Scratch* E.P., would end up defining a whole aesthetic adopted by some of punk's more musically-challenged wannabes (Desperate Bicycles, anyone?); while the seven-inch format – two tracks per side at 45 rpm – necessitated it be played loud, fucking loud.

The punk genie was out of the bottle, and there was no way he was going back in his glass prison. For starters, Punk now had a dozen working bands, four times the number needed for a movement and all inspired by the Pistols. And alongside the likes of The Adverts, Buzzcocks, The Clash, The Damned, Generation X, The Jam, Penetration, Siouxsie & The Banshees, The Slits, Subway Sect, Wire and X-Ray Spex were a few dozen pretenders in equally garish gear.

The common cause that drove punk in 1976 was disappearing into the winter mist. The diaspora of punk would have separate, contradictory gospels to guide them – some redemptive, some apocalyptic, one that accorded with punk's own Antichrist. But if English Punk as a collective musical form was done'n'dusted, the battle for the public image of 'punk' had only just begun.

OUTRO: EVER GET THE FEELING YOU'VE BEEN CHEATED?!

One of the first things I was ever quoted as saying was, 'I'd like to see more bands like us.' … I didn't mean *exactly* like us.

– John Lydon,* NME, *December 23rd, 1978

Captain Sensible … thinks Punk was a working-class movement, but for me it started out like an art thing, where you have a manifesto.

– Pete Shelley, 2002

In the early days there was an original hardcore of creative people that were aware of the [generational] gap and decided to fill it with a pool of people – artists, musicians, managers. And we always thought it'd continue in that vein … But now I just find myself with that same original heart of creative people … It didn't work the way it should have done.

– Joe Strummer,* Melody Maker, *July 15th, 1978

Between November 6th, 1975 and November 26th, 1976 – the day 'Anarchy In The UK' was released into the world – Punk was not only a dirty word, it was a nasty secret. One of the most glorious periods in popular music passed most folk by because it was only found between the cracks left by a crumbling post-war consensus as to the role of youth culture in society. For an increasingly alienated generation it represented an irrevocable breaking of the bonds which had bound British society since the Victorian era. Slackened by the sixties, they were still in need of melting down.

And they called it Punk. If Malcolm McLaren started out pulling the strings, his punk Pinocchio turned out to be a real boy, with an attitude all his own. For a year and a bit, Malcolm and Johnny managed to pull in the same direction as they wrought a revolution of the mindful. But by the end of 1976, the contradictions that would make punk a roman candle of a musical movement ended up roasting the Pistols in the town square.

The outcome for what had been – for most of 1976 – an 'art thing' with its own elitist manifesto, would be a populist movement, but it was not the one McLaren had sought to create; even if it would provide steady employment for sociologists with nothing better to do than miss the point for decades to come.

By March 1977 – three months after the Anarchy tour crashed and burned, but a mere month after main Pistols tunesmith Glen Matlock and Buzzcocks frontman Howard Devoto both quit their respective outfits – the first wave of punk had already struck home.

In fact, such was the confusion that when at the end of that month *Sounds* attempted a roundup of those bands constituting the 'Sounds of the New Wave', they came up with thirty-four names without mentioning The Adverts, The Prefects or Sham 69. They did, however, include two of the biggest bands of the eighties, conjoined for the first and last time – Iron Maiden and The Police! So much for ring-fencing the barely-born movement.

NME's own Rent-A-Punk Guide, published the previous week, seemed slightly less confused about the term's remit. They did namecheck The Adverts, while reserving tongue-in-cheek mentions for Ultravox and Tom Petty who 'could conceivably qualify as new wave if you've been lost in the jungle for a decade or so'.

The beginning of the end may have been the term itself. When critics started calling it 'New Wave', it gave permission to crowbar the likes of The Boys, The Cortinas, The Drones, The Only Ones, Squeeze, The Stranglers and The Vibrators into this amorphous construct, so much more *marketable* than Punk.

Tellingly, the entry for the Pistols in the magazine which had been their greatest champion suggested a band almost moribund: 'Credit where it's due – none of this would have happened without the Pistols ... Annoying though that they haven't done a show in months ... Not to mention dangerous from the point of view of the number of fans who'll ultimately get sick of waiting for the Pistols to materialise and place their allegiances elsewhere.'

The rebranding of rock's most revolutionary musical movement had begun. It was 1967 all over again. A musical genre that threatened to topple the mother country's pyramid of propriety was first set upon by the rabid dogs of the gutter press then neutered by commerce.

Back then, it was not so much the connection between sex and rock & roll as between drugs and rock & roll which had set off society's fire alarm. As a result, Psychedelia in its unrefined state – containing (as it did) an overt, celebratory connection to *psychedelics* – lasted barely a year. By 1969, it had been successfully rebranded as 'Prog', shorthand for Progressive: forward-thinking music for cerebral folk. Which is where the trouble started; and proof provided that every action has an equal but opposite reaction – even in pop culture.

Punk was that opposite reaction. The most profound difference between Psychedelia and Punk is that Psychedelia began as the brainchild of rock's increasingly detached nobility, sparked by an album that became a global sensation, sold millions, and became the soundtrack for a summer of love that convinced a generation to tune in, turn on, drop out. But the music itself was as conformist as could be. (Surface sound-effects and fading band-unity were all that really separated *Sgt Pepper* from its two superior predecessors.[52])

On the other hand, Punk in 1976 was a roots movement cultivated from the ground up, a secret dossier whose contents only truly became public as the light of communal inspiration was being turned on all over the island. Punk's demand to shake some action was the inevitable e.b.o. reaction to the hippy mantras of peace, love and understanding. That it coincided with a far more diffuse explosion of self-expression in all the arts across the entire island (and beyond) was not so much coincidence as serendipity.

It took the Pistols to show punk's essence to the young at heart; and they did it the only way they knew how. A travelling band of chaos-accepting communalists, they spread musical sedition wherever they went. And for fourteen months they drew them all to a common cause, cajoling the like-minded to embrace the aesthetic and join the circus. Buzzcocks, Clash and The Damned each strutted across

[52] For those who feel a need to revisit the full argument re *Pepper*, I refer them to *The Act You've Known For All These Years* (Canongate, 2007).

a different tightrope to draw the crowds until they felt confident enough to start up revues of their own.

The message all acolytes received was the same – DO IT YOURSELF – but the music the Pistols' immediate apostles made was as contradictory as the gospels of Matthew, Mark, Luke, John and Thomas. Unfortunately for these blessed apostles, they would not have it their own way for long. For those determined to claim the sonic summit, it would prove an uphill battle maintaining a clear distinction between Punk – i.e. 'bands like us' – and a new wave of bands who had picked up on the general buzz of excitement in the air.

The conformity of sound and tedious sloganeering of the many who took the name of punk in vain as of 1977 reflected an entirely distinct constituency: those who found inspiration in their own bedroom/bedsit reflections, with their Dansettes set to max.

For those shouting 'Oi, look at me', the speed of the Ramones and The Clash's catchphrases were valid exemplars of Britpunk. And with no modern Council of Nicaea to decide the matter, Punk became a dirty word again. Only this time it was the original punks who disowned it; setting out their own stalls in opposition to the new wave, preferring to be Something Else. The sonic successor to Dadapunk would have to chunder on nameless for a while yet as the music papers squabbled about what to call it; and whether to embrace it. But one thing was for sure, the term punk had outlived its usefulness.[53]

★ ★ ★

[53] The etymology of the term post-punk, and its precursor, after-punk, is discussed at length in my earlier book, *Babylon's Burning: From Punk To Grunge* (Penguin, 2006), which takes the story up to Nirvana's gunshot blast.

I was getting fed up with punk, which I got involved in because I was fed up with music. Of course it wasn't called punk then. It was a particular style in which the Sex Pistols played, and then we played … There was a certain identification, because it did provoke. People would go to see the Sex Pistols and say, 'They were awful,' as if it really did disturb them. We wanted to share that. [Then] that became a style of its own. So I wanted to push against that.

– *Howard Devoto,* New York Rocker, *September 1979.*

If punk had once been a convenient banner for 'bands like us', as early as the winter of 1977 it was no longer fit for purpose, prompting the search for some different brand name. As the first to read the writing on the wall, Howard Devoto by his own admission had already 'started to feel frustrated … at the perpetual regurgitation that seemed to be going on'. The official reason he gave for quitting Buzzcocks in February 1977 was as paradoxical as his future plans: 'What was once unhealthily fresh is now a clean old hat.'

That (slightly premature) gesture actually doubled the number of core Mancunian punk bands overnight. Meanwhile, rehearsal rooms from Deansgate to Denton began to fill with the shell-shocked survivors from the depth charge the Pistols had laid under the Free Trade Hall a mere nine months earlier.

After the first wave, the aftershock. Actually, a series of aftershocks – none of which were as strong and enduring as the seismic one the Pistols set off. A few lingered long enough in the collective memory to codify some of the biggest bands of the eighties: The Pretenders, Adam & The Ants, New Order, The Smiths, The Pogues, ABC, Visage, the Pet Shop Boys; all of whom once drunk from the same faucet.

By the time Devoto himself was ready to debut his latest sonic solution, the futuristic Magazine, at the last night of the Electric Circus in October 1977, Mancunian punk's ranks had swelled to include The Fall and Warsaw (and, lest we forget, those anti-rock twins of atonality, John The Postman and The Negatives).

Appropriately enough, it was here at the Circus on this October night that the campaign to reclaim punk's higher ground got up a real head of steam. The three-song debut of Devoto's periodical art-rockers vied with the first hints Ian Curtis was hiding a Joy Division inside his heart and that Mark E. Smith had a plan above and beyond getting pissed and pissing off audiences.

For all these individuals, the Pistols had succeeded in redrafting the very parameters of pop culture and reintroduced the cult of unbridled self-expression to a self-indulgent, self-satisfied music scene, albeit at the expense of their own existence.

By the time a parodic Pistols Mk.2 made their ill-advised procession through the USA's southern states in January 1978, on their way to the west-coast HQ of the summer of Acid, the music had become a mere backdrop to Vicious's onstage antics as Jones tried to beef up the guitar-sound to compensate for a bass that was not even in the live mix. It was to prove the last of McLaren's travelling circuses when Rotten reached for the parachute chord.

After Winterland, the Pistols vacated the building. By then, The Clash had found their live mojo. Indeed, for a while there they also seemed all-conquering – thanks to a trio of genre-defining singles and some storming national tours – until the release of that difficult second album took all the wind out of their sales.

The punk crown would sit no more easily on 25-year-old Strummer's head than on a recalcitrant Rotten. And like the Pistols, The Clash would be ultimately torn apart by the contradictions placed there at the outset by their maverick manager, Bernie Rhodes. In the meantime, they had time enough for Guy Stevens to demonstrate he was not the problem back in November 1976, by jointly producing the oft-acclaimed *London Calling*, a bog-standard rock album – title-track excepted – by any other name.

Namechecked endlessly in 2015, The Clash's influence has not been so obviously enduring, or musically endearing, as the band they set out to emulate. Wholly magnificent debut albums from themselves, The Ruts and Stiff Little Fingers still do not stack up against the likes of *Germ Free Adolescents, Pink Flag, Another Music In A Different Kitchen, Cut, The Scream* and *Crossing The Red Sea*, to name half a dozen classic punk platters cast by the Pistols' paradigm.

By summer 1978, The Clash's so-called manager started issuing memos to the media criticising 'his own' band for selling out, i.e. straying from his own ill-conceived brief. After their association ended in the usual recriminations, the four Clash city rockers read the CBS contract to which they had put their names, and found out Bernie, for all his extra-curricular reading, was still some way off passing his accountancy exams.

* * *

I'm not purist about it, but there was nobody as good as the Sex Pistols … The Sex Pistols never preached, they made statements, they made them tough, they accused, and they hated and irritated and they got up people's noses but they never told you what you should do, giv[ing] you these rules … And of course it came from the attitude and the clothes, but mostly it was a vital combination … [And] artistic control is a difficult thing to keep when some [record label] is paying. It took great fortitude on Malcolm's part to keep them as they were intended to be.

–Jordan, to Jon Savage, 1986

When John Lydon finally sought to cut the Gordian knot with his erstwhile manager in a high profile court case, Malcolm McLaren simply shrugged his shoulders and moved on to embrace a different future. He had trampled down the dirt on rock's corpse. It was time to spout some Double Dutch, leaving Lydon to endlessly refine his now-patented method of putting the music press on.

By the time His Rottenness returned to the land of his birth in the spring of '78 – to reclaim his own name and public image – a second Pistolean wave was already washing across the Thames Barrier. After suburban chancers had threatened to drown out that first wave of apostles with A to D to E chord changes and football chants for choruses, remnants of the original punk legion refilled their borrowed pistols and sprayed scorn on these Ramonesian ranters, in the Banshees' case via a December 1977 letter to *Sounds*:

> Sorry we don't subscribe to the standard 'Punk ethic'. 'Mimicry is the sincerest form of flattery' [now] seems to be the maxim to judge 'interesting unknown bands'. Maybe they should remain unknown if they sound 'like' the Pistols, Ramones or Clash.

These 'anti-rock' aggrandizers closed ranks and detuned their guitars, determined to generate a response emulating the one from 'people [who] would go to see the Sex Pistols and say "they were awful" as if it really did disturb them'. This phalanx of former punks included attendees like Adam Ant, Marco Pirroni (The Models and The Ants), Shanne Hasler and Shane McGowan (The Nipple Erectors), and Mark P (Alternative TV), as well as the founder members of those twin battalions of noise, the Banshees and Subway Sect.

All had taken their original instructions from the Pistols and their inspiration from a few dozen shows they saw in the year of Our Lord nineteen seventy-six. One and all set about carefully formulating the way forward. This time, though, they were prepared to stay underground until they were good and ready.

There was no shortage of like-minded cohorts. Wire, after making a pitch-perfect punk platter, *Pink Flag*, were another band of would-be apostles determined to be 'the fly in the ointment' even as they documented a near-circular journey from St Martin's to the Electric Ballroom. And while the Sect released 'Nobody's Scared' and 'Ambition' as markers to their own development, Alternative TV called for some 'Action – Time – Vision' from *Sniffin' Glue*'s former readers.

Two others who had seen more Pistols gigs in 1976 than they had hot dinners decided to form an even more radical post-punk collective. Jah Wobble had stopped hitting people for a living and picked up a bass guitar, tutored initially by the ever-curious Keith Levene. By May 1978, they had begun rehearsing with the boy Johnny, fresh from the Pistols' dissolution.

Public Image Limited adopted punk's fiercest frontman and most challenging wordsmith, setting him to a soundtrack which was more free-form than Can, more atonal than Beefheart and more Dub than Rock. The four-piece PiL would last no longer than the Pistols, but at least they would leave behind two significant signposts to a left-of-centre sonic future: *First Issue* and *Metal Box*.

By the end of 1978, while the children of Sham fought over the pocket money of the puerile, the more experimental side of the Pistolean paradigm was being perpetuated by outfits far removed from the sounds and attitudes of these late-comers who had summoned up the nerve to call themselves punk. Post-punk was the rock on which the likes of Rotten, Howard Devoto, Siouxsie Sioux, Mark E. Smith and Ian Curtis would build their churches of sound.

Out in the provinces, Manchester's futurists – Magazine, The Fall and Joy Division (in that order)[54] – were content to lead the way. Gang of Four and The Mekons in Leeds, Bristol's The Pop Group and the ever-improvisational Prefects (traversing Birmingham's M6 corridor) – all anointed by Rotten's phlegmatic rite of passage – were also signed up for the post-punk recruitment drive.

Meanwhile, The Jam and The Clash perpetuated the sonic status quo, making often-compulsive rock music designed to appeal to provincial punks for whom Year Zero held little or no meaning and punk concerts were an extension of the football terraces.

By 1979, many outlanders preferred the indie route to the chequebook wielding majors. Labels like Factory, Fast and Rough Trade sprang up to cater to these anti-pop pioneers. Geoff Travis's Rough Trade proved particularly keen to snap up what they could of The Pop Group, Wire, The Slits, Subway Sect and The Prefects – sometimes after the fact.

But long before it became a record label for the hip and the hubristic, Rough Trade had already performed perhaps its greatest service to the future of punk ideals by disseminating industrial quantities of *Spunk* to the home counties (and beyond). With *Spunk*, McLaren bequeathed a legacy that hinted at everything to come on a single bootleg album, comprising the best of Dave Goodman's studio work with the boy band he cast in his own image.

And when Travis and co. had finally exhausted their supplies of that anarchic artifact, they obtained a limited supply of the shattering

[54] Those who think Joy Division led the way check your historian credentials at the door. PiL, Magazine, the Banshees and The Fall had all made records well before Curtis and co. found the key.

live experiences offered by *No Fun*, a homemade bootleg of the June '76 Manchester show that sounded all the more unearthly for its lack of production values; *Indecent Exposure*, an edit of the September '76 Burton upon Trent gig; and then, in quick succession, the formative demos of Howard Devoto's Buzzcocks (*Time's Up*), Siouxsie & The Banshees with Pete Fenton (*Love In A Void*) and the pre-Factory Joy Division (*Warsaw*).

Every one of these titles, pressed surreptitiously in the UK, subverted the idea of product for product's sake and reminded all like-minded souls as to the rough'n'ready roots of this revolution of the mind. They also acted as a necessary counterpoint to the monosyllabic speed merchants who, in hijacking punk's good name, seemed determined to prove the appositeness of Lenin's maxim, 'Whoever expects a pure revolution will never live to see it.'

For those who felt the world owed them a living, punk would be a convenient banner. For the few who had lived through the halcyon days and had a common route map, it was time to abandon this flag of convenience. Neither camp seemed predisposed to reference the sound of '76 explicitly. On each side of the barricade a namecheck for the Pistols was deemed to suffice.

It would take a decade and a half for *Time's Up* to receive a fully authorized official release and two decades for *Spunk* to get similar treatment.[55] At the same time, the surprisingly plentiful archive of live 1976 recordings has remained largely untouched by the official archivists of the Pistols, Clash and Buzzcocks. So perhaps it is no wonder the Year Zero of punk has been written off as a mere prelude to 1977's summer of hate.

[55] Yes, *Spunk* and *Time's Up* finally received their official CD releases – in the nineties – as did the Pistols' Screen On The Green performance (crudely lifted from the 1996 bootleg CD) in the noughties. But a proper release of the Chelmsford Prison desk-tape, the Burton audience tape and the Paris soundboard – all from the Pistols' September '76 heyday – should be a no-brainer to the band now that they have regained control of all things Pistolean. The magical Manchester audio also survives only on bootleg – via the rare vinyl original, or on two separately sourced CDs, the appositely named *Aggression Through Repression* in the nineties and, in the noughties, the equally pummelling *I Swear I Was There*. The Clash have proven even more reluctant to issue a live document of the era – even though the 25% of their two dozen 1976 shows to have been recorded breaks every record for an unsigned band. Perhaps all those pre-slogan songs, that rough and ready musicianship and the vocalist's rabble-rousing

In fact, the *real* Year Zero is still viewed – in and out of academia – as something contradistinct from itself; as if it was *not* the bookends to punk as a communal cause, or the be-all and end-all of why the Pistols and the people they *directly* influenced in those manic months ultimately redeemed the form they set out to dee-stroy.

We shall not see its like again.

mess with the myth. They certainly suggest Strummer was a sinner long before he became a saint. Even the November Polydor demos – about which the band bitched endlessly – only slipped out officially in 2013 on a three-figure boxed-set of largely lifeless repackaging, the third such exercise in living memory. Buzzcocks have also missed a trick by not releasing their contagiously anarchic sets from The Screen On The Green and the Electric Circus, both of which were surprisingly well-recorded and bootlegged with a welcome attention to detail. At least The Damned's 1976 performances are well represented 'on catalogue' – their debut gig at the 100 Club and the Mont-de-Marsan meltdown both having been released on readily accessible official releases, along with their November 1976 Peel session, a high watermark for a band just nine months away from dissolution themselves.

A YEAR ZERO CHRONOLOGY

All gig-listings are for The Sex Pistols, unless otherwise stated.

In all cases where tapes are known to exist, I have provided full track-listings even if they are not in general circulation. The tracks of relevant shows/tapes are highlighted in bold.

So much of the early Pistols history remains a source of dispute, more than a quarter-century after Lee Wood's Sex Pistols Day By Day *(Omnibus, 1988), for which I provided much of the information. If a previously reported gig is not here, it is because I can find no evidence it ever happened.*

1975: NOVEMBER

6 NOV P1
ST MARTIN'S SCHOOL OF ART, LONDON
Photos purporting to be from this gig and taken by Rotten's best friend, John Grey, were included in *No Irish, No Dogs, No Blacks*. Grey has confirmed they are not from this gig, but from a later performance.

7 NOV P2
CENTRAL SCHOOL OF ART, HOLBORN, LONDON

?14 NOV P3
HERTFORDSHIRE COLLEGE OF ART AND DESIGN, ST ALBANS

21 NOV P4
WESTFIELD COLLEGE, FROGNAL, LONDON

28 NOV P5
QUEEN ELIZABETH COLLEGE, KENSINGTON, LONDON
ALL NIGHT BALL
The band's first, brief mention in the music press: 'The [Social] Sec. [lists the bill, and then says,], "There are [also] the Sex Pistols. You missed them." "Were they good?" I asked brightly. "They played for expenses," he countered. The Sex Pistols were huddled against a far wall of the dance floor. They are all about 12 years old. Or maybe about 19, but you could be fooled. They're managed by Malcolm, who runs "Sex" in the King's Road, and they're going to be the Next Big Thing. Or maybe the Next Big Thing After That.' – Kate Phillips, *NME* 27/12/75.

29 NOV P6
THE NATIONAL COLLEGE OF FOOD TECHNOLOGY, WEYBRIDGE
A piece by Simon Wright in *The Guardian* 14/11/14 recalls this previously undocumented gig.

DECEMBER

5 DEC P7
CHELSEA SCHOOL OF ART, CHELSEA, LONDON
Photographed by legendary rock-photographer Mick Rock.

9 DEC P8

RAVENSBOURNE COLLEGE, CHISLEHURST, KENT

A track-listing has appeared for this gig – but no tape – which fits with the likely set they were playing. It is as follows:

Set: Did You No Wrong. Don't Give Me No Lip Child. Understanding. Through My Eyes. Seventeen. New York. Whatcha Gonna Do About It. I'm Not Your Steppin' Stone. Submission. Pretty Vacant. No Fun.

10 DEC P9

FAIRHOLT HOUSE, LONDON CITY POLYTECHNIC

This was presumably the gig in Aldgate Paul Cook mentions in *No Irish, No Dogs No Blacks.* Also mentioned, by Rotten, in the same memoir are gigs at a Hounslow Teddy boy convention and at the West Ham Utd social club. No confirmation of either has been forthcoming.

1976: JANUARY

23 JAN P10

WATFORD COLLEGE, WATFORD, HERTS

JAN-FEB P11

NORTH EAST LONDON POLYTECHNIC, LONDON

This was a gig mentioned by Jonh Ingham in his 24/4/76 *Sounds* profile. See also a letter from a 'Bill Dyke' to *Melody Maker* 9/10/76. This may be the rumoured early show when they supported Kilburn & The High Roads, which might also explain how they got the gig in the first place.

FEBRUARY

EARLY FEB P12

RAVENSBOURNE COLLEGE, CHISLEHURST, KENT

Both Steve Severin and Siouxsie Sioux missed the Pistols set at the same college on December 9, but according to Severin they both saw the Pistols at a 'return' show, a week or so before the Marquee. Nigel Williamson, who was at one of the Ravensbourne shows, remembers meeting Siouxsie, so he also presumably attended this second show.

12 FEB P13

MARQUEE CLUB, SOHO, LONDON

Reviews: *Evening Standard* 20/2/76; *NME* 21/2/76 [reprinted in *Creem*, June 1976; partially reprinted in *New York Rocker* #3]. A mention, the following week, in *NME*'s 'Teazers', suggested, "The Sex Pistols [were] dismissed as support band to Eddie and the Hotrods on the Rods' current tour after only one gig (reviewed last week)." This is the only time such a possibility was mooted. Additional oral recollections appeared in Pistols features in *Mojo* #76 and *Uncut* #37.

14 FEB P14

ANDREW LOGAN'S PARTY, BUTLERS WHARF, LONDON

Review: Nick Kent in *NME* 27/11/76.

Famously photographed by Joe Stevens, as Rotten wrestled with Jordan's underwear.

19 FEB P15

HERTFORDSHIRE COLLEGE OF ART AND DESIGN, ST ALBANS

The first time the Pistols were photographed by Ray Stevenson, at McLaren's behest.

20 FEB P16
COLLEGE OF HIGHER EDUCATION, HIGH WYCOMBE
Additional oral recollections appeared in Pistols feature in *Uncut* #37.

21 FEB P17
WELWYN GARDEN CITY
Set: Did You No Wrong. No Lip. Understanding. New York. Seventeen. Whatcha Gonna Do About It. Submission. I'm Not Your Steppin' Stone. Pretty Vacant. No Fun. Substitute.
The show is recorded by Howard Trafford and Pete McNeish after seeing the previous night's performance in High Wycombe.

FEB P18
CENTRAL SCHOOL OF ART, HOLBORN, LONDON

MARCH

MARCH ??
INSTITUTE OF CONTEMPORARY ARTS, LONDON
Though cancelled at the last minute, the Pistols turned up for the occasion. Mentioned as forthcoming in Neil Spencer's review of the Marquee show, so presumably early March.

20 MARCH P19
NASHVILLE ROOMS, WEST KENSINGTON, LONDON.
'Teazers' 27/3/76; Letter to *NME* 3/4/76.
The Giant Kinetic Wardrobe was the support-act/co-headliner.

25 MARCH P20
ST ALBANS COLLEGE OF ART AND DESIGN, ST ALBANS

30 MARCH P21
100 CLUB, OXFORD ST, LONDON
'Jaws' 10/4/76; photos in *Sounds* 24/4/76. Photographed by Ray Stevenson. At least one photo does appear to show Rotten trying to 'spear' Matlock with the microphone stand. Additional oral recollections appeared in Pistols feature in *Mojo* #76.

APRIL

1 APRIL B1
INSTITUTE OF TECHNOLOGY, BOLTON
[Buzzcocks Mk.1's debut gig]
'Buzzcocks played their first gig last night. We were great. The music was pretty awful. A third of the way through the set, they, the management, switched off the PA and started up the disco. It was only after our last number that the audience clapped … It was our first rehearsal, live.' – Letter from Howard Devoto to Richard Boon, 2/4/76.

3 APRIL P22
NASHVILLE ROOMS, WEST KENSINGTON, LONDON
Ads in *NME* + *Melody Maker* 3/4/76. Reviews in *Melody Maker* 10/4/76 by Allan Jones and *NME* 17/4/76 by Geoff Hutt.
Another show photographed by Ray Stevenson and probably by Eve Dadomo. The headliner was The 101'ers. Previously cited as the source for the '1st Nashville Tape', see 23 April. Additional oral recollections appeared in Pistols feature in *Uncut* #37.

4 APRIL P23

EL PARADISE STRIP CLUB, SOHO, LONDON

Plugged in 'Teazers' a week early, on 27/3/76, the first El Paradise gig was photographed by Ray Stevenson and Joe Stevens. It was also reviewed by Jonh Ingham in the 10/4/76 *Sounds*.

11 APRIL P24

EL PARARDISE STRIP CLUB, SOHO, LONDON

Though many sources cite only a single El Paradise gig, the *Sounds*' gossip section, 'Jaws', for 17/4/76 specifically says, 'Sex Pistols keep going down a storm at their regular venue, Soho's Burlesque Strip Club. But sadly, the venue is already proving to be too small and gigs are about to be deferred until a suitably raunchy but larger dive can be found ...,' suggesting a second show did happen.

18 APRIL GIG

THE ROUNDHOUSE, LONDON

Van Der Graaf Generator/ The Spiders From Mars/ The 101'ers.

19 APRIL GIG

THE ROUNDHOUSE, LONDON

Van Der Graaf Generator/ The Spiders From Mars/ The 101'ers.

23 APRIL P25

NASHVILLE ROOMS, WEST KENSINGTON, LONDON

NME 8/5/76; 'Jaws' 8/5/76.

Set: Did You No Wrong. No Lip. Seventeen. I'm Not Your Steppin' Stone. No Feelings. New York. No Fun. Submission. Substitute. Problems. Satellite. Pretty Vacant.

The famous fight was photographed by at least three photographers there that night, Joe Stevens, Kate Simon and Eve Dadomo. The headliner was again The 101'ers. A contemporary reference in 'Jaws' 8/5/76 notes that 'fisticuffs broke out' during 'Pretty Vacant' and that 'voice-man John Rotten quipped, "Ease up, we haven't finished the song yet."' This corresponds with the so-called 'First Nashville Tape', usually attributed to the 3rd. When I compiled and circulated a Sex Pistols tapeography in 1979-80 I listed it thus. The tapeography was appropriated by a 'gentleman' and published as his own work in *Sounds* in 1982. When Lee Wood began work on his *Sex Pistols Day By Day* (1988), I provided him with an updated tapeography, from which he drew much of the information. I again attributed the First Nashville Tape to 3/4/76, not the 23rd. Mea culpa.

29 APRIL P26

NASHVILLE ROOMS, WEST KENSINGTON, LONDON

Set: Did You No Wrong. No Lip. Seventeen. New York. Whatcha Gonna Do About It. I'm Not Your Steppin' Stone. Submission. Satellite. No Feelings. Pretty Vacant. No Fun. Substitute. Problems. Understanding. Did You No Wrong.

Billed as 'Party With The Sex Pistols', flyers for this gig were distributed at the April 23rd show. For the re-dating of the tape, see above. Given that the 'Second Nashville Tape' includes an encore, and is evidently the later gig, one must assume it is in fact their 4th and last at the Nashville Rooms. There is certainly no fight on there, though something odd is going on during 'Substitute'. Bootlegged extensively on vinyl and CD at invariably the wrong speed.

MAY

5 MAY P27
BABALU DISCO, FINCHLEY RD, LONDON
Photographed by Ray Stevenson. Famously ill-attended. Additional oral recollections appeared in Pistols feature in *Mojo* #76.

6 MAY P28
NORTH EAST LONDON POLYTECHNIC, LONDON

11 MAY P29
100 CLUB, OXFORD ST, LONDON
Previewed in *Time Out* (7/5/76) by Giovanni Dadomo. Probably the source of photographs by Jo Faull. Support act: Krakatoa. Additional oral recollections appeared in Pistols feature in *Mojo* #76.

12 MAY REC
MAJESTIC STUDIOS, LONDON w/ Chris Spedding.
Problems. No Feelings. Pretty Vacant.
Bootlegged in the early eighties on a 7" E.P., all three tracks were finally released officially on the *This Is Crap* 2-CD set in 1996. A news story on the session in the following week's *Sounds* featured a photo of the band unloading their equipment outside Majestic, taken by Ray Stevenson and used as the cover for said bootleg E.P.

12 MAY GIG
THE RED COW, HAMMERSMITH, LONDON
The 101'ers. Attended by Glen Matlock, Mick Jones, Paul Simonon + members of The Stranglers.

16 MAY GIG
THE ROUNDHOUSE, LONDON.
Patti Smith Group w/ The Stranglers.

17 MAY GIG
THE ROUNDHOUSE, LONDON
Patti Smith Group w/ The Stranglers. There were at least two bootleg albums from the PSG Roundhouse 'residency', one a single, the other a double.

18 MAY P30
100 CLUB, OXFORD ST, LONDON
Ad in *NME* 15/5/76. Reviewed, rapturously, by Greg Shaw for the June issue of US music monthly, *Phonograph*. Support act: Strange Days.

19 MAY P31
NORTHALLERTON, YORKSHIRE
Photographed by Peter Lloyd, who attended the show with his girlfriend, Pauline Murray. Additional oral recollections appeared in Pistols feature in *Record Collector* #407.

20 MAY P32
PENTHOUSE, SCARBOROUGH
Photographed by Peter Lloyd, who attended the show with his girlfriend, Pauline Murray. Additional oral recollections appeared in Pistols features in *Uncut* #37 and *Record Collector* #407.

21 MAY P33
TOWN HALL, MIDDLESBROUGH
The Pistols were support to Doctors of Madness. Additional oral recollections appeared in Pistols feature in *Mojo* #76.

22 MAY ??
BISHOP GROSSETESTE COLLEGE, LINCOLN [?]
This gig was certainly advertised – as was a show at the Manchester University Union, on the same night – but no band-member seems to remember this show, and no eye-witnesses have come forward with corroborative evidence it ever took place. I find it hard to believe that the band drove from Middlesbrough to Lincoln and then back to Hull.

[23/24] MAY P34
HULL

[23/24] MAY P35
BARNSLEY

25 MAY P36
100 CLUB, OXFORD ST, LONDON
Reviewed by Jonh Ingham for *Sounds* (5/6/76), opening with the immortal line, 'The Sex Pistols, teen savages and Britain's answer to the Captain & Tennile, were good but not great.' Support act: Dogwatch.

25 + 26 MAY GIG
CHAPTER ARTS CENTRE, CARDIFF
The Subterraneans. This was Nick Kent's short-lived band featuring three-quarters of The Damned: Brian James, Rat Scabies and Captain Sensible. According to Brian James, three Damned originals were performed each night: 'Fan Club', 'I Fall' and 'New Rose'.

30 MAY P37
ART EXCHANGE, READING UNIVERSITY, READING

JUNE

4 JUNE P38
LESSER FREE TRADE HALL, MANCHESTER
ad *NME* 5/6/76; *New Manchester Review* preview 29/5/76; *Out There #1*; *Penetration #8*; *NME* letter 19/6/76; *Sounds* letter 26/6/76; photos *New York Rocker* #3.
Set: Did You No Wrong. No Lip. Seventeen. I'm Not Your Steppin' Stone. New York. Whatcha Gonna Do About It. Submission. Satellite. No Feelings. No Fun. Substitute. Pretty Vacant. Problems. No Fun.
As a gig for which everyone seems so keen to rely on unreliable oral memory for the facts, this is a remarkably well-documented show. Having paid for a display ad in *NME* and run a preview in the *New Manchester Review*, Devoto and Shelley booked Solstice as a last-minute support act. Aside from the very good audience tape of the show – bootlegged on vinyl as *No Fun* and on CD as *Aggression Thru Repression* and *I Swear I Was There* – the young Morrissey wrote two separate letters to the music papers, both published, in *NME* 19/6/76 and *Sounds* 26/6/76, respectively. Paul Morley's review ran in issue one of *Out There*. Also there was Paul Welsh, editor of Stockport 'zine *Penetration*, who reviewed the concert in issue eight. The opening paragraph of Welsh's review ticks all the boxes: 'Well, at last our prayers have been answered with the "Sex

Pistols". They are musically everything that a Velvet Underground, Stooges, New York Dolls freak could wish for, while visually they look like poor customers at a jumble sale, tacky, sleazy, distasteful and yet somewhat natural. They attack their numbers as if they were attacking a gang of thugs in a street fight, viciously.' Additional oral recollections appeared in Pistols feature in *Mojo* #76.

5 JUNE GIG
CLARE HALLS, HAYWARDS HEATH
Last gig of The 101'ers.

12 JUNE D?
LISSON GROVE, LONDON
[Also June 19th, 26th, July 3rd]. It is alleged that The Damned played four consecutive Sundays at a youth club in Lisson Grove. Neither Scabies nor James remember any such occurences.

JUNE REC
DANGERFIELD STUDIO, LONDON
The Damned w/ Matt Dangefield.
I Fall. See Her Tonite. Feel The Pain.
These demos appear on the 2012 *Damned Damned Damned* boxed-set.

15 JUNE P39
100 CLUB, OXFORD ST, LONDON
NME 3/7/76; 'Jaws' 3/7/76. According to *Time Out*, The 101'ers were scheduled to headline, but they had disbanded ten days earlier. The Pistols appear to have ended up playing it on their own. The infamous occasion when Nick Kent was assaulted by Jah Wobble and Sid Vicious.

17 JUNE P40
ASSEMBLY HALL, WALTHAMSTOW, LONDON
Headlined by Ian Dury & The Kilburns, what was in fact their final gig. The Sex Pistols and The Stranglers also shared a bill for the first and last time. 'I prepare myself properly for beloved Walthamstow … I polish the razor-blade ear-piece, oil the knife, primp the barnet … and spray and splash until I smell like a moose … We were magnificent and the Sex Pistols are smashing.' – Ian Dury, *Melody Maker* 17/7/76.

29 JUNE P41
100 CLUB, OXFORD STREET, LONDON
Set: Flowers of Romance. Seventeen. No Lip. I'm Not Your Steppin' Stone. New York. Whatcha Gonna Do About It. Submission. I Wanna Be Me. Satellite. No Feelings. No Fun. Substitute. Problems. Pretty Vacant. Did You No Wrong.
The support act is Seventh Heaven.

JULY

3 JULY P42
PIER PAVILION, HASTINGS
Letter in *NME* 16/10/76.

4 JULY P43/C1
BLACK SWAN, SHEFFIELD
Sex Pistols w/ Clash. Letter from Reg Cliff, 'A real music lover', published in *NME* & *Sounds* 17/7/76. According to Pat Gilbert's Clash bio the Clash set-list included 'Protex Blue', '1-2 Crush on You', 'Keys To Your Heart', 'a couple of Kinks and Who numbers', 'I Can't Control Myself', 'Too Much Monkey Business' and 'Junco Partner'.

5 JULY GIG
DINGWALL'S, LONDON
The Ramones w/ Flamin' Groovies. Attended by assorted members of the Pistols, Clash, The Damned and The Stranglers.

6 JULY P44/D1
100 CLUB, OXFORD ST, LONDON
Sex Pistols w/ The Damned.
Damned Set: One of the Two. New Rose. Alone. Help. Fan Club. I Feel Alright. Feel The Pain. Fish. Circles. See Her Tonite. I Fall. So Messed Up. Pistols Set: I Wanna Be Me. No Lip. Seventeen. I'm Not Your Steppin' Stone. New York. Whatcha Gonna Do About It. Submission. Satellite. No Fun. Substitute. Pretty Vacant. Problems. [poss. encore – Did You No Wrong]
The Damned set appears on the 2012 *Damned Damned Damned* boxed-set.

9 JULY P45
LYCEUM BALLROOM, THE STRAND, LONDON
Ad in *Melody Maker* 10/7/76; *Melody Maker* 17/7/76; *Sounds* 9/10/76. The Pistols played support to The Pretty Things and Supercharge. Additional oral recollections appeared in Pistols features in *Mojo* #76 and *Uncut* #37.

10 JULY P46
THE SUNDOWN, CHARING CROSS RD, LONDON

13-19 JULY REC
DENMARK STREET, LONDON
Sex Pistols w/ Dave Goodman.
Submission. Seventeen. Satellite. Pretty Vacant. Anarchy In The UK. No Feelings. I Wanna Be Me.
These seven 'Goodman demos' have appeared in a bewildering number of guises, bootleg, semi-official and official. Six of the seven (minus 'Pretty Vacant') appeared on *Spunk*, all seven appeared on *No Future UK*, both of which subsequently appeared as quasi-legit CDs (on Sanctuary and Receiver respectively). The full tape also appeared on the CD edition of *The Mini Album*, a vinyl version of which appeared first in 1985. Six songs again appeared on the *Studio Daze* CD, though only 'Pretty Vacant' and 'Submission' were used on the supposedly definitive 2002 boxed-set, *Sexbox1*. The CD version of *The Mini Album* provides the most complete, best sounding version of the final demo tape, after post-production at Riverside and Decibel Studios. Pre-overdub versions of 'Satellite', 'Pretty Vacant' and 'Submission' have appeared on a particularly dodgy Receiver Records CD called *Wanted – The Goodman Tapes*.

[MID-] JULY D2
ART COLLEGE, ST. ALBANS
The Damned.

[MID-] JULY D3
NAG'S HEAD, HIGH WYCOMBE
The Damned.

15 JULY D4
NASHVILLE ROOMS, WEST KENSINGTON, LONDON
The Damned.
Sounds 24/7/76.

20 JULY P47/B2
LESSER FREE TRADE HALL, MANCHESTER
Sex Pistols w/ Buzzcocks and Slaughter & The Dogs.
Sounds 31/7/76; *NME* 2/10/76. Photos are taken at this show by Peter Oldham and Al McDowell. Unlike the previous Manchester show, this gig, featuring the live debut of 'Anarchy In The UK', does not seem to have been recorded.

AUGUST

6 AUG D5
NASHVILLE ROOMS, WEST KENSINGTON, LONDON
The Damned

10 AUG P48
100 CLUB, OXFORD ST, LONDON
Sex Pistols w/ The Vibrators.
Sniffin' Glue #3; 'Jaws', 21/8/76. Additional oral recollections appeared in Pistols feature in *Mojo* #76.

12 AUG B3
THE RANCH, MANCHESTER
Buzzcocks.

13 AUG C2
REHEARSAL REHEARSALS, CAMDEN TOWN, LONDON
Clash.
Sounds 21/8/76. 'If you think the H-Bomb's hot, wait till you see The Clash. Risen from the ashes of The 101'ers, King Joe Strummer and his cohorts … unveiled the results of two months intensive rehearsal at an exotic soiree in their swank rehearsal studio before an exclusive assembly of hard Mach-Rock fans.' – 'Jaws', 21/8/76.

14 AUG P49
BARBARELLA'S, BIRMINGHAM
Set: Flowers of Romance. I Wanna Be Me. Liar. Substitute. Seventeen. New York. I'm Not Your Steppin' Stone. No Fun. Satellite. No Feelings. Pretty Vacant. Problems. Anarchy In The UK.
Additional oral recollections appeared in Pistols feature in *Mojo* #76.

19 AUG B4
THE RANCH, MANCHESTER [?]
Buzzcocks.
This gig was certainly advertised but may not have taken place.

19 AUG P50
WEST RUNTON PAVILION, RUNTON, NR CROMER, NORFOLK

20 AUG D6
MONT-DE-MARSAN PUNK FESTIVAL, FRANCE
The Damned.
'The Raver' *Melody Maker* 28/8/76; *Melody Maker* 4/9/74; Sounds 28/8 + 4/9/76.
Set: One of the Two. New Rose. 'Equipment Failure'. Help. Fan Club. 1970/ I Feel Alright. Feel The Pain. Fish. See Her Tonite. I Fall. So Messed Up.
Released on the Sanctuary 2008 boxed-set, *Play It At Your Sister.*

21 AUG P51
BOAT CLUB, NOTTINGHAM
Zob the Tuffdart, letter to *Sounds* 11/9/76.

28 AUG B5
THE COMMERCIAL HOTEL, STALYBRIDGE
Buzzcocks.

29 AUG P52/B6/C3
THE SCREEN ON THE GREEN CINEMA, ISLINGTON, LONDON
The Sex Pistols, Clash and Buzzcocks.
NME 11/9/76; *Sounds* 11/9/76; letter in *Sounds* 18/9/76; *Sounds* 9/10/76.
Buzzcocks Set: Breakdown. Friends of Mine. Time's Up. Orgasm Addict. Peking Hooligan. Lester Sands (Drop In The Ocean). Oh Shit. You Tear Me Up. Love Battery. I Can't Control Myself. I Love You Big Dummy/ Don't Mess 'Round.
Clash Set: Deny. I Know What To Think About You. I Never Did It. Janie Jones. Protex Blue. Mark Me Absent. What's My Name. Bernie's Shakedown. 48 Hours. I'm So Bored With You. London's Burning. 1977.
Pistols Set: Anarchy In The UK. I Wanna Be Me. Seventeen. New York. No Lip. I'm Not Your Steppin' Stone. Satellite. Submission. Liar. No Feelings. Substitute. Pretty Vacant. Problems. Did You No Wrong. No Fun.
A double-CD bootleg appeared in the mid-nineties sourced direct from a master cassette of the complete show. The Pistols set was subsequently copied from said bootleg for the *Sexbox1* boxed-set. Additional oral recollections appeared in Pistols feature in *Mojo* #76.

31 AUG P53/C4
100 CLUB, OXFORD ST, LONDON
The Sex Pistols, w/ Clash & Suburban Studs.
Letter in *Sounds* 18/9/76; *Sounds* 11/9/76 [part of Screen On The Green review].
Set: Anarchy In The UK. I Wanna Be Me. Seventeen. New York. No Lip. I'm Not Your Steppin' Stone. Satellite. Submission. Liar. No Feelings. Substitute. Flowers of Romance/Pretty Vacant. Problems. No Fun. Anarchy In The UK.
[I Wanna Be Me].
The show, minus three songs, was bootlegged on vinyl in 1979 as *100 Club Pistols Party.*

?AUG REC
4-TRACK REHEARSAL TAPE, STOCKWELL
Wire w/ George Gill.
Prove Myself. Mary Is A Dyke. Bad Night. Can't Stand It No More. Love. Midnight Train. What Is This Feeling Called Love. TV. Lost Boy. Johnny Piss Off. After Midnight. Fade. Bitch. Roadrunner.

SEPTEMBER

1 SEPT P54
GRANADA TV *SO IT GOES* TV SHOW, MANCHESTER
Anarchy In The UK. [Problems].
Broadcast on September 4th, 1976, this performance has been repeated a number of times, and even appeared on an official VHS punk compilation. It seems unlikely that the rehearsal version of 'Problems' remains in the Granada vaults.

2 SEPT P55
NAGS HEAD, HIGH WYCOMBE

3 SEPT P56
CLUB DE CHALET DU LAC, PARIS, FRANCE
Melody Maker 11/9/76; *I Wanna Be Your Dog* #1.

5 SEPT P57
CLUB DE CHALET DU LAC, PARIS, FRANCE
Beat magazine; *Sounds 9/10/76.*
Set: Flowers Of Romance. Anarchy In The UK. I Wanna Be Me. Seventeen. New York. No Lip. I'm Not Your Steppin' Stone. Satellite. Submission. Liar. No Feelings. Substitute. Pretty Vacant. Problems. No Fun. Did You No Wrong. Anarchy In The UK.
This (supposedly soundboard) tape remains uncirculated.

5 SEPT C5
THE ROUNDHOUSE, LONDON
Clash.
Set: Deny. 1-2 Crush on You. I Know What To Think About You. I Never Did It. How Can I Understand The Flies. Protex Blue. Janie Jones. Mark Me Absent. Deadly Serious. 48 Hours. I'm So Bored With You. Sitting At My Party. London's Burning. What's My Name. 1977.

11 SEPT P58
THE ROYAL BALLROOM, WHITBY

12 SEPT P59
FFORDE GRENE, LEEDS

13 SEPT P60
QUAINTWAYS, CHESTER

15 SEPT P61
LODESTAR, BLACKBURN
Set: Anarchy In The UK. Did You No Wrong.
This gig was rescheduled from August 18th, Two songs from the encore appear to have been preserved at the end of the first reel of Goodman's soundboard tape of the Chelmsford Prison show, misassigned to the latter. Additional oral recollections appeared in Pistols feature in *Mojo* #76.

17 SEPT P62
H.M. CHELMSFORD PRISON, CHELMSFORD
'Pistols in Prison', by Jonh Ingham, unknown fanzine, reproduced in *Sex Pistols Day By Day.*

Set: Anarchy In The UK. I Wanna Be Me. Seventeen. New York. No Lip. I'm Not Your Steppin' Stone. Satellite. Submission. Liar. Substitute. No Fun. Pretty Vacant. Problems. [Anarchy in the UK].
Released initially with fake audience noise and between-song banter by a Johnny Rotten impersonator – I kid you not – the show has subsequently been released on CD with said extraneous matter removed. Caveat emptor.

20 SEPT P63/C6
100 CLUB, OXFORD ST, LONDON (Punk Festival)
The Sex Pistols w/ The Clash.
This show generated more press than any punk gig to date, with reviews in the following: *Sounds* 2/10/76; *Melody Maker* 2/10/76; *NME* 2/10/76; *Evening Standard* 23/9/76; *New Society* 7/10/76; *Sounds* 9/10/78 and *Sniffin' Glue* #3 1/2, a special 'Punk Festival' supplement.
Clash Set: White Riot. London's Burning. I'm So Bored With You. How Can I Understand The Flies. Protex Blue. Deadly Serious. Deny. 48 Hours. What's My Name. Janie Jones. 1977.
Pistols Set: Anarchy In The UK. I Wanna Be Me. Seventeen. New York. No Lip. I'm Not Your Steppin' Stone. Satellite. Submission. Liar. No Feelings. Substitute. Pretty Vacant. Problems. No Fun. [Anarchy In The UK].
Additional oral recollections appeared in Pistols feature in *Mojo* #76.

20 SEPT B7
HOLDSWORTH HALL, DEANSGATE, MANCHESTER
Buzzcocks w/ Eater.
Paul Morley, *NME* 2/10/76; Martin Hannett, *NMR* 22/10-4/11/76.

20 SEPT REC
PATHWAY STUDIOS, LONDON
The Damned w/ Nick Lowe
New Rose b/w Help.

21 SEPT B8/D7
100 CLUB, OXFORD ST, LONDON (Punk Festival Night #2)
Buzzcocks, The Damned, w/ The Vibrators.
NME 2/10/76; *Sounds* 2/10/76 + 9/10/76; Caroline Coon, *Melody Maker* 2/10/76.
'On stage, the Buzzcocks, undismayed by scant audiences, don't give a shit. Their first number, "Breakdown", showed forcefully what they're about. Devoto, with cropped orange tinted hair, stands twisted in front of the mic, his head always turned away from the audience. Pete, with a razorblade earring dangling about his head, clasps his guitar and throttles out riff after riff that proves he don't need no solos. John's drumming in "Oh Shit" couldn't have been better, whacking away without a trace of feeling, while Steve maintains the pace on bass. Rumbling away on such goodies as "Big Dummy". The audience don't know, the Buzzcocks don't know and even we don't know what they're about – but we all know they're good, very good!' – Steve Mick, *Sniffin' Glue* #4.

21 SEPT P64
TOP RANK, CARDIFF, WALES

22 SEPT P65
STOWAWAY CLUB, NEWPORT, WALES
South Wales Echo 24/9/76.

23 SEPT P66
CIRCLES CLUB, SWANSEA, WALES

23 SEPT D8
NAG'S HEAD, HIGH WYCOMBE
The Damned w/ The Vibrators.

24 SEPT P67
76 CLUB, BURTON UPON TRENT
Set: Anarchy In The UK. I Wanna Be Me. Seventeen. New York. No Lip. I'm Not Your Steppin' Stone. Satellite. Submission. Liar. Substitute. No Feelings. No Fun. Pretty Vacant. Problems (false start). Problems.
The legendary *Indecent Exposure* bootleg, released in 1978 (minus 'Satellite'), made this remarkably fine audience tape the definitive audio document of the original band. Dave Goodman later lied about the origins of the tape to justify his repeated editions of the same tape – off the bootleg – on quasi-legit CDs. Again, it was a bootlegger who accessed the original, complete tape for the *Truly Indecent Exposure* CD in 1996, which remains the definitive edition.

25 or 26 SEPT P?
MIDDLESBROUGH
Possible Pistols gig/s.

27 SEPT P68
OUTLOOK CLUB, DONCASTER

28 SEPT P?
THE PLACE, GUILDFORD [?]
Another date consistently cited in Pistols gigographies, but the idea that the Pistols drove from Doncaster and/or Derby to Guildford to Stoke stretches credulity, and there is surely no way the London-based EMI A&R man Nick Mobbs drove himself to Doncaster/Derby if the Pistols were playing Guildford the following night.

29 SEPT P69
STRIKES CLUB, BURSLEM, STOKE-ON-TRENT

30 SEPT P70
CLEOPATRAS, DERBY

OCTOBER

OCT PE1
ROCK GARDEN, MIDDLESBROUGH
The Points [a.k.a. Penetration]
The debut gig for Pauline Murray's punk band. The band is then renamed Penetration.

1 OCT **
DIDSBURY COLLEGE, MANCHESTER
[Cancelled. Rotten's voice shot.]
A great deal has been made of the so-called Didsbury College gig. It certainly never happened as a trawl through that week's music papers – a simple enough procedure one would think – shows the Sex Pistols, minus Rotten, were at the Roundhouse to see The Runaways that night.

5 OCT **
400 CLUB, TORQUAY
[Cancelled?]

6 OCT **
WOODS CLUB, PLYMOUTH
[Cancelled?]

7 OCT **
WINTER GARDENS, PENZANCE
[Cancelled?]

2 OCT **C7**
INSTITUTE OF CONTEMPORARY ARTS, LONDON
The Clash.

EARLY OCT **C?**
[THE PLACE?], GUILDFORD
The Clash.

8 OCT **B9**
ST. BONIFACE CHURCH YOUTH CLUB, SALFORD
Buzzcocks.

8 OCT **D9**
THE WHITE SWAN, LUTON
The Damned.
Letter to *Sounds* 23/10/76.

9 OCT **D10**
CANLEY TEACHER TRAINING COLLEGE, COVENTRY
The Damned.

9 OCT **C8**
TIDDENFOOT LEISURE CENTRE, LEIGHTON BUZZARD
The Clash.

9 OCT **P?**
COUNTY CRICKET GROUND, NORTHAMPTON [?]
One assumes this gig was cancelled because the Pistols went straight into the studio after signing with EMI on the eighth.

9-11 OCT **REC**
LANSDOWNE STUDIOS, LONDON
Sex Pistols w/ Dave Goodman.
Substitute. No Lip. I'm Not Your Steppin' Stone. Johnny B. Goode/ Roadrunner. Whatcha Gonna Do About It?. Through My Eyes. No Fun. [Anarchy In The UK.]
The first five tracks were released with overdubs on *The Great Rock'N'Roll Swindle* in 1979. The first six tracks were then released on *Pirates of Destiny* in 1991, and the first seven tracks were released on the 2002 *Sexbox1* boxed-set.

12 OCT **P71**
COLLEGE OF TECHNOLOGY, DUNDEE, SCOTLAND

13 OCT P72
LAFAYETTE CLUB, WOLVERHAMPTON

14 OCT D11
NAG'S HEAD, HIGH WYCOMBE
The Damned.
Sounds 23/10/76.

14 OCT P73
MR DIGBY'S, BIRKENHEAD
Mary Harron: How do you feel about [tonight's] set?
Johnny Rotten: It wasn't a good one. We can do much better than that. We were in Wolverhampton last night and Dundee the night before. Travellin' around in the back of a van is no fun. It fucks you up. – Interview after Birkenhead gig, *Punk* #8 [March 1977]

15 OCT P74
ERIC'S @ GATSBY'S, LIVERPOOL

15 OCT C9
ACKLAM HALL, LADBROKE GROVE, LONDON
The Clash.

16 OCT C10
UNIVERSITY OF LONDON UNION, LONDON
The Clash.

16-17 OCT REC
WESSEX STUDIO, LONDON
Sex Pistols w/ Dave Goodman.
Anarchy In The UK.
Released on *Spunk, No Future UK* and *The Great Rock'N'Roll Swindle* in the original Goodman mix.

16 OCT J1
SOHO MARKET, LONDON
The Jam.

[MID-] OCT CH1
CHELSEA POTTER PUB, LONDON.
Debut gig for Chelsea.

18 OCT CH2
INSTITUTE OF CONTEMPORARY ARTS, LONDON
Chelsea w/ Throbbing Gristle.
Tony Parsons, *NME 30/10/76.*

18 OCT REC
REVOLUTION STUDIO, MANCHESTER
Buzzcocks [Engineer: Andy MacPherson].
You Tear Me Up. Breakdown. Friends of Mine. Orgasm Addict. Boredom. Time's Up. Lester Sands (Drop In The Ocean). Love Battery. I Can't Control Myself. I Love You Big Dummy. Don't Mess Me 'Round.
The legendary *Time's Up*, first bootlegged on vinyl in 1979 and subsequently issued offcially on CD, most recently in 2000, with enhanced packaging.

20 OCT P75
BOGARTS, BIRMINGHAM
Letter to *Sounds* from Steve Horton, Birmingham, 6/11/76.
Set: Anarchy In The UK. I Wanna Be Me. Seventeen. Satellite. Substitute. Liar. No Feelings. No Fun. Pretty Vacant.

21 OCT P76
QUEENSWAY HALL, DUNSTABLE
The Sex Pistols w/ The Jam.
Additional oral recollections appeared in Pistols feature in *Mojo* #76

21 OCT D12
RED COW, HAMMERSMITH, LONDON
The Damned.

22 OCT REL
Stiff release of **New Rose b/w Help.**

23 OCT C11
INSTITUTE OF CONTEMPORARY ARTS, LONDON
The Clash w/ Subway Sect.
Miles, *NME* 6/11/76.

26 OCT D13
VICTORIA PALACE, LONDON
The Damned w/ Graham Parker & The Rumour.
NME; 6/11/76; 'Teazers' 13/11/76.

27 OCT C12
BARBARELLA'S, BIRMINGHAM
The Clash w/ The Suburban Studs.
Jonh Ingham, *Sounds* 13/11/76.
Set: White Riot. Birmingham's Burning. I'm So Bored With The USA. How Can I Understand The Flies. Protex Blue. Going To The Disco. Deny. Career Opportunities. 48 Hours. What's My Name. Janie Jones. 1977. 1-2 Crush on You.
Jonh Ingham credits this gig to a Wednesday, which would mean the 27th, not the commonly attributed 26th.

29 OCT C13
FULHAM TOWN HALL, LONDON
The Clash w/ The Vibrators.
Giovanni Dadomo, *Sounds* 6/11/76.
Set: White Riot. I'm So Bored With The USA. Career Opportunities. How Can I Understand The Flies. London's Burning. Protex Blue. Deny. Mark Me Absent. What's My Name. 48 Hours. Janie Jones. 1977. 1-2 Crush On You. I Know What To Think Of You. White Riot.

30 OCT D14
TIDDENFOOT LEISURE CENTRE, LEIGHTON BUZZARD
The Damned.

[LATE-] OCT REC
WESSEX STUDIO, LONDON
Sex Pistols w/ Chris Thomas.
Anarchy In The UK I. Anarchy In The UK II.
The official EMI 45 version. An alternate take appeared on the 2002 boxed-set *Sexbox1.*

NOVEMBER

2 NOV D15
HOPE N ANCHOR, ISLINGTON, LONDON
The Damned.

3 NOV D16
UNIVERSITY OF KENT, CANTERBURY
The Damned w/ Eddie & The Hot Rods.

3 NOV C14
HARLESDEN COLISEUM, LONDON
The Clash.

5 NOV C15
ROYAL COLLEGE OF ART, LONDON
A Night of Treason.
The Clash w/ Subway Sect.
Set: White Riot. I'm So Bored With The USA. Career Opportunities. How Can I Understand The Flies. London's Burning. Protex Blue. Deny. Mark Me Absent. What's My Name. 48 Hours. Janie Jones. 1977. White Riot.
'By the time they play the Royal College of Art … emotions are running way too high. They play a set under the rubric "A Night of Treason" … Some of the audience, when not lobbing fireworks around, take an extreme dislike to The Clash and start bunging bottles at the stage. The rest of the audience is split between Clash fans who already think their band can do no wrong and the uncommitted whose previlaing attitude is, "Well, they are playing violent music and if you play violent, well, you know what they say about what you sow…" The band are certain how they feel about playing in a rain of bottles. Strummer lurches off stage and tries to sort out those responsible … personally.' – Pete Silverton, *Trouser Press* 2/78.

8 NOV B10
BAND ON THE WALL, MANCHESTER
NMR's 1st Anniversary Party, featuring Buzzcocks.
Set: Time's Up. Orgasm Addict. Friends Of Mine. Boredom. Breakdown. You Tear Me Up. Love Battery. I Can't Control Myself.

NOV? REC
WOKING
Three 8-track demos by the 4-piece Jam. Unreleased.
Soul Dance. Back In My Arms Again. I Got By In Time.

9 NOV J3
100 CLUB, OXFORD ST, LONDON
The Jam w/ The Vibrators.

10 NOV B11/CH3
ELECTRIC CIRCUS, MANCHESTER
Buzzcocks w/ Chelsea Mk.1.
Paul Morley, *NME* 27/11/76; *Sniffin' Glue* #5.

11 NOV C16
THE LACY LADY, ILFORD
The Clash.

11 NOV REC
BBC STUDIOS, LONDON
NATIONWIDE, [b/cast 12/11/76] **Anarchy In The UK**.

11 NOV D17
COATHAM BOWL, REDCAR
The Damned w/ Flamin' Groovies.

12 NOV D?
ERIC'S, LIVERPOOL
The Damned. [Almost certainly cancelled.]

13 NOV D?
BARBARELLA'S, BIRMINGHAM
The Damned. [Almost certainly cancelled] 'The Groovies pulled out after the first show. The second was at The Roundhouse [sic] … [I believe] the remainder were cancelled but were rescheduled for The Damned.' – Rat Scabies.

14 NOV D18
THE ROUNDHOUSE, LONDON
The Damned.

[MID-]NOV REC
'THE POLYDOR DEMOS'
The Clash w/ Guy Stevens, Chris Parry & Vic Smith.
Janie Jones. Career Opportunities. London's Burning. 1977. White Riot.
Released on the *Sound-System* boxed-set in 2013.

15 NOV P77
NOTRE DAME HALL, LEICESTER PLACE, LONDON
Sniffin' Glue #6; *Time Out*.
Set: Anarchy In The UK. I Wanna Be Me. Seventeen. Pretty Vacant. No Feelings. No Lip. No Fun. Whatcha Gonna Do About It. Did You No Wrong. Seventeen. I'm Not Your Steppin' Stone. Satellite. Problems. New York. Submission. No Fun.
Partial versions of 'Anarchy In The UK', 'Submission', 'Pretty Vacant' and 'No Fun' are included in the *London Weekend Show* broadcast on 29/11/76. Additional oral recollections appeared in Pistols feature in *Uncut* #37.

16 NOV SH1
100 CLUB, OXFORD ST, LONDON
The Count Bishops w/ Sham 69. [replacing The Jam].
NME 27/11/76.

18 NOV D19
THE LACY LADY, ILFORD
The Damned.

18 NOV C17
NAG'S HEAD, HIGH WYCOMBE
The Clash.
Sounds 27/11/76.

19 NOV P78
HENDON POLYTECHNIC, MIDDLESEX

19 NOV REL
Anarchy In The UK b/w I Wanna Be Me. [often cited as 26/11]

19 NOV D20
MANOR HILL UPPER SCHOOL, FINCHLEY, LONDON
The Damned w/ Slaughter & The Dogs + Eater.

20 NOV D21
FRIARS, AYLESBURY
The Damned.

21 NOV CH4
NASHVILLE, WEST KENSINGTON, LONDON
Chelsea w/ The Stranglers.

21 NOV D22
THE GREYHOUND, CROYDON
The Damned.

23 NOV J4
UPSTAIRS AT RONNIE SCOTT'S
The Jam's last gig as a 4-piece.

26 NOV D23
ERIC'S, LIVERPOOL
The Damned.
Sounds 4/12/76.

27 NOV D24
TEESIDE POLYTECHNIC, MIDDLESBROUGH
The Damned.

28 NOV D25
ELECTRIC CIRCUS, MANCHESTER
The Damned w/ Slaughter & The Dogs.

29 NOV P79/C18
LANCHESTER POLYTECHNIC, COVENTRY
The Sex Pistols w/ The Clash.

30 NOV REC
BBC STUDIOS 4, MAIDA VALE, LONDON
John Peel Session. The Damned w/ John Walters.
Neat Neat Neat. New Rose. So Messed Up. I Fall.

DECEMBER

EARLY DEC G1
SUMMA STUDIOS, LONDON
The Only Ones w/ Generation X.

2 DEC W1
NASHVILLE ROOMS, WEST KENSINGTON, LONDON
Wire w/ The Derelicts.
[Reviewed by Julie Burchill in *NME 13/11/76*, but she fails to mention Wire.]

3 DEC W2
ST MARTIN'S SCHOOL OF ART, LONDON
Wire.

6 DEC P80/C19/D26
LEEDS POLYTECHNIC, LEEDS
Anarchy in the UK Tour. The Sex Pistols w/ The Clash, The Damned & The Heartbreakers.
John Shearlaw, *National RockStar* 11/12/76; Caroline Coon, *Melody Maker* 11/12/76; Tony Parsons, *NME* 11/12/76; Steve Kendall, *Record Mirror* 11/12/76; James Johnson, 'Sex Pistols Insult Queen', *Evening Standard* 7/12/76.
Pistols Set: Anarchy In The UK. I Wanna Be Me. Seventeen. I'm Not Your Steppin' Stone. No Future (God Save The Queen). Substitute. No Feelings. Liar. Pretty Vacant. Problems. [Tony Parsons claims in his review they encored with 'Whatcha Gonna Do About It' and 'No Fun', but if so the taper missed them.]

7 DEC D27
HOPE N ANCHOR, ISLINGTON, LONDON
The Damned w/ Eater.

9 DEC P81/C20/B12
ELECTRIC CIRCUS, MANCHESTER
Anarchy in the UK Tour. The Sex Pistols w/ The Clash, Buzzcocks & The Heartbreakers.
Sounds 18/12/76.
Buzzcocks Set: Orgasm Addict. Breakdown. Time's Up. Boredom. You Tear Me Up. Friends of Mine. Love Battery/ Stop Messin' 'Round. Oh Shit. I Can't Control Myself.
Clash Set: White Riot. I'm So Bored With The USA. London's Burning. Hate & War. Protex Blue. Career Opportunities. Cheat. 48 Hours. Janie Jones. 1977.
Pistols Set: Anarchy In The UK. I Wanna Be Me. Seventeen. I'm Not Your Steppin' Stone. Satellite. Submission. Substitute. No Feelings. Liar. Pretty Vacant. No Future (God Save The Queen). Problems.

10 DEC G2
CENTRAL COLLEGE OF ART & DESIGN
Generation X w/ Eater
Set: Ready Steady Go. Prove It. New Order. Your Generation. London Life. Trying For Kicks. Listen. Youth Youth Youth. Instant Karma. Paranoid. [from Tony James' diary]

[MID-] DEC W3
ROYAL COLLEGE OF ART, LONDON
Wire.

[MID-] DEC SI1
THE RED DEER, CROYDON
Siouxsie & The Banshees.

14 DEC J5
100 CLUB, OXFORD ST, LONDON
The Jam.

14 DEC G3/SI2
CHAGUARAMAS, COVENT GARDEN, LONDON
Generation X w/ Siouxsie & The Banshees. [Sometimes dated 21st December]

14 DEC P82/C21
CASTLE CINEMA, CAERPHILLY, WALES
Anarchy in the UK Tour. The Sex Pistols w/ The Clash & The Heartbreakers.

15 DEC G4
CHAGUARAMAS, COVENT GARDEN, LONDON
The Heartbreakers w/ Generation X.

17 DEC G5
ELECTRIC CIRCUS, MANCHESTER
Generation X w/ Martin Ellis & The Drones.

19 DEC P83/C22
ELECTRIC CIRCUS, MANCHESTER
Anarchy in the UK Tour. The Sex Pistols w/ The Clash & The Heartbreakers.
Paul Morley, *NME* 25/12/76.

20 DEC P84/C23
WINTER GARDENS, CLEETHORPES
Anarchy in the UK Tour. The Sex Pistols w/ The Clash & The Heartbreakers.
Pistols Set: Anarchy In The UK. I Wanna Be Me. I'm Not Your Steppin' Stone. Satellite. No Future (God Save The Queen). Substitute. Liar. No Feelings. Pretty Vacant.

21 DEC P85/C24
WOODS CENTRE, PLYMOUTH
Anarchy in the UK Tour. The Sex Pistols w/ The Clash & The Heartbreakers.

22 DEC P86/C25
WOODS CENTRE, PLYMOUTH
Anarchy in the UK Tour. The Sex Pistols w/ The Clash & The Heartbreakers.
'To Woods [Centre] about 9. Only about ten people have arrived. Ergh … It is clear no one will turn up so Clash go on and play brilliant. Ditoo HBs. SPs play well but the sound is up the creek.' – Sophie's diary 22/12/76.

22 DEC G6
HOPE 'N' ANCHOR, ISLINGTON, LONDON
Generation X.

27 DEC REC
MANCHESTER SQUARE STUDIOS, LONDON
The Sex Pistols w/ Mike Thorne.
No Feelings (backing track). No Future. Liar. Problems.
Broadcast on Italian radio in the 1980s, one song ('No Future') appeared on the *Agression Thru Repression* CD. Released complete on the 2002 boxed-set, *Sexbox 1.*

28 DEC REC
INDIGO SOUND STUDIO, MANCHESTER
Buzzcocks w/ Martin Hannett.
Breakdown. Time's Up. Boredom. Friends of Mine.
The legendary *Spiral Scratch* E.P., issued on vinyl in February 1977 and on CD in 1991.

[LATE-] DEC REC
REHEARSAL ROOMS, WEST LONDON.
The Adverts.
One Chord Wonders. Newboys. Quickstep. We Who Wait I. Bored Teenagers. Great British Mistake. Safety In Numbers. New Church. We Who Wait II.
These tracks have been made available as a download on the TV Smith website.

[LATE-] DEC REC
PATHWAY STUDOS, LONDON
The Damned w/ Nick Lowe.
Neat Neat Neat b/w Stab Your Back.

BIBLIOGRAPHY

The main written sources for a work like this must be the weekly music press in 1976. I have drawn on the relevant issues of New Musical Express, Sounds *and* Melody Maker *continually. The live reviews are individually cited in the Year Zero Chronology; but may I also pay particular tribute to the* NME *and* Sounds *gossip columns, 'Teazers' and 'Jaws', a mine of useful information.*

For my purposes, the oral histories that have been published in the last fifteen years have been invaluable. The other reference works have usually helped with a particular piece of this jigsaw, but I once again tip my hat to Jon Savage's pioneering work for laying a trail for all punk historians to follow.

Oral Histories:

Colegrave, Stephen & Sullivan, Chris – *Punk* (Cassell Illustrated, 2001)

Martin, Gavin – 'Anarchy In The UK', *Uncut* #37 pp42-65.

Nolan, David – *I Swear I Was There: Sex Pistols & The Shape of Rock* (Milo Books, 2001)

Robb, John – *Punk Rock: An Oral History* (Ebury Press, 2006)

Savage, Jon – *The England's Dreaming Tapes* (Faber, 2009)

Eds. of *Mojo* – 'All You Need Is Hate', *Mojo* #76 pp60-77.

Other Reference Sources:

Albertine, Viv – *Clothes, Music, Boys: A Memoir* (Faber, 2014)

Blaney, John – *A Howlin' Wind: Pub Rock & The Birth of the New Wave* (Soundcheck Books, 2011)

Bromberg, Craig – *The Wicked Ways of Malcolm McLaren* (Harper Collins, 1989)

Coon, Caroline – 1988: *The New Wave Punk Rock Explosion* (Omnibus Press, 1982)

Crancher, Steve – *Eddie & The Hot Rods: Do Anything You Wanna Do* (pp, 2009)

Curtis, Deborah – *Touching From A Distance: Ian Curtis & Joy Division* (Faber, 2007)

Diggle, Steve – *Harmony In My Head* [w/ Terry Rawlings] (Helter Skelter, 2003)

Dudanski, Richard – *Squat City Rocks* (pp, 2014)

Eden, Kevin – *Wire...Everybody Loves A History* (Omnibus Press, 1991)

Frame, Pete – *The Complete Rock Family Trees* (Omnibus Press, 1983)

Gilbert, Pat – *Passion is a Fashion: The Real Story of The Clash* (Aurum, 2004)

Goodman, Dave – *My Amazing Adventures with the Sex Pistols* (The Blue Coat Press, 2007)

Gorman, Paul – *In Their Own Write: Adventures In The Music Press* (Sanctuary Publishing, 2001)

Heylin, Clinton – *From The Velvets To The Voidoids: A Pre-punk History For A Post-Punk World*
- *Never Mind The Bollocks, Here's The Sex Pistols*
- *Babylon's Burning: From Punk to Grunge*

Hook, Peter – *Unknown Pleasures: Inside Joy Division* (Simon & Schuster, 2012)

Idol, Billy – *Dancing With Myself* (Simon & Schuster, 2014)

Kent, Nick – *Apathy For The Devil* (Faber, 2010)

Marshall, Bertie – *Berlin Bromley* (SAF Publishing, 2006)

Matlock, Glen – *I Was A Teenage Sex Pistol* [w/ Pete Silverton] (Omnibus Press, 1990)

McGartland, Tony – *Buzzcocks: The Complete History* (Music Press Books, 1995)

McNeil, Legs & McCain, Gillian – *Please Kill Me: The Uncensored Oral History of Punk* (SOS, 1996)

Middles, Mick – *The Fall.* [w/ Mark E. Smith] (Omnibus Press, 2003)
- *Factory: The Story of The Record Label* (Virgin Books, 2009)
- *Torn Apart: The Life of Ian Curtis* [w/ Lindsay Reade] (Omnibus Press, 2006)
Morrissey – *Autobiography* (Penguin Classics, 2013)
Neate, Wilson – *Wire's Pink Flag* (Continuum, 2009)
Nice, James – *Shadowplayers: The Rise & Fall of Factory Records* (Aurum Press, 2010)
O'Shea, Mick – *The Anarchy Tour* (Omnibus Press, 2012)
Panciera, Mario – *45 Revolutions: UK 1976-79* (Hurdy Gurdy, 2007)
Parker, Alan & Burgess, Paul – *Satellite: Sex Pistols Memorabilia* (Abstract Sound Publishing, 1999)
Paytress, Mark – *The Art of Dying Young: Sid Vicious* (Omnibus Press, 2010)
Perry, Mark – *Sniffin' Glue* (Sanctuary Books, 2003)
Rotten, Johnny [né Lydon] – *No Irish, No Blacks, No Dogs* [w/ Kent Zimmerman] (St Martin's Press)
- *Anger Is An Energy.* (Simon & Schuster, 2014).
Salewicz, Chris – *Redemption Song: The Definitive Biography of Joe Strummer.* (Harper Collins, 2006)
Savage, Jon – *England's Dreaming: The Sex Pistols and Punk Rock* (Faber, 1991)
Southall, Brian – *Sex Pistols: Ninety Days At EMI* (Bobcat Books, 2007)
Stevenson, Nils – *Vacant: A Diary of the Punk Years 1976-79* [w/ Ray Stevenson] (Thames & Hudson, 1999)
Stevenson, Ray – *Sex Pistols Scrapbook* (pp, 1977)
Strongman, Phil – *Pretty Vacant: A History of Punk* (Orion, 2007)
Strummer, Joe; Jones, Mick et al – *The Clash* (Atlantic Books, 2008)
Sumner, Bernard – *Chapter & Verse: New Order, Joy Division & Me* (Bantam Press, 2014)
Sykes, Bill – *Sit Down! Listen To This!* (Empire Books, 2012)
Temple, Julien et al. – *The Filth & The Fury: The Voice of the Sex Pistols* (St Martin's Press, 2000)
Thompson, Dave – *Johnny Rotten In His Own Words* (Omnibus Press, 1988).
Vermorel, Fred & Judy – *Sex Pistols: The Inside Story* (Corgi Books, 1977)
- *Sex Pistols: The Inside Story* (Omnibus Press, 1987) [revised ed]
Wood, Lee – *Sex Pistols Day By Day* (Omnibus Press, 1988)
Wreckless Eric – *A Dysfunctional Success: The Wreckless Eric Manual* (The Do-Not Press, 2003)

<u>Unpublished materials:</u>
Garside, Andy – 'Talkin' 'Bout Myth Generation': How could two nights in Manchester in the summer of 1976 come to influence the development of Anglo-American rock music throughout the next thirty years? (MA thesis, 2006)
Robb, John – transcript of interview w/ Glen Matlock, courtesy of author.
- transcript of interview w/ Mick Jones, courtesy of author.
Savage, Jon – full transcript of interview w/ Simon Barker, courtesy of author.
- full transcript of interview w/ Mary Harron, courtesy of author.
- full transcript of interview w/ Shanne Hasler, courtesy of author.
- full transcript of interview w/ Jordan, courtesy of author.
- full transcript of interview w/ Morrissey, courtesy of author.
- full transcript of interview w/ Joe Stevens, courtesy of author.
- full transcript of interview w/ Nils Stevenson, courtesy of author.
Wood, Lee – draft version of *Sex Pistols Day By Day*, circa 1987.

<u>Articles (excluding live 1976 reviews):</u>
Anon. – 'Pistols: small bore', letter to *Sounds* 22/5/76.
Clarke, Steve – Interview w/ Bernie Rhodes, *NME* 4/11/78.
Coon, Caroline – 'Punk rock: Rebels Against The System', *Melody Maker* 7/8/76.
Dadomo, Giovanni – 'In The Pub Across The Road With The Damned', *Sounds* 27/11/76.

Gilbert, Pat – 'Punk '76', *Mojo* #267 2/2016.
Hannett, Martin & Harries, Andy – 'Punk Rock … The Boys in the Bands', *New Manchester Review* 22/10-4/11/76.
Harron, Mary – 'Johnny Rotten – To The Core', *Punk* #8. [3/77]
Ingham, Jonh – 'The Sex Pistols are four months old…', *Sounds* 24/4/76.
- 'Welcome to the (?) Rock Special', *Sounds* 9/10/76.
- 'Single of the Week: New Rose', *Sounds* 23/10/76.
- 'Sounds' Star Single, *Sounds* 27/11/76.
Jaspan, Andrew – 'Rocking On The New Wave', *New Manchester Review* 11-24/2/77.
Jones, Allan – 'Rotten!', *Melody Maker* 4/6/77.
Kelly, Danny – 'Mick Jones Remembers', *The Word* 11/2006.
McCullough, Dave – 'The Northern Soul of Vic Godard', *Sounds* 2/12/78.
McLaren, Malcolm – Interview w/…, *Melody Maker* 9/7/77.
- Interview w/ …, *NME* 9/8/80.
- 'Punk and History', transcript of discussion at Fashion Institute of Technology, New York, September 24, 1988.
McNeill, Phil – Rent-A-Punk Guide, *NME* 26/3/77.
Morley, Paul – 'They mean it, M-a-a-a-nchester', *NME* 30/7/77.
Morley, Paul & Penman, Ian – 'Calm & Confusion', The New Howard Devoto Interview, *NME* 2/12/78.
Morrissey, Steven – 'Who Is This Band, Anyway?', *New York Rocker* #10.
Needs, Kris – 'Konkrete Klockworl', *ZigZag* #71.
- 'Silver Jubilation', *ZigZag* 6/77.
Nemeth, Cathy – 'Musings of Magazine's Main Man', *New York Rocker* 9/79.
Nicholds, Andrew – 'It's The Buzz, Cock!', *Time Out* 21/2/76.
Salewicz, Chris – 'Generation X Rock & Roll Soul', *NME* 8/4/78.
- 'Johnny's Immaculate Conception', *NME* 23/12/78.
Savage, Jon – 'The Future Is Female', *Sounds* 17/12/77.
Silverton, Pete – 'What did you do on the Punk tour, daddy?', *Sounds* 18/12/76.
- 'The Clash: Greatness From Garageland', *Trouser Press* #26. [2/78]
- 'Sid Vicious crashed my twenty-first', *The Observer* 1991 [accessed from *Rock's Backpages* website]
'Sounds' [ed.] -'Sounds of the New Wave', *Sounds* 2/4/77.
'Siouxsie & The Banshees' – 'Siouxsie sez!', letter to *Sounds* 31/12/77.
Turner, Steve – 'Sex Pistols: The Anarchic Rock of the Young and Doleful', *The Guardian* 3/12/76.

<u>Online postings:</u>
Albiez, Sean – 'Print the Truth, Not The Legend: Sex Pistols Lesser Free Trade Hall', posting dated 4/3/2012.
Anon. – online posting re Whitby gig 11/9/76, posted on Vintage-rock website 26/5/2014.
Peter S. – online posting re Whitby gig 11/9/76, posted on 10/10/2012.
Taylor, Barry – online posting re Hastings gig 3/7/76, posted 30/10/2013.
Walker, Bobby – online posting re Hastings gig 3/7/76, posted 4/4/2014.

DRAMATIS PERSONAE

Below are the characters who populate this book, and contribute their voices to it. Those in bold are those whom I have interviewed myself. Their 'punk credentials' and the date of their first Pistols gig are given in square brackets.

ADVERT, Gaye [The Adverts – 29/8/76]
ALBERTINE, Viv [The Slits – 5/12/75]
ANT, Adam [Adam & The Ants; Bazooka Joe – 6/11/75]
ARMSTRONG, Roger [Chiswick Records – 5/12/75]
BAINES, Una [The Fall – 4/6/76]
BARKER, Simon [Bromley Contingent – 9/12/75]
BIRCH, Will [Kursaal Flyers]
BOON, Richard [Buzzcocks manager – 20/2/76]
BRAMAH, Martin [The Fall – 4/6/76]
BROWTON, Ben [audience member – 29/11/76]
BURKE, Steve aka Steve Shy [fanzine editor/audience member 20/7/76]
BURNHAM, Hugo [Gang of Four – 6/12/76]
CHAPEKAR, Robin [Bazooka Joe – 6/11/75]
COOK, Paul [Sex Pistols]
COOKE, John [audience taper – 14/8/76]
COON, Caroline [*Melody Maker* journalist – 20/3/76]
CURTIS, Deborah [audience member – 20/7/76]
CZEZOWSKI, Andy [Damned manager/Roxy owner – 6/11/75]
DEMPSEY, Martin [The Yachts – 15/10/76]
DEVOTO, Howard [Buzzcocks – 20/2/76]
DIGGLE, Steve [Buzzcocks – 4/6/76]
DRUMMOND, Bill [audience member – 15/10/76]
DUDANSKI, Richard [The 101'ers – 3/4/76]
EATON, Bob [audience member 11/9/76]
EDWARDS, Alan [audience member – 3/4/76]
FIELDS, Danny [Ramones manager]
FORD, Nigel [audience member 3/7/76]
FOXTON, Bruce [The Jam – 20/10/76]
GARRITY, Ed [Ed Banger & The Nosebleeds – 4/6/76]
GODARD, Vic [Subway Sect – 12/2/76]
GOODMAN, Dave [Sex Pistols soundman – 3/4/76]
GRAY, Iain [audience member – 4/6/76]
GRIMSHAW, Margaret [Lodestar owner – 15/9/76]
HARRON, Mary [*Punk* journalist – 14/10/76]
HASLER, Shanne [The Nipple Erectors – 14/11/76]
HAWKINS, Pete [Social Secretary Weybridge College – 29/11/75]
HOOK, Peter [Joy Division – 4/6/76]
HYNDE, Chrissie [The Pretenders – 12/2/76]
IDOL, Billy [Generation X – 30/3/76]

INGHAM, Jonh [*Sounds* journalist – 4/4/76]
JACKSON, James [Cleethorpes promoter – 20/12/76]
JAMES, Brian [The Damned – 14/2/76]
JAMES, Tony [Generation X – 5/12/75]
JONES, Allan [*Melody Maker* journalist – 3/4/76]
JONES, Steve [Sex Pistols]
JORDAN [Sex worker – 6/11/75]
KENT, Nick [*NME* journalist – 14/2/76]
LEVENE, Keith [The Clash; PiL – 3/4/76]
LEWIS, Graham [Wire – 23/4/76]
LLOYD, Peter [Penetration manager – 19/5/76]
LLOYD, Robert [The Prefects – 14/8/76]
LURE, Walter [The Heartbreakers – 6/12/76]
LYDON, John aka Johnny Rotten [Sex Pistols]
MATLOCK, Glen [Sex Pistols]
MAY, Phil [The Pretty Things – 5/76]
McDERMOTT, Peter [audience member – 15/10/76]
McLAREN, Malcolm [Sex Pistols manager]
MOBBS, Nick [EMI A&R man – 29/8/76]
MORLEY, Paul [fanzine editor/journalist – 4/6/76]
MORRISSEY, Steve [audience member – 4/6/76]
MOSS, Ian [The Hamsters – 4/6/76]
MURRAY, Pauline [Penetration – 19/5/76]
NEWMAN, Colin [Wire – 20/9/76]
O'KEEFE, Tracie [Sex worker – 11/75]
PARKER, Graham [Graham Parker & The Rumour]
PARRY, Chris [Polydor A&R man – 14/8/76]
PERRETT, Pete [The Only Ones – 5/12/75]
PERRY, John [The Only Ones – 20/9/76]
PERRY, Mark [fanzine editor/Alternative TV – 10/8/76]
PIRRONI, Marco [Siouxsie & The Banshees/ The Models/ Adam & The Ants – 4/4/76]
POVEY, John [The Pretty Things – 9/7/76]
PYE, Chris [*So It Goes* producer – 1/9/76]
RITON ANGEL FACE [Angel Face – 5/9/76]
ROBINSON, Tom [Tom Robinson Band – 11/5/76]
ROMERO, Paloma aka Palmolive [The Slits]
RYTLEWSKI, Joe [sound guy – 3/7/76]
SCABIES, Rat [The Damned – 30/3/76]
SEVERIN, Steve [Bromley Contingent; Siouxsie & The Banshees – 2/76]
SHELLEY, Pete [Buzzcocks – 20/2/76]
SILVERTON, Pete [*Sounds* journalist – 23/4/76]
SIMON, Kate [*Sounds* photographer – 4/4/76]
SINCLAIR, Martin [audience member – 4/6/76]
SIOUX, Siouxsie **[Bromley Contingent; Siouxsie & The Banshees – 2/76]**
SMITH, Tim 'TV' [The Adverts – 20/9/76]
SPEDDING, Chris [Sex Pistols producer – 30/3/76]
SPENCER, Neil [*NME* journalist – 12/2/76]
STEVENS, Joe [*NME* photographer – 14/2/76]
STERLING, Linder [designer/audience member – 20/7/76]
STEVENSON, Nils [Sex Pistols road manager – 12/2/76]
STRANGE, Steve [audience member – 22/9/76]
STRUMMER, Joe [The 101'ers; The Clash – 3/4/76]

STYRENE, Poly [X-Ray Spex – 3/7/76]
SUMNER, Bernard [Joy Division – 4/6/76]
SYMMONS, Rob [Subway Sect – 12/2/76]
TAYLOR, Barry [Torquay promoter – 3/7/76]
TAYLOR, Ian [audience member – 4/6/76]
THOMAS, Chris [Sex Pistols producer – 29/8/76]
THOMPSON, Howard [Island A&R man – 12/2/76]
THORNE, Mike [EMI producer – ?29/8/76]
TYLA, Sean [Ducks Deluxe – 14/2/76]
VEGA, Arturo [Ramones road manager]
WALKER, Bobby [audience member – 3/7/76]
WALKER, Peter [*So It Goes* cameraman – 1/9/76]
WELLER, Paul [The Jam – 9/7/76]
WILLIAMSON, Nigel [journalist/audience member – 2/76]
WILSON, Tony [*So It Goes* presenter – 4/6/76]
WIMBLE, Jane [Trash – 29/11/75]
WITTS, Richard [The Passage – 20/7/76]
WOBBLE, Jah [PiL – ?30/3/76]
WRIGHT, Simon [Trash – 29/11/75]
ZERMATI, Marc [Skydog Records – 14/2/76]

ACKNOWLEDGMENTS

If time passes slowly up here in the Quantocks, even I can't quite believe it is forty years since the (real) year of Punk. And still the debate rages on. This is a book I have wanted to write for a long time. I genuinely believe it is as necessary to that debate in 2016 as *From The Velvets To The Voidoids* was, in 1993. That book was correctly subtitled *A Pre-Punk History For A Post-Punk World* (at least it was until the US publisher of the second edition decided they knew better). So, welcome reader, to *A Punk History for a Post-Punk World*.

The punk interviews I draw on here are mainly ones I have personally conducted over the past twenty years. Sadly, but inevitably, the ol' Reaper has claimed a couple of the voices so represented. But I thank you one and all, and hope and pray everyone below feels it was worth the investment of your precious time:

Gaye Advert, Una Baines, Will Birch, Richard Boon, Martin Bramah, Steve Burke, Hugo Burnham, John Cooke, Andy Czezowski, Howard Devoto, Richard Dudanski, Bob Eaton, Vic Godard, Dave Goodman, Pete Hawkins, Jonh Ingham, Brian James, Tony James, Nick Kent, Graham Lewis, Pete Lloyd, Robert Lloyd, Walter Lure, Glen Matlock, Ian Moss, Colin Newman, Peter Perrett, John Perry, Mark Perry, Marco Pirroni, Chris Pye, Paloma Romero, Rat Scabies, Steve Severin, Kate Simon, Martin Sinclair, TV Smith, Chris Spedding, Linder Sterling, Rob Symmons, Ian Taylor, Chris Thomas, Howard Thompson, Jane Wimble, Richard Witts, Simon Wright and Marc Zermati.

I'd also like to thank the invaluable staff at Manchester Central Reference Library and at *Time Out* in London, for allowing me free rein of their written archives. Ditto Barney and Mark at *Rock's Backpages*, who are providing a service the world needs. I encourage you all to subscribe, lest we forget that without rock writing – and especially fine rock writers like Nick Kent, Jonh Ingham, Caroline Coon, Paul Morley, Jon Savage, Tony Parsons and the late great Lester Bangs – punk almost certainly would never have happened.

Given the strong oral history component to this tome, I cannot fail to acknowledge the fulsome help I received from those who have trod this path in tandem, or indeed before. Nina Antonia was kind enough to lend me interviews from 25 years ago that she conducted for a book on the Roxy Club that was never published. Stephen Colegrave encouraged me, some years back, to write just such a book; his oral history cum visual punkfest, *Punk*, remains a must for all iconoclasts. John Robb was his usual gregarious, engaging, opinionated self as we chewed the fat on all things punk; and was his usual generous self when I asked for complete transcripts of important interviews from his own oral history of punk. And that archdeacon of Punk History, Jon Savage, after years out of touch, responded to my heartfelt plea for full transcripts of his own interviews with certain key figures I could not find or would not talk as if we'd spoken the week before. A true scholar and gentleman.

(Almost) finally, a personal thanks to the friends and fellow believers who made the calls and sent the e-mails that tracked down the figures that had fallen through the cracks, and who shared my enthusiasm for the facts – just the facts – and the remarkable music that resulted. I thank you all: Paul Bradshaw, Peter Doggett, Pat Gilbert, June Hony, Susie Hulme, Jonh Ingham, Dave and Julie Knight, C.P. Lee, Richard Lysons, Mick Middles, Mark Paytress, John Perry, Steve Shepherd, Martin Sinclair, Howard Thompson, Simon Warner, Simon Wright and, wherever you may be, Lee Wood. And especial thanks to Peter Lloyd, whose generosity of spirit shines through in the photos he so kindly allowed me to use as a visual record of Year Zero.

Also a votive thanks to Thurston Moore, Steve Shelley & Lee Ranaldo for a) carrying the torch and b) encouraging me to give my enthusiasm for the year 1976 rein again.

And though no book is ever finished, only abandoned, Ian and Isabel at Route saw the book through to the 'bitter end', and made it better in the process. As did my good friend, the eagle-eyed Mike DeCapite. Bless you, one and all.

Till the next time,

Clinton Heylin, March 2016.

www.anarchyyearzero.wordpress.com
www.route-online.com

route™
SPECIAL EDITION